Occult Aesthetics

THE OXFORD MUSIC / MEDIA SERIES

DANIEL GOLDMARK, SERIES EDITOR

Tuning In: American Narrative Television Music
RON RODMAN

Special Sound: The Creation and Legacy of the BBC Radiophonic Workshop
LOUIS NIEBUR

Seeing Through Music: Gender and Modernism in Classic Hollywood Film Scores
PETER FRANKLIN

An Eye for Music: Popular Music and the Audiovisual Surreal
JOHN RICHARDSON

Playing Along: Digital Games, YouTube, and Virtual Performance
KIRI MILLER

Sounding the Gallery: Video and the Rise of Art-Music
HOLLY ROGERS

Composing for the Red Screen: Prokofiev and Soviet Film
KEVIN BARTIG

Saying It With Songs: Popular Music and the Coming of Sound to Hollywood Cinema
KATHERINE SPRING

We'll Meet Again: Musical Design in the Films of Stanley Kubrick
KATE MCQUISTON

Occult Aesthetics: Synchronization in Sound Film
K. J. DONNELLY

Occult Aesthetics: Synchronization in Sound Film

K. J. Donnelly

OXFORD
UNIVERSITY PRESS

OXFORD
UNIVERSITY PRESS

Oxford University Press is a department of the University of Oxford.
It furthers the University's objective of excellence in research, scholarship,
and education by publishing worldwide.

Oxford   New York
Auckland   Cape Town   Dar es Salaam   Hong Kong   Karachi
Kuala Lumpur   Madrid   Melbourne   Mexico City   Nairobi
New Delhi   Shanghai   Taipei   Toronto

With offices in
Argentina   Austria   Brazil   Chile   Czech Republic   France   Greece
Guatemala   Hungary   Italy   Japan   Poland   Portugal   Singapore
South Korea   Switzerland   Thailand   Turkey   Ukraine   Vietnam

Oxford is a registered trademark of Oxford University Press
in the UK and certain other countries.

Published in the United States of America by
Oxford University Press
198 Madison Avenue, New York, NY 10016

© Oxford University Press 2014

All rights reserved. No part of this publication may be reproduced, stored in a
retrieval system, or transmitted, in any form or by any means, without the prior
permission in writing of Oxford University Press, or as expressly permitted by law,
by license, or under terms agreed with the appropriate reproduction rights organization.
Inquiries concerning reproduction outside the scope of the above should be sent to the Rights
Department, Oxford University Press, at the address above.

You must not circulate this work in any other form
and you must impose this same condition on any acquirer.

This volume is published with the generous support of the AMS 75 PAYS Endowment of the
American Musicological Society, funded in part by the National Endowment for the Humanities
and the Andrew W. Mellon Foundation

Library of Congress Cataloging-in-Publication Data

Donnelly, K. J. (Kevin J.)
Occult aesthetics : synchronization in sound film / K. J. Donnelly.
pages ; cm
Includes bibliographical references and index.
ISBN 978-0-19-977349-7 (hardcover : alk. paper)—ISBN 978-0-19-977350-3 (pbk. : alk.
paper) 1. Motion picture music—History and criticism. 2. Music and occultism. 3. Sound
in motion pictures. I. Title.
ML2075.D664 2013
781.5'42117—dc23
2013017331

9 8 7 6 5 4 3 2 1
Printed in the United States of America
on acid-free paper

TABLE OF CONTENTS

Preface   vii
Acknowledgments   xi

1. Introduction: The Lock of Synchronization   *1*
2. Synchronization: McGurk and Beyond   *14*
3. Sound Montage   *44*
4. Occult Aesthetics   *70*
5. Isomorphic Cadences: Film as 'Musical'   *94*
6. 'Visual' Sound Design: The Sonic Continuum   *123*
7. 'Pre' and 'Post' Sound   *154*
8. Wild Track Asynchrony   *181*
9. Conclusion: Final Speculations   *200*

Notes   210
Bibliography   236
Index   249

PREFACE

The initial impetus for this project came to me not when engaged with films or music, or when reading theorists such as Eisenstein or Chion, but while looking out of the window. Upon moving to the seaside town of Aberystwyth in mid-Wales in the early 2000s, I was struck, as many cannot fail to be, by the intermittent bursts of sound and vision afforded by jet aircraft of the Royal Air Force. I learned rapidly that it was one of the principal areas of Britain for air conflict simulation. I had been told that there were strict guidelines on how low these planes were allowed to fly in populated areas, but these were not adhered to. In the run up to another of Britain's seemingly regular punitive actions overseas, these jet planes disconcerted me by appearing to use the building in which I was teaching (the tallest on campus) as a target for bombing runs during my classes. On one highly memorable occasion, I was standing in the marina when a jet came in from the sea to land at a height that would not have cleared buildings. I saw the pilot's face and could even make out the intricacies of his headgear. At this point, the jet obliquely shot upward at an angle of about 60 degrees. What was so shocking about this incident was not the proximity of the activity, but the fact that it initially took place in an eerie, disconnected silence, a fraction of a second before the devastating blast of sound from the plane. This was a more extreme instance of the unremitting experience of having jet planes in the vicinity, where the key aspect of their presence was the disconnection between sound and image. In most cases, one hears the sound and then has to look for the presence of the plane, which is most successful if one looks well ahead of where the brain informs us that it might be. On rare occasions, we might see a plane fractionally before the sound reaches us. This disparity of perception dictated by the different speeds of sound and light imparted a disconcerting and uncanny aspect to the planes, where they seemed to be lacking something essential and then appeared to leave behind more than they should. The most disconcerting moments were those where, in a fraction of a second, one could see the plane and anticipate its sound, but in that split second wonder if the sound was ever going to arrive. Furthermore, this division emphasized to me the essential and sensual difference between sound and image: The image appears cognitive whereas the sound appears physical.

This experience was complemented and enhanced by moving to a part of town where there was anomalous and often notably poor television reception. Owning an antiquated TV set did not help. After getting advice, I found that I could not plug together my old, small set with my new home-cinema sound and video system, and that while the latter could plug into the building's external aerial, the TV could not and had to run off its own mini-aerial. This meant that when I wanted to switch channels, I had to change both the TV and the sound system. This situation led to many moments of ambiguity, when I was not sure whether I had changed both to the same channel. This happened far more often than I ever would have imagined. Depending on what was on television, sometimes there was a coherence between the image track and the sound track of radically different programs, while, less commonly, there was a seeming disjunction that I perceived in a show with its actual soundtrack, merely because I was anticipating such by not feeling secure in knowing whether the image and sound were from the same channel.

Sometimes research has a long genealogy and deep roots. My grandmother was a tasseomancer—a tea-leaf reader—and a fanciful interest in the unapparent and bizarre has been a characteristic of my family. Yet this was also allied with a strong sense of practicality and understanding that was more 'scientific' than superstitious. This is far from unique, but it inculcated in me an assumption that there is a hidden world underneath the banal surface and a desire for the specialist knowledge that might unlock it or emanate from it. These might be unfounded assumptions, perhaps little more than prejudices. Critical theory has a generative function in that, in its best form, it grapples with unknowables, making them into something more tangible—although never quite making them unproblematically understandable, in other words, never making them into a simplistic reduction. Theory also has something of medieval alchemy about it. I can vividly remember the first time I came across psychoanalytic theory as an undergraduate student. Admittedly, some of Freud's ideas had long been ensconced in popular culture beyond the academy and the hospital, but nevertheless, the more detailed and more outré versions still had a significant impact on me. We were required to read some of Freud's case studies, and I was gripped. There was something absolutely compelling in Freud's grappling with problems that were initially beyond comprehension with theoretical tools that were beyond immediate logic. I sometimes think back to Freud's case studies in the face of so much instrumental and prosaic 'research' being completed in universities these days. Freud's 'research questions' are fairly straightforward, but his methods and his 'research answers' are so far beyond, so much more imaginative than the sorts of answers these same questions might receive if they wanted to remain fundable under today's circumstances (in the UK but elsewhere too). I was never sure whether these conclusions, or indeed the methods, were to be taken as unassailable truths. But I was sure that there were answers that were worth debating and a potential door being opened to different ways of thinking. I say this because to some, in these times, the use of psychoanalysis as a device in the study of film is anathema. Some declare that it has an 'unproven' scientific status, while others suggest that its insights might be obtained elsewhere and through other means, and others still merely see it as an obfuscatory discourse that provides nothing concrete for the study of film or wider culture. I am far from a 'psychoanalytic' theorist. However, I can see the value of such an approach and am fully convinced that its alchemical ability to turn some base symptoms into philosophical/theoretical gold is beyond doubt. If I wanted a simple, definitive answer, then perhaps I would not value its magical operation. But I realize that the nature of my inquiry and object of scrutiny make it unlikely that there is an absolute and unassailable answer, and I would be happy with some conceptualizations that can allow us to address some of the questions rather than supply an outright answer.

There is something of the occult about 'theory,' particularly the form that is being used in this book. It is in some ways closer to acts of divination than it is to instrumental 'social' research. An important inspiration is Walter Benjamin's dictum that open-minded research cannot dismiss soothsaying from coffee grounds.[1] I might add tea leaves. And I want to play a little along the line dividing rational 'science' and inquiry, and more 'irrational,' imaginative speculation. As psychological underpinnings and inspiration, this study uses scientific, functional, neurological, and physiological ideas about human beings and sound to develop its argument about the perceptual primacy of cinema's dynamic interplay across synchronized and unsynchronized sections of film. The process of synchronizing image and sound is Pavlovian in that, in many cases, there is an expectation of one corresponding with the other, and their relationship can be wholly defined by learned associations. For example, the sound of wood blocks clashing together is the accepted conventional sound of someone being punched or kicked in an action film, whereas the actual act of doing this involves no such sound. Michel Chion notes that the seeming unity of sound and image, what he calls 'synchresis,' is Pavlovian, and that "[t]he effect of synchresis, is obviously capable of being influenced by cultural habits. But at the same time, it very probably has an innate basis."[2] There is a strong physical foundation to the yoking of eye and ear through image and sound synchronization, but it is perhaps more profitably approached as an essentially psychological process. Maurice Merleau-Ponty characterized embodied perception as a more important stage than abstracted cognition,[3] and the dominance of cognitive film theory in recent years has tended to atomize analysis—reducing activities and objects to minute subcomponents, while avoiding the 'bigger picture.' Such reduction has been happier dealing with narrative development than with more general aspects of the film experience. The whole point of synchronization is that, at heart, diverse components (sound and moving image) are unified by the phenomenological experience of the audience member. Furthermore, as I have noted already, these components might well embody different impulses: the image as cognitive and the sound as more physical and more readily perceived.

ACKNOWLEDGMENTS

Some material in this book has appeared in a different form in "On the Occult Nature of Sound-Image Synchronization" in *Cinephile*, vol. 6, no. 1, Spring 2010, 39–43; "*Saw* heard: Musical Sound Design in Contemporary Cinema" in Warren Buckland, ed., *Film Theory and Contemporary Hollywood Movies* (London: Routledge, 2008), 103–123; "Europe Cannibalizes the Western: *Ravenous*" in Kathryn Kalinak, ed., *Music in the Western: Notes from the Frontier* (London: Routledge, 2012).

Included are my own musical transcriptions of John Carpenter's main theme from *Assault on Precinct 13* (Jack-O-Lantern Music Publishing Co.) and Iron Butterfly's *In-A-Gadda-Da-Vida* (written by Douglas Ingle, published by Alfred Publishing Ltd.).

It has been suggested to me that in my previous books I have been minimal, perhaps even parsimonious, in thanking people. I will try harder to be a more thankful person.

OUP editor Norm Hirschy went well beyond the call of duty in helping the birth of this book. Although I was inspired by too many filmmakers and musicians to list here, my research was consistently given energy by the theoretical writings of Theodor Adorno, Walter Benjamin, Michel Chion, Sergei Eisenstein, and a few less obvious ones who remain half-hidden. The following people were very kind, reading and commenting on at least some of the material: Daniel Goldmark (a great series editor), Liz Weis, Warren Buckland, Kathryn Kalinak, Tim Bergfelder, Claudia Gorbman, Royal S. Brown, Lisa Coulthard, and readers at *Cinephile*, as well as two very helpful but anonymous report writers for OUP. These people helped in some way: the Film and Music departments at the University of Southampton, Mila Cai, Beth Carroll, Michael Chanan, Michel Chion, Carol Churchouse, Glen Creeber, Andy Curtis-Brignell, Leah Curtis, Jack Curtis Dubowsky, Mark Goodall, Ian Q. Hunter, Neil Lerner, Dan Levene, Wilfred Marlow, Isabelle Munschy, Michael Nyman, Mike Pearson, Becca Roberts, Ron

Sadoff, Jamie Sexton, Ann-Kristin Wallengren, and anyone else I failed to mention. Very importantly, these people tried to keep me sane: Portsmouth F. C., Robert Donnelly, Joan Donnelly, and Mandy Marler. Heartfelt thanks to all of you.

CHAPTER 1

Introduction

The Lock of Synchronization

<blockquote>
Art is magic delivered from the lie of being truth.
—T. W. Adorno[1]
</blockquote>

In Michelangelo Antonioni's *Blow Up* (1966), there is a highly illustrative and notably singular moment in cinema. David Hemmings is entertaining Vanessa Redgrave in his apartment. He puts on a jazz record as they light cigarettes. He then exhorts her to smoke "against the beat." They then both attempt to smoke, drawing in and exhaling out of synchrony with the rhythm of the music. In effect, they simply smoke slowly and avoid the conspicuous synchronization of drawing in or exhaling on an emphasized beat.[2] In this sequence, screen time is undermined as a coherent unity, while corresponding with the rest of the film where space and time are made 'occult'—blown-up, re-experienced, and made ambiguous: A 'new world' is revealed underneath the quotidian everyday. It might be argued that the way the film re-presents banal time-spaces as mysterious and compelling reveals how film in general is all about radically rethinking the idea of time and space.[3] A focus on synchronization can do the same for the 'space' between sound and image. In essence, the discussion about synchronization here is not merely aesthetics or a problem of cognitive activity, but rather a way of thinking about the world. Thus, matching or not matching sound and image (so-called parallel and counterpoint) might be construed as different ways of thinking. This is not too fanciful. Important theoretical work has already opened up some of the territory. Sergei Eisenstein's primary interest was aesthetics in service of political and social opportunities. Similarly, Hanns Eisler and Theodor Adorno's discussion of film music was concerned with social and political aspects of culture and aesthetics.[4] In recent years, these concerns have receded, in favor of political discussion merely being the domain of positivistic approaches to a wider notion of culture or, perhaps worse, culture merely being approached as a weak symptom of the social. As part of this equation, aesthetics have been relegated to a very minor role of importance, which at least has bolstered a tendency to hermetically sealed aesthetic research.

Film is an audiovisual medium except for isolated cases. This book would like us to remember this more often, and to think of the music of sound and the sound of music as defining features of the experience, through the registering of the centrality of sound's momentary interaction with image. There are a handful of crucial, defining characteristics that mark out sound film (and indeed audiovisual culture more generally[5]) as a unique aesthetic and perceptual entity. They are all thought via sound although defined via image: non- or extra-diegetic status (where sound appears not to emanate from the world on-screen), off-screen sound (where the audience does not see the origins of the sound but assumes it to be near to what we see on screen), and synchronization and asynchrony (where sound can match events on-screen or appear to a lesser or greater degree to be unconnected). Although there has been some interest in the first two categories, there has been no notable or sustained research about the last.

In this book, I have used the term 'occult' because film sound can often have an effect that is not immediately apparent and sometimes rather mysterious, but almost always powerful. Although the term means 'hidden,' it often connotes something unapparent and magic. Film sound can often have such an effect, but it also became one of the hidden aspects of film in criticism and analysis, where it has often been treated as something that is not quite real and of little import next to the seemingly all-important image. While my use of the word in this book follows from the definition provided, it inevitably has something of its other implication. The aesthetics of film—particularly when dominated by sound and music—can work in an unapparent and 'magic' manner, yielding startling results from the product of sound and visuals that do not succumb to easy explanation. We should remember that while on the one hand, synchronization is a technical process, on the other, it is a psychological state engendered by film and something beyond simplistic and banal description. The word 'occult' merely means hidden or unapparent; it should not be equated with sinister or evil characteristics. Things that can be hidden away might be deemed 'occulted,' and the term has some currency in medical circles for events taking place inside the body that remain unseen. However, I also rather like the connotations of mystical and secretive ritualistic activities, which are far from being a stranger to the processes of cinema. My starting point is that aesthetics *are* occult. The way they work is far from being simple, logical, or easily understood, and, particularly in the case of film, they strive to conceal their processes and foster the impression that something else is going on instead. The 'occult aesthetics' of this book revel in the mysteries of the irrational at the heart of the film experience: desiring never to lose the texture, the feel, of the aesthetic while hoping to know something of its intimacies and secrets. One of its open secrets is the separation of sound and image and their union through mechanical (and increasingly digital) synchronization. This operation is occult in the sense that it is knowledge that *must* be kept hidden and secret. Synchronization of sound and image has to be hidden as a process to allow for sound cinema's function as an engaging medium that appears to render a coherent world on-screen and in sound. Beyond this, there is also something occult about the process generally, where two radically different media can be fused in perception, generating something that is infinitely more than the sum of its parts.

THE FUNDAMENTAL LIE: ILLUSION

The essence of the overwhelming majority of films is the combined illusion of eye, ear, and brain: that of a coherent image and sound, often premised upon the depiction of human beings on-screen. As Rick Altman notes, "...the sound film's fundamental lie [is] the implication that sound is produced by the image when in fact it remains independent of it."[6] This audiovisual sleight of hand is so central to films that it is beyond being considered remarkable. However, at certain times, we can be made painfully aware of its importance. When a film or television program goes 'out of synch,' our enjoyment can be ruined and the spell of the diegetic effect (the 'illusion') broken. We cannot fail to notice immediately when sound is momentarily out of synch with images, especially on television (or, for that matter, if we have become accustomed to dubbed dialogue in the cinema[7]). If it is only a slight delay—it is *nearly* in synch—we can mentally 'overlook' the discrepancy by 'compensating' and concentrating less on the conduct of dialogue and lips on-screen. Because of this unconscious/pre-conscious mechanism, other elements like sound effects and music can get away with very slight delays, often without notice or comment.

Ever since initial attempts to accompany recorded sound with image (and vice versa), there have been concerns about synchronizing the two, realizing that out-of-synch sounds and images tend to undermine the film experience. While films could have soundtracks of music that were only vaguely in synch, the development of the 'talkie' was premised upon precise synchronization, creating an illusion of a world on-screen of space, movement, and corresponding sound. Thus sound cinema became founded upon such so-called synch points, around which the fixed matching of image and soundtracks cohered. These are commonly moments of dialogue, where the on-screen character's mouth movements should be consistent with the sounds of the words, as if they were being produced directly. However, there are also many other notable synch points, such as sound effects, particularly when an action seen on-screen has an anticipated sonic counterpart (for instance, a gun being fired). Similarly, incidental music also provides a number of synch points with the action on-screen, marking an activity most obviously with an emphasized 'hit,' a stinger or sonic punch, indicating the conclusion of a sequence or narrative segment with music that offers a degree of closure, or entering at a significant point to provide and enhance dramatic aspects of the narrative.

These moments serve to anchor the images and sounds together, forging the illusory unity of the sound film as a medium. Michel Chion provides a definition of such 'locking' moments:

> ...[a p]oint of synchronization or synch point [is the] audiovisually salient synchronous meeting of a sound event and a sight event. Example: a dramatic cut in both image and soundtrack, sound effect or striking musical note, or cadence, or emphasized word of dialogue, coinciding with an action, a zoom in, etc.[8]

He also notes that it is "...like an accented chord in music."[9] These are significant moments of punctuation in film, but in their solidifying of the primary association of image and sound into an illusory whole, they are ontologically essential to sound cinema. Such events are not usually registered consciously by a film audience. They seem unremarkable, normal in fact. Apart from non-diegetic music, film sound overwhelmingly attempts to give the impression that it is a natural state of affairs, doubling the way things are in the world outside the cinema. Mary Ann Doane noted that in classical Hollywood films and beyond, "The invisibility of the practices of sound editing and mixing is ensured by the seemingly 'natural' laws of construction which the sound-track obeys."[10] The illusion of cinema, and its fundamental perception as something closely related to the real world, has undoubtedly been one of the most fundamental characteristics of the medium. However, it has also militated against certain types of analysis.

As time-based art forms, film and music have many fundamental attributes in common, despite clear differences. Isomorphic structures on large and small scales, and patterns of build-up, tension, and release are most evident in both, as are strong conventional concepts of 'what fits with what' and dynamic patterns of presentation, re-presentation, development of material, planes of foreground and background, withholding closures and marking minor as well as final conclusions to the musical piece or film. Film, both in terms of its conceptualization and practical production, embraces sound and image analogues (in terms of rhythm, both literally and metaphorically), 'Mickeymousing' in music, or gesture and camera movement being matched by or to the 'sweep' of music, to name but a few instances.

This book is concerned with sound and image synchronization and the associated psychology and its implications. I aim to reassess film from the point of view of it being less a representational medium at heart and more about the combination of sound and image. This might move analysis into abstraction and away from dealing with film as a recognition and comprehension. As part of this, another of my concerns is to detail how far 'musical' procedures have an impact on film more generally, not only on sonic aspects, but also on the rendering of images. Taking a lead from neuroaesthetics, I partially address the notion that culture emanates from or is determined by patterns in the human brain and physical human perception.[11] This is less than controversial, but it does pull analysis away from cultural/ideological traditions and re-engages with matters of the physical and perceptual. It is broadly clear that sound and image (and their synchronization) in cinema are modeled on sight, hearing, and synchronization processes in human hardware. Indeed, art and cultural objects might well emanate from basic perceptual-cognitive requirements more than 'higher level' ones. For instance, Leonard B. Meyer notes that short musical phrases come from the ability of the human memory to retain that specific amount of material, rather than any accrued convention of musical culture.[12] Similarly, Philip Ball's *The Music Instinct* argues that modernist classical music undermined principles that make music understandable to all, not because these principles were traditional but because the convention derived from patterns readily recognized by the human brain.[13] In terms of film, analysis has tended to look for determinants in narrative and neglects the likelihood that film structures are derived from some innate perceptual-cognitive requirement. It is striking how extraordinarily well certain visual configurations work with certain music when wearing an iPod or similar personal stereo. Human senses and brains have powerful pattern-seeking abilities and tendencies, which allow for rapid cognition but also can lead to confusion in complex environments. Apophenia (originally considered only a psychotic condition) entails finding unapparent connections and significance in things—seeing patterns where they do not exist.[14] A particular version of this relating to images and sounds is called pareidolia and is outlined further in chapter 4. Albert Bregman discusses the notion of 'chimeric percepts,' named after the mythological composite beast that had a lion's head, a snake's tail, and a goat's body.

> An example of an auditory chimera would be a heard sentence that was created by the accidental composition of the voices of two persons who just happened to be speaking at the same time. Natural hearing tries to avoid chimeric percepts, but music often tries to create them. It may want the listener to accept the simultaneous roll of the drum, clash of the cymbal, and brief pulse of noise from woodwinds as a single coherent event with its own striking emergent properties.[15]

Yet when sound is added to vision, there is a further dimension. More than simply moments when filmmakers, musicians, and others involved in the process have designed the keying of sound to image, there is the phenomenon of 'synchresis,' a neologism Michel Chion coined that combines 'synchronism' with 'synthesis' and which is "...the spontaneous and irresistible weld produced between a particular auditory phenomenon and visual phenomenon when they occur at the same time. This joins results independent of any rational logic."[16] Illusion is founded upon synch points where sound and image match each other precisely, be it spoken words or music and screen dynamics. Chion's synchresis describes the appearance of a perceived connection between sound and image, pulling them into a seeming unity of either illusion or aesthetics.[17] The rivets holding the process together are moments of precise synchronization between simultaneous sound and image events.[18] Furthermore, these points involve mutual implication of sound and vision, as discovered in the 1970s by McGurk and MacDonald.[19] Moments of sonic and visual unity work around distinct perceptual phenomena for sound and image (which are detailed in chapter 2). These suggest that the sum of seeing and hearing is not a simple, transparent access to reality at all due to hearing affecting vision and vice versa. Consequently, there is no such thing as 'pure music' or a pure visual discourse. This underlines audiovisual culture as a radical object, as a mixture of the exploitation of cross-referencing and the synergy of the human senses.

As I noted, there is a tendency for synchronization to be perceived where it was not necessarily intended, at points in the film where sound and image cohere in an effective manner that establishes a sense of their marriage. What appears to be a diverting example of precisely this is the phenomenon known as 'Dark Side of the Rainbow' or 'Dark Side of Oz.' If one begins to play a DVD or video of *The Wizard of Oz* (1939) and mutes the sound while playing Pink Floyd's album *Dark Side of the Moon* (1973), the two seem to fit together surprisingly well. Some contend that it is no coincidence that there appears to be a synchronization, and that it is the hidden logic of the rather esoteric Pink Floyd record.[20] Others have pointed to Jung's concept of synchronicity, where there is a seemingly meaningful coming together of two disparate elements.[21] Rather than happening by chance, as a so-called coincidence, there is a logic to the event that is not quite apparent.[22] Others still have had recourse to the explanation that the human mind wishes to find unity and cohesion, even in situations where there is little likelihood of finding much. Without necessarily trying to alight on one explanation, what interests me is that there appear to be synchronizations, and these appear to hold together a loose structure of sound and image in an astonishingly coherent fashion. Elements seem to gel, and synchronization is less a matter of consistently precise 'hits' of notable elements, than more a sense of flow being met by similar dynamics and notable portals of development being matched, as well as the words to songs appearing to comment on the screen action. So, there is some magic in Oz. The wizard in *The Wizard of Oz* might serve as an apt metaphor for cinema. Having heard about the wizard's powers throughout her time in Oz, Dorothy meets him at the film's conclusion. He is large, loud, and impressive. She and her companions assume the unity of the booming voice and strange visuals as a 'real' and highly singular, powerful being. This is all an illusion, achieved by a man with a machine. Once the illusion is removed, so is the power of the wizard.[23] The overwhelming majority of films exploit the illusory characteristics of the medium to present a world that on some level is taken to be reality by its audience. The combination of sound and image is a mechanical operation that appears to render a perceptual reality. Also like the wizard, cinema makes the audience wide-eyed, unable to see and hear beyond the thin veil of the illusion to the mechanism that grips them in a state of such awe. An awareness of the illusion of cinema ought to lead us to be concerned with perception and artifice. On one level, of course, cinema is a miracle of illusion, allowing us to see and hear the world in a magical manner. But on the other, it is a huckster's trick, underlined by Richard Pryor playing the Wiz in the film of the same title (1978) as a failed politician. In the 1930s, Sergei Eisenstein and Sergei Yutkevich expressed surprise that the United States despite all its sophistication had not overcome the simplistic desire for 'illusionism' in film.[24] Their pronouncement remains valid today, and analysis has to step back to break the illusion. Maurice Merleau-Ponty stated that

> It is because we are through and through compounded of relationships with the world that for us the only way to become aware of the fact is to suspend the resultant activity, to refuse it our complicity... [and]... in order to see the world and grasp it as paradoxical, we must break with our familiar acceptance of it.[25]

Mary Ann Doane elucidates the process of illusion forged by sound in mainstream cinema, observing that the synchronization of image and voice is 'sacrosanct' and that 'invisible' synchronization is to obscure the medium's 'material heterogeneity' (and hide its origin in artifice and industry). Conventional construction, founded upon synchronization, set up a stable auditory-spectatorial position, "...holding at bay the potential trauma of dispersal, dismemberment, difference."[26] The crucial element in this process is the point of synchronization, or synch point, which holds it all together. It is the crucial lynchpin in the process of retaining a sensible, often comforting discourse from a collapse into disturbing meaninglessness and chaotic psychological and material disorder.

So, the absolute essence of sound film is the synchronization of image and sound at key moments that hold together the film experience. I should note here that I am essentially discussing cinema, where a big screen and big sound can produce an overwhelming effect rather than merely minor interest, rather than television. The basis of cinema in a precise synchronization of the audio and the visual is evident to the degree that it has been considered unworthy of serious or sustained consideration. Furthermore, film tends to move between moments of synchrony between sound and image and points where there is no synchronization. This is quite likely the beating heart (or breathing lungs, perhaps) of cinema as an audiovisual medium. Regarding audiovisual culture from this perspective illuminates it in a form that removes the overly familiar aspects that militate against sustained and detailed theorization, from a sonic point of view at least. I would suggest that synchronization offers a form of repose, moments of comfort in a potentially threatening environment that is overwrought with sound and image stimuli. In consequence, the lack of synchronization between sound and images has to be characterized as potentially disturbing, perhaps even moments of textual danger. Thus the interplay between the two becomes the central dynamic of audiovisual culture, and its objects can be reconceived and newly understood along these lines. Film might then be seen as a series of dynamic plays of plenitude and rupture across film's audiovisual synchronization that manifest film as a psychological, as well as aesthetic, drama.

THE MUSIC OF VISUALS: ASYNCHRONY AND THE DYNAMIC

As almost an opposite of synchronization, asynchrony refuses the moment of synchronization. Sergei Eisenstein was one of the first theorists to articulate a notion of film image and sound working through difference and contrast rather than mutual representation. This desire for asynchrony was evident in his theory of film and sound working either in parallel, doing the same thing, or in counterpoint, marking an independence of image and soundtracks. This notion of parallel and counterpoint as descriptive of the relationship of image and sound can be traced back to the famous and often-cited "Statement on Sound" by Eisenstein, Pudovkin, and Alexandrov. Using musical metaphors, this endorsed counterpoint as a manifestation of the montage principle they espoused, stating that film sound should aim at a "...sharp discord with the visual images..." to realize the audiovisual potential of cinema.[27] They were interested in the space between image and sound communication.[28] On an aesthetic stage, however, cutting-edge music of course can be accompanied by banal and conventional visuals, and vice versa. In the vast majority of cases, the weld between music and image is strong enough to furnish something of the qualities of sound and image to each other, to the point where it is rare to come across a notably banal song with an interesting video or an interesting song with a banal video. This situation illustrates vividly that there is a significant creative potential in the space between the music and the image as accompaniments to one another. Questions of what images should accompany certain pieces of music predated recording, let alone the complementing of screened images with recorded music and vice versa. Yet there always has been some idea of conventional and acceptable matches of images with sounds. Illustrative images for music have always had a certain ambiguity, although the closer the images relate to a reproduction of a live performance of what can be heard on the soundtrack, the less ambiguous the relationship of sound and image. In this book, I wish to remove what at times might be arbitrary divisions between sound and music, allowing us to think of film soundtracks as essentially 'musical' rather than simply representational.

In terms of film production, key sequences (such as dialogue) tend conventionally to have action matched to sound through direct synchronization, yielding the illusion of a coherent reality. However, many sequences (sometimes including dialogue sequences) are not shot with location or synchronized sound. This habitually is added later, as part of the post-production stage (not just the musical score but also dialogue re-recording or dubbing, recorded sound effects, and Foley[29]). Consequently, there are plenty of points where visuals and sound do not match directly, sometimes only vaguely, and sometimes in a manner that is not immediately apparent. The cinema is less concerned with capturing reality than it is with producing a composite of sound and image that will be accepted by audiences, and is thus essentially conventional in character.[30] At heart, this process uses the same time to pull often different spaces together. As well as the process of their interaction, the aesthetic nature of both sound and image tracks regularly gets overlooked. A film soundtrack might be conceived in musical terms. After all, centuries of development in musical theory have furnished one of the most highly developed means of analyzing sound and thinking in sonic terms. Film scores have their own synch points, which delineate momentary junctures where music synchs directly with action. The most extreme form of this is Mickeymousing, where music directly and slavishly mimics screen action, often for comic effect. These synch points are the keystone moments in sound film. We might reconceptualize films as a forward movement though time from moments of synchronization of image and sound through unsynchronized moments and back to synchronized moments. In musical terms, this is reminiscent of the harmonic movement of classical tonality, where music in the tonic key then 'develops' by modulating into different keys before returning home to the tonic key. Indeed, it is advantageous to think of temporal progression in musical terms, where images form notable cadences conjoining or ending sections of space, narrative, or activity. In fact, as an abstract ordering of time, music ought to prove an important analytical approach for understanding film. This process can be fleeting or take longer and unfold in a more leisurely manner.

Noel Burch observes that "The fundamental dialectic in film, the one that at least empirically seems to contain every other, is that contrasting and joining sound with image."[31] Audiences and analysts may not focus on it, but Burch is correct to point to relations of proximity or distance between sound and image as crucial. Furthermore, the synchronization of sound and image constitutes a drama of play between order and chaos, or perhaps between safety and uncertainty. Asynchrony threatens to pull apart the contract of film's illusion of sound and visual unity into a miasma of disparate and potentially meaningless elements.

The overwhelming majority of films are constructed with synchronization in mind, either through conscious points of synchronization that guide sound and image editing or through less clear notions of aesthetic choice. There is a concrete status to such synch points and dynamic hits (from an aesthetic and perceptual, as well as an industrial point of view). Traditions of editing techniques and staging techniques, added to the relations of shots and gestural aspects of shapes and characters on-screen, all coalesce into a sense of synchronization of sound and image in film. On the other hand, synchronization is also a perceptual phenomenon, and the finished object of the film is received by audiences as an object that, among other things, involves rapid shifting and oscillation between precise synchronization and asynchrony.

Theories of film have emphasized the need for continuity, yet films are clearly a dynamic relationship between conventional continuity and novel, discontinuous elements. This is nowhere more evident than in the 'whodunit' detective film, where we are shown certain events but not others, and important clues are withheld until late in the film. Perhaps we should spend less time thinking of films as a progression from start to finish and more as a containment of energy, of balance between elements that a skillful filmmaker is able to hold in precise relationship, making a deft blend of light and dark, energy and repose. Large sections of film retain a sense of balance, but this can be undermined or exploited for effect. Yet this dynamic and psychological balance wards off disturbance, and a concentration of asynchrony with less resolution in synchrony is a characteristic of certain tense and disturbing sequences in avant garde, art, and horror films. Despite a regular desire for thrills, Freud's 'Nirvana Principle' proposes that people ultimately want to be tranquil.[32] The nervous system functions to make the tension caused by extreme emotion dissipate, to be discharged as soon as possible. Yet film audiences only want questions posed that are answerable by the film, and mainstream audiences tend to be upset at narrative and representational ambiguities. The anxiety that may well arise during long passages of asynchrony might be disquieting, as it reminds us on some level of antiquated silent cinema, mime, and ancient cultures back from the grave, like the eponymous Knights Templar villains of *The Tombs of the Blind Dead* (1971), who are silent, relentless, and malevolent manifestations of the long dead, an upsetting outburst of silence in sound cinema.[33] There is, of course, an important historical genealogy to this dynamic between synchrony and asynchrony. Movement between synchrony and asynchrony clearly derives partly from a movement between the talkies (dialogue-based cinema) and earlier silent cinema, where sound and image were more independent and music was able to take the lead in some situations. Some sequences have minimal amounts of synchronized sound and maximum un-synched sound. The relation of sound and image makes an unregistered dynamic play of plenitude and rupture across time that manifests film as a psychological and aesthetic drama irrespective of the events depicted.

BRIDGE

The construction of sound in the cinema, while incorporating music, might also be seen to have a certain musical impetus more generally. Film editor Ernest Walter has stated, "...the sound editor assembles his sound effects to create an almost musical effect in some sequences...."[34] Although this book spends less space scrutinizing dialogue and voices in detail, it looks to how sound and image are orchestrated across time ('horizontally') through great investment in moments or sustained sections of synchrony ('vertically'). Whereas it might easily be argued that all sonic aspects in cinema are sound effects, and I agree that they are, I approach sound effects and dialogue more as music, or at least as retaining an aesthetic sensibility that might in some way be related to music. The aim of this book is to provide a view of cinema as an audiovisual medium through a focus on the central characteristic of synchronization of sound and image into a seeming single event. The book's thesis argues that the crucial essence of sound film is the synchronization of image and sound at key moments that hold together the film experience.

Generally speaking, although there have been a welter of recent studies on film sound, there has been little thought about the relationship of sound and image beyond its production and narrative function. Apart from moments in Michel Chion's work, there is almost nothing written about cinema as a synchronization of sound and image. I think this should be approached as a central issue in the study of film sound. After all, the audiovisual lock is the lynchpin of sound cinema. Most writing about cinema has abided by the illusionist perspective that encounters it as a coherent object or, worse, has assumed that it is in essence visual. It is high time that deliberation on the matter attempted to rethink and restate the medium and phenomenon in more sophisticated terms.

In this book, I concentrate overwhelmingly on mainstream narrative films and only fitfully address documentaries, experimental and avant garde films, musicals, and animated films. One reason for this is the fact that film production and exhibition are dominated by such films, and they retain a dominant place in the psychology of cinema. Furthermore, some of these other genres and formats tend to have highly specific processes, which would have taken far more space to address than available for a book such as this. Later in the book, I suggest that film musicals have had a distinct influence on films that are not musicals, while I also point to the impetus of avant garde aesthetics evident in many films with more mainstream characters.

It seems almost inconceivable that there has been no major study of film sound and image synchronization. However, this book does not manifest a full and systematic treatise on the subject, or even a general introduction, but instead attempts to theorize film as an audiovisual medium by addressing the synchronization of moving images with recorded music, sound effects, and voices. Although this may initially seem to be a high-concept book with a couple of wild ideas about 'how cinema works,' it actually aims to take a sideways look at film and music aesthetics in order to see and hear cinema differently: precisely as an audiovisual enterprise with a highly particular aesthetic that derives from this essential fact. By necessity, this book does not evade dealing with relevant issues that define our considerations here, but it does not lose the principal theoretical and aesthetic arguments at the expense of peripheral concerns. Note that while the discussion touches many bases, the constraint of space does not allow for a systematic working through of large topics such as technology, industrial practice, and historical developments. The focus is to remain on theoretical matters, but with a foot on those concrete moments of synchronization.

CHAPTER 2
Synchronization

McGurk and Beyond

Although there are many books that provide a basic outline of how films are made from the point of view of filming and editing footage, few focus on the soundtrack and its combination with the images. Indeed, many of the techniques involved are even unfamiliar to those well versed in filmmaking. The inclusion of a historical backdrop and technical description is important for this book, as the emergence of synchronized sound and image chiefly followed an industrial imperative enabled by developing technology. This chapter provides some technological information but concentrates more on outlining aesthetic procedures and addressing the psychology of synchronizing sound and image.

Synchronization has been at the heart of cinema since the implementation of recorded sound, yet scholarship has regularly ignored this essential but not immediately visible aspect of cinema. The dominant approach has been to deem film a visual medium, ignoring the significant sonic component and, crucially, ignoring the fact that sound and image are yoked together at the center of the filmmaking process.[1] General studies of film persist in marginalizing sound, and it appears to remain viable for authors to proclaim film as a visual medium, although perhaps less sanguinely than their forebears.[2] Across the history of serious writing about film, isolated writers such as Kurt London, Sergei Eisenstein, and Hanns Eisler and Theodor Adorno exhibited strong concerns with sound and sound-image aesthetics. In more recent years, however, Michel Chion's writings (particularly in their English translation and condensation by Claudia Gorbman) appear to have built a foundation by pulling sound processes to the center of discussions of film aesthetics. Chion's writings have been highly influential, and virtually all writings about film sound published in the last few years draw heavily upon his ideas and analyses. Other writers such as Elizabeth Weis, John Belton, and Rick Altman have also voiced concerns about the process at the heart of film and all contemporary audiovisual culture, while Claudia Gorbman and Royal S. Brown have been isolated but authoritative spokespersons for film music. Yet these have been practically voices in the wilderness. Indeed, interest in film sound and film music remained peripheral until the turn of the second millennium, with the implication that these were roundly unimportant aspects of film. Despite exponentially increasing interest in these matters, there remains a tendency merely to approach synchronization as a fact to produce the illusion of talking characters on screen. The illusionistic aspect of cinema—undoubtedly one of its foremost defining characteristics—is taken for granted rather than interrogated as a mysterious process that is able to both effortlessly hide and call attention to itself. In my discussion here, I engage with most of these writers but have accorded a particular position of importance to Eisenstein, who, more than any other, was concerned with the synchronization of sound and image and had a number of striking ideas about synchronization as a practice and also as a political-psychological process. In this chapter, I deal with theoretical and practical aspects of synchronization. It is important to provide something approaching a description of the technical process of synchronization and illustrate how this developed and what impact it had on film aesthetics.

The synchronized recorded sound film may well predate cinema as we know it. Thomas Edison's assistant W. K. L. Dickson claimed to have demonstrated synchronized sound and moving image on film as early as October of 1889.[3] In 1900, Gaumont more famously exhibited its 'Phono-Cinema-Theatre' at the Paris Exposition. These short song films matched sound to image using recording cylinders and acoustic amplification, while in 1904, Oskar Messter distributed the similar 'Biophon' song films and Georges Mendel distributed short films of operatic arias.[4] In 1906, Eugene-Auguste Lauste patented a device that recorded sound and image simultaneously. All of these did not culminate in talking films but became something of a historical dead end. Warner Brothers' showing of its Vitaphone system in the late 1920s caused the wide-scale adoption of films with synchronized recorded sound, although the newest part of the technology was in fact electric sound amplification. The Western Electric sound-on-film system, using variable density imaging on celluloid, became the Hollywood standard after an agreement in 1928 and by February of 1930, 95 percent of Hollywood's output had synchronized recorded sound.[5] In the earliest years of sound cinema, 'synchronized' or 'synched up' originally meant essentially fitting music to a film, rather than matching sound effects and dialogue to images. At the end of the 1920s, a number of silent films were retrofitted with recorded music in this manner, with the music conceived very much as a supplement to the images. The conjunction of silent films with recorded sound in the late 1920s marked a highly momentous intersection of existing industries, bringing together film, music, and communication companies. For instance, Warner Brothers merged with Western Electric (which was the telegraphy company AT&T) to form the sound film company Vitaphone, while in 1928, RKO was formed from merging RCA (Radio Corporation of America) with Keith-Orpheum. Although not its origin, such multimedia conglomerates were the blueprint for the form of cultural industry cross-platform enterprises that are evident today. Many film histories have failed to register that events outside the film industry were the central deteminant. As Rick Altman noted but few still seem to acknowledge, "...*Don Juan*, the Vitaphone shorts, and *The Jazz Singer* were an outgrowth of the record industry."[6] The conjoining of the capabilities of the sound recording industry with moving image-based film studio output not only forged a new aesthetic object; it also created a new psychological experience.

Sound provides the dimension of space for film, serving a crucial function in expanding the surface of its flat images. Illusion is keyed to notable synch points that are sometimes used to sound-edit a film and provide an underlying logic to the film as perceptual object and abstract aesthetic. Michel Chion coined the term 'synchresis' to describe the spontaneous appearance of synchronized connection between sound and image.[7] This is a lock that magnetically pulls together sound and image in the same perceptual space. We expect the two to be attached. While this can be in evidence outside of the world of electronic screens or projectors allied with electronic speakers, for the purposes of discussion here, it is worth noting that the effect seems particularly strong and solid when sound and image are perceived as a potential unity in a film, television program, or video game. Chion goes on to declare synchresis 'Pavlovian' and capable of cultural influence, "[b]ut at the same time, it very probably has an innate basis."[8] While we the audience assume a strong bond between sounds and images occupying the same or similar space, the keystones of this process are moments of precise synchronization between sound and image events.[9] This illusion of sonic and visual unity is the heart of film and related media. Being perceived as an utter unity not only disavows the basis in artifice, but also has dissuaded much in the way of serious questioning of film as more than simply a visual medium. The commonsense notion among writers dealing with film is that image dominates and sound is often little more than its supplement. There is no reason why this should be the case for film analysis and criticism, despite constant assertion of film as being a visual art. As Roy Armes noted, "Sound is not 'subordinated' to image—but industrial discourses... compartmentalized sound."[10] It is therefore not easy to think beyond these ingrained limitations.

THE PSYCHOLOGY OF SYNCHRONIZATION

The branch of neuroscience that is referred to as 'sensory neuroscience' investigates the brain processes that underpin perception. Through neuroimaging, different areas of the brain can be seen to be activated when dealing with specific pursuits or when faced with certain situations.[11] Although this may suggest a form of compartmentalization in the brain, with certain parts dealing with particular things, it seems that in most cases, more than one area is activated. The brain increasingly has become understood as a parallel processor, where brain sections might deal simultaneously with different sensory information, but not in a totally separate manner. These sections are also intimately connected, so that one can influence the other (such as odor and taste), so the brain's functions are not compartmentalized or fully separated.[12]

Should we draw a line between perception and cognition? An approach that has dominated cognitive film theory assumes that such a division is futile and that all brain processes and understanding should be housed under the rubric and conception of cognition. For the purposes of this book, I am happier to adopt a division that retains a sense of perception's physical basis and a distinction from cognitive processes as being 'higher order.' Perception is in essence physical in that it involves transferring sound waves and light into electrical impulses in the brain through a process known as 'transduction.' This makes a 'proximal stimulus' (the raw signals entering the brain) that is processed on a basic level as sensory information *before* the cognitive processing of that information (thinking). To illustrate this, our ancestors' understanding that an animal may be a predator or possible food would be a cognition, whereas simply registering the animal's presence and basic physical aspects would be at the level of perception. This higher level activity is sometimes called 'judgment,' and such mental activity has more to do with thought as it is commonly recognized than to do with a basic level of understanding or reaction: lower order activity dealing with stimuli that is more physically based but an essential and foundational precursor to cultural contemplation.[13] Grasp of synchronization is surely at this primary level.

According to Joseph Ledoux in *The Emotional Brain: The Mysterious Underpinnings of Emotional Life*, brain states (unconscious affect) and physical body states (conscious or unconscious expressions of emotion) are stored in and retrieved from the amygdala in the brain's limbic region.[14] These emotional memories are associated with the particular perceptual situations in which they initially arose and are then triggered by similar ones. These are not simply cognitive memories, and indeed the associated process of cognition takes place elsewhere in the brain; stimulus recognition takes place *before* cognition. Unconscious affect always creates emotion, whereas conscious cognition does not necessarily do so, and "...emotion and cognition are best thought of as separate but interacting mental functions mediated by separate but interacting brain systems."[15] Ledoux's work suggests that emotion is less concerned with a cognitive response so much as an immediate and almost physical reaction to a situation with a preexisting emotional state. Debates that have endeavored to blanket the whole human process from stimulus to response as cognition do a disservice to cognitive psychology by watering down the strong foundations of the theory and the ideas involved.[16] Cognitive psychology's notion of perception is that there is a small amount of stimulus and the 'work' all takes place as a cognitive process in the brain. This so-called mental model affirms that stimulus requires the considerable brain input of 'enriching' through hypothesis-testing. On the other hand, there is the notion of direct perception, sometimes called the body model, a 'realist' approach that posits there is much stimulus that is translated directly into an isomorph in the brain.[17] Traditionally, perception was seen as passive—until Gestalt experiments made significant steps in proving otherwise.[18] But can we have one without the other? While much takes place at a primary, perhaps essentially physical or physiological level, it necessarily precedes higher level thinking processes, yet is crucial in defining the courses these might take.[19]

Cognitive psychology has tended to deemphasize the process of perception, often merely declaring it an instrumental part of the more general cognitive process. Inspired by Gestalt psychology, in this book, I try to place more emphasis on perception. This reinstates a physical aspect to the process denied by cognitive psychology-inspired approaches.[20] It also makes for a more solid demarcation between lower order and higher order brain processes, between those of basic understanding and a more culturally acquired sense of registering relationships between things and ensuing implications. This division might, in a simple way, be seen as that between general human hardware and more specific human software that is uploaded later.

The dominance of cognitive psychology in debates about culture and the unregistered slippage of the term 'cognitive' into notions wider than ideas governed by cognitive psychology have muddied the waters in terms of debating aesthetic effect. Although I am more than happy to accept the insights provided by cognitive psychology (or cognitive science as it is sometimes called), there are distinct aspects of the aesthetic process (for film especially) that are poorly accounted for by such an approach. The reader might appreciate that this book's concern with the process of synchronizing sound and image as the central aspect of sound cinema means that a cognitive approach along such lines might be less attractive. Instead, I prefer to proceed from a psychological position that has solid foundations in scientific experimentation: Gestalt psychology.[21] It is also not a 'big theory that explains everything with a couple of basic tenets,' but it provides a number of principles that can offer insight. Taking its origins from experiments addressing human perception, often of visual objects, Gestalt psychology has proven itself adept at dealing with this most basic level of human activity. However, it has not been widely exploited to provide significant insight beyond this, into more complex forms of understanding. Perhaps this is why Gestalt psychology has proven unattractive in the study of film or narrative-based culture like literature. As an empirical endeavor emanating from repeatable experimental situations, Gestalt psychology appears more scientific than the forms of psychology that have dominated analysis and interpretation in the arts. The others have seemingly proven themselves better at dealing with narrative and representation, two ideas that have dominated critical approaches to film. Yet Gestalt psychology has not been without influence in other arts such as fine art, architecture, and music. It is also not as if Gestalt psychology has had no impact in the study of film. Max Wertheimer theorized 'phi phenomenon,' where broken movement is perceived as continuity: the epicenter of film. This gradually replaced the notion of the 'persistence of vision,' which was thought to account for the illusion of movement in successive frames.[22] It is also not without some significance that one of the earlier classical film theorists was a follower of the principles of Gestalt psychology. Rudolf Arnheim wrote important books such as *Film as Art* (1958) where he discusses the 'partial illusion' of film and focuses on 'expressive' aspects at the nexus of the formal and the representational. Arnheim wrote more about other arts than film, although his theories have valence across media and approaches. In "The Gestalt Theory of Expression" (1949), he theorized that expressive aspects of art objects have a form of 'structural kinship' with corresponding mental states.[23] This notion of isomorphism, or 'psychophysical parallelism,' between mental state and object/situation perceived has some currency in how we understand the world, as well as art. However, as Meraj Dhir convincingly argues, the designation of Rudolf Arnheim's writings as 'classical' or of historical merit has prevented current film theorists from seeing the enduring viability of his approaches.[24]

Although Gestalt psychology does not begin from 'given' concepts like much empirical analysis, there are some core concepts to Gestalt approaches that emanate from experiments and are proven to be essences of human perception. Absolutely central is the act of perception itself (defined as becoming aware of or grasping sensory information/stimulus). Gestalt psychology was one of the first approaches to posit 'active perception,' whereby a dynamic relationship is posited as existing between description in the brain and impulses arriving in the senses, rather than the realist position of simple and passive processing between sensory input and mental understanding. For Gestaltists, the brain is approached as holistic (self-organizing with the whole different from the sum of its parts), processing in parallel and with analogue procedures that have similarities to outside events.

Analytical approaches include the principles of totality, psychophysical isomorphism, and experimental analysis (starting from the phenomenon itself), which privilege actual experimental activity and experience. There are a number of laws for Gestalt psychology that work to group together similar or proximate objects. These include the laws of closure, similarity, proximity, symmetry, continuity (continuation of patterns), and common fate (where objects moving in the same direction are perceived as a unity). Among the most useful insights of Gestalt psychology are that we attempt to order the stimuli we perceive in as simple and regular form as possible (called the 'good Gestalt').[25] Perhaps the most well-known Gestalt characteristics are so-called reification, whereby we 'finish off' incomplete shapes (proving that perception is generative) and multi-stability, whereby single objects might be perceived in alternation as two different yet stable entities. As can be seen from the images of the Necker cube and the Rubin vase (figures 2.1 and 2.2), perception is active, rather than passive and merely representational. The existence of planes of figure and ground on a perceptual level demonstrates the ability to construct three-dimensional space from the two-dimensional, along with our mental ability to flip between two mental constructions of the same flat image. These well-known diagrams not only illustrate precisely how the process of perception and cognition is bound up in us imagining the missing parts that make up the

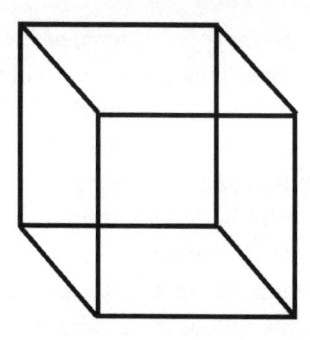

Figure 2.1: Necker Cube.

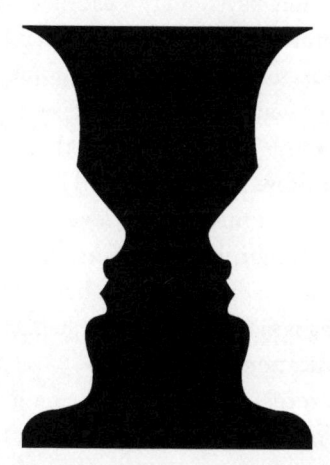

Figure 2.2: Rubin Vase.

crucial whole, but also show how central the process of pattern-finding is to human endeavor.

Despite the fact that most Gestalt theories and experiments from its halcyon era in the early part of the 20th century were based on purely visual aspects, there is evidence of aural objects following similar processes. Hearing is not a purely physical process. A sound wave hits the ear and is converted immediately into a neural signal, but the processes of perception and the brain develop it into something more. This is illustrated by the dominance of psychoacoustic phenomena in current processing of audio signals: We hear what is geared precisely to our hearing process (psychoacoustics) rather than to what is a good reproduction of an actual sound (as in the old hi-fi approach). One audio phenomenon that is sometimes taken advantage of in audio equipment is 'phantom fundamentals.' These are low pitches heard when there is no signal of the sort present. The brain produces a sense of an underlying pitch from patterns in the differences of frequencies present. Such principles work for the perception of sound too, although not in precisely the same manner. It is possible to hear and register two sounds simultaneously, whereas usually one sound will be registered over another or even be hidden (physically masked) by the other. Dual hearing—or 'dichotic listening' as it is sometimes known—takes place more effectively when we are able to segregate audio streams more easily because of noticeable spatial, pitch, and tonal differences in the two sound sources.[26]

Recent scientific activity has found some proof of sensory-neural processing fitting with Gestalt psychology's estimation of perception, which was established well before current scientific capabilities. The Zürich group has had recent success in relating Gestalt phenomena to activities of neural networks and single neurons, correlating neurophysiology with phenomenological deductions.[27] Thus the theory that events are apprehended through an analogue process is strengthened by empirical work on physical aspects of the brain on a microscopic level. It is not far to jump from some sort of analogue isomorphism between stimulus and registering in the brain to imagine that the isomorphism between real world and sound and image in the cinema is significant, as would be a sense of isomorphism across art and communication forms.

One of the central processes of sound cinema is the unifying of image and sound into a single Gestalt perception. When the unity is not apparent, we have a desire for it and in some cases 'connect the dots' to complete a coherent picture, as illustrated most vividly in the general impression provided by montage. Our desire for a unity of perception—sound and image appearing as a seamless, unproblematic representation of reality—has been exploited mostly unwittingly by the cinema. According to Gestalt psychologist Kurt Koffka, "An incomplete task leaves a trace which is unstable, compared to a non-closed figure. Such figures possess, as we know, a tendency towards closure, and we find that this tendency is also a characteristic of the trace of an incomplete act."[28] So, just how much do we imagine? Cinema is often about 'giving an impression' and sleight of hand in terms of making us register something emotionally and cognitively from elements that add up to something rather less. A fine example of this occurs, for example, in the murder in the shower in *Psycho* (1960), which never shows an impact of knife on skin, even though that is our abiding impression. Our perception follows the 'law of minimum principle,' according to John Benjafield: "We do not perceive what is actually in the external world so much as we tend to organize our experiences so that it is as simple as possible...simplicity is a principle that guides our perception and may even override the effects of previous experience."[29] At this point, we should remember that film consists of a limited repertoire of standardized shots in standardized relationships, with highly focused and structured sound. This pared-down basic audiovisual language rendering of the real world is a correlation of our perception and understanding of the world as simple and understandable. In this way, film embodies the law of minimum principle, emanating perhaps less from any direct representational relationship of film material to the world outside and more from the human mechanisms of pattern-seeking and the Gestalt processes of 'filling in the gaps.' Kurt Goldstein notes that

> ...the tendency toward the good Gestalt finds its explanation as an organismic phenomenon. The explanation lies in the tendency toward preferred behavior, which is the essential prerequisite for the existence of a definite organism. It is a special expression of the general tendency to realize optimal performances with a minimum expenditure of energy as measured in terms of the whole. The operation of this tendency includes the so-called 'prägnanz', the closure phenomenon, and many other characteristics of Gestalt. In fact, they are only intelligible from this tendency."[30]

So the grounding of the process is physiological, based in the body's hardware and basic mechanisms rather than a 'thinking' part of cognition. A common criticism of Gestalt psychology is that, for the purposes of humanities and arts research, it furnishes answers that tend toward the merely descriptive and provides little mileage for analysis. Perhaps it does not have readymade answers at hand for traditional interpretive film studies, but its central principles lie at the heart of film as a medium and thus, I would suggest, are a crucial key to unlocking the physical, as well as the cultural and social, mechanisms of cinema.

Methods inspired by Gestalt approaches adopt fundamental positions in relation to film as an object and research as a process. Human perception has a tendency to 'join up' elements of an object into a meaningful, coherent—and seamless—whole. This offers an explanation, therefore, of why representational cinema seems *like* reality. We ask no further questions of it. We take in the whole and do not pay attention to all the elements individually. This grasping of situations as a whole is one of the most profound insights of Gestalt psychology. The mechanisms by which this takes place are empirically proven (and sit uneasily with the 'atomistic' approach of cognitive psychology-inspired analysis). In tandem with this, when confronted with an object, structures appear for us no matter what is actually physically present. Human hardware is determinedly pattern-seeking, looking for—and inevitably finding—some sort of sense, be it narrative, representational, relational, or whatever. A Gestalt-inspired approach might find something more or at least make us more aware of the process.

It is crucial to note the desire for unity among audiences, who aim at concretizing 'the good Gestalt' of an object, taking it as a unity rather than a fragmented ragbag of disparate elements. No matter how abstract a film might be, human beings search for patterns of meaning and understanding. Perception is an active process and might be differentiated from higher level cognition. It also has a physical character rather than necessarily consisting of a purely logical and computational process. We perceive sounds and images as part of a whole, not separately, except in certain situations when a single sense is heightened by a paucity of impulses from the other senses. This is, of course, why silence is so compelling in films and why horror films regularly exploit darkness or impinged vision and make the audience focus on sonic aspects. The *conceptual lock* of sound and image in films is mental rather than technical, but it is essential to investigate the technical procedures that render sound cinema as an object that can be apprehended with such effect by the human senses.[31]

SOUND AND VISION MULTIPLIED: BEYOND THE MCGURK EFFECT

Although the understanding of our physical processing of sound and image is probably still quite primitive, there have been some important insights from research into our perception and cognition of sound and image in combination. These studies are often focused on so-called cross-modal effects, when one sense is implicated or changed by the input of another sense. What some have termed 'congruence studies' proceed from the congruence-associationist model established for analysis of film music by Sandra Marshall and Annabel Cohen.[32] This identifies structural congruence, particularly temporal congruence, between film and music as having the power to 'cement' the sound and visual elements together, although perhaps not necessarily all of them. After this initial marriage, the perceiving subject will likely associate similar sonic elements with the on-screen object. (For example, slow, sad music might in a Pavlovian manner become associated with a single character on-screen.) When sound and image on-screen are synchronized, we associate the two, perceiving them as a single entity, or at least as directly and intimately related. Once this takes place, other attributes of sound become attributed to the visual object too. Although this has been a foundational study of massive influence, there have been some criticisms and caveats. Marshall and Cohen's experiment involved using human subjects who gave responses to moving shapes on a screen alongside sounds. Their conclusions extrapolate from this to make general pronouncements about film that are not borne out by their study. One response to their study by Scott Lipscomb and Roger Kendall staged a similar experiment but this time used moving film images.[33] They found that music has the ability to shift perception/cognition of moving images. Particularly in the ranges of potency (how strong a reaction might be to images) and activity (affecting the degree that image events are perceived as more extreme in terms of speed or movement, or non-movement). However, a high degree of congruence is required for these effects, without which sound and vision will be perceived as running on separate independent channels. One of the significant points to be drawn from their conclusions is that synchronization is an absolutely central element in achieving congruency between sound and image, and thus crucial in achieving the dramatic effects of the synergy of sound and image.

There are further important points of perceptual-cognitive reality that should be approached as highly significant for any study of film that accepts the audiovisual basis of the medium. Some of the most famous phenomena include the 'McGurk effect,' whereby the visual influences the sonic; the 'ventriloquist effect,' whereby the sonic and the visual spontaneously appear to cohere; and the 'bounce-inducing effect,' whereby sounds reformulate our perception of visual activity. I will adumbrate a few of these to illustrate how far relations between sound and image do not follow simple, commonsense patterns, and thus why the fundamentals of the relationship need more concentrated and subtle thought.

The McGurk effect (occasionally called the McGurk-MacDonald effect) is an audiovisual phenomenon that demonstrates the interaction of sound and image stimuli in perception and cognition. Rather than being totally separate channels, our vision is able to affect our hearing, suggesting that the senses are never fully autonomous when used in combination. First stated explicitly in an article in *Nature* in 1976, McGurk and MacDonald pointed to the perceptual phenomenon whereby images of a person's mouth making a sound, when added to a recording of a different vocal sound, added up to the perception of a different sound.[34] In other words, despite being the same, the sound appears to change when accompanied by visuals of different mouth movements. This is highly evident in the cases of particular combinations. The most-often cited is the use of a visual image of a mouth saying 'ga' and the sound of a person saying 'ba,' which is perceived as sounding like closer to 'da.' A phoneme (sound) combined with an almost matching viseme (image of sound being produced) when seen and heard together yield a different phoneme for the perceiver. Illustrating that visuals can change perceptions of sounds, this phenomenon also significantly demonstrates the fundamental interrelatedness of sound and image. Indeed, it suggests that fully isolating sound or image may be invalid. It certainly suggests that blanket assertions of film being a purely or mostly visual medium should be long banished. The implications for sound may in fact be more profound. Indeed, any appeal to the purity of musical experience is thrown into question.

The ventriloquist effect is another instance of the phenomenal effect of sound and vision combined. When images and sound relations are ambiguous, sound compels the perceiver to try to make sense of elements by integrating sound and vision into a single event. The perceiver will aim at obtaining a 'good Gestalt,' following ease of understanding and simplicity of organization. Consequently, when presented with images and sounds that might possibly be construed as the same source, we assume it is so.[35] This, of course, is the basis of film sound synchronized with image, where so much of the sound is not a direct recording of a unified pre-filmic/recording event, but unified at the point of perception by the audience. This is part of the phenomenon that has been called 'auditory capture,' when sound appears to attach itself immediately to image. The term was used in the 1994 special issue of *Psychomusicology* by Annabel Cohen with John Fentress and Valerie Bolivar, where their experiments used images with certain narrative content but varied musical accompaniment.[36]

'Motion bounce illusions' include the bounce-inducing effect, which was demonstrated by Sekuler, Sekuler, and Lau by having two concentric target shapes moving toward and through each other on a screen.[37] Once sound is added at the point of coincidence, it seems as if they are bouncing off each other, whereas without sound, it does not appear this way. This illustrates how sound affects, indeed radically changes, visual perception. It shows a sense of congruence whereby adding two media together produces the effect of their direct relationship. It also vividly illustrates the centrality of precise temporal synchronization in the primary perceptual-cognitive effects.

An experiment by O'Leary and Rhodes demonstrated that a succession of high- and low-pitched tones can influence the perception of a series of fast-moving dots on a screen. The dots alternated high and low positions, being perceived as moving up and down or as continuous and unmoving.

Adding alternating high and low sounds led to the perception of two separate unmoving dots in high and low positions on the screen (without the sound, they would not have appeared so). Change in perception of objects in a scene (through sound addition) can lead to changes in perception of movement.[38] Along similar lines, an experiment by Shams, Kamitani, and Shimojo concluded that lone flashes of light on a screen accompanied by multiple beeping sounds became perceived as regular, faster flashes of light.[39]

It seems that there are some fundamental aspects of the human brain that aim not only to join together sound and image stimuli, but also aim to assign a certain significance to the marriage of the two at vital points. These effects are without doubt at the center of cinema and have been exploited consistently, albeit unsystematically and with only an intuitive and unconscious awareness of their importance. A clear example would be cinema's exploitation of dramatic moments of synch very obviously, such as the loud entry of music at an emotional moment of revelation in a film. One might argue that there seems little point in founding the study of film on an objective inventory of elements that are 'there' as part of the film. It seems far more prudent to proceed from the point where we understand that film is an amalgam of effects, many of which precisely add up to more than the sum of their evident parts. We would do well to be aware of this more often. These findings have profound implications for understanding sound cinema. We should remember that it is problematic to deal with sound and image as separate entities—and thus with the commonplace assertion that film is a visual medium. The synergetic effect of the sound and image amalgam is the heart of cinema, and indeed it is why its illusory character can be so convincing. These experiments also underline the absolute centrality of those precise moments of synchronization. It is in these momentary links that the heart of cinematic effect is animated and invigorated.

As previously noted, the brain functions as a parallel processor. Neuroscience has made momentous discoveries about our mental hardware, displacing a simple notion of a single 'processor' and modular parts for different senses. Senses are not compartmentalized: There is a mutual implication of hearing and seeing, as testified to by the McGurk effect and other sound-image phenomena. There are some vivid illustrations of the synchresis of sound and image that are marked as exceptions to the rule of convention. In these cases, the audience is not supposed to trust its perception of the voice and moving lips appearing as a unity. An absolutely extraordinary case in point is in the version of Fritz Lang's *Metropolis* (originally released in 1927) that was assembled, re-edited, and provided with music by Giorgio Moroder (released in 1983). In one memorable sequence, Bonnie Tyler sings "Here She Comes" as accompaniment to the false Maria whipping the crowd of downtrodden proletarians into a frenzy in order to make them rise up against their oppressive social masters. What appears most bizarre about this sequence in the Moroder version is that on a number of occasions, the vocals of the song appear to synchronize precisely with the mouth of Maria on-screen goading the crowd. The effect is uncanny, and this must stand as one of the very few examples of post-synching a song to action when moments of direct synchronism join sound and image in an 'impossible' mixture of the diegetic and non-diegetic. Indeed, the synchresis of Tyler's singing voice and Maria's mouth movements cannot have gone without discussion during the Moroder version's construction. Indeed, it almost looks like a mistake. The marriage of the song and the diegetic action at times look almost like a song sequence in a film musical. Yet as soon as it does, the vocal synchronization becomes lost as quickly again. This adds up to a bewildering sequence in which the synchronization oscillates between synchrony and asynchrony.

This illustrates the tendency of human perception-cognition to seek—and almost always find—patterns of meaning. This is similar to the occasional mistake in cheaply made and rapidly produced television, when a person on-screen moves their mouth at the same time as a voiceover commentary. The momentary effect is disquieting: a moment of confusion quickly replaced by realization that voice and person on-screen are not one and the same.[40] These phenomena are illustrated vividly in films that depict ventriloquism.[41] The celebrated ventriloquist doll section of the Ealing portmanteau film *Dead of Night* (1945) exploits the mechanism at the heart of sound cinema. Indeed, ventriloquism more generally is premised upon human perception and the desire for sound and visual unity through the process of pattern-seeking and Gestalt organization of external world objects into the most logical, aesthetically and cognitively pleasing arrangement. The story segment concerns a ventriloquist (played by Michael Redgrave) whose act, it increasingly becomes apparent, is not one of matching his voice to the doll's movements but his pretending to operate a living doll. Or is he psychologically disturbed? The uncanny potential of synchronized sound and image is clear, and its exploitation underlines how far matching sound and image is more than an unsophisticated mechanism to render a sense of reality in films. The McGurk effect informs us that the addition of image track and soundtrack is not a simple product. Two and two make five, or the two tracks add up to something different: a third thing that is more than each individually and quite possibly the magic product at the very heart of cinema itself.

OPTIONS FOR JOINING SOUND AND IMAGE

Although I have been emphasizing the contrived character of the majority of seemingly unified sounds and images in films, there is also a strong tradition of retaining a sense of sound that actually belongs with its image. Such 'direct sound' (or *son direct* in French) has remained a strong tradition in documentary filmmaking and television, where shooting takes place with live sound recording, and editing endeavors to enshrine the direct connection between sound and image as a recorded event. In more mainstream filmmaking, direct sound is less common except in certain national film production traditions, such as in France. John Belton notes that

> The initial practice (ca. 1926–29) of mixing sound while it is being recorded and recording it (except for music that was often added later) at the same time as the image is recorded locks the sound indexically into the pro-filmic event of which it is the record, giving it an immediacy and integrity resembling that of the image. The introduction of rerecording and mixing in the early thirties breaks that indexical bond of sound to the pro-filmic event.
>
> ... The building of the sound track, using the image rather than the pro-filmic event as a guide, now becomes a final stage in the 'realization' of the image.[42]

Charles O'Brien points to the French preference for *son direct*, sound recorded simultaneously with the image, as suggesting an alternative to the Hollywood model. Sound reproduces a performance staged for the recording (rather than the U.S. procedure of assembling different components). O'Brien notes that direct sound almost defines a national French filmmaking style.[43] It is highly evident in films by Straub and Huillet, Godard, Rivette, and Eustache, among others, and marks a startling contrast with Hollywood: "Instead of the recording of the actors' performances, sound-film work in 1930s Hollywood was understood in terms of a process of assembly, whereby scenes were constructed from separate bits and pieces—shot by shot, track by track." [44] A *son direct* approach equates the microphone with the camera, with the assumption of a parity of space and time between the two. The desire for less in the way of artifice chimes with André Bazin's notions about the ability of cinema to catch and retain something of reality. Rick Altman describes the adoption by Hollywood of uniform volume single-position sound (as in radio) rather than matching the scale of the image.[45] This has implications for sound editing, when the soundtrack editor need not worry too much about retaining a single position of recording and can mix elements from diverse sources more easily into the whole.

The traditional functions of sound in cinema are as an agent of 'dialogue cinema' (the talkies, the basis of much television), allowing us to hear actors talking, and to provide a sense of the real where objects on-screen have a correspondingly believable or at least congruent sound, clarifying image events. This anchorage dispels ambiguity, although sound has the equal capability to contradict visual events. In certain genres, such as horror, off-screen sound also appears consistently as a device.[46] The last case aside, film sound almost always aims to be unremarkable, part of the seamless continuity demanded by the illusion of a coherent world on- screen to which we are party.

Film production usually involves three options for dealing with sound. First, there is shooting with location sound that is synchronized to the visual footage. This is live, as for television events and broadcasts, and was the norm on classical Hollywood soundstages. Second, there is the less common use of prerecording sound, where shooting takes place to an existing soundtrack. This is where a recorded playback is acted along to, as in musical song sequences, and the image track is usually edited later to fit the sound recording. The third method is post-synch sound, where sound is added afterward. This can be in the form of dialogue replacement and adding ambient sounds if the difficulties of location shooting had led to a poor recording or filming without location sound. Also, this is the procedure where preexisting music can be added and the film edited to accommodate their duration and dynamics, and where special sound effects can be added, such as the sound of the light sabers in *Star Wars* (1977). (See further discussion of this matter in chapter 7.)

The film soundtrack comprises three elements. In terms of production, these can often be compartmentalized until they are united in the film's final mix. They are dialogue, sound effects, and music. Traditionally, these areas have had different responsibilities and origins: dialogue (actors, sound recordists), sound effects (sound recordists but until the last couple of decades primarily the sound editor), and music (composer, performer, music editor). In recent years, the position of bringing all these activities together in the film soundtrack's final mix falls to the sound designer, although in many cases, that person will retain the less grand and more traditional title of supervising sound editor. In terms of synchronizing sound and image, there are massively strong conventions as to how broadly a film might be synchronized with its soundtrack. Dialogue is often synchronized in a conventional way that renders most of the lip movement precisely synchronous with the vocal sounds that make up the whole of the person talking on-screen. Sound effects vary, with some requiring precise synchrony with an image or event on-screen, while others are more ambient. Music often retains only a loose synchrony with the mood of events on-screen, but it will make precise, dynamic emphases at certain points in concert with notable image events.

Broadly, there are three types of sound and image relation. These run on a spectrum from tight synchronization at one pole and total asynchrony at the other. In between, there is the possibility of plesiochrony, where sound and image are vaguely fitting in synchrony, but lack precise reference points. Focusing on dialogue, Siegfried Kracauer noted four possible forms of synchronization and asynchrony derived from real-life situations and transferred to the cinema. First is the 'norm' in talkie films, where we see and hear a person speaking simultaneously. The second is where we hear a speaker's words but see something else in that space, in a cutaway to something else. The third option is off-screen sound, where we hear something and try to find its origins. This example is inspired by Pudovkin, and Kracauer describes it: "We hear a cry for help from the street, look out of the window, and see the moving cars and buses without, however, taking in the traffic noises, because we still hear only the cry that first startled us."[47] The fourth is extra-diegetic sound, where a voiceover without any notable connection with the diegetic world guides us through the film.[48] Sergei Eisenstein has much to say about synchronism in sound cinema. In the well-known essay "Synchronization of Senses" from *The Film Sense*, he has a section he describes as the "ABCs of every sound-cutter," which takes his persistent musical metaphor for cinema to an extreme. He sets out different musical descriptions of what he identifies as levels of synchronization[49]:

(1) Natural. This is 'purely factual synchronization', matching diegetic events on screen with suitable sounds (voice matches moving lips, sound of door slamming as event takes place on screen). This is in no way artistic, but merely serves to relate sounds and images in the most direct manner.
(2) Metric. From these simplest circumstances—simple 'metrical' coincidence of accent (film 'scansion')—it is possible to arrange a wide variety of syncopated combinations and a purely rhythmical 'counterpoint' in the controlled play of off-beats, shot-lengths, echoed and repeated subjects, and so on.[50] This is the abstract play of rhythm of sound and image elements.
(3) Rhythmic—...shots cut and edited together to the rhythm of the music on the parallel sound-track[51] This provides a sense of rhythmic movement through making the cuts correspond with the beat of the music, or is rhythmic structure (the first beat of a bar, the opening beat of a two- or four-bar unit, etc).

(4) Melodic—as a melodic line; the successive movement of a linear element where we are able to understand there is a higher unity to a succession of elements
(5) Tonal—changes in the emotional tone of a succession of related items. (In a rough analogy pitch can correspond to the play of *light*, and tonality to *colour*."[52])

Any of these may become the determining compositional concern, and dissonance between elements is an option.[53] These distinctions have rarely been taken up by recent film analysis. As montages, Eisenstein has focused on editing aspects, as well as other developmental elements, while interest in sound-image relations is less important in this instance. Conventions of precise editing, spotting, and placement are the keys to riveting images and sounds together. We can take these divisions of sound and image further:

(a) Dialogue based. This is where we see people speak and the words regularly match mouth movements on screen. This was the innovation brought to the cinema by the coming of synchronized recorded sound in the late 1920s, the so-called talkies, and still evident in many films or most obviously on television soap operas or interviews. This marks the 'degree zero style' of most sound films.
(b) Sound effects based. We see and hear activities that occur simultaneously. Good examples here are single gun shots, doors slamming, body punch impacts, or the turning of a key starting a car engine.
(c) Punctuation. In these cases, there are sonic emphases on an element such as a cut, a piece of dialogue (such as a revelation), a particular shot, or dramatic camera movement. The impetus is from narration rather than representation and consequently it often (although not always) takes place in the non-diegetic music and tends to 'underline' narrative activity.
(d) Mickeymousing music. On-screen activities are doubled precisely by music. The term originated in a pejorative term for music that simply aimed to mimic or 'double' events on-screen like the music in some cartoons. Perhaps the most evident example of this is the 'stinger' (or 'shock chord') used in horror films to accompany a shocking or violent act. For example, at the moment when Michael Myers stabs a character in *Halloween* (1978), his act of knife-thrusting is accompanied by a blast of non-diegetic electronic keyboard sound.
(e) A general and vague musical matching. Rather than corresponding to the fall and momentary dynamics of each minor event in a precise manner, music often marks a distinct change in screen activity, or merely

the tenor of that activity. General developments on screen inspire and are matched by a corresponding change in musical activity.

Less concerned with editing than Eisenstein, the five-point list below enumerates options for sound-image relations. Although all forms of screen activity unmatched with sounds constitute asynchrony in a way, there are some quite particular forms that asynchrony regularly takes:

(1) Mechanical or electronic faults. In this instance, there is a lack of direct synchrony between images and their sounds when the projector goes out of time to a separated soundtrack or when electronic algorithms are insufficient to keep image and sound in precise time. The 'slip' so that sound or image slightly lags behind is one of the most noticeable forms of asynchrony, as it is an error. This plagued early sound film and is still evident in many audiovisual files on the Internet. Robert Spadoni notes on the transition to sound film: "Every synchronization mishap served to remind viewers that the bodies speaking on the screen constituted whole entities only tenuously, ones that had been pieced together in a movie studio and that could come apart quite easily once inside the movie theater."[54]

(2) Voiceover narration. This is almost always 'synched' on some level, fitting with the on-screen activities or commenting upon them. Indeed, it is the rare voiceover that has no fairly direct connection with the images, even though it usually has extra-diegetic origin.

(3) Off-screen sound. This will often be 'resolved' by showing its origin fairly rapidly. Sustained passages of off-screen sound are traditional to many horror films, where a monster will not be shown but be cued by isolated part images and sounds.

(4) The pace of representation varies between sound and image. Some films use slow- motion sequences at their most dramatic points, but the mainstream film convention is that sound should not follow the image into slowed down speed but remain at the conventional (normal) tempo. Hence, synchronization in slow- motion sequences is often almost nonexistent. (See further discussion of this disparate synchronization in chapter 8.)

(5) Images from one space-time are accompanied by sounds from another space-time; for instance, when the story of a past event is being narrated by a character in the present and it is accompanied by images of the event in the past, while the narrating voice continues. Images swap diegetic status—and become extra-diegetic (as a memory or illustration) while sound remains diegetic.

(6) When the dynamics and mood of the images are accompanied by music of different dynamics and character. Examples of this would include 'classic' sound and image counterpoint as described by Eisenstein, Pudovkin, and Alexandrov,[55] or anempathetic music, where music is 'out of step 'with the character and dynamic of the narrative and images.

(7) Images on-screen are accompanied by a total lack of sound (a 'dead soundtrack'), or vice versa. In these situations any precise synchronization clearly is out of the question.

(8) When there is an ambiguity of connection, but no perceptible synchronization of screen and sound speaker, although it may not 'jar.' This can be the case in many montage sequences, or also when a pre-recorded song accompanies a sequence with little structural or semantic connection to the accompanying images.

(9) When there is no discernible connection whatsoever. Even with creative application to the riddle, we have trouble making a solid and lasting connection between sound and image.

SYNCHRONIZATION TECHNOLOGY: 'RUBBER NUMBERS'

In recent years, the digital dominance of audiovisual industries has meant that sound and vision in projection, as well as production, has increasingly become the dominant practice. The development of synchronized recorded sound in the late 1920s had a direct requirement for both precise and standardized playback and synchronization between image and sound. Warner Brothers made an indelible impact on the film world with its synchronized sound films; first, *Don Juan* (1926) with its recorded music and later, *The Jazz Singer* (debuting at the end of the same year) with its passages of synchronized dialogue and songs. These both used a sound system called Vitaphone, which added large shellac discs of recorded sound to the existing film projection apparatus. Synchronization was achieved by means of pulleys and drive shafts, was mechanical, and regularly presented plenty of difficulties for the securing of precise synchronization of sound and image. This system was swept aside by a competitor that had far less of a problem with synchronization, the so-called sound on film system (developed first by Fox/Western Electric as Movietone and RCA's Photophone). Although Vitaphone's discs produced better sound quality, the marriage of images and sound on a single celluloid reel not only made for ease of projection but, significantly, also prioritized a sound and image system in which loss of synchrony was a rarity. Instead of cutting sound into the grooves of a disc, this system used optical sound, which is premised upon a light camera converting sound into image by allowing light controlled by a microphone or other voltage to imprint onto celluloid film with a standard surface of emulsion. Variations in electrical pressure derived from microphones were applied to a light valve (either from a microphone or an existing recording) that controlled the amount of light hitting the film. Once on film, it could be edited, mixed, and then added to the edge of a film print. Once developed, the soundtrack part of the film has an image of light and dark, which is then either a variable density recording, where the density or opacity varies in successive sections, or a variable area recording, where the transparent track bordered by opaque bands varies in its width.[56] The quality of sound depends on the resolution of the photosensitive emulsion on the film, and later, on the quality of the reproduction equipment in the film theatre. Optical sound on film is a highly practical system in that it is not easy for sound and image to fall out of synch or for the soundtrack to become physically damaged. The sprocket holes on the edge of the film itself enable a direct mechanical coupling that became the key to synchronized sound and image. This also enabled editing with much more ease. Barry Salt notes:

> The basic tool for sound editing had already been introduced at the beginning of sound filmmaking, and this was the multiple synchronizer just as we know it today in its unadorned form without track reading heads. Originally its purpose had been to keep the several simultaneous picture tracks obtained from multiple cameras filming in synchronism with each other during the editing, and hence finally with the sound-track on disc, but by 1930 both multiple camera filming and sound-on-disc were abandoned. The synchronizer was then used just to manipulate the series of pairs of picture track and sound track, and keep them in synchronism during editing. This simple procedure gave no way of hearing the words on the sound track, was extremely inefficient, and was not conducive to scene dissection into a large number of shots. But in 1930, the sound Moviola became available, and from 1931 the Average Shot Lengths in Hollywood films started to drop.[57]

The flat bed Moviola editing desk remained virtually unchanged, but with an addition to the soundless one of a photoelectric sound head reading the tracks, all with a rigid shaft drive for precise synchronization. This device remained in nearly the same form until the 1970s. Certain developments allowed for the absolute precision required in the process of synchronization. For example, electric clocks were developed with motor mechanisms that rotate in relation to the speed of the power station alternators that produce electricity, either as an integral multiple or a sub-multiple. This allowed for precision in chronography without minor interferences from the nature of electricity itself, indeed exploiting its precisely periodic nature. In terms of film production, a rapid development was the clapperboard or slate, which was recorded as a sonic snap by the sound recordist and the visual counterpart of that action by the film camera. This single event then becomes the precise reference point to check and establish for alignment of filmed images and location sound into a single unity of sound and vision in the editing process. The frame where the sound and image are matched thus was called the synch frame.

In terms of synchronizing music to images, Mickeymousing is perhaps the most obvious form. This describes music that mimics movements in the image like cartoon music that doubles the comic movements of a screen character like a shadow. A lesser degree of correspondence is more common, where action and mood are matched by the dynamics of music. For example, a sad and quiet scene is accompanied by undynamic and soft music, while an energetic fight scene is accompanied by kinetic music, sometimes with a strong pulse and often making rhythmic punches or emphases. Indeed, the relationship of music and image often directly follows the principle of analogy, a vestige of silent film's intermittent provision of sound effects with musical accompaniment. Sound and image analogues take the form of rhythm, gesture, and movement. For instance, a broad turn of camera movement can often synchronize with a palpable sweep of music.

Music almost always needs to fashion precise synchronizations with images. In the 1930s, Hollywood composer Max Steiner was instrumental in the development of what became known as 'click tracks,' which enabled the precise synchronization of sound and image. The process initially involved punching holes in the film to make bursts of light (punches and streamers) when it is projected for the musicians to synchronize to as they perform.[58] The click track not only allows for the composer to write precisely to the image but also works as a metronome, allowing the conductor to synchronize musical performance with precision.[59]

In the 1950s, magnetic tape on reel-to-reel machines took over from optical sound, most notably on expensive productions with stereo sound. At first, this procedure involved a large sprocketed tape, which was quickly replaced by 6.25mm tape with a coordinating synch pulse derived from the camera motor speed and also present in the projector motor. Blackham describes the process:

> The 6.25mm recording is transferred to sprocketed tape and the sync pulse on the tape used to control the speed of the sprocket recorder motor. In the case of

sprocket recorders with mains sync motors, the reproduced sync pulse is locked to the mains and the 6.25mm replay machines varied in speed to keep the mains and the sync pulse in step.

The sync pulse from the camera can be the mains frequency (in the case of a camera with a mains sync motor) or may be obtained from a small AC generator driven by the motor. The most modern systems use a camera motor whose speed is locked exactly to the divided-down output of a crystal oscillator. The sync pulse at the sound recorder is derived from an oscillator of the same frequency. This then eliminates cable or radio links between the camera and the recorder.[60]

The development of more flexible handheld cameras demanded sound capabilities that could be used to catch events as part of a whole. In 1960, the Nagra portable tape recorder became available; it was based on a quartz clock mechanism controlling the motor, which allowed precise timing in the face of the unreliability of earlier portable tape recorders.[61]

The widescreen film format, which became prominent in the 1950s, meant that sound again became uncoupled from the single roll of celluloid. In many cases, projection adopted magnetic tape, which afforded better quality than optical sound and was a suitable counterpart to the large, epic images on-screen. In most cases, it was also in stereo rather than the cinema norm of monophonic sound up to this point. In order to achieve mechanical synchronization, film exhibition was dominated by the process of 'direct coupling' using motors (such as Selsyn or Syncrostart motors) that are interlocked, or alternatively by a flexible coupling between projector and tape player. The drive motors of the two machines share a common central shaft that keeps both sound and image in constant synchrony.[62] Each Selsyn motor must be powerful to control and regulate the driving motors in the different devices. The drawback is that the whole mechanism is large and unwieldy, with gears and timing belts, large rotating mechanical components, and a big external distributor. Constant speed motors replaced governed motors. These are induction motors, based on the frequency of mains electricity, and so run at 50 Hz in the U.K. Projectors also used stroboscopes, which gave a static signal when the image on the projector was in synch with the audiotape. The shutter speed of the projector can be varied, as can the speed of the film reel's movement through the projector—but not the speed of the magnetic tape, illustrating that synchronization was forced to follow the audio requirements more than those of the visuals. Electrical synchronizers were in some cases a replacement for mechanical synchronizers, which had a phase relationship between tape speed and film speed. If the projector changed speed, then so did the phase relationship, which was then automatically compensated for. Similarly, the electronic version uses unheard or visual pulses to hold the two tracks together, derived either from a control track on the tape or the projector's shutter speed.[63]

In the 1950s, there were notable developments for sound and image in cinema, particularly the increased use of stereo sound and widescreen images. The requirement for multiple projectors and a desire for higher quality and multitrack sound led, as I have noted, to an uncoupling in some cases of sound and image from the single piece of celluloid. John Belton points out:

> The advent of wide-screen cinematography—whether the Grandeur system (1929–30), Cinerama (1952), CinemaScope (1953), or Todd-AO/70mm (1955)—provides a wider visual field for the sound track to duplicate, necessitating multiple track, stereo sound. In Fox's CinemaScope process, for example, four different tracks play on three separate speakers behind the screen and on one 'surround' speaker.[64]

This 'surround' speaker usually contained off-screen sounds, and most obviously voiceover narrations, indicating that sound from an off-screen source was thought to occupy a different physical, as well as mental, space. This seems to compound the use of asynchrony, yet such aspects were quickly integrated as unproblematic parts of film style. On a physical level, the use of magnetic tape for sound allowed for better sound quality but reengaged precisely the problems of synchronizing two machines that had plagued Vitaphone at the beginning of synchronized sound cinema. Things were less problematic this time around, though, with electronic coupling allowing for precise synchronization.[65]

While sound on film remained dominant in smaller and less sumptuous film theatres, television's small speaker and poor frequency range used different image formats. The regular option was 16mm film, but from the late 1950s, videotape increasingly became used for audiovisual culture, although television remained primarily a live broadcast medium well into the following decade. Videotape also increasingly became an option for editing film footage. As Ashley Shepherd notes,

> Many projects are shot on film for the look but edited on video for ease, then are delivered to the public on video, whether on television or on videotape and DVD.... Typically, film will be transferred to video for editing, effects, and computer manipulation. Then, once the film is in final form, it will be transferred back to a celluloid film print for presentation in theatres.[66]

In recent years, almost all sound and synch work is done on digital workstations. In 1967, 'timecode' for videotape was introduced by the Society of Motion Picture and Television Engineers (SMPTE). It allowed for absolute precision in synchronization, as well as precise film editing. This is an 80 bit code, which works from a displayed eight-digit, 24-hour clock (hours:minutes:seconds:frames) that also presents frame rate measured in frames-per-second.[67] Timecode is the fast-advancing number on the bottom of the screen in rough-cut footage that can be seen sometimes in DVD extras, for example. This is crucial for precise synchronization, mediating between the separate devices. Exploiting this, 'Genlock' is a generator lock that synchronizes at least two video/sound sources, such as cameras, and allows direct switching between them without loss of continuity and image rolling. This synchronizes color, frame, vertical and horizontal aspects of the image, as well as the soundtrack. It contains a shared 'reference synch' across hardware, involving a 'trigger synch' on the master device being connected to the internal clock of studio hardware. This clock can be an atomic clock or one based on an external standard (more recently based on GPS for shooting cameras).[68]

It is no exaggeration to state that the advent of digital sound and image equipment has revolutionized production of films. In terms of post-production, there have been radical changes with the rapid movement toward nonlinear editing (on computer rather than physically cutting up film and tape). Processing is now completed largely by computer software, with suites of programs such as those by AVID and Pro Tools dominating.[69] For synchronization, Pro Tools uses an internal audio clock but is also able to use an external reference point, such as Sync I/O or USD, which provide the most reliable time clocks to hold together pace and synchronization of sound and image. In terms of digital distribution, MPEG digital video format is standard (along with AVI, MOV, and others very prominent on the Internet).[70] While celluloid film may still be used for shooting, in many cases, it will still be digitized to allow for nonlinear editing and sound construction and treatment. Films now use an electronic clapperboard called a 'smart slate' that displays information in numerals rather than chalk written on the older snapping version. Significantly, the electronic form also carries a timecode. This allows for easy synchronization by the film (and sound) editor. Instead of manually lining up the sound and image, the editor, after the transfer from film to videotape, merely notes the timecode and punches the details into a synchronizer that matches the code of sound and image and thus automatically puts the two in synch. Despite radical change, the basic concept of filmmaking has remained remarkably constant.

Analogue video with an LTC (longitudinal timecode) is able to be fed directly to a synchronizer linked to musical software. This was still roughly synchronized by hand from the video deck, while a more sophisticated system allowed control from the software via MMC (MIDI machine control) or through nine-pin serial machine control (these tend to have different decks that use VITC, or vertical interval timecodes. This process was simplified dramatically by the advent of totally digital editing capabilities. Once the image is held as digital, it is simply imported into the musical software program, such as Logic or Pro Tools.[71] Indeed, the conversion from analogue to digital sound and image processing has changed the system radically in terms of the possibility of manipulation, while retaining the basic process of sound and image matching and mixing that was already in place. As a development of the analogue electronic synching system, Pro Tools uses a system of synchronization called 'synch beep' or 'two pop.' This has a single frame audio signal (1kHz at −20dB), where a tone is inserted into each audio file two seconds before the picture begins. Less expensive 'soft studios' (aka Digital Audio Workstations, or DAWs) such as Logic, Cubase, and Ableton Live allowed for quick and easy creation and fitting of music to images from the mid-2000s onward. The composer is given a digital file of film in rough-cut form and composes to it, with any precise temporal changes required taking place later. Precise numerical references for synchronization are called 'timestamps' and mark when certain added sounds (such as a music or sound effect) should be placed or begin. This is an update of the 'spotting' process for composers (working out which sequences need music). For sound effects as well as music, 'hits' can be entered into the sequencer as temporal markers, around which the music can be written and constructed. The options for Pro Tools are to link it to a separate visual machine (a digital video or videotape deck or film projector) or to import the film and synchronize it in Pro Tools and then put in 'markers' for where sounds will be 'laid in.' More specialized programs exist for dealing with voices, with dialogue-aligning software such as Synchro Art's VocALign plug-in, which analyzes original sound and adapts new recording to fit it.[72] Despite far-reaching developments, it remains largely a process of having a clapperboard for synching film and sound using markers in a counting system for indicating where sounds will be placed.

Writing about technological developments often focuses on multi-channel (spatial) sound and Dolby high-definition sound quality.[73] Sound diffusion through the theatre space developed dramatically in the late 1970s, with films such as *Apocalypse Now* (1979) being released with Dolby Split Surround, which had six discrete sound channels, adding up to an overall impression of dramatic three-dimensional sound space. The creative process of deciding how to synchronize sound and image involves personnel such as the film director, sound designer, editor, sound editor, and dubbing mixer. In some cases, these jobs might be shared or doubled. A so-called 'hit list' is compiled (often by the music editor) that details important image events for the sound editor, music editor, and music composer. For the latter, it defines the space of each cue they are to write and details all the points the music has to 'hit.' *Star Wars* (1977) was remarkable for its sound, with sound designer Ben Burtt creating new sounds and expanding the sonic palette exponentially. In terms of music, despite technological developments making the process much quicker and easier, procedures have in essence remained pretty much the same. The tradition of matching music to film broadly has been in place since the 1930s and either involves music being composed to fit images or existing recordings being edited to fit images.[74] The former involves 'spotting' followed by the construction of charts of music timing breakdowns and requirements (known as 'cue sheets'). After this the composer then 'lays out' the empty score onto manuscript paper (sometimes on computer), setting tempos and bar structures, and then composes the music and records it; then it must be edited to fit the film. All of these developments illustrate the critical importance of precise synchronization in production and exhibition. As well as delineating historical events, this chapter has endeavored to detail the older processes that were the origins of the current methods and conventions of synchronizing sound and image.

CONCLUSION

With the advent of electronic synchronization, the filmmaking process became less mechanical and ultimately more easily achieved with recourse to wholly digital equipment. Indeed, it is now possible to have music produced for images by a computer program that constructs and fits sonic accompaniment to the footage fed into it.[75] The total integration of filmmaking processes through digital programs has opened up the possibility of dictating the outcome, although this has not been taken up on a large scale. Such programs also indicate how far conventions dominate, in that they follow a number of rudimentary rules that are deemed to be important in audiovisual culture. The key appears to be the dynamics of music, as it is actually far easier for the program to auto-edit footage to fit its music.

Nevertheless, the assumption is of *equivalence* of dynamics, and finding corresponding aesthetics between music and film footage.

Fostering the sense of cinematic illusionism remains at the heart of mainstream film, and this has conventionally led to sound naturalism and its correspondent audiovisual naturalism. This marks a zero degree of style for mainstream cinema, an unremarkable stylistic given, but crucially also an expectation, which some films intermittently work to confound if for only a short period of time. Of course, there is no reason why films should not be accompanied by music that appears almost totally unsynchronized with the screen. However, in mainstream cinema, convention dominates to the point where even slight divergences from the norm come to be considered remarkable. The aim of conventional approaches, by and large, is to remain almost imperceptible, one might say. Most mainstream narrative cinema follows a conventional blueprint of 'transparent' style, where aesthetic aspects refuse to call too much attention to themselves in order to function primarily as vehicle for content, rather than comprising the content themselves. The corresponding 'togetherness' of non-diegetic music and the rest of the film is the overwhelming aim, as taught by courses on filmmaking and film music the world over. Too much divergence is often considered unproductive, and limits are set by Eisenstein's notions of parallel and counterpoint (which are discussed in detail in the following chapter), although the latter is considered more of an occasional effect on the former's norm. So despite the range of possibilities offered by sound and image synchronization, mainstream film has been happy to remain within a relatively narrow band of aesthetic possibilities. Avant garde film and video art have not,[76] but consequently they have at some point sacrificed the 'illusionism' of representational cinema, one of its most powerful aspects. There is an assumption that sound's relationship to image is either (a) a homology *or* (b) a supplement. Although it is not quite the same, this appears remarkably similar to Eisenstein's formulation of parallel and counterpoint relationships.

A good number of experiments into the perception of simultaneous audio and visual events have been completed by psychologists, scientists, and neuroscientists. Conclusions seem to be that people are not absolutely precise in their perception of simultaneous events, and their acceptance of synchronization varies in different situations.[77] However, differences of synchronization of less than 20 msecs do not register.[78] Clearly, watching a film in the cinema requires close synchrony of voices with mouth movements, whereas on a small television this is not so imperative. However, this is far from maintaining that people will accept asynchrony. Indeed, it appears to be the opposite. Although these experiments are certainly relevant, they are not dedicated to film material. There is a narrow margin of perception, with a difference between point of objective equivalence and accepted point of perceived equivalence being 35 msecs for audio, 30 msecs for audio delays, and 85 msecs for video delays.[79]

In a 1960s book about making sound films, D. M. Neale noted: "Synchronization can be divided into three categories: loose sync, where an error between sound and picture of five or even ten seconds can be tolerated; close sync, where the error cannot exceed more than one or two seconds over the whole length of the film; and lip-sync, where there must be no error at all."[80] This underlines the fact that there are films where synchronization matters little—such as some avant garde and amateur films—and the fact that most writers about film follow the tacit assumption that all films are based on dialogue. This goes so far that film theorists can continue to discuss film as essentially visual when the vast majority of films are dialogue-centered talkies. Furthermore, writers about film sound have tended to focus on sound effects and music and implicitly bracket off dialogue as part of the rest of the film and somehow less 'sonic.' Yet dialogue is the most tangible point of seamless union between sound and image tracks, and the central endeavor of editing in most films.

The fusion of elements that takes place at synch points is highly significant and should not be underestimated. This coalescence is taken by the audience as an assumption of relationship, an admittance of direct connection. This is essentially a psychological process, even if there are different forms of synchronization that might yield psychologically different situations. Yet these points should not be mistaken merely for edits; many are on-screen events that are matched to the occurrence of particular sounds. Over the past two decades, the development of mobile cameras has led to less cutting, and the use of high-quality spatialized stereo has also encouraged more independence of sound and image, as well as less need to constantly orient the audience spatially.

Traditionally, film meaning has followed the notion of the Kuleshov experiment's montage in conceiving of film's crucial interior relationship as a succession, where different images arranged in order add up to a third idea not necessarily present in either constituent. However, as theorists like Eisenstein noted, music's simultaneous relationship of elements (harmony, counterpoint) offers an important means of understanding film as simultaneity. Furthermore, like the Kuleshov effect, the McGurk effect illustrates that a similar montage process takes place between sound and image, producing a protean synthesis that is beyond mere constituent elements and not only a strong illusion of reality, but also a magical embodiment of ideas and emotion unlike any other.

CHAPTER 3
Sound Montage

Although it is commonplace to assume that so-called new technology has radically shifted the aesthetic and theoretical terrain, a few highly influential studies have pointed to direct continuity with earlier concerns. For instance, Lev Manovich's highly influential book *The Language of New Media*, published just after the turn of the second millennium, contains a significant section on the 1920s and '30s Soviet film director Dziga Vertov and extrapolates his pioneering theoretical and filmmaking concerns into modern screen and speaker culture.[1] Montage theory also remains at the heart of filmmaking and cinema studies, although many of its original concerns and insights have perhaps receded from view. Sound montage, theorized with the arrival of recorded synchronized sound in films, was the first theory of sound, as well as image, and sometimes explicitly derives ideas and inspiration from music-based theory.

Montage theory of the 1920s and '30s feted asynchrony, looking to gaps between components and discourses that could manifest easily as gaps between image track and soundtrack. This was a film-specific theory that has had an influence in other arts, setting film at the heart of more recent multimedia theory. It emerged at a point when synchronized recorded soundtracks had just become an integral part of cinema and an unencumbered initial view of potential was achieved that was perhaps more difficult once the medium was established with pervasive conventions. Rather than focusing exclusively on representation, these early theorists, most notably those in the Soviet Union, looked into the linguistic and expressive possibilities of film and, significantly, straddled what later became an insurmountable divide: that between mainstream narrative cinema and avant garde cinema. This enabled the questioning of conventions, and we should remember that many cinematic conventions were in a state of flux in the late '20s and early '30s, although expediency for achieving good quality sound meant that films soon became more conventionalized than ever, particularly in the U.S.A., where filmmaking followed a Fordist model of industrial production.

The continued relevance of this body of theory from the first part of the 20th century resides not only in its concern with complex processes at the heart of film,[2] but also in that it had an interest in synchronism of sound and image that has not been followed up significantly by later film theory, or indeed even become a point of minor interest for most recent filmmakers. As Siegfried Kracauer noted, these early sound cinema theorists assumed that counterpoint between elements and asynchrony were intimately related.[3] Their focus was on the gap between image and sound aesthetics, something that inevitably is always present to some degree, although narrative films put much effort into eliding any gap and warding off the dangers of such fissures. Indeed, the overwhelming majority of films feign that there is no gap to open and that film is a unified output not reliant upon the hidden synchronization of sound and image.

THE COMING OF SYNCHRONIZED SOUND

As noted in the previous chapter, in 1926, *The Adventures of Don Juan* used discs to provide a musical accompaniment for the film, while the more celebrated *The Jazz Singer*, which premiered at the close of the same year, also used discs but concentrated more on the synchronized performances of songs and particularly dialogue.[4] Within five years, silent films had been pushed to the margins in many countries and almost forgotten in some. Yet, at what point did a strong sense of how synchronized image and sound emerge? Of course, there was already a strong sense of how sounds, especially music, should fit with the moving image, yet this changed with the addition of recorded sound. It seems that almost immediately, there was an intuitive notion of how recorded sound and image should coalesce, emerging from a sense of verisimilitude. Moving lips were expected to match appropriate sounds precisely. For a time, Hollywood produced some films not only in English but also in other languages, such as the Spanish-language version of *Dracula* (1931) shot simultaneously with different actors. In Europe at the same time, multi-language versions of films were produced; yet within a few years, the dubbing of films became the norm, with some national audiences accepting a certain discrepancy between mouth movement and vocal sound. Some temporary techniques to ameliorate the gap of sound and vision included editing the length of shots so that they better matched the sounds of the new overdubbed language. The projection of silent films had not only regularly involved the use of live music but also other sonic elements, including live sound effects.[5] Indeed, in the 1920s, there were carefully synchronized live accompaniments that mixed effects and voices spoken from behind the screen, with a number of commercial companies supplying this service in the U.S.A.[6] Such practices went some way toward creating the blueprint for sound in the cinema.

Rapidly, there emerged a sense, allied to industrial expediency, of dividing the responsibilities of the soundtrack into elements: dialogue (which was and is the most important), sound effects, and music. The first was the key to the emergence of sound cinema as a new object, and technicians sourced from the telecommunications industry aimed to make voices as intelligible as possible. Musicians had their own associated technicians derived from the music performance and recording industry. Sound effects had more in common with the former than the latter, although it quickly grew into something of its own division and specialty. The key person holding all these together was the sound editor, who, in conjunction with other film technicians such as the principal editor and director, was responsible for pulling the mélange of elements into a coherent whole that complemented the filmed images. Seamlessness and the need for the soundtrack not to call attention to itself as an element in any way not attached directly to the illusion of image and sound were the most important considerations. The means for achieving these were, as with every other element of the Hollywood studio system of the 1930s and to a lesser degree every other popular national cinema, through industrial standardization. The strategy for sound was almost never to approach it as a creative element within the system of the film but more so as merely a conventional element. Thus written discourses existed to standardize best practices and establish film sound as a process that had a right and wrong way of doing things, along with particular examples of difficult problems solved and outstanding instances of good craftsmanship that were held up as models for continued sound technician activity. Rick Altman details the debate during the 1930s about whether sound should match its volume to the proximity of the image, or whether it should retain a fixed position in the face of camera mobility through cutting.[7] The latter won out, despite the former appearing more logical.

As with Hollywood film products of the studio era, conventions led not only to speed and ease of production but also to an ease of audience consumption of material when standardized aspects made style seem almost transparent, and audiences had to expend a minimum amount of mental energy thinking about sound and image elements that were not part of the illusionistic developments on-screen. The 1938 book *Motion Picture Sound Engineering*, which stemmed from a series of lectures, states that "The listener should hear by means of the recording the same sound he would have heard had he been present when the original was created."[8] This seems naïve, particularly by the later 1930s.[9] Some earlier discussions were more sophisticated. Kenneth F. Morgan noted in the 1931 book *Recording for Motion Pictures*:

> The dubbing of sound is analogous to trick photography and duping which have long since been adopted as useful adjuncts in the composition and editing of the motion picture...the art of dubbing has developed with great rapidity and is already a fundamental part of sound pictures.[10]

Morgan then goes on to emphasize the illusionistic status of what is seen and heard. He points to the established status of music accompanying film and its technological foundation through unsynched discs of sound effects and music that were made available in the wake of the earliest synchronized sound films.[11] He noted that "The addition of music...was known as 'scoring'; when sound effects or dialog were added the process came to be known as 'synchronizing.'"[12] The process of fitting music was not simply matching timing, as with the precise spotting of dialogue and sound effects. It was arguably a more artistic affair, of fitting mood and broader movement and emphasizing the most emotional moments.

The debut of *The Jazz Singer* in Britain showcased a number of converged concerns. The program at London's Piccadilly Theatre on September 27, 1928, included a number of other films with synchronized sound. One was a film of the New York Philharmonic Orchestra performing the overture to *Tannhäuser* by Wagner. The reviewer in *Melody Maker*, the journal aimed at cinema and popular musicians, noted that the orchestra pit at the theatre was covered in flowers, perhaps not only to hide the absence of musicians but also to signify the "graveyard of musicians' hopes." The reviewer also noted that when the film showed oboes in close-up, the audience expected a rise in their volume.[13] The review detailed how the audience laughed each time the image and sound went out of synch, which clearly was an intermittent problem.[14] Another film screened was a British-made African travelogue called *Simba*, which used the Phonotone system. The reviewer noted,

> ...the Phonotone music to 'Simba' must be said to be a comparative failure. No special synchronization was noticeable, and an equally satisfactory result

SOUND MONTAGE [47]

could have been produced from ordinary 'radio amplified' gramophone records played on a machine which had no means of synchronizing it with the film.[15]

Indeed, the transition period from silent to sound films not only included talkies but also so-called sound films that were shot silently and then 'fitted up' with recorded music with varying degrees of artfulness and success. This aesthetic remained as a technique inside the new sound cinema. Originating in silent film musical accompaniment, this synchronizing of music to non-speaking sections of films marked a persistence of a silent filmmaking style lacking direct connection between sound and image track. In many films, there is still a division of sorts between regimes derived from talkies and sound films.

EISENSTEIN AND MONTAGE

At this time, technological possibilities excited many filmmakers and theorists alike. Sergei Eisenstein's conception of montage touches on the gap between two pieces of film.[16] According to him, the juncture of the edit is the key moment when the real work of cinema takes place. These gaps regularly are glossed over by mainstream film. Gaps between shots often aim to register as nothing, as something that we don't see. In theory, these voids are 'black hole' collapsed spaces of time and space, negated by the classical continuity system (and its more recent variants). However, for Eisenstein, these are the points when there is the most *potential*, in aesthetic, emotional, and political terms. Eisenstein's notion of montage is based on dialectic, a clash between seemingly disparate elements making for a physical and mental jolt. This conception differs from the idea of montage practiced by some other influential Soviet filmmakers of the time, such as Vsevolod Pudovkin, who also saw montage as the key to cinema, but rather as a more passive joining of ideas, which is still not the same as the invisible editing system promulgated by classical Hollywood.[17] Pudovkin suggested that contrasting sound and image allows for perception that doubles the spectator's physical perception of real life, and thus was a mode of realism able to make complex representations and expressions. He discussed asynchronism in his book *Technique of the Film* (translated into English in 1929).[18] While Pudovkin saw montage as 'linking,' Eisenstein, in "A Dialectic Approach to Film Form" (1929), saw it as 'collision' (and thus dialectical, leading to a higher synthesis of clashing elements), and compared it to an engine that drives the film forward.[19]

For Eisenstein, art is about conflict, with a mission to make manifest the contradictions of modern existence. In "Methods of Montage," written in 1929 before sound was an option in Soviet films, Eisenstein makes a distinction between 'metric montage' and 'rhythmic montage.'[20] The former is based on similar lengths of film used (using a specific number of frames). This involves regular shots irrespective of their content, and was used regularly by Dziga Vertov and Vsevelod Pudovkin. Rhythmic montage, on the other hand, has frame content of the same significance as the film length, so its practical length derives from the specifics of content and movement within the frame. 'Tonal montage' is based on the characteristic emotional tone of the film, communicating an emotion directly through the image, while 'overtonal montage' (also known as 'associational montage') has an abstract effect due to the conglomeration of the film's metric, rhythmic, and tonal attributes. The most complex, and also the most effective, form of montage was 'intellectual montage,' whereby the juxtaposition of intellectual affects would lead to a new synthesis of the aspects of the film, creating an impression of an idea or object not present. Eisenstein saw this as a potential synthesis of science, art, and the class conflict, and its awareness that motivated Soviet cinema, exemplified by the end of his film *Strike* (1925), where images of a violent attack on striking workers are intercut with footage of a bull being killed in a slaughterhouse.[21] This audacious moment in cinema also corresponded with Eisenstein's description of the 'montage of attractions,' which should be premised upon the use of non-contextual, seemingly unconnected images for emotional impact.[22]

Eisenstein's insightful deliberation about the capabilities of editing in film remains a striking piece of theory, although it has only been influential for film scholarship as a general notion about the power of editing, rather than persisting as a range of production strategies or as an accepted mode of aesthetic analysis. In his later "Synchronization of Senses," Eisenstein considers sound as a part of this montage system. He comprehends it as essentially empowered when it becomes 'vertical montage,'[23] when there is an opportunity for divergence in the content of image and sound. Sound montage extends the system but retains the basic principles. Eisenstein describes the addition of a soundtrack as "...a new 'superstructure' [that] is erected vertically over the horizontal picture structure."[24] The implication of this explicitly Marxist language is that sound can elucidate a more significant structure than the more basic visual one. Indeed, it is clear that the possibilities offered by sound montage in addition to visual montage seriously expanded the expressive capabilities of cinema. Eisenstein emphasized the sophisticated abilities of cinema, seeing it as more than simply a storytelling device, as arguably the view that had become dominant in Hollywood cinema. Although film montage first concerned the dominant aspect or tendency in the frame, secondary stimuli, overtones, and/or undertones were also of significant concern to Eisenstein. Overtones only emerge in the dynamics of interaction and development of diverse elements. These visual and aural overtones mark what he referred to as the 'fourth dimension' of film, which is *felt* rather than necessarily registered directly.[25]

Eisenstein's theories have always proved attractive, although often more to film theorists than filmmakers, perhaps. At the turn of the fourth decade of the 20th century, Eisenstein's concept of montage embraced the possibilities of the new sound cinema, looking for a dialectic interaction among the ensemble of elements. This is much more complex and less satisfactory than his earlier theories, simply transporting the potential of the gaps between their (quantifiable) meanings. It is the coming of sound that allows for the concept of counterpoint to bloom (although it could conceivably have been theorized in relation to elements within silent film as well). In 1930, Eisenstein, along with Pudovkin and Alexandrov declared in their famous "Statement on Sound":

> It is well known that the principal (and sole) method which has led cinema to a position of such great influence is *montage*.... And so for the further development of cinema the significant features appear to be those that strengthen and broaden the montage methods of influencing the audience. If we examine every new discovery from this standpoint it is easy to distinguish the insignificance of colour and stereoscopic cinema in comparison with the great significance of *sound*.[26]

This is a remarkably sanguine manifesto, luxuriating in the aesthetic possibilities afforded by the new capabilities opened up by sound cinema. The "Statement on Sound" is careful, however, to note how synchronized sound is likely to be used in a banal manner. The key for Eisenstein, Pudovkin, and Alexandrov is the massive potential for montage in the form of asynchrony between sound and image and, more precisely, in dialectical contradiction of meaning and association between sound and image. First experiments should aim at "...sharp discord with the visual images...[resulting in] a new orchestral counterpoint of visual and sound images."[27] The diametric opposite of this is likely what they dismiss as more banal ways to use sound in film. These follow "...an incorrect understanding of the potential for the new technical invention [which] might not only hinder the development and improvement of cinema as an art form but might also threaten all its formal achievements to date."[28] In aesthetic terms, this might well be borne out with recourse to the standardized practices of mainstream cinema since that time. But, of course, the potential of any aesthetic or technology is almost never fully in constant use. At heart, this potential that Eisenstein, Pudovkin, and Alexandrov are writing about is montage, broadly conceived. While they might fete asynchrony and its radical possibilities, they fail to register the massively effective illusory character of synchronized sound and image. This is dismissed as being an application 'along the lines of least resistance' and making cinema into a form of ersatz theatre. They note that the initial period of sound adoption will likely involve "...synchronizing exactly with the movement on the screen and creating a certain 'illusion' of people talking, objects making a noise, etc."[29] This is a prescient description of the sound-image relations that dominated early sound cinema, and some might argue still dominates certain forms of film and television. They argue that sound destroys montage. Capturing an object on film 'neutralizes' it, cutting it off from its context and time and allowing it to be used as an icon. The inclusion of an associated sound reinstates its sense of self and place, giving it an independence and aesthetic 'inertia.' According to Eisenstein, Pudovkin, and Alexandrov,

> Sound used in this way will destroy the culture of montage, because every mere *addition* of sound to montage fragments increases their inertia as such and their independent significance; this is undoubtedly detrimental to montage which operates above all not with fragments but through the *juxtaposition* of fragments. *Only the contrapuntal use* of sound vis-à-vis the visual fragment of montage will open up new possibilities for the development and perfection of montage.[30]

Adding significant amounts of non-diegetic sound or emphasizing simultaneity mitigates the combined sound and image's tendency toward inertia. The assumption—which quickly became dominant to the point of invisibility—was that the shot should come with its own sound, and that the sound-image composite was the central pillar of sound cinema and its younger relations. The "Statement on Sound" suggests that the only way to halt the slide into such naturalism and away from the aesthetic possibilities of cinema is by the use of asynchrony. Montage in synchronized sound film should come from

> ...finding *an inner synchronization between the tangible pictures and the differently perceived sounds.*... this is far beyond that external synchronization that matches the boot with its creaking—we are speaking of a 'hidden' inner synchronization in which the plastic and tonal elements will find complete fusion. To relate

these two elements, we find a natural language common to both—movement. Plekhanov has said that all phenomena in the final analysis can be reduced into movement. Movement will reveal all the substrata of inner synchronization that we wish to establish in due course.[31]

There is undoubtedly a sense of movement in both music and film, although it is elusive as to how far these might cohere or be workable on a logical level.

Eisenstein developed this notion further in an essay that appeared in *The Film Sense*, where he created a diagram of the movement as he saw it in a piece of film and its accompanying music. The diagram is impressive but not built on a solid foundation. Eisenstein's correlation of movement in music and images seems too direct and without basis. However, it is a diagram that has an important historical place in the study of film and in the study of film music, in that it makes direct correspondence between still frames of film and notated music, illustrating precise aesthetic developments in the celebrated battle-on-the-ice sequence from Eisenstein's own *Alexander Nevsky* (1938). Eisenstein had noted the power of vertical montage, which the tabulation makes plain, and pointed out that sound montage necessitated the addition of a new part to the instrumental musical score: that of the image, to create an 'audiovisual score.'[32] However, despite this being impressive, Robert Robertson's analysis of it rightly finds some small discrepancies and some 'flights of fancy' that mean that the description and corresponding explanation are not as precise as one initially might imagine.[33] Despite the problematic status of his diagrams, Eisenstein's aspirations toward aesthetic integration and analysis are still laudable. A crucial aspect of the *Nevsky* diagram is that it focuses on events point-counter-point, illustrating the synchronization of elements rather than simply enumerating aspects that add to narrative development.

PARALLEL AND COUNTERPOINT

The notions of parallel and counterpoint as descriptive of the synchronous relationship of image and sound can be traced back to the famous "Statement on Sound" by Eisenstein, Pudovkin, and Alexandrov. Their essay introduced this strong and widely used theoretical concept to both cinema analysis and filmmaking. It postulated that sound works either in parallel with or in counterpoint to the visuals. These terms are elaborated on by Eisenstein and have formed a foundational, but not unproblematic, approach in both analysis and production of film. Eisenstein, Pudovkin, and

Alexandrov warned about the dangers of parallelism and feted the potential of counterpoint. Their interest was in the gap that might be opened up in terms of both meaning and aesthetics between sound and image, rather than merely having both working toward the same end.

The term 'parallel' has predominantly been used to describe sound 'doing the same thing' as image rather than going off on its own path. This indicates providing the same meaning as, or directly supporting the meaning of, images. Equally, though, it can mean aesthetic 'doubling' when more abstract aspects in the image are paralleled by sound. So, on the one hand, parallel might designate meaning and tone when, for example, a sad scene is accompanied by apparently sad music. On the other, it might mean dynamics, when an extreme example would be the Mickeymousing of action by music, with on-screen movements triggering the rise and fall of musical dynamics in a tight accompaniment.

Dialogue and sound effects conventionally parallel activities in the image track. Synchronism is therefore of paramount importance for films that are premised upon dialogue scenes and the illusion of a pro-filmic event being captured by camera and microphone. Non-diegetic music, however, is not restricted by such concerns. David Bordwell notes that film scores have a pleonastic character, which allows them to simply double the meanings of what films are supplying through other means of narration.[34] If scores are conceived as simply furnishing the same message, in narrative terms, they are therefore redundant or at best merely a reinforcement of the film's general message. However, much of the time, music is not sending any such quantifiable message; yet regularly the film's score appears consonant with the images and dialogue, marking a seeming parallel of sound and image. Perhaps a better formulation would be that sound works as a parallel when it is not aiming at contradicting the existing meaning in other elements. It is indeed difficult to gauge how far music in films might double existing information or add to narrative development. However, as Royal S. Brown rightly notes:

> ...film music can contribute in an overwhelming way, via its tendency to hyper-explicate, to passivity in the viewer/listener. In other words, a given passage of music, instead of leading the viewer/listener towards an open and/or paradigmatic reading of a given situation, imposes a single reading by telling the viewer/listener exactly how to react to and/or feel that situation.[35]

This is a crucial point. Thus film incidental music is a device that aims to destroy ambiguity and multivalence, and to help ward off any potential worries, not only about asynchrony but also about other gaps in the images and sounds and their possible psychological implications. Considerations of film music have tended to retain a focus on the narrative (and an associated cognitive effect) at the expense of any material, physical, and emotional effect. Yet, the classical film score and its more recent relations had clear material functions, most obviously to aid in aesthetically 'papering over the cracks' to join film fragments (spaces, edits, etc.), but also as a soporific, enveloping and cocooning the audience in a womb of sound. Rather than discussing matters on a communicative level, I prefer to discuss matters on a level of perception of 'togetherness.' After all, synchronization is more or less a fact. The overwhelming majority of film scores produce film sequences that are corresponding and congruent, with occasional, sometimes very occasional, forays into counterpoint, be it of an anempathetic or dynamically contrasted nature.

Mickeymousing is the most obvious manifestation of the parallelism of film scoring with on-screen action and dialogue, following the rise and fall, mood, pace, etc. It is often decried but it is effective and has proved a highly resilient strategy for film music composers. Its name derives from the tendency in cartoon music for the music to provide (often comic) sounds for movements of characters on-screen. It can be highly efficacious when not used in a crass and crude manner. One example is at the opening of *Atonement* (2007), when the Briony character's purposeful walking along a corridor is accompanied by music that includes a regular typewriter beat that matches the pace of her stride and derives from her earlier use of a typewriter. The sonic derivation is clearly that of a typewriter, although it has more of the character of a multi-firing sample than a diegetic typewriter sound that is synchronized to on-screen action. Later in the film, composer Dario Marianelli also uses the sound of a ball bouncing against a wall around which his music coheres, and mixes soldiers singing diegetically with the non-diegetic score during the highly dramatic Dunkirk beach sequence. Film score composer Ernest Gold once declared:

> When I first started in the business, the old school of thought was that you go for the physical thing—somebody closing a door, somebody hanging up the phone, that sort of thing. I prefer to find a meaning or a change in the dramatic line to justify a musical entrance. [One might call the former]...the faucet form of movie scoring—you turn it on and you turn it off.[36]

He seems to suggest that this method is more a thing of the past, but in a broad sense, film scores still regularly follow activity, making the sort of dynamic moves that emanate directly from screen action, and in the most crass situations aim for an imitation of screen action, even if only for comic effect. Such precision of parallel between music and image activity was enabled by composer Max Steiner's development of a synchronization system premised upon a hole in a single frame providing a visual pulse when projected, becoming the industry standard click track to allow accurate matching of sound and image.[37]

Dialogue and sound effects are less likely to counterpoint activities in the image track. However, as a sparing device, mainstream cinema utilizes counterpoints of certain kinds. For example, voiceovers might be characterized as counterpoints to the diegetic world depicted on-screen, particularly when they are from the point of view of a dead protagonist as in *Sunset Boulevard* (1950) and *American Beauty* (1999). However, these are often not a counterpoint but seemingly fully integrated. More confusing is the voiceover that opens *L'Aneé derniere a Marienbad* (1961), which has an elusive connection with the images on-screen. Michel Chion states:

> Audiovisual counterpoint will be noticed only if it sets up an opposition between sound and image on a precise point of meaning. This kind of counterpoint influences our reading, in postulating a certain linear interpretation of the meaning of the sounds.[38]

Such a form of oblique commentary seemingly undermines a Bazinian sense of unity in film and its representational veneer. Eisenstein's musical approach to film aesthetics considered elements as abstract entities with an almost infinite range of combinatory possibilities. Dialectical clashing of components would be brought to some form of resolution. Yet the 'antiphony' between voices that he advocated is not really contradictory, and it is clear that in some ways, Eisenstein was more interested in the potential for clashing and contrasting aesthetics. Therefore, anempathetic sound or music is almost the perfect example of counterpoint between sound and image. As discussed by Claudia Gorbman, this occurs when music is indifferent to the emotion of a situation on-screen and marks a definite effect.[39] Counterpoint in terms of meaning leads to contradiction; in terms of tone, it leads to anempathetic sound or music; and in terms of dynamics, it results in effective contrasts; but it rarely leads to any sense of incommensurability between sound and image. There is, of course, much more opportunity in mainstream narrative film for music as counterpoint than there is for diegetic sound.

Caryl Flinn noted that film music composers' use of thematic techniques and orchestrations to work around dialogue and sound effects "...suggest[s] that a more *contrapuntal* (as opposed to parallel) relationship exists between film music and other elements of the classical film's complex: indeed, several composers state that they consider their most successful scores to be those which are 'integrated' most wholly with the film."[40] Thus Flinn argues that the practice of classical Hollywood scoring exceeds the dominant view that the soundtrack must parallel the image and/or the narrative. George Burt discusses film music's contrapuntal aspect, in which music and film interact, each having an impact on the other:

> In music, counterpoint evokes the transfer of attention from one voice to another as an enrichment of the total experience.... This happens in film as well, though to a limited extent. There are occasions when the score takes on a more noticeable role, if only for a short period of time—even a few seconds. This can occur at the beginnings and endings of scenes or at climactic points where dialog and action come to a momentary pause. Still, this momentary transfer of attention in no way mitigates our preoccupation with what is on the screen. Under the best of circumstances, it substantiates what is on the screen by filling in where dramatic extension is required.[41]

In music, the term 'counterpoint' tends not to designate superimposition but rather the independence of musical voices or lines that nevertheless still make sense together. A notable subcategory is 'contrary motion,' when one voice modulates upward in pitch while another simultaneously goes downward in pitch, both retaining a pleasing relationship melodically (temporally) and harmonically (simultaneously). Theoretical counterpoint in film appears to describe something more extreme. For example, film historian Richard Maltby noted that during the silent cinema, live musical accompaniment had potential for deviation:

> In some venues,... such as the movie theaters catering to African-American audiences, which employed jazz-based 'race orchestras,' the relationship between sound and image was one of deliberate counterpoint, as the orchestras played music 'against the grain' of the movie, ignoring the narrative and the sheet music library, undermining or satirizing the white cultural forms of the movie....[42]

An exemplary instance of music counterpointing film was the phenomenon early in the second decade of the 20th century, when silent film musicians would 'fun' the film they were accompanying by applying inappropriate music. This practice of burlesquing a film's original intentions caused a debate in the U.S. about the nature of music's relation to film exhibition.[43] The practice persisted into the era of synchronized sound films, although in a different form in comedy films and cartoons.

A similar but unrelated phenomenon, derived from the potential for music not to fit the film it accompanied, persisted as an occasional device in sound cinema: namely anempathetic music. In a sense, anempathetic music is the opposite of Mickeymousing in that, rather than following the rise and fall of screen dynamics, it aims to directly contradict the emotional tone of the on-screen narrative and representations. Probably the best-known instance is a sequence in Quentin Tarantino's *Reservoir Dogs* (1992), which I further discuss later. Here, Mr. Blonde (Michael Madsen) cuts off the ear of a tied-up policeman to the accompaniment of the banal and jaunty pop song "Stuck in the Middle with You" by Stealer's Wheel. Most examples involve diegetic sound or music, often with a mechanical character. For instance, in Hitchcock's *Psycho* (1960), the sound of the shower continues indifferently as the camera focuses on Marion's static face after she is stabbed to death. In another Hitchcock film, *The Birds* (1963), crows gather threateningly on a jungle gym outside the school as we hear the children inside singing a repetitive nonsense song. A particularly good example is in the Coen brothers' *Miller's Crossing* (1990), where gunmen are coming to kill gang boss Leo (Albert Finney) as he relaxes while listening to the sentimental Irish song "Danny Boy." Their relentless approach is intercut with his repose in close-up until the point when they arrive and an extremely violent fight with machine guns takes place. The song carries on over the action without interacting on a level of dynamics, its emotional tone at odds with the violent action it accompanies.

Cases of non-diegetic music working anempathetically with the image track tend to come across as self-conscious irony: for instance, Stanley Kubrick's use of the sentimental song "We'll Meet Again" (sung by Vera Lynn) at the conclusion of *Dr. Strangelove* (1964) as nuclear bombs explode; or his use of the overture from Rossini's opera *La Gazza Ladra* to accompany, indeed choreograph, a fight between Alex and his droogs and Billyboy's gang in the theater, among many other instances of musical anempathy in *A Clockwork Orange* (1971). Often, non-diegetic music working in an anempathetic manner appears as a direct ironic commentary. For instance, the thriller *Shallow Grave* (1994) concludes with Alex (Ewan McGregor) lying either dead or dying with the money everyone has been pursuing hidden under the floorboards beneath him. This is accompanied by Andy Williams's jolly song "Happy Heart," while in *Trainspotting* (1995), the same actor has a drug overdose to Lou Reed's "Perfect Day," a song that already appears ironic.

Though not usually anempathetic, music for a contrasting or problematic character might be construed as a form of counterpoint, perhaps making a subtle commentary on the action: for example, self-consciously anachronistic film scores such as Michael Nyman's for *The Draughtsman's Contract* (1982) and Craig Armstrong's for *Plunkett and Macleane* (1999), particularly the dance sequence in the latter. Musical anachronisms abound in film but are rarely noticed by audiences if the music fits general conventions for drama or period representation. Sofia Coppola's *Marie Antoinette* (2006) includes some period music but intersperses it with contemporary rock and pop music, including electronic music by Squarepusher and Aphex Twin, along with songs by Adam and the Ants, Bow Wow Wow, and The Strokes, among others. Anachronisms such as this can short-circuit audience expectation by undermining convention, potentially producing a Brechtian alienation that emotionally distances the audience from the film.[44] Yet often, contrasting aesthetics can have a pleasing effect, with a different dynamic tone, such as in the opening of *Candyman* (1992), when a vertical downward helicopter shot moves the frame slowly and inevitably along Chicago's streets accompanied by Philip Glass's fast, rhythmic music. A more celebrated instance of this is the use of Strauss's *The Beautiful Blue Danube* waltz to accompany a slow-moving spaceship in *2001: A Space Odyssey* (1968). Although not contradictory, in this last case, the image and soundtracks are far from conventional and amount to a shock in expectations. These last examples appear less concerned with providing a sense of commentary than fashioning explicit instances of 'horizontal freedom,' where soundtrack and image track appear highly independent of each other.

THE PERSISTENCE OF THE SILENT AND EARLY SOUND FILM MODES

Some early sound filmmakers were adamant that the capabilities for the application of sound to cinema were only fulfilled by making films that eschewed the conventionalized talkie format. The Russians previously discussed were not the only concerned people. The fear articulated in the "Statement on Sound" that the path of least resistance for cinema with synchronized recorded sound was likely filmed stageplays was realized quickly, aided by Hollywood's industrial production-line approach to making films. British documentary filmmaker Basil Wright made a distinction between the talkie and the sound film. He suggested that the talkies are not cinematic and that they should be seen as wholly exclusive categories.[45] Wright noted that sound was an essential part of silent cinema and that among filmmakers with ambitions beyond the merely conventional, there was a fetishization of counterpoint and asynchrony, stating, "If you put any natural sound which doesn't correspond with the visual action, you make a dull highbrow film!"[46] French filmmaker René Clair noted that "The talking film is not everything. There is also the sound film—on which the last hopes of the advocates of silent film are pinned."[47] In such films as *Sous le toits de Paris* (1930), *Le million* (1931), and *A nous la liberté* (1932), Clair championed the idea of the 'sound film' as opposed to the 'talkie', attempting to integrate asynchrony rather than slavishly matching sound to screen content. He noted that dialogue scenes in which the director showed a reaction shot of the listener rather than simply synchronizing with the speaker were important for moving beyond the demonstration "...that the actor's lips opened at exactly the same moment as the sound was heard—in short, that their mechanical toy worked beautifully."[48] However, some early sound film experiments were less aimed at integration with mainstream narrative film than Clair's work. David Bordwell cites Pudovkin's *Deserter* (1933), where the sounds of sweet music and children's voices accompany shots of the bourgeoisie in cars, culminating in a sound bridge of a woman's voice shouting "The truth about the strike!" before we see her handing out leaflets. "For many cinéphiles such sonic montage—much more hard-edged than Clair's ingratiating auditory metaphors—pointed the way to true sound technique."[49] Perhaps the clearest example of this is Dziga Vertov's first sound film *Enthusiasm* (1930). Near the beginning of the film, Vertov startlingly juxtaposes images of drunks with the sounds of Eastern Orthodox religious services. Similarly, Joris Ivens's *Song of Heroes* (1931) was an early Soviet sound documentary about industrial activities in the new town of Magnitogorsk in the Urals. The film's music by Hanns Eisler was conceived more as a collaboration than an added-on feature and was aimed at explicit counterpoint with the images.

Ironically, the advent of recorded sound invented 'silence' in the cinema. Although there may have been quiet at times in film theatres, it was rarely a part of the highly atmospheric and distinctive quietness of some early sound films. Along with Universal's *Dracula* (1931) and *Frankenstein* (1931), with their long periods of near silence, which within a few years would have been broken by incidental music, Fritz Lang's *M* (1928) is also a strikingly quiet film. Similarly, Carl Theodor Dreyer's *Vampyr* (1932) has long, spooky passages of silence that suggest that the film's synchronization might have failed and that the film atavistically returned to the modes of silent cinema. It is these very sequences without staged dialogue that allow for a strong aesthetic effect, moving beyond character identification into dreamlike ambiguity.

While Eisenstein lauded the image flexibility of silent film, Siegfried Kracauer noted that a return to image takes place in many films with synchronized sound:

> If speech is in the lead, even the most knowing film maker cannot avoid synchronizing it with the images in ways which disqualify the latter as a source of communication. Conversely, if the visuals predominate, he [sic] is free to avail himself of modes of synchronization which, in keeping with the cinematic approach, advance the action through pictorial statements.... In case verbal communications prevail, the odds are that the imagery will parallel them. The reverse alternative—speech being de-emphasized—greatly favors counterpoint, which stirs the visuals to become eloquent. Eisenstein and Pudovkin were of course not wrong in advocating a contrapuntal use of sound. But from the present viewpoint they did so for the wrong reasons.[50]

Near the start of the Spanish horror film *Tombs of the Blind Dead* (1971), the character Virginia jumps off a train and visits a deserted village where, after a while, she encounters the Knights Templar ghosts of the film's title. This sequence lasts nearly 22 minutes and includes only two lines of dialogue when Virginia shouts to ask if anyone is there, but the soundtrack is not silent by any means. Virginia's activities make distinct (often hollow and echoing) diegetic sounds, while atmospheric music proceeds throughout the second part of the sequence, halting only momentarily for an anticlimax when Virginia encounters a stray cat. The resurrection of the skeletal monsters involves deep rumbles and the music by Anton Garcia Abril (which has retained a regular 4/4 rhythmic loop with bass notes alternating a tritone apart) becomes denser as accompaniment to the silent figures. Organ and piano bass are accompanied by religious choir music and noises from percussion, glissandi, and tape effects. Metallic-sounding echoes dominate the soundtrack, not only in elements of the music but most noticeably on the diegetic sounds made by Virginia. While the ghosts appear silent (and move in slow motion), Virginia appears to hear something—quite possibly the loud choral music that accompanies the monstrous but serene figures. This extended dialogue-free section of *Tombs of the Blind Dead* can be accounted for by a number of determinants. One is that sounds and action are more atmospheric than dialogue, and thus the horror film is often a repository of the traditions of the sound film. Another is that films made to be dubbed into foreign languages can often depend less on dialogue scenes. In cases like this, it is immaterial which language the film is in, making light work of subtitling duties.

Kracauer states that "All the successful attempts at integration of the spoken word have one characteristic in common: they play down dialog with a view to reinstating the visuals."[51] He might have suggested that they also allowed for loud, dominant music, a predominance of sound effects, and dramatic interactions between sound and vision that are more often able to take a counterpoint approach to their relationship.

While Eisenstein's description of the movements of multiple lines, as he notes, is perfectly possible without sound, a soundtrack proliferates elements and their complexity of interaction. Dialogue, sound effects, and music often interact subtly in films, although their relationship may be formulaic in many cases. In less common cases, there is a montage of sonic elements that does not mesh into a distinct unity but pulls the soundtrack apart into separate lines.[52] An interesting case in point occurs in John Carpenter's *Assault on Precinct 13* (1976): a highly memorable sequence entailing a seemingly chaotic soundtrack that mixes diegetic sound, including music, with non-diegetic incidental music, and works across the integrity of the diegetic music in a slow but extremely tense sequence that concludes with a little girl being shot dead.

All music for the film is derived from the title theme or a quieter and more reflective theme. The film's opening title theme reappears across the film and begins with a ticking drum machine beat, which often appears alone in the film as a tense element (associated with the threatening gangs in the film). Director Carpenter regularly writes and performs his own film music, usually using synthesizers and led by a strong sense of musical minimalism. His main theme for *Assault on Precinct 13* is minimal in the extreme, based on the repetition of a single five-note rhythmic figure in minor mode (figure 3.1), which is then moved up a minor third, down a fourth, and then up a whole tone. This generates a four-bar structure based around the (non-functional) harmony of I-III-VII-I. The regularity sets up certain expectations in terms of time, while Carpenter also uses simple, instantly apparent and modular elements: bass, fanfare-like melody, mechanical percussion. All of the music apart from the beatbox is played on an analogue synthesizer and has a highly distinctive timbre. The main theme motif is played in the bass register, which is well differentiated from other musical activity through the distinctiveness of the timbre and

Figure 3.1: *Assault on Precinct 13* (1976) Main Theme (John Carpenter).

pitch register. There is a gradual entrance from higher-pitched synthesizer chords matching each harmonic change, with a featured suspension of the fourth resolving slowly to the (major) third of the VII chord. This suspension resolution is redolent of church organ music, and indeed has become something of a clichéd representation of the religious in Western popular culture, and perhaps hints at the faith and martyrdom of those under siege in the film.

In probably the film's most startling sequence (see figures 3.2–3.12 and table 3.1), a man in an ice cream truck fears being shot by passing gang members. He serves a girl an ice cream cone but she comes back for a different flavor and is shot dead by one of the gang members. Diegetic sound is sparse in the sequence, which is often dominated by the continuous ticking sound of an echoed beatbox (continuous sixteenth notes of artificial-sounding hi-hats); this persists and drifts in and out of focus as a continuous beat throughout the action without dynamic change in relation to image events. The diegetic tinny bell-like music-box tune of Strauss's "Emperor Waltz" is played by the ice cream truck, at times masked by the beatbox pulse and at other times creating a cacophonous aural fabric. While these two musical tracks fade in and out, they are also superimposed. A strategy of cross-fading would be the conventional way of dealing with two competing sonic discourses. However, here, they are left to fight it out between themselves. Despite stereo separation adding clarity, the intermittent effect is of chaotic sounds running on top of one another.

This sound-on-sound montage makes the sound and image synchronization highly confusing. An immediate effect is that the non-diegetic music does not appear synchronized with the diegesis in any meaningful way. Beyond traditional sound montage, this might be approached as montage from a distinctly musical point of view, even though the montage of sounds might initially seem musically contradictory. Rather than any sense of musical polyphony, this appears simply as simultaneity, mixing diegetic and non-diegetic music in a manner that refuses to harmonize them directly. Although upon first appearance together, the ice cream truck waltz and beatbox are virtually in time, later the meters differ and at other times merely come across as chaos. The pulse of each is often unsynchronized, with the two channels of music simply appearing as a random superimposition. This sequence establishes a unified pulse, but then introduces another with the effect of 'de-synching,' making things extremely disorienting. This incidence of multi-voiced polyphony involves a range of channels (visuals, dialogue, sound effects, diegetic music, and non-diegetic music) that undermines the traditional hierarchy between the latter two and allows their almost

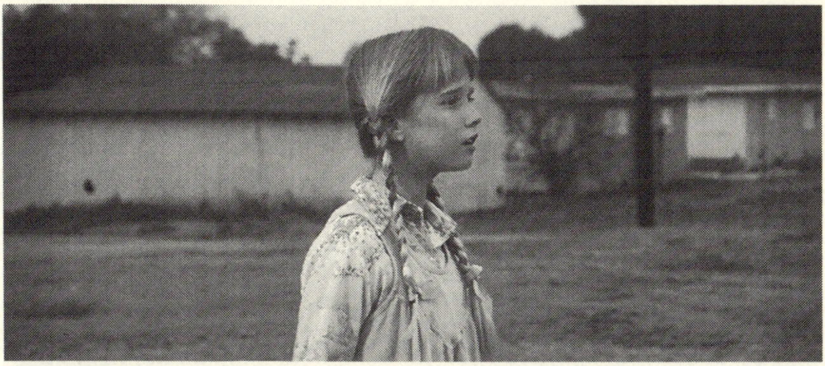
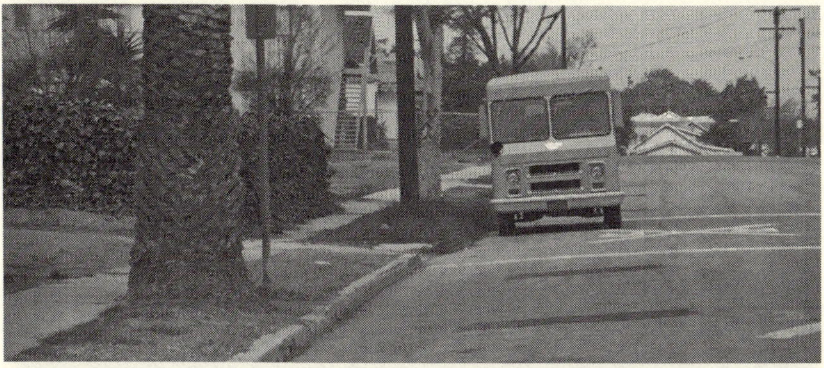
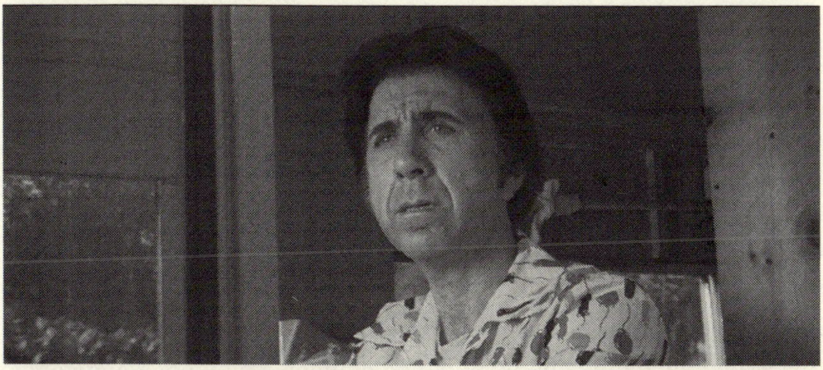
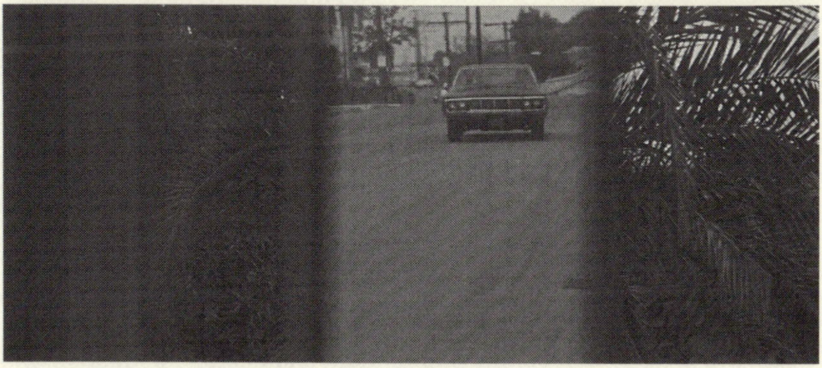

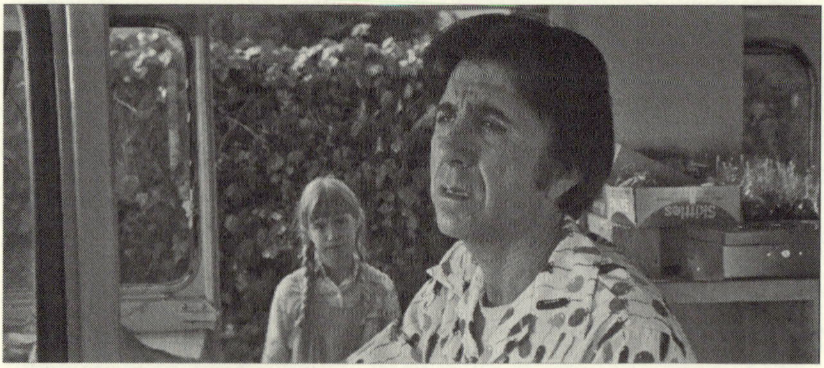

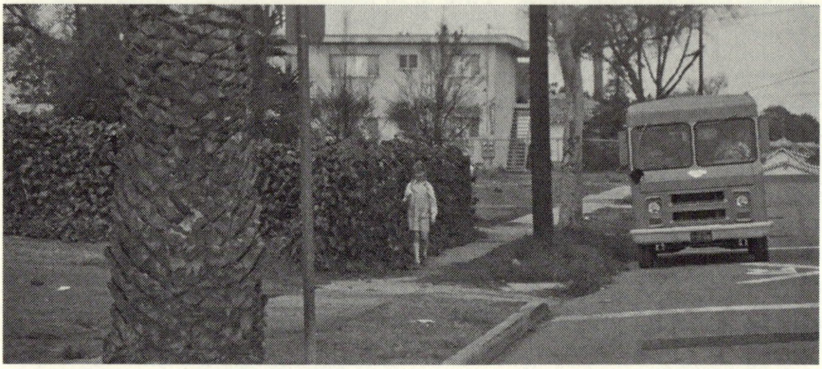

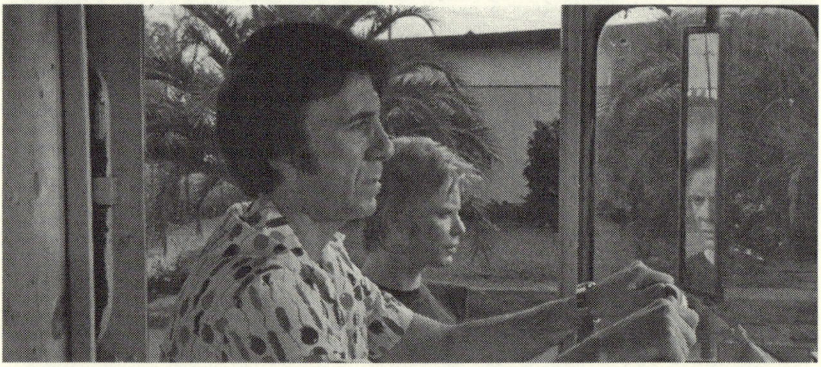

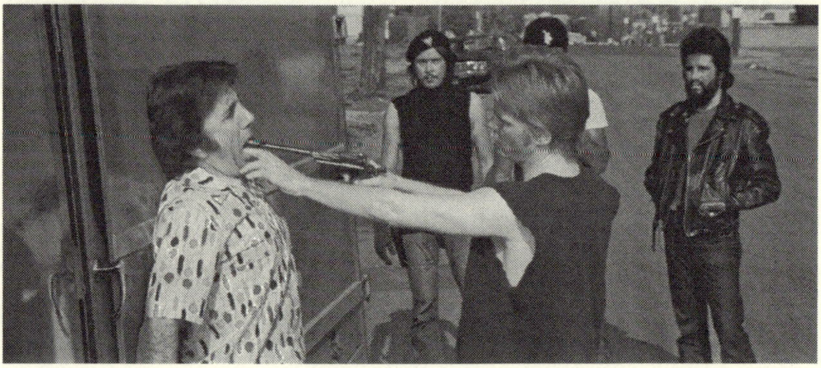

Figures 3.2–3.12: *Assault on Precinct 13* (1976): Ice Cream Truck Sequence.

independent coexistence. This sequence also has two strands of narrative in operation: the little girl getting her ice cream unaware of the danger and the ice cream man's concern about the slow passing of a car of gang members up and down the road. The narrative trajectory is to conclude the sequence with the two strands coalescing with the gunshot. This also marks the 'musical' closure of the sequence.

Table 3.1. TIME NARRATIVE: EVENTS AND MUSIC.

0.27:54	The girl sees the ice cream truck: "Daddy…." (figures 3.2 and 3.3)	Diegetic sound of ice cream truck tune, playing Strauss waltz: tinny, resonant, and slightly flat.
0.28:19	Ice cream man's point of view shot in truck side mirror. (figures 3.4 and 3.5)	Sounding across the diegetic ice cream truck music, the presence of the gangsters' car is indicated by the non-diegetic score, which consists of ticking regular sixteenth notes on a drum machine (closed hi-hat sound). These commence as two bars of 3/8, one with emphasized sixteenth notes, the other not. Starting out almost in time with the ice cream truck waltz, they 'pull it' into being heard as following their tempo.
0.29:17	The car turns as the girl runs to the ice cream truck.	The sixteenth note beat almost imperceptibly changes pulse, so that the emphases are not regular and the beat becomes merely a continuum of mechanical sixteenth notes, with a chaotic series of emphases. It sounds as if the music was cut. As she runs, the deep bass notes of the main theme enter briefly and quietly (in 4/4) alongside the regular beating pulse (in 3/8 at this point). All the time, the ice cream truck music has persisted—out of time with the pulse— although often masked by other sounds and the non-diegetic music.
0.29:20	Ice cream man: "…I'm closed." Girl: "Your music's still playing." He gets her an ice cream. (figures 3.6 and 3.7)	After she points it out, he switches the truck music off abruptly.
0.29:31	The ice cream man looks in side mirror and watches the gang car disappear.	The sixteenth note non-diegetic pulse continues briefly until he sees the gangsters' car disappear, whereupon it fades and halts.
0.29:42	A gang member appears in the door gap behind the ice cream man. (figure 3.8)	Droning, sustained deep synthesizer notes enter (making an A minor chord with the lower A and higher C most audible). Despite pitch remaining constant, intensity varies through filtering of the overtones.
0.29:58	The gang member puts the gun barrel in the ice cream man's mouth. (figure 3.9)	The pitch of the lower note raises to B$\flat$ as the chord sustains. A deeper synthesizer tone with filter sweep dominates, anticipating a gunshot.
0.30:13	Girl: "Hey, this is regular vanilla." (figure 3.10) She returns to the truck: "I want vanilla twist."	The intensity of the sustained chord increases, with constituent tones varying in volume.
0.30:25	Gang member shoots the girl. (figures 3.11 and 3.12)	The gunshot (with a silencer and sounds like a blast of white noise) is the cadence that resolves the sustained chord. Silence ensues.

In musical parlance, these two independent and rhythmically oriented musical discourses construct a polyrhythm that is complex and not coordinated. While each is its own magnetic center of activity that pulls for the listener's attention, they also manage to make occasional and almost-random momentary harmony. Musical superimposition is often a complex and not immediately pleasing effect. In art music, it has most readily been associated with the American composer Charles Ives, whose music sometimes borrowed melodies from elsewhere and then played them simultaneously in different keys.[53] A more recent and more obscure example is V/Vm Test Record's Dimitri Shostakovich adaptation *The Missing Symphony*, which digitally time-stretched and superimposed all 15 of Shostakovich's symphonies so that they all fit into a single cacophonous duration.[54] It emerges as utter chaos, with no division into significant moments and no possibility of finding (and recognizing) coherent streams, the whole movement of sonic dynamics being lost in the melee. This strategy is equally rare in film music, although another example takes place in Wojchiech Kilar's score for *Bram Stoker's Dracula* (1992), where, at a few points, two different themes of radically different character are simply played at the same time over one another. Kilar's score quite rigidly pursues a leitmotiv structure, and in the concluding chase of Dracula, a deep minor mode ostinato bass in the strings is overlayed by the superimposition of a violin playing the melody of the love theme, with a full string crescendo to conclude the cue, and with no concession to mixing them together.

One reason for the rarity of such sonic superimposition is that it is difficult for the brain to process. As Bregman's auditory scene analysis suggests, the mind works to segment and differentiate sonic elements by finding a hierarchy in the sounds present.[55] Coherent melody lines are difficult to process when simultaneous, although a degree of dual listening is possible. Simultaneous lines can lead to schizophrenic listening, where we listen to some of one and then some of the other, or strain to try and hear both at the same time. Furthermore, such musical superimposition marks something of an asynchrony in that it loses the rhythm of the film, creating a musical cross-rhythm that does not mesh satisfactorily. A notable effect of this is that synch points appear redoubled by their existence in such an uncertain environment. Strangely, the 2005 DVD (and later Blu Ray) release of *Assault on Precinct 13* with isolated music track option allows the removal of the ice cream truck music, leaving a more conventional and unremarkable effect.[56]

CONCLUSION

The crucial notion of parallel and counterpoint, while perhaps not generating a tremendously robust analytical method, [57] nevertheless remains an important analytical lens for filmmakers and film criticism. As descriptive of the fundamental relationship of image and sound, these terms and ideas can be traced back to the massively influential "Statement on Sound" by Eisenstein, Pudovkin, and Alexandrov. Using musical metaphors, this endorsed counterpoint as a manifestation of the montage principle they espoused, stating that film sound should aim at a "...sharp discord with the visual images" to realize the audiovisual potential of cinema.[58] They were interested in the space between image and sound communication. On an aesthetic stage, however, cutting-edge music can be accompanied of course by banal and conventional visuals, and vice versa. In the vast majority of cases, the weld between music and image is strong enough to furnish something of their qualities to each other, to the point where it is rare to encounter, for instance, a notably banal song with an interesting video or an interesting song with a banal video. This situation illustrates vividly that there is a significant creative potential in the space between the music and the image as accompaniments to one another. Questions of what images should accompany certain pieces of music predated recording, let alone the accompaniment of screened images with recorded music. Yet there always has been some idea of conventional and acceptable matches of images with sounds. Illustrative images for music have always had a certain ambiguity, although the closer the images relate to a direct reproduction of a live performance, the less ambiguous the relationship of sound and image.

An insistent strand in early film theory (often referred to as classical film theory) was interested in the conjunction and disjunction of sound and image and how the effect of sound relies upon its nature being unperceived, in order to lull the cinema audience into a sense that they are beholding a seamless audiovisual entirety. There were crucial theoretical writings in the 1930s (shortly after the onset of synchronized sound cinema) that attempted to grasp the complexities of the sound film in theoretical and practical terms. Since then, with one or two notable exceptions, there has been a conspicuous paucity of theory concerned with the soundtrack and its relationship to the film image. Making a return to classical film theory is significant. The theoretical ideas generated at the birth and early years of sound cinema are still relevant and cast a shadow, if sometimes only faintly, over more recent theory. The loss of original aesthetic concerns of film analysis to imports from other disciplines arguably has hamstrung the aesthetic analysis and theorization of film as an audiovisual medium.

Although I started this chapter by noting the centrality of Soviet montage cinema to recent theorizations of new media, specifically in Lev Manovich's writings, the influence from this earlier historical period is also evident among filmmakers. For instance, Alexander Graf notes of German director Wim Wenders that a characteristic "...in all of his films, is a relative autonomy of the soundtrack from the image. In this Wenders' position is a development on the film-ideological debate among Soviet directors Sergei Eisenstein, Vsevolod Pudovkin and Grigori Alexandrov in 1928...."[59] Soviet montage cinema is taught in film schools and universities, although the implications of its ideas about asynchrony rarely appear to have had more than a passing influence. Yet momentary counterpoints are more common than ever in recent films. According to Béla Balázs, film sound has the potential to open up new experience. At its most expressive, when sound is asynchronous to the picture, the lack of necessity for it to appear natural allowed it a more symbolic deployment open to greater artistry.[60] However, following Eisenstein, Pudovkin, and Alexandrov, he also opined that synchronized recorded sound dissipated this potential habitually by the overwhelming convention of making film into an illusion of theater. Yet counterpoint has remained, sometimes appearing determinedly as asynchronous moments in films that are dominated by dialogue scenes, at points when music comes to dominate or action pushes aside the spoken word, or when the film's narration takes a dramatic and bold turn from the zero degree of film style that Eisenstein characterized as a simple parallel for sound to its master, the image. These might be often characterized as being residuals from films that were not talkies, the earlier silent film regime, and the transition period of sound film with its interest in sound but not in dialogue.

CHAPTER 4

Occult Aesthetics

As I noted in the opening chapter, 'occult' does not necessarily mean 'satanic,' pagan, or in any way evil or negative; it merely means unapparent. The term can be used to describe any hidden workings or processes that are unable to be observed. For example, 'occult bleeding' is a medical term for bleeding that takes place out of sight. Occult tends to have connotations of magic and the mystical, and invokes the notion of mysterious ritualistic underpinnings of the everyday world. All these aspects are relevant for the discussion of what I call 'occult aesthetics' in this book.

Aesthetics can work in mystical, magical, and unapparent manners, and the synchronization of sound and image in the cinema is an exemplary case in point. It is far from straightforward. Despite the impression of an unproblematic composite of sound and image, the relationship of the two is always more complex than it initially might seem. Horror films appear to know more about the occult of aesthetics than other films: They play around with this lynchpin of cinema far more than other genres. There is something potentially disturbing about the cinema's illusion that has a determinedly supernatural character. Film could be understood as a conjuration: as a magical act of illusionism that dazzles the audience into believing it.[1] This was a persistent notion in the early days of film. One of early cinema's alleged effects was known as the 'train effect,' where audiences feared physical impact upon seeing the Lumière brothers film *L'arrivée d'un train en gare de la Ciotat* (1895), specifically when the train on-screen travels toward the camera.[2] The illusionism of this phenomenon was burlesqued in *Uncle Josh at the Moving Picture Show* (1902), when a country rube visiting town gets up next to the screen in a cinema, thinking that he can interact with the uncanny shadows of people depicted. Although it may have been a cause for mirth, the illusion of film has an impact: We believe it on some level. In fact, to a degree, film keeps us as children, constantly amazed and engrossed in its magic. Perhaps it is no surprise then that there has been a glut of 'magic' films recently that are almost as popular with adults as they are with children, such as the *Harry Potter* films, the *Narnia* films, *The Golden Compass* (2007), and *The Lord of the Rings* films. The success of the literary originals aside, some might argue that the degree of magic portrayed in films has risen with the capacities for computer animation, but this has always been an insistent strand of cinema, certainly since Georges Méliès's startling conjuring tricks and wild special effects in films at the turn of the 20th century.[3] The 'hidden' aspect of all such magic is crucial: In his discussion about melodrama, Peter Brooks invokes what he calls the 'moral occult,' which

> ... is not a metaphysical system, it is rather the repository of the fragmentary and desacralized remnants of sacred myth. It bears comparison to unconscious mind, for it is a sphere of being where our most basic desires and inner dictions lie, a realm which in quotidian existence may appear closed off from us, but which we must accede to since it is the realm of meaning and value. The melodramatic mode in large measure exists to locate and to articulate the moral occult.[4]

The weakening of religious belief in the wake of the Enlightenment and industrial revolution led to the seeming disappearance of religious representations of good and evil, which became hidden or partially masked by the surface of reality. Brooks argues that melodrama as a form engages this repository of ideas, and similarly, I argue here that there is a half-hidden 'occult' in the fundamental aesthetics of sound cinema: one that plays across representational and emotional concerns with basic perceptual movements between synchronization and asynchrony. The marriage of sound and image is a form of hidden rite, matching the occultist belief that clandestine rituals control and underpin the world while remaining hidden to the naïve and unsuspecting population. Furthermore, the secret marriage of sound and vision includes the fragmentary residuals of silent cinema, as well as the promise of wholeness. Tom Gunning suggests that recorded and synchronized sound cinema was likely a product of the desire to reunite hearing and vision, which had been divided by technology a few decades earlier, "... a desire to heal the breach."[5]

In this book, I approach theory as having something of the occult in itself. When dealing with culture as intangible as the shadows of film and the fleeting squeaks of musical sounds from a speaker, theory can take on something of the form of divination, trying to find something not immediately apparent or obvious. Indeed, theory has a generative function in that, in its best form, it grapples with unknowables, making them into something more tangible—although never quite making them unproblematically understandable. In other words, theory can never make them into a simplistic reduction that passes itself off as guaranteed knowledge. Retaining a sense of the occult means realizing that hidden aspects might be the most important ones, and by their obscured nature, the most difficult to pin down.

Despite its concealed formation, there was a determinedly ritualistic element to the synching up of sound and image in the early years of cinema—before it was achieved mechanically—that remains at the heart of cinema. To achieve convincing and immersive illusion, the ritual of synchronization must be completed to satisfaction. Yet similarly, theoretical investigation, as well as scientific experimentalism, involves clear, ritual aspects, including following certain strict and quasi-religious procedures to open the portal from the known to the unknown.

As noted previously, there were some highly specific meanings ascribed to the term 'synchronization' at the time of the arrival of sound cinema, derived specifically from fitting music to a film. These had implications beyond simply making a unity of sound and image. Robert Spadoni notes:

> Synchronized voices are understood to *accompany* moving lips rather than to issue from them. This connotation helps to explain instances in which the word is applied, during the early sound period, to describe sloppy post-dubbing and even foreign speech that has been dubbed over English-speaking mouths. The sense of synchronization as something more provisional than essential accorded well with a viewer's impression of synchronized speech as a marvelous mechanical gimmick. The novelty of the technique guaranteed that even if there had been no discernable problems with the synchronization, the quality of the sound, or the disparity between the locations of the loudspeakers and the speaking mouths, viewers still would have experienced a heightened awareness of the artificial nature of cinema as a direct result of sound.[6]

He points to the audience's sensitivity to material aspects of the film medium at this historical juncture, and suggests that this was exploited by films at the time, particularly horror films. According to Spadoni, the uncanny nature of film sound in transitional period cinema is translated into supernatural, seemingly monstrous bodies on screen, such as that of Frankenstein's monster, Dracula, or the characters in Tod Browning's *Freaks* (1932). Thus technology offered a potential for complex representation through the uncanny assemblage of sound and image. Rather than improving the illusion, Spadoni suggests that it initiated a form of reception interference or static, with an effect more intense than mere illusion, expressing an embodiment of the aesthetic disturbance afforded by the cultural possibilities of technological developments.[7] The illusionism of cinema is doubtless a profound effect, but the potential disturbance invoked by asynchrony can also be an extreme effect, although different in nature. I would argue that there is a residual psychological disturbance to the divorce of sound and image in cinema, despite the conventional use of asynchrony for passages of films. There appears to be some evidence that early sound films unsettled audiences—who had a heightened awareness of the new formulation of cinema—as images appeared less real than silent, but more uncanny because sound was a strange new addition to the familiar images on the screen. In addition, David Toop points to the sonic at the core of the notion of the uncanny more generally.[8] The heart of cinema then contains a potential disturbance at the center of one of its most enduring and engaging aspects: the illusion of sound and image unity.

THE DYNAMIC OF SYNCHRONIZATION

Sound film routinely tends to travel in the midst of moments of synchrony between sound and image, and points when there is no apparent synchronization. Approaching audiovisual culture from this more abstract perspective illuminates it in a form that removes the overly familiar aspects that have militated against sustained and detailed theorization of sound in films, and the notion of sound cinema more generally.

Points of synchronization constitute something of a repose, a default position of normality that furnishes moments of comfort in a potentially threatening environment that can be overwrought with sound and image stimuli. Correspondingly, the lack of synchrony between sound and images has to be characterized as potentially disturbing for the audience, perhaps even as moments of aesthetic and representational danger. Indeed, McGurk and MacDonald noted that asynchrony tends to prove upsetting.[9] Thus, from this perspective, the interplay between the two becomes the central dynamic of audiovisual culture, and its objects can be reconceived and newly understood along these lines. Indeed, contemporary mainstream film is sometimes conceived as movement from set piece to set piece, with filler material in between. (Indeed, the exigencies of film finance and production dictate that certain 'featured' sequences are nodes where the budget is concentrated.) We can rethink film, though, as a different form of temporal movement, between moments of synchronized repose and unsynchronized chaos. Films contain a large amount of asynchronous sound that we tend not to notice or register consciously: They aim to ensure that we do not linger on these moments. However, every film that has a synchronized soundtrack will evince this sort of forward development or movement. Rather than merely conceiving of this as an industrial process and a byproduct of the conventions of framing, recording, and post-production, I mean to engage this as something potentially more profound. It can be approached as an abstract, unconscious, and aesthetic drama, where film might play out momentary and instinctual understandings of and responses to the world. Within this system, precise synchronization and complete asynchrony represent different extremes of film and extremes of experience for the viewer/auditor. Asynchrony (non-synchronization), or at least an uncertain relationship of synchronization between images and sounds, renders the audience uncertain, making them uneasy or anxious. At the opposing pole, (absolute) synchronization suggests to us, or dramatizes for us, a situation where all is well with the world: Everything is in its rightful place. Ambiguity about synchronization (or a total lack of it) is potentially unsettling. At the very least, it is a different 'mode' from synchronized 'normality' on screen. Scientific insights and biological determinism might help to understand how synchronization appears to serve films. Human beings likely react to discontinuity between what is seen and what is heard on an unconscious or preconscious level. According to developments in neuroscience and sociobiology, we possess physical, hardwired processes whereby we are informed about the space we occupy through a combination of the senses. A disparity between visual perception of a space and its apparently attached sound (or vice versa) will have an instant effect. Such unprocessed reactions likely set in process an unconscious unease or dissatisfaction. This mechanism may have evolved for human defense and might inform us, for example, that a dark ravine with no echoes might contain a large, unseen predator. Such biological concerns about sound's perception and its place in our survival were doubtless transposed into cinema and exploited by that most sensual of audiovisual media. Since the advent of 5.1 Surround Sound cinema, soundtracks have spatialized their elements as never before. Features such as the in-the-wings sound effect still can, if used in an unsubtle and crass manner, make us partially turn our heads, forcing an involuntary physical reaction to sound. It is worth remembering that in psychobiological terms, sounds that emanate from anywhere except directly in front of us, initially at least, are perceived as a potential threat. Indeed, as these points attest, there is something absolutely primal about the synchronization of sound and image. Clearly, the senses of hearing and seeing are not totally separated.

The cross-referencing of the two, making for a seamless continuum of perception, would have to be taken as the normality of human physicality. The exigencies of the human body clearly are partially activated and altered in significant ways by the cinema. I suspect that moments of synchronization between sound and image provide feelings of coalescence, joining up, and ultimately integration. Integration on an aesthetic level homologizes feelings of integration on a level of well-being and ultimately social integration. Following Adorno's approach to culture as 'concentrated social substance,'[10] I would suggest that the abstract play of synchronization in films (indirectly at least) mirrors the social and psychological processes of understanding our place in the world and our perception of risk in modern life.

Film manipulates audience emotion and desires. Gestalt psychology concerns similar 'vectors' of energy, and film appears to marshal audience energy in its movement from tension to repose, sometimes very crudely.[11] Similarly, the movement between asynchrony and synchronization forms vectors of emotional and psychological dynamics. These ideas are evident in some musical theory. For example, music theorist Leonard B. Meyer notes that

> Both music and life are experienced as dynamic processes of growth and decay, activity and rest, tension and release.... Emotional behavior is a kind of composite gesture, a motion whose peculiar qualities are largely defined in terms of energy, direction, tension, continuity, and so forth. Since music also involves motions differentiated by the same qualities, 'musical mood gestures' may be similar to behavioral mood gestures. In fact, because moods and sentiments attain their most precise articulation through vocal inflection, it is possible for music to imitate the sounds of emotional behavior with some precision. Finally, since motor behavior plays a considerable role in both designative emotional behavior and in musical experience, a similarity between the motor behavior of designative gestures and that of musical gestures will inforce [sic] the feeling of similarity between the two types of experience.[12]

The analytical dominance of a model of film as being essentially narrative or representational has marginalized approaches that attempt to think of film as dynamic movement or emotional cathexis. Cathexis usually describes an investment of emotional or mental energy in something (or a form of channeling psychological and emotional energy). Of course, certain types of film have been founded very explicitly upon the direction of emotional energy and manipulation of audience anxieties and desires. Synchronization is only one of the ways that energy is cathected, while there are a plethora of dynamic devices that regulate tension and release in arousal and emotional terms, alongside narrative revelations and cathartic outlets of extreme excitement, etc. In an isolated article that discusses synchronization, John Belton noted:

> This perceptual process of testing or attempting to identify sound can, through a system of delays that postpone the synchronism of sound and source, be manipulated to create suspense, both in the area of voice/dialog and in that of sound effects, calling attention to sound *as a device* by playing with our perception of it. The identification of a voice with a body can be delayed, as in the case...of *The Wizard of Oz* (1939), in which the Wizard's unmasking occurs at the precise moment that synchronization is established; the achievement of synchronization creates a unity whose completeness spells the end of a hermeneutic chain within which an enigma is introduced, developed, prolonged and resolved. Or in the more complex case of *Psycho* (1960), in which off-screen sound is employed to create a nonexistent character (Mrs. Bates), the particular revelation of the sound's source carefully avoids synchronism: we never see Bates speak in his mother's voice; even at the end, his/her request for a blanket comes from off-screen and his/her final monologue is interiorized. Image and sound here produce a tenuous, almost schizophrenic 'synchronization' of character and voice, which precisely articulates the fragmented nature of the enigma's 'resolution' and completes an 'incompletable' narrative.[13]

Belton reaffirms the importance of the moment of synchronization as a point of stability in the film's development but significantly also in the film's dynamic landscape. This 'pull' is so strong that we not only search for that unity but also desire it deeply in its absence. Consequently, we often imagine that simultaneity equates with causality; in other words, sound appearing at the same time as image is often understood as a single event. This is more the case in cinema than in the real world, where visual and sonic aspects have limited characteristics of quality, space, movement, and conventional relationships. An example that occurs on television sometimes is when a news report with a voiceover is accompanied by an image of a person on-screen speaking. We have a desire to match the two into a unity. This is further illustrated by the confusion caused by the difference in speed between sound and light: a gunshot that is heard after someone is hit by a bullet; jet planes that fly by dragging their roars behind them. The drifting apart of the components of single events are an ontological disruption and a cognitive disturbance. This is why a confusing confluence of sound and image at the same time can short-circuit our perception momentarily. This principle of simultaneity often suggests that a causal connection might easily be related to the Gestalt principles of proximity, whereby objects that are close together are construed as belonging together; continuity, whereby elements that appear to create a united form are perceived as intimately connected; or common fate, whereby objects seemingly moving in the same pace and direction are perceived as unified.

SYNCHRONIZING SOFT MACHINE(S)

The physical hardware of human beings is of paramount importance for understanding how sounds and images are perceived, despite being largely ignored by film theory. After all, concepts do not merely materialize in consciousness from nowhere. The grounding for all understandings is the physical limitations set by the human body, and these are exploited explicitly by sound and image culture. The mechanism of the human ear involves a succession of physical processes initiated by sound striking the eardrum before a neural signal is sent to the brain. Sound waves vibrate the eardrum, which articulates a mechanism of small bones that impart movement impulses to the cochlea, the spiral-shaped canal of the inner ear. The eighth cranial nerve runs from the cochlea directly to the cerebral cortex.[14] Human hearing conventionally has a range from 20 Hz to 20 kHz (this is ten octaves, although it decreases with age), and frequencies below 20 Hz are not processed by the ear but can be felt by the body. We would do well to remember the physical basis of our dealings with the outside world, particularly in the case of sound, which actually imparts a physical impact upon us: We are touched and vibrated by sound waves. Vision, of course, is no less mechanical in its operation. Yet despite the regular assertion of film as a visual medium, it seems conventional to approach it as a cerebral medium, one that appears almost ready-formed in our consciousness.

Neuroscience supports the notion that the brain functions as a parallel processor, with different brain locations specializing but often dealing with matters simultaneously rather than in a simple modular manner where certain parts of the brain deal exclusively with specialized functions.[15] Although scientists increasingly know more about the brain, its processes are still beyond detailed and definitive account. Sometimes understanding may be forced into a déjà vu, splitting the signal in the brain with a delay in reception and processing, particularly as a discrepancy exists between the speeds of aural and visual perception and processing. This lapse could be compounded by the physical makeup of the brain as a parallel processing device that channels impulses to different regions and works on them simultaneously. Asynchrony in sound and image might lead to a divided and fragmented state approaching schizophrenia. This schizoid state is embodied by the aesthetic fact of a division between the unsynched sound (i.e., non-diegetic music) and the co-temporal image (the illusion of people talking on-screen in two-dimensional space).

Brains appear to be able to go 'out of synch.' Normally, the left temporal lobe receives messages from the right, but if the parietal regions of the brain (which have a spatial role) go quiet, the frontal lobe (often thought of as the 'executive') can think that the body has disappeared.[16] Asynchrony between the two hemispheres of the brain can impart the impression that something strange is happening, and bizarre occurrences such as out-of-body experiences can take place.[17] Such hemispheric asynchrony can divide and confuse broad cerebral functions. Many functions and activities in the brain involve more than one location. Broadly speaking, however, emotion and music processing take place predominantly in the right hemisphere of the brain (the 'creative' side that is associated with the left ear). Indeed, there is a surprisingly strong division of brain activities in different hemispheres of the brain. While the left hemisphere is predominantly 'verbal' and concerned with language and logical thought, the right hemisphere is predominantly 'nonverbal' and deals with more emotional matters.[18] Music is mostly (but not exclusively) processed by the left hemisphere, unless it is essentially a vehicle for words.[19]

The human brain seeks and finds patterns, and this has clearly had a central determining role on structures and formations in art and wider culture. A similar perceptual process to the 'cocktail party effect' (named after the fact that people can hear their own name mentioned across a noisy room at a party) called psychoacoustic masking is utilized regularly and unconsciously by people to focus on certain sonic elements in a complex soundscape, while managing to ignore other sounds to the point of their not registering. This ability also enables us to phase out crackly noise on an old record or poorly tuned radio and listen to the music as if it is not obscured, or for people who live next to a noisy road to not register the background drone of traffic. This is part of essential pattern-seeking mechanisms in the human brain that are easily best illustrated with reference to sonic phenomena. The brain appears to use a correlative process for recognizing sonic patterns in a similar manner to how electrical circuits look for signal patterns.[20] Schemata are held up to the complex of sounds looking for a fit. This can lead to a so-called psycho-acoustic phantom effect, where we hear what is not there through over-concentration on expectations of hearing certain sounds. A low threshold of acceptance will lead to a finding of the patterns too easily and in places where they might not exist. The brain can fill in the missing parts of the pattern, although white noise allows for elements to be singled out into a distinct pattern where one might not exist independently. There is a similar process with vision, which can take place in situations of very low light. Heightened states of perception (as a result of anxiety, for example) can lead to this effect, such as in situations of potential danger or in houses that are supposedly haunted.[21] The term 'pareidolia' describes the phenomenon of the brain discovering patterns where none exists, or the perception of significant meaning or a pattern in something ambiguous: in other words, the act of finding sense in the senseless.[22] A more extreme form is 'apophenia,' originally a psychotic condition of finding unapparent connections and significance in things where meaningful patterns actually do not exist. This is particular to images and sounds.[23] In perceptual terms, this involves a vague stimulus being perceived as distinct, often seeing animate objects in the inanimate. Examples could be a cloud being construed as a human form and the famous Rorschach blot test, which is projective of the patient's personality and state of mind as the blots are ambiguous but standardized.[24] Yet such pattern recognition is of course also responsible for extreme detective work and scientific breakthroughs as much as it is for illusions and delusions. In some cases, sound can be interpreted more readily for patterns than visual aspects. For example, 'phantom fundamentals' are low-pitched sounds heard where none is present. In this situation, the brain interprets patterns from differences in present sounds' audible harmonics and 'creates' the impression of a lower note.[25]

If pareidolia suggests a misinterpretation of stimuli, it goes some way toward explaining the illusion of sound and image as unified and living on-screen.[26] As discussed in chapter 2, the McGurk effect is concerned with the matching of phonemes (basic units of speech sound) and visemes (basic units of speech in visual terms). Perception of speaking involves both sound and visual cues, rather than simply the former as many might expect. This phenomenon demonstrates that there is not a solid perceptual-cognitive division of sound and image. Chion describes the process of synchresis as a phenomenon of almost gravitational 'pulling' of sound and image together.[27] An associated form or mode of psychology is attached to the synchronization of sound and image. The illusion of unity is enough to engender a sense of reality on some level. This is not quite the same as outside the cinema, yet it has its own situation, rules, and beliefs. Such organization, according to Wolfgang Köhler, "... refers to the fact that sensory fields have in a way their own social psychology."[28] Such Gestalt psychology confirms (rather than is inspired by Kantian idealism), which suggests that we do not perceive the world as it is but impose a sense of cause-effect relationships on it that are derived from something approaching ideal forms inside our head. Aesthetics have solid psychological implications. Indeed, one might imagine that it is their heart. Moreover, such forms might have materiality as proformas or templates, and these can sometimes become confused and misapplied. Being 'out of synch' is arguably a mental state. In essence, a similar malady relates to sound. 'Schizophonia' describes the splitting of sounds from their original contexts. The founder of acoustic ecology, R. Murray Schafer, is the originator of the term:

> I coined the term schizophonia in *The New Soundscape* intending it to be a nervous word. Related to schizophrenia, I wanted it to convey the same sense of aberration and drama. Indeed, the overkill of hi-fi gadgetry not only contributes generously to the low-fi problem, but it creates a synthetic soundscape in which natural sounds are becoming increasingly unnatural while machine-made substitutes are providing the operative signals directing modern life.[29]

Schafer makes many relevant points. His notion relates directly to technology and its ability to foster a disjunction of spatial perception. This state is a little like permanent existence in an uncertain echoing environment, where the precise origins of sounds are not immediately apparent and are difficult to pinpoint.[30] Such a sense of uncertainty about the source of a sound can be a cause for anxiety. Acoustic ecology's answer to current stressful environments is to limit sourceless sound or to emphasize sound that is continuous and fairly predictable, so that we know where we are with it. The same applies to other areas of culture: Music that aims to promote relaxation habitually lacks any startling sound events or surprising elements. There should be no sounds that demand us to enquire of their origins. As we might expect, music that targets the opposite effect will often contain precisely what is lacking in such relaxing music. Cinema also exploits these characteristics. A startling sequence in David Lynch's *Lost Highway* (1997) involves the spectral 'mystery man' (as the film's credits call him) using a mobile telephone. Here, despite standing next to him, this obscure character, played by Robert Blake with a ghostly whitened face, informs the film's protagonist Fred (Bill Pullman) that he is at Fred's home 'right now.' He entreats Fred to call and speak to him on a mobile phone and verify this statement. Fred calls and then speaks to the very man who nevertheless appears to be standing opposite him. The film might have suggested to us that it was some sort of ventriloquist trick but instead plays it seriously. The audience is left in little doubt that there are some bizarre, supernatural machinations afoot. The mystery man's entrance and exit are marked by a sound dissolve, whereby the diegetic music at the party is removed to leave silence as the backdrop to his conversation with Fred. On one level, this is telegraphing the extraordinary narrative situation, but on another level, this sequence is emphasizing the artificiality of the illusion created by sound and image synchronization.

Fred's reaction to the mystery man's division of sound and image is one of shock. Such a rupture of asynchronous division within a film premised upon conventional sound and image relations inaugurates something of a trauma. Indeed, it is through the undermining of the established audiovisual normality in a film that such a contrast proves traumatic. At least partly, this extreme example under discussion works precisely as a rupture to audiovisual naturalism, the unremarkable sound and image relations that the audience grasps as normal and does not register as an organized discourse. Asynchrony more generally can mark a degree of psychological trauma in films through its negation of the contract of illusory unity in sound and image relations. The clinical state of psychological trauma is damage to the psyche, often occurring when an event overwhelms an individual's ability to deal with the emotions, ideas, and memories of that experience. It might be a horrifying experience or a violation of familiar ideas about the way the world works that leads to confusion and anxiety. Indeed, dangers may always be perceived as potentially present even when they are not. So trauma can range from the extreme to the mild, with causes that also vary correspondingly.[31] Trauma can invoke feelings of low self-esteem, depression, and possibly even a sense of loss of identity.

People suffering from trauma need to avoid triggers or stressors. If we transpose this psychological condition to film perception, we might imagine that audiences could crave the normality of mainstream cinema while finding overtly challenging aesthetics or difficult avant garde films as something to avoid as stress producers. Indeed, it is reasonable to suggest that there is much about mainstream cinema that provides a sense of reassurance for audiences, who know where they are with the conventional regime of mainstream representational films.[32] Perception and its limitations can inspire anxiety and agitated mental states. For instance, there are highly disturbing states such as the neuropsychological disorder akinesthesia (sometimes called akinetopsia), which is the inability to perceive movement, in which the sufferer perceives instead a series of still images. This motion blindness is a rare condition, often arising from brain damage. Another perceptual-cognitive state of anxiety appears far more commonly: Cognitive dissonance involves holding two seemingly contradictory ideas simultaneously. This leads to anxiety and stress (or other negative emotional states). Normally, ideas held simultaneously by an individual are considered consistent and thus 'consonant' with one another, and moments of dissonance short-circuit the functioning system to a greater or lesser degree. Lionel Festinger's original theory from the late 1950s stated that cognitive dissonance occurs when two cognitions that are absolutely inconsistent with one another are held by an individual.[33] This position is a highly anxious mental state to occupy, and the mind's desire is to attempt to negate one of the notions as soon as possible. We have a drive to ameliorate such cognitive dissonance and thus limit the amount of mental stress to which we are subject. Processes to reduce such cognitive dissonance include ego defense mechanisms such as rationalization. Indeed, self-justification procedures become central in allowing a cohabitation of such incommensurable concepts.[34] The so-called double bind is a situation in which a subject receives different and contradictory messages or impulses, and this untenable situation of cognitive dissonance often produces a state of physical arousal, a tangible state of anxiety, where the individual is visibly upset or disconcerted. Similarly, motion sickness can occur when the brain receives conflicting messages from the eyes and ears about acceleration. Ears detect only changes in acceleration, rather than movement itself—totally failing to notice constant movement. If a train journey is not smooth, focusing on the page of a book during acceleration leads to the brain deciding that the disjunction between sonic and visual information is illness of some sort, triggering a vomiting reflex. States of arousal, as psychologists term heightened awareness and physical symptoms of anxiety or excitement, have become an essential component of certain leisure activities. The proximity of disturbed and aroused states can also be exploited. For instance, amusement park rides are founded upon the concept of anxiety as stimulating and enjoyable. Despite taking place in a controlled situation and environment, there is the threat of physical danger, which is at the heart of the extremity of experience and enjoyment derived from that. Films also offer this experience on a number of levels, so it would be no surprise if anxiety derived from cinematic aesthetics was not also, in its own way, enjoyable and exciting while also being physically and emotionally anxious.

The denial of sound and image synchronization at crucial points in films manifests something similar to a momentary episode of cognitive dissonance. The lack of synchronization potentially offers a disunified communication to the film audience. Though in some cases, this is not consciously exploited by filmmakers, in others, it clearly inaugurates a short-term policy for the purposes of cinematic impact. An illustration of sound and image disjunction leading to cognitive dissonance is evident in Michelangelo Antonioni's *The Passenger* (*Professione Reporter*, 1975). There is an astonishing sequence in which the reporter (Jack Nicholson) is assuming the identity of the man he met the previous day who has now suddenly died. As he pastes his own picture into the dead man's passport, the soundtrack consists of a conversation between the reporter and the dead man that is temporally unconnected to what we see. After some minutes, the camera focuses on a reel-to-reel tape, revealing that we are listening to a conversation that was recorded the previous night. If we think of this sequence in terms of a classical sound counterpoint, the key is in the space between the meaning of the soundtrack and image track and their seeming temporal dislocation. However, thinking of it in more abstract terms, the key moment becomes the renewed unity of the sound and image at the point when we realize that we are listening to a tape. Indeed, this is a very dramatic moment, but it is also an imperative instant in structural and perceptual terms.

The initial audience reaction is likely to imagine that the sequence is taking place in the character's head. We might think this for a while, but the sequence sustains and proceeds beyond the conventional for subjective sequences, and the expected return to normality fails to appear. Of course, the return to film style normality does appear after a long period, but with the retrospective motivation of the uncoupled soundtrack as an audiotape running. The shot of the reel-to-reel tape machine is the visual answer to the question that has been posed by the film's asynchrony. The ambiguity of sound and image relation asks to be addressed by the audience and retains their mental state in a split frame of mind, holding what we expect to be a unity apart and short-circuiting cognition until this dissonance is resolved.

An ostensibly mainstream narrative film, *Point Blank* (1967), directed by British director John Schlesinger, effects a chaotic sound and image style. The film has an elusive narrative about the seeming return from the dead of Walker (Lee Marvin) to avenge himself on his former partner and wife, both of whom double-crossed him. As we might expect from a film premised upon disconnection, embracing narrative ambiguity, dream sequences, flashbacks, and subjective images, there is an intermittent but insistent appearance of asynchrony. At the film's beginning, Mal Reese is talking to the film's protagonist Walker, telling him about the situation at a prison. As his voice continues, the image track transforms to Reese literally showing Walker around the prison itself. During this shot, Reese is gesticulating and clearly addressing Walker, but this is not synchronized as a voiceover continues. This opening section contains a number of incoherencies if the film is approached in traditional terms, including temporal confusion and repetition. At the point when Walker is approaching his wife's (and Reese's) house, the sequence begins with Walker in a medium shot walking purposefully toward the camera with loud and echoed footsteps making an insistent beat. This sound continues as the image track moves though a succession of shots lacking any synchronized sound, with the footstep beat persisting relentlessly, until the point when Walker smashes through the front door of the house and grabs his wife in a simultaneous blast of sound and movement. This is the moment when synchronization returns, as the lead-up to this has contained images and spaces that clearly were not related to the sounds of the footsteps, apart from in a symbolic sense of determined advance upon his wife. *Point Blank* begins in a most confusing manner, following a poetic path, but one that is intent on setting up a confused state in the audience. A less immediately challenging beginning to a film (but one with a similarly problematized synchrony) is *Sunset Boulevard* (1950). It begins and concludes with a voiceover from a dead man, whom we see floating inertly in a swimming pool. This is a curious and rare effect that appears to confound or challenge cinema's sense of credible illusion. *Sunset Boulevard* does not emphasize the impression or indeed ask the audience to work it out, but rather just uses it as a mildly troubling frame for the rest of the film's action.

Such asynchrony can sometimes act like Brechtian alienation (*Verfremdungseffekt*). It has the ability to alienate the audience from the comfort of the illusion of a habitually coherent world of sound and image on-screen. This strategy usually aims to make audiences momentarily 'stand outside' the film and take a critical distance from the film as an illusion. It is premised upon assumptions about audiences and their expectations of cinematic convention, meaning that it is largely only effective as an occasional device in the context of illusionistic and immersive film style. If this strategy is used in avant garde films, it is often immaterial as audiences suspend the expectations of mainstream film conventions and often replace them with others more particular to avant garde cinema.

Some of the French New Wave films exploited both the engaging illusion afforded by film and the potential for undermining it for aesthetic and political reasons. In Jean-Luc Godard's *Pierrot le fou* (1965), for example, there is a mock battle sequence that consists of a diorama of model soldiers and planes that is accompanied by seemingly real war sounds. This self-conscious disjunction of sound and image wields the realistic sounds of war to alienate any emotional immersion and destroy any illusion of the models as representative of a war. This approach appears less poetic and more parodic. Perhaps on one level, it is even poking fun at the film convention of using model shots in large-scale battle scenes. Whatever its actual aim, it alienates the audience from the illusion of the world on-screen as a reality to which they are unseen perceivers, causing a disconcerting effect.[35]

In recent years, such stylistic approaches have become more widely utilized as a specific artistic technique in films. The British biographical film of the celebrated eponymous violent prison inmate, *Bronson* (2009), uses a variety of sound and image dislocation techniques to tell a complex and static story in an engaging but semiotically rich manner. The film opens with a stylized shot showing Bronson (Tom Hardy) facing the camera in a medium shot. He addresses the film audience: "I'm Charlie Bronson." The shot cuts to a reverse shot that is immediately behind him, then to a different medium shot (with a different camera angle and different lighting). His voice retains the same acoustic quality, but now it becomes a voiceover, no longer synchronized as his mouth remains closed. The shot returns to the original frontal medium shot with the voice synchronized again. Accompanying this shot is some minimal non-diegetic music consisting of a single tone of deep bass to which is added a high string tone. As this proceeds, the image cuts to a shot of Bronson naked behind the bars of a cell doing push-ups, lit with an unlikely and stylized red light. Singing begins on the soundtrack at the precise moment when an image appears of a warden opening a door in long shot. An immediately ensuing shot of fighting in a cell is accompanied by a lack of any diegetic sound but the song persists. The image track then cuts to the original medium shot of Bronson as he laughs (with synchronized diegetic sound having returned), and the film's title is superimposed beneath his face. This sequence revels in its visual discontinuity, but in terms of sound, the song continues throughout much of it while synchronized sound alternates between matching unity and dislocation. Sonic continuity is often the foundation for visual discontinuity, emphasizing the semiotic inter-reliance but aesthetic divergence of the two tracks.

Extreme forms of disjunction are highly disorienting, particularly when there is sustained sound and image independence. Here, synch points become much more important, as something to hold onto in a wash of perceptual ambiguity. A more extreme example is evident in Gus Van Sant's controversial film *Elephant* (2003), which was based on the events of the Columbine High School massacre. The film uses some sound art/soundscape recordings to startling effect. Hildegard Westerkamp's recordings "Türen der Wahrnehmung" ("Doors of Perception") (1989) and "Beneath the Forest Floor" (1992)[36] and Frances White's "Walk Through Resonant Landscape #2" (1992) appear in the film without adaptation, although at times with some diegetic sound appearing simultaneously. These are not music in the traditional sense, but more assemblages of sound field recordings in a structured whole. At one point in *Elephant*, student Nathan (Nathan Tyson) walks to meet his girlfriend, traversing a sports field, into school corridors, out into a yard in between, and then back inside the school to meet her. The sequence begins with diegetic sounds from the sports field, as well as what appears to be the distant non-diegetic sound of Beethoven's "Moonlight Sonata" played on a piano. At the point of the cut when Nathan crosses the threshold to enter the building, there is a radical shift in the film soundtrack. While the non-diegetic Beethoven remains, instead of different ambient diegetic sounds for the school interior, the Westerkamp piece ensues. It begins with the sound of a choir that could almost be diegetic sounds but then progresses into the body of the piece, which incorporates most notably many sounds of doors opening and closing along with other field recordings that clearly have no connection with what the audience is seeing on-screen. The expectations of diegetic sounds are confounded as events happen silently until a degree of diegetic sound reappears later in the sequence. Yet the sounds on the soundtrack are clearly not music in the conventional sense, nor are they existentially connected to any origins on-screen. This sets up a sense of dislocation through the dichotomy of representational images and unrelated sounds as a replacement for those that we might imagine as 'belonging' to the images. When Nathan is in the courtyard, Westerkamp's piece presents the expansive soundscape of a train station, which, although its appearance matches the change in space back to exterior, the expected change in diegetic sound is instead replaced with a radical disconnection. Some of the sounds are almost fitting, but never quite, while much of the sound confounds expectations about sound film synchronization conventions. As Nathan opens the door back into the school's interior, the sound of the door is synchronized with the sound of a door in Westerkamp's piece, returning a sense of synchronized unity of sound and vision and restoring the illusory effect of narrative film.[37] This is an example of 'musical' sound in film, with what might be construed as film sound effects ceasing to be mere sound emanations from the world on-screen and becoming a musical aspect of the whole. It makes plain the artificiality of the welding of sound to image as an illusionary unity but also emphasizes the aesthetic interplay of elements evident in most films.

UNPROBLEMATIC ASYNCHRONY AND SOUND BRIDGE TRANSITIONS

Asynchrony is not a problem for cinema, far from it. It is one of the natural states of sound cinema. When set in a dynamic relationship with synchrony, it creates a powerful effect. Yet at other times, it can be simply a strategy for industrial reasons. Cheaply made films, not prestige products or mainstream blockbusters, often appear to have long passages of unapparent synchrony when all sound has clearly been added in post-production. Such films often have their own sense of psychology. For example, films screened in the middle of the night on the Horror Channel tend to have fewer and more Spartan scenes with precise synchronization than mainstream films. This is a type of production with its own psychological world molded by sound and image style as much as is the most sumptuous Hollywood production. Indeed, some areas of film production do not aim for solid synchrony but nevertheless work perfectly.[38]

In terms of music and image, anything potentially goes with anything. Synchronization here has less to do with maintaining the illusion of cinematic representation than it has with forming a different aesthetic whole. This is most clearly illustrated in sequences that remove most diegetic sound to allow a pure and strong interaction between a loud piece of non-diegetic music and a succession of images. Discussing the use of recorded songs on film soundtracks, Alan Williams notes:

> Kenneth Anger's *Scorpio Rising* includes recorded popular music on its soundtrack without raising issues of dominance or veracity. In that film, image and sound run *parallel*, with frequent points of rhythmic and semantic coincidence; yet the two channels remain separate because a common origin (reference to a diegesis) is never posited—except inasmuch as it is the film-maker who has matched them. Music cannot dominate the image, nor vice versa, since they do not share any common ground to do battle.[39]

A good example of this and the parallel running of audio and visual tracks is the conclusion of Michelangelo Antonioni's *Zabriskie Point* (1970). The final sequence is startling and in many ways disconnected from the rest of the film. Indeed, it can stand up as a short film in itself, and almost operates as an avant garde film inserted into a more mainstream narrative film. After multiple shots from different angles of an exploding house, the sequence settles into a succession of highly singular images of exploding household items in slow motion, with the pro-filmic events recorded with a high-speed camera. These include, perhaps most memorably, a working television set and a frozen chicken, the latter of which flies through the air with the grace enabled by slow-motion photography. There is little sense of screen direction and continuity, merely a succession of shots with the premise of showing the unusual explosive imagery. It is accompanied by a piece of music by Pink Floyd called "Heart Beat Pig Meat" (a version of "Careful with that Axe, Eugene"). This is a wordless two-part piece that is relaxed and organ-led until it bursts out with vocal screams and guitar noise. It is a remarkable piece of music in many ways. John S. Cotner wrote a chapter about "Careful With that Axe, Eugene" in Kevin Holm-Hudson's book *Progressive Rock Revisited*, noting that "...the beauty of the piece is that it allows for multiple readings."[40] It certainly has a general ambiguity, bringing together Pink Floyd's tradition of improvisation with the more conceptual character their music would take on in the future. Most versions contain the same core musical elements, including a single chord harmony, a continuous beat and bass line, an improvisatory organ melody, a build-up in dynamics with whispered vocals that go back down again, and a section of climactic vocal screaming. The musical aspects of the song encapsulate Pink Floyd's evolution in that there is no real musical development in the traditional sense. Instead, the piece is based on atmosphere, dynamics, and, most notably, concept. This loose musical format lent itself to a fair degree of improvisation, and the piece's lack of traditional song focus certainly makes it more conducive to being used as an accompaniment to images.[41] Although it is not based on song form, the song retains four-bar structures and has an unwavering pulse in 4/4 time. It never has the flexibility of a traditional film score, yet "Careful With that Axe, Eugene" proved itself a durable piece of music for accompanying moving images. A version of the piece had already appeared in *The Committee* (1967), underlining the ability of the music to be both accompanying (fitting with images) and foregrounded (standing on its own, like absolute music). Although there is no direct connection between sound and image in the concluding sequence of *Zabriskie Point*, there is a shared sense of aesthetic movement that comes from the undulation of the music and the slow trajectories and visual vectors of moving items on-screen. The music keys the altering of the diegesis, which becomes indistinct and of a metaphorical character, while the music, remaining non-diegetic, retains its integrity. Significant developments in the music appear to articulate the sequence as a whole, proceeding from the point when the music starts and the images settle into a pattern of regular shots of explosions. There is a significant dynamic change in the music some way through, when it builds to a crescendo surmounted by sustained screaming and heavier and louder articulation by the instruments. The only synch point of note is at the moment of the harrowing scream in the music, which coincides with one of the explosions. The conclusion of the sequence is a crude cut that simply amputates the music in mid-phrase as it abruptly halts the images of the explosions. This is a remarkable sequence that may well be more familiar to people these days as a sequence in itself than as a part of Antonioni's film.[42] Although *Zabriskie Point* is not quite a mainstream film, by and large, it follows

Figure 4.1: *Zabriskie Point* (1970).

the conventions of narrative filmmaking—apart from the concluding sequence of explosions (figure 4.1), which exhibits many characteristics of avant garde cinema, including repetition of filmed events, lack of directional continuity, and lack of synchronized diegetic sound. In the context of the rest of the film, this style and the dramatic asynchrony appear disruptive. Indeed, this poetic sequence appears to be inspired by the celebrated insert shots in Eisenstein's *Strike* (1925), with this sequence as a larger non-diegetic insert, here seemingly representing the destruction of consumerism and bourgeois society. It signals the conjoining of narrative representational film with more abstract film. Asynchrony in avant garde cinema is far from always being disruptive. There is often less of a solid sense of diegetic and non-diegetic too, a corollary of the fact that many avant garde films lack a sense of a strong diegetic world.

Sound bridges are the points when the joins are problematized but also dramatized. They manifest a form of montage and fashion a momentary asynchrony quickly resolved by the payoff of returning to synchrony. Sound bridges are one of the best illustrations of the principles of montage, where different ideas or spaces can be joined through a transition that is more than simply functional. A lack of synchronization potentially offers an incoherent and dislocated communication to the film audience. Commonly, the sound of a particular scene is replaced by the sound of another while the former remains visually on-screen. In most cases, the change of diegesis will be signalled strongly by sound; in other words, the sonic character of the two different scenes will be marked rather than sounding similar. At the point when the audience is confronted by visuals and sound that do not match into one illusory space, there is clear cognitive dissonance in the disjunctive messages, with the possibility of the production of anxiety that will then be dissipated once the images of the first diegetic space catch up with the sound and match the second diegetic space in a seeming unity of spatial perception.

In the Atom Egoyan film *The Sweet Hereafter* (1997), main character Stephens (Ian Holm) and his daughter's friend (called Alison) are on a plane, in a sequence that includes visual and sound flashbacks. He tells her about having to rush his daughter to the hospital after a potentially fatal spider bite. To calm her, he sang her lullabies. As he narrates this story on the plane, the sound of a lullaby sung by a man is heard. Later, when Stephens meets the Otto family, he talks to them and we hear his voice from elsewhere saying, "I did everything that the loving father of a drug addict is supposed to do." Then the image moves to the plane where Stephens is saying this to Alison. This film has a particularly malleable approach to sound's matching with image. This final example is a sound bridge between two different times, rather than the more prevalent movement between two spaces. The free relationship between sound and image gives an impressionistic account of the personal psychology of litigation lawyer Stephens as he deals with a tragedy that has killed a town's children, and his ongoing troubled relationship with his own daughter. Egoyan's use of confused sound and image augurs a trauma in the film's principal character and his engagement with others who have experienced a similar trauma. Stylistically, trauma is not only expressed through disengagement of sound and image synchronization; it is also instilled in the audience through that same process. *The Sweet Hereafter*'s intermittent flashbacks move backward and forward but less to explicate character information in a coherent manner than to perhaps give some of the schizoid impression of trauma. Indeed, this is a profoundly disturbing film, obscured partly by the sound and image relations, which at times have similarities to the opening of *Point Blank* previously discussed.

Comedy films have often exploited the seemingly irrational conventions of cinema for the purposes of humor. In *Scary Movie 3* (2003), there is a dramatic sound bridge shock cut as a joke at the point when Cindy Campbell (Anna Faris) realizes she must visit a place that requires taking a ferry. There is a shot of a boat crossing water. At the point when she has this realization, a sound bridge allows the boat's horn to shock her, before the image cuts to the boat again. This is, of course, a parody of one of the most famous and earliest of shock cuts, that in Alfred Hitchcock's *Blackmail* (1929).[43] Protagonist Alice's scream cuts to the scream of the landlady as she finds the dead body. This is a highly self-conscious effect at a precise synch point. Although it is solidly synchronized, it remains a disjunctive effect. This was during sound cinema's absolute infancy and illustrates that the play of synchronizing sound and image was at the heart of the narrative sound film as an effect and variation from the domination in this period of showing talking heads. Rather than alienating the audience, this homology of the shock of screaming works to heighten the effect of shock in the film. This moment marks a modest form of montage and moment of chaos, but with retrospective motivation—a normalizing realignment—after a moment of potential confusion. It is not so much a narrative strategy as an effect emanating from the possibility of image and soundtrack's convergence and divergence

Sound bridges can move outward to an elsewhere while retaining a foot in the established diegesis. *Picnic at Hanging Rock* (1975) is about the mysterious disappearance of some schoolgirls at a remote rock. The sung hymn *Rock of Ages* begins over images of the Australian countryside, during a scene where such a sound clearly cannot emanate diegetically. The images of the countryside in long shot are then replaced by close-up images of a 'missing' poster, and finally, after some time, the visual diegesis reaches the aural diegesis as we are shown synchronized images of a congregation singing the hymn in church. We also hear some disconnected sounds of people searching for the girls before they are lost. The soundtrack has remained constant, and the image track has modulated. This is an extreme form of sound bridge where, instead of spanning two different times and spaces, it traverses three, while belonging only to the final one.

Adorno and Eisler noted that songs appearing in films were good examples of the principle of montage undermining illusionism.[44] In Michael Powell's *Wings of the Morning* (1937), for example, famous Irish tenor John McCormack appears and sings a song, which cues stereotypical landscape images of Ireland appearing as non-diegetic inserts. This breaks the film's diegesis (and its illusion) for the duration of the song, but no lasting damage is incurred. This is an example of what film historian Charles Barr has called 'Montage Anglais' because of its strength of tradition in the British (or should that be English?) cinema.[45] This involves a song being the vehicle for a montage of diverse images. The song is usually of diegetic origin and thus allows for images that are from outside the more common use of non-diegetic song as accompaniment to a traditional montage sequence, when time is collapsed and a long period is shown compressed in a short succession of shots. Another prime example of this occurs in *Chariots of Fire* (1981), where the singing of "To be an Englishman" leads the image track into a montage of non-diegetic inserts of other locations while the sound track remains firmly diegetic and follows the temporal arrow of the film's diegetic world. Similarly, in Joseph Losey's *The Go Between* (1970), in the sequence of celebration in the barn after the cricket match, the song "Take a Pair of Sparkling Eyes" is sung diegetically by Ted (Alan Bates) accompanied by Marian (Julie Christie) on the piano. Once the song begins, the established sound of the music continues, but the image cuts away to the modern day of the film, when the camera looks from outside the window as the adult Leo (the 'go between') is waiting to see the aged Marian in a flat. These images have no corresponding sound. As the song progresses, the image track returns to reengage the visual diegesis of the song. This is an example of the sound and music remaining diegetic while the image in effect becomes a non-diegetic insert. The song's production is depicted at the start with precise vocal synchronization, and the time shift marks a radical movement into asynchrony. However, because of the song, we know that the lost diegesis is bound to return, and that marks the flash-forward imagery as only temporary and lacking the uncertainties that characterize some sound and image asynchronies.

CONCLUSION

Asynchrony has potential to disturb, whether it is through sustained loss of the synchronized norm or through momentary anomalies. For instance, in a lengthy sequence from the Australian thriller *Black Water* (2008), a woman walks through trees in a swamp accompanied by echoed and rather tuneless music and well-defined sounds of her footfalls and grasping of trees. As she reaches the end of the trees, we hear isolated sounds of water gurgling—suggesting that there might be something there—but the water in the shot appears calm. This minor disjunction causes some disquiet, but it is not blatantly 'telegraphed' so it is not immediately evident to the audience, perhaps merely setting up an unconscious anxiety. In their initial article about the McGurk effect, McGurk and MacDonald note that asynchrony tends to be upsetting.[46]

Alternation between asynchrony and synchrony is far from uncommon, although it rarely registers as a specific device of film. At times, it marks a fundamental dynamic movement that functions largely by its processes remaining unconscious rather than on the surface of the film. There is a significant difference between not having precise synch points and clear asynchrony as a policy. Asynchrony as a policy is evident in many avant garde films and in a fair number of music videos. However, in narrative films, there is a strong tradition of movement between clear synchronization of sound and image and situations when the relationship between the two is more equivocal.

While Eisenstein stressed the montage potential of asynchrony, where it can open up the possibility of different meanings, I am more concerned with a lack of synchronization as a potential breach in the fabric of illusion, where ambiguity might disrupt the immersion of cinema's unity of sound and image. We cannot assume that a lack of synchronized sound and image is 'radical aesthetics' as the alternation between precise moments of synchronized sound and image, and degrees of movement away from this, is endemic in audiovisual culture. This alternation augurs cinematic normality, with some films playing around with latent psychological disturbance. So, while conventional, this is a step beyond the illusionistic processes of film and constitutes a dramatic movement by film style only, through the crucial but unacknowledged 'occult' lynchpin upon which cinema is reliant.

CHAPTER 5
Isomorphic Cadences

Film as 'Musical'

The notion of the 'music of the spheres' often referred to a sense of balance and geometric proportion rather than necessarily to music. It derives from a belief about the assumed relationship between celestial bodies and was elaborated by Johannes Kepler in his 1619 book *Harmonices Mundi*, although its origins derive from mystical ideas of proportion in creation expressing its celestial creator. This ancient notion was founded on an assumed hidden mathematical relationship between elements in the skies and was also embodied in musical relationships as something of a prime and mysterious emanation from existence. According to Kepler, these moving bodies produce sound. However, this music of the spheres was not actually audible and was perhaps not even sound, let alone music. However, the idea of music as being more than simply an aural phenomenon, which drifted out of fashion with Renaissance learning, returned in a different form in avant garde culture of the 20th century. This chapter might be the point when this perhaps illogical impression meets the wrongheaded notion that film is essentially a visual medium, rather than an audiovisual medium. It takes an interest in how far film might be musically inspired and how far a focus on sound and music can—and indeed, already does—'think' film. Moving bodies on-screen are rarely silent. The chapter begins by looking into perceived similarities among film, film sound, and music, and then looks at film's aesthetic elements in a more abstract manner than has often been the case in the study of film.

In an interview, Michel Chion declared: "...I think you have to understand music to be able to talk about sound in cinema."[1] Broadly speaking,

I have to agree. There are different forms of knowledge about music, and though some may be of less help than others, a musical sensibility and sensitivity are doubtless of benefit for addressing sound in the cinema. I am far from the first to note the similarities between music and film,[2] from the standpoint of aesthetics, as well as from analysis. Indeed, musical analysis has much in common with other forms of cultural analysis—something that is not often registered, particularly by musicologists.

Music and sound sometimes dominate films, determining the aesthetic patterns and having particular ramifications for sound and image synchronization. The obvious case is film musicals (and their television cousin, the music video), but such techniques are also apparent in films that are not musicals, and this chapter focuses on some of these. Dominance by music is not surprising, perhaps, given that there has been a perceived close relationship between the processes of the moving image and music. Indeed, on some levels, there appears to be a shared core of aesthetics and assumptions. Many discussions of audiovisual culture fail to live up to the description. Those that do manage illustrate a sense of equivalence of sound and image in terms of production and consumption. This supports a sense of the value of using for each 'channel' analytical techniques that are usually reserved for one or the other. After all, if the two can be so intermingled on an aesthetic level, then surely the use exclusively of one or the other analytical approach is ultimately doomed to failure or at least to banal conclusions. It is not unreasonable to assume that human physicality/mentality has defined the form of culture. Indeed, film, music, and other culture have indelible similarities on differing levels and in some cases tangibly similar underlying aesthetics. If, as is likely, these derive partly from similar underlying perceptual-cognitive structures in the brain, then not only are different media more closely related in essence than has previously been registered, but more abstract principles can also most profitably be used for the analysis of film. Although it is not unreasonable to approach film music as film aesthetics rather than music per se, film, especially certain types of film, might be approached as 'musical' with the visual forming an extension of the heard aspects. As Royal S. Brown notes, the analysis of film has suffered at times from an overwhelming focus on representation and narrative, and conversely, music analysis has been dominated by a focus on abstract formal elements to the detriment of representational or significatory aspects.[3] What happens when we consider the two together? There is a persistent tradition of likening the two, with film and music evincing structural similarities such as cadences, which in both tell the audience where they are with events, often marking some sort of conclusion to a passage and cutting time into consumable segments.

EQUIVALENCE: SYNAESTHESIA AND ISOMORPHISM

In Eisenstein's analyses, he looked for a common denominator between music and image, and touched at first upon the notion of movement.[4] His sense of equivalence between film images and music was informed by a sense of structural resemblance at a profound level, allied to a sense of synaesthetic mixing of stimuli and sensation.[5] Synaesthesia is a medical condition whereby stimuli from one sense can seemingly supply stimuli in another. An example of this is the ability that some have to taste sounds, or at least to have certain taste impulses when confronted with certain sounds. This condition increasingly has been invoked to account for close interactions and seeming equivalents between different media, perhaps most particularly between music and the visual arts.[6] I would suggest that one of the advantages of thinking along these lines is that it emphasizes the bodily (perceptual-cognitive) aspects of sound and image relations, where the effect is physical rather than simply analogous or metaphorical. The concept of synaesthesia tells us something: that there is an agreement of the possibility of equivalence between sound and image.

The history of music's coupling with the moving image has built up a sense of conventional synaesthesia, an equivalence of music and image; at least, there is a tradition of using particular forms of music to accompany certain images (and vice versa). Certain sounds appear to invoke certain images. There is without doubt a strong sense of what fits what. Figurative images aside, there is a tradition that marries certain visual kinetics with certain types of sound and rhythm. Energetic music tends to complement energetic images. Busy music gives an impression of movement, although fast repetition can also give the impression of stasis. The cross-rhythm of the beat and edits or other punctuations in the image can furnish an abstract sense of aesthetic play or a compelling mesh and feeling of movement. Either smooth and gliding or sudden and abrupt screen motions often seem to fit the movement of music well. The former can be seen in films like *An American in Paris* (1951) as much as in recent music videos.

As temporal media, film and music have a good degree in common, and the two can be conceived in similar terms. Musical development relies on aspects such as cadence, dynamics, presentation, re-presentation, development of material (themes can be narrative or theoretical as much as musical), and use of foreground and background planes, etc. Often a degree of equivalence might be found between music and image: Music might well be image or might manifest it. There is, of course, a whole tradition of programmatic music, which aims in essence at evoking images or ambiences of a specific place or event. Fine examples would be William Bax's "Tintagel" or Debussy's piano prelude "La cathedrale engloutie." A strong tradition exists of matching certain sounds with particular representational notions as much as certain sounds become associated with particular images more strongly in film music. Peter Kivy discusses the matter:

> ...as I am using the phrase 'musical picture', musical pictures can be divided into two kinds: those, like the cuckoo in the *Pastoral* [Beethoven's 6th symphony], or (I believe) [Honegger's] *Pacific 231*, where the illustration would be recognized as such without text, title, or even minimal information that one is listening to an illustration; and those like *The Iron Foundry* [1928 Mossolov piece], perhaps, or the thunderstorm in the *Pastoral*, where one only needs to *know* that one is listening to illustrative music in order to identify the object of the illustration, but would need no information other than that...."[7]

Honegger's *Pacific 231* aims to evoke a train through analogous rhythmic figures that instantly suggest similar illustrative images, while Mossolov's *The Iron Foundry* needs more information to point the listener in its intended direction. Kivy's second type of musical picture often does not need too much direction for its audience, although on occasion, titles or verbal information can be crucial in establishing the object of representation that the composer desired to express through the music. Such musical pictures clearly feed in to the modes of representation in film incidental music, and indeed have expanded the existing equivalences of music and image in the tradition of illustrative and impressionistic program music. The addition of images to the tradition of programmatic music forms a redoubled sense of specificity to representation or, some might argue, produces a high degree of redundancy.

Furthermore, there are some important areas of intersection between film and music on a conceptual level, where one is reconfigured in the form of the other. The most notable of these would be the film musical and its younger relation, the music video. Film musicals, like operas, are structured into featured song sections and sections of narrative importance. In operas, these are arias and recitative, while in film musicals, production numbers or song sequences are interpolated with sections of the film that use conventional dialogue and music in the background as in mainstream dramatic films. This alternation provides a wider film structure that has nothing to do with the requirements of the narrative material and everything to do with the conventions of presenting songs in a film format. A third analogue is the leitmotiv as used in Wagnerian opera and the classical film score. In the latter case, the drama might be 'read' to a greater or lesser degree by interactions between leitmotivs that register the presence and interaction of characters on-screen. This distinctive process is perhaps paracinematic in that it might make sense outside cinema. After all, it is possible in many cases to listen to the cues from a classical film score in order and follow the film's development. Mickeymousing, the precise mimicking of visual movement, gesture, and action by music, is evident in an extreme form in many cartoons. However, it might be conceived more as a sliding scale from precise momentary copying to only occasional matching. Horror film stingers are sometimes simply an isolated blast of Mickeymousing. Such precise matching is similarly related to more vague action matching by the music, where it might follow kinesis, surface, or even more vaguely the emotional and energetic mood on-screen. Conceptions of scoring the moving image run from matching *action* (dealing with the surface) to matching *emotion* (the film's underlying level). Such correspondence is at a fundamental level and illustrates how far a direct equivalence is thought to exist between moving images and music.

Music and film as moving image certainly have aspects in common: Both are temporal structures of dynamics and both have manifested highly conventional mainstream forms. The Kantian idealist formulation suggests that materials may differ but underlying aesthetics are the same: Culture has a common essence and is different merely in its surface manifestations.[8] Such structural similarity is often identified as isomorphism. This term has had a loose history in the analysis of film but a more solid antecedence in Gestalt psychology, where isomorphism is a central principle. Here it has a more precise meaning: that there is an analogy between brain activity and stimulus input. The implication is that similar structures in different media are related in a way not dissimilar to the relation between an artistic stimulus and the configuration of the brain activity it causes. Certain arts have clear essences in common with others. This assumption is hardly new: For example, there is an assumption that television and film are closely related, and even a notion that film and novels are quite similar. Are all narrative-based arts similar in essence? The industry of adaptation might suggest so. According to Rudolf Arnheim,

> Gestalt psychologists hold that expressive behavior reveals its meaning directly in perception. The approach is based on the principle of isomorphism, according to which processes take place in different media may be nevertheless similar in their structural organization. Applied to body and mind, this means that if the forces which determine bodily behavior are structurally similar to those which characterize the corresponding mental states, it may be understandable why psychical meaning can be read off directly from a person's appearance and conduct.[9]

This sense of analogue perception can be very close to a notion of unproblematic realism in conceptualizing our senses' relation to the real world. However, it need not be. Furthermore, this takes place on a primary physical level rather than being unimpeded access to the world as direct thought, as realists aver. So, perception-cognition does not just shape understanding; the interior of the brain dictates formal and comprehensive aspects of culture, at the very least.

Assumptions about the equivalence of sound and image on a structural and material level are most evident in less than mainstream culture. Indeed, 'visual music' is a term often applied to abstract films that make some form of equivalence of their visual aspect with the abstract processes of music. Some, like Norman McLaren and Len Lye, aimed at a complete synthesis of music and image into a whole inspired probably more by music than anything else. McLaren is most renowned for abstract animations often instigated explicitly by pre-recorded music. Good examples of this are *Fiddle-Dee-Dee* (1947) and *Boogie-Doodle* (1948), both of which involve shapes move around continuously on-screen as accompaniment to music. His later film *Canon* (1964) illuminates three musical canons (starting with "Frere Jacques") in images of moving blocks, animated people, and manipulated filmed images of people. Such illustration assumes an equivalence of music and moving image. Going further into positing an essence of music and other art, McLaren's *Synchromy* (1972) was premised upon the filming of various shapes on both the film and the optical soundtrack at the edge of the film. The images from these shapes therefore comprise the film's sound and thus the film and soundtrack are the same in terms of material, although that does not add up to an equivalence of the final product of sound and vision.

One of the most consistent figures working with musical conceptions of film is Austrian avant garde filmmaker and artist Peter Kubelka, who made a series of short 16mm films that question the mainstream convention of synchronizing sound and image. His policy of asynchrony is evident in his early films such as *Mosaik im Vertrauen* (1955), where regularly discontinuous images have a soundtrack that is also not seemingly directly connected. Probably his most well-known film, *Unsere Afrikareise* (1966) consists of documentary 'records' of hunting trips in Africa, where the focus on certain visual elements is set in collision with the sounds of those same elements, usually through non-synchronization of images with their corresponding sounds. In describing *Unsere Afrikareise*, Kubelka noted:

> Vertov and Buñuel had worked already with the same postulate, namely that natural synchronism is not the ideal, that there is the possibility of separating

> this natural synchronism and speaking through a sound which is not going naturally with the image. Here is the great possibility of sound in film.... In *Afrikareise*, if you attentively look at it, each movement of the body, and animal, a hand or a plant corresponds to the sound, as if it were created by this movement. It is different from Vertov: my film is, so to speak, an artificial naturalist film. I use the habit of the spectator to believe in synchronism.[10]

Organized into elements of hunting (animals, places, hunters, natives, etc.), Kubelka's *Unsere Afrikareise* has the sound from one accompany the image of another, yielding an initially confusing but ultimately highly analytical effect. Asynchrony is hardly a rarity in avant garde film. For example, British avant garde filmmaker Guy Sherwin tends not to use sound in the manner of mainstream films. One review of his work noted:

> Sherwin's films are often silent, and some that use soundtracks, such as *Filter Beds* or *Under the Freeway*, feature sound that's asynchronous from image. This alienation effect ideally leads the audience to question their expectations of both the noise inherent in the image, and the correlation of sound and vision.[11]

Of course, such use of sound in avant garde cinema is not the exception. Kenneth Anger had a propensity to use unsynchronized musical accompaniments in many of his films, such as *Scorpio Rising* (1964) and *Kustom Kar Kommandos* (1965). Similarly, Andy Warhol's films, such as *Sleep* (1963), *Screen Test #1*, and *Screen Test #2* (both 1965), have no synchronized soundtrack and can be screened silently or with some form of live or mechanical music added.

Perhaps more often, film has attempted to integrate music on a more profound level. Oskar Fischinger made a number of abstract animated films that had only musical soundtracks. For example, *An Optical Poem* (1937) accompanied Liszt's *Second Hungarian Rhapsody* and *Motion Painting No. 1* (1947) used Bach's *Brandenburg Concerto No. 3*, the latter of which paralleled the structure of the music but was not closely synched as if Mickeymoused. Franziska and Stefan Themerson's 11-minute *The Eye and the Ear* (1945) was made to fit musical pieces by Karol Szymanowski, creating visual aspects to accompany individual musical elements. For example, pulses in the music are accompanied by rhythmic aspects in the image such as water dripping and ripples on the water's surface. In the third piece, geometric shapes on-screen form direct analogues of the musical elements.[12] The Canadian film *Thirty-Two Short Films About Glenn Gould* (1993) was a highly singular account of the concert pianist's life. It consists of 32 variations, portrayed on film, as a series of fragments about Gould based on the structure of one of the musical pieces that made him famous: Bach's *Goldberg Variations*. Some of these short films are interviews and others are reconstructions of episodes from Gould's life. There is a section called "Gould Meets McLaren: Animation by Norman McLaren" where a fugue is accompanied by animated moving circles that turn and divide, following the activity of the music. Almost all the music for the film consists of recordings of piano music played by Gould, and the film aims to express that the structures of the music and film are shared.

Indeed, such technical equivalence is also evident in films by Walter Ruttmann, Len Lye, and Stan Brakhage, among others. The goal of stylistic and thematic autonomy in these films makes many of them appear superficially similar to absolute music. It is not difficult to make comparisons among musical minimalism, Mark Rothko's paintings, Michael Snow's *Wavelength* (1967), or Andy Warhol's slow and static films like *Sleep*. Technical equivalence *across* the arts is not necessarily due to cross-fertilization or inspiration but may be due to *underlying* similarities emanating from available technologies, prominent ideas of the time, influences of art/artists individually or in groups—perhaps even down to a sense of trying to alter human perception. There is a strong undercurrent in the assumptions of many 20th-century artists and musicians that intellect offered the possibility of undermining traditions that have been built upon evolutionary processes, thus halting pandering to the most basic in human perception and the simplest forms of cognition.[13]

Although we ought to be careful not to assign too much to the abilities of music, it does appear to have a fundamental and powerful effect on most people. Discussing culture more generally, Suzanne K. Langer suggests that musical structures directly resemble human emotional structures. Correlations are certainly evident: "There are certain aspects of the so-called 'inner life'—physical or mental—which have formal properties similar to those of music—patterns of motion and rest, of tension and release, of agreement and disagreement, preparation, fulfillment, excitation, sudden change, etc."[14] In essence, this notion posits that the outside (culture) corresponds with the inside (the psyche). This is perhaps not too surprising when considered in a general sense. After all, broadly speaking, tonal structures follow a number of simple principles based on showcasing sonic material, repeating and developing, contrasting dynamics, and bringing elements to partial and ultimately full closure. These are principles that might be mapped onto much time-based art and culture. It is certainly not too bold a suggestion to indicate these aspects of structuration as being evident in the audiovisual procedures of film. Some might say that studies of culture have lauded (bourgeois) individualism or celebrated the capabilities of our species to the detriment of stronger understanding. Humanist interests have limited potential answers. So culture is the way it is less because of creativity and tradition than because of the *physical* structures of our heads and senses. While it is perhaps an antiquated assumption, without necessarily having accumulated much in the way of empirical evidence to back it up, the notion that music's essential form corresponds on some physical/emotional level with the interior of the human body and mind has remained surprisingly robust. Aristotle posited that art imitates, and likely imitates human emotions and states of mind, while for Kant in his *Critique of Judgment*, music manifested an art of "the beautiful play of sensations," thus conceived as lacking representational, semantic, and expressive properties. This position on music remains a dominant one, what Peter Kivy has called "musical purism."[15] Indeed, this characteristic (even if something of a misnomer) is one of music's attractions as an aspiration and inspiration for other arts and media. As a pure art, art music has become a figurehead for other arts, with the assumption that other arts can share its essence, spirit, or aesthetics. In its abstraction and sense of self, can we use it for analyzing other media? The fact that it has been used as a metaphor for so long means that it has valence in the domain of other art forms. In the case of cinema, music has been a partner since its inception. Yet the hermetically sealed character of much musicological technique and analysis has made the insights of the academic discipline inaccessible to other areas of culture, and has militatedagainst the sustained use of musicology as a tool for the analysis of culture beyond music.

Hitchcock saw himself as being like a conductor of an orchestra, and also likened a trumpet solo to a close-up shot while he equated a long shot with muted orchestral accompaniment.[16] In his 1963 article "On Style," Hitchcock wrote: "[Film] Construction to me, it's like music. You start with your *allegro*, your *andante*, and you build up."[17] One might argue that it was his own particular conception of what music was, but we might also wonder if he confused the nature of music and the nature of film and perhaps his own relationship to music.[18] Nevertheless, Hitchcock was persistent in his interest in music: Eight of the central protagonists in his films were musicians of one sort or another.

It is only a short leap to see further equivalences between films and pieces of music. The musical processes of repeated and developed leitmotiv themes can easily be compared with narrative or iconic elements of films or television dramas. Narrative structure might then be rethought as a succession of elements that interact, appear, and disappear over time. For instance, Robynn Stilwell noted that the 13-episode first series of 'new' *Doctor Who* (2005–) "... can bear the load of functional narrative leitmotifs, and itself demonstrates a structure reminiscent of music: perhaps nothing as strict as sonata form but a fantasy on various leitmotifs, both narrative and musical."[19] The ingrained notion of film being like music has strong roots. A filmmaking manual discusses what sort of music to use in films:

> In selecting music for a film, analyse the plot very broadly. Decide which points constitute the crises and which to treat as interludes. In a story film, see if there are two main themes: hero and heroine, or hero and villain. Many successful plots are constructed on the same plan as a sonata movement in music. The first theme (hero) and a second theme (villain). These are established separately and then you have interplay or development of the two themes. This reaches the main climax, followed by a repetition of the original themes. In music this repetition is called the recapitulation.[20]

On a more theoretical level, Noel Burch has pointed to a deep-structure equivalence between film and music. Following Eisenstein's lead, he finds equivalent or analogue processes between film and music.[21] Indeed, Burch emphasizes the claim for an existential relation rather than a merely vague similarity between the two different arts. His influence as a film theorist is often not openly recognized in recent years despite his influence on a whole generation of film theorists and theory. David Bordwell, in "The Musical Analogy," pointed to how music had been used as metaphor by filmmakers and critics precisely because it is an abstract system of organizing elements in relation to each other.[22] The fact that much music appeared to refer only to itself rather than elements 'outside' suggested a pure art. Bordwell followed Burch in seeing the systematic abstraction of integrated serial music as a mode that would have had clear attractions for filmmakers, particularly those working in a more abstract mode.

Yet it seems possible to move beyond metaphor to verge upon a direct *equation* of film and music. Eisenstein discusses 'plastic music,' where sounds and music are expressed by almost equivalent visual elements. This was a commonplace activity in silent cinema, and in sound cinema it was most clearly evidenced by landscape shots, which lack the narrative burden of other images and function more as a vehicle for emotion than narrative information. He writes about "...a similar emotional landscape, functioning as a musical component...."[23] In this way, the visual might be conceived as musical, and a more intimate connection between moving images and sound might be sought. Eisenstein also discussed the musically inspired 'polyphonic montage,' with its simultaneous advance of multiple series of lines, each with an independent compositional course.[24] Following the example of musical polyphony, Eisenstein looks at his film *The Old and the*

New (1929), where he develops seven themes throughout the film's procession sequence. Indeed, he tended to sustain his musical conception of film throughout his writings. In a lecture to filmmakers, Eisenstein declared:

> Where you set action to music or song, you lead it towards purely musical resolution.... If you do not work on the metrical relationships between depiction and music, that is, if there is no primitive, direct relationship between musical and visual accents, between the 'lines' of music and the montage segments of expression, that makes it doubly difficult."[25]

And of course, a tension or question in the music might be resolved or answered in the images as well. A most tangible instance of this notion of build-up and resolution between musical and visual elements is related by composer Geoffrey Burgon, who declared that dramatic cues can be at their most effective when they finish early and allow the event taking place on-screen to function as the musical cadence or resolution.[26] Eisenstein clearly thought carefully about the musical implications of filmic developments and was constantly concerned about the music-like aspects of film. He even discussed a more esoteric notion about direct correspondence among qualities of sound and image and representations. His "Theory of Ocular Music" declared a correspondence of words, music, and colors through standardized cultural associations. He supplied examples such as 'sun shines on valley' being rendered as softly descending tones that suggest violet and green coloring.[27] Of course, his contentions are not easily verified and might be more profitably approached as an aesthetic aspiration, a technique that might allow for enhanced cinematic effect rather than direct communication of distinct ideas. Eisenstein's famous diagram of the relationship of music and image in a sequence from *Alexander Nevsky* (1938) has inspired but also infuriated and frustrated scholars.

Eisenstein's considerations involved sound and to a degree image, as well being conceived in basic musical terms. He was far from alone in considering all sound as music. Although the film soundtrack might be approached as if it were music, this is surely enabled by increasing awareness of the sonic and material aspects of music. Founder of acoustic ecology R. Murray Schafer, points to the situation in the wake of modernist avant garde and experimental music, where music might be taken as synonymous with all sounds:

> To define music merely as *sounds* would have been unthinkable a few years ago, though today it is the more exclusive definitions that are proving unacceptable. Little by little throughout the twentieth century, all the conventional

definitions of music have been exploded by the abundant activities of musicians themselves.... Today all sounds belong to a continuous field of possibilities lying within the comprehensive dominion of music.[28]

After all, if music is able to include all sorts of sounds, then why shouldn't the organizational and analytical principles of music be brought to bear on soundscapes—both inside and outside of films? Surely this can offer some insight into the sonic complexities that are taken for granted in the experience of films. Those working on sonic aspects of films need something of a musical appreciation of sound, including care with sonic details and attention to the precise relationship of simultaneous and successive sounds. Speaking in 1937, John Cage noted:

> Wherever we are, what we hear is mostly noise. When we ignore it, it disturbs us. When we listen to it, we find it fascinating.... We want to capture and control these sounds, to use them not as sound effects but as musical instruments. Every film studio has a library of 'sound effects' recorded on film. With a phonograph it is now possible to control the amplitude and frequency of any one of these sounds and give it rhythms within or beyond the reach of the imagination. Given four film phonographs we could compose and perform a quartet for explosive motor, wind, heartbeat, and landslide.... If this word 'music' is sacred and reserved for eighteenth- and nineteenth-century instruments, we can substitute a more meaningful term: organized sound.[29]

Cage's celebrated definition of music as organized sound was influential (and apparently followed a similar formulation by Edgard Varèse). His discussion already, before the Second World War, suggested the possibility of film sound effects and music being unified. It is of paramount importance to recognize that Cage's statement on the one hand expands the idea of what constitutes music, but on the other opens up a conceptualization of film sound as essentially musical rather than representational.

DOWNBEATS AND HYPER-SYNCH

Music is more often recognized as an art of time than an art of space. George Burt notes that "...a given musical form can provide a supra rhythmic structure on a broad scale."[30] As an example, Burt cites director Richard Fleischer's claim that Hugo Friedhofer's fugue on the "Dies Irae" in *Between Heaven and Hell* (1956) was not cut to the music, but nevertheless it all fitted together extremely cohesively.[31] Music coheres the other elements, often irrespective of direct synchronization. The celebrated sequence in *Psycho* (1960) of Marion (Janet Leigh) driving in the rain until reaching the Bates Motel has little clear synchronization between music and image. According to Nicholas Cook:

> Herrmann's angular, repetitive music does not connect in a literal manner with anything that is visible on the screen; it does not obviously synchronize, for instance, with the regular rhythm of the wiper blades, or the irregular rhythms outlined by the lights of oncoming cars. And whereas its busy quality, its high level of activity, could be seen as corresponding to the speed of the car and the rain, the music continues at its own pace as the car slows and stops. Rather than corresponding to anything that is visible, the music jumps the diegetic gap, so to speak, 'seeking out' and uncovering the turmoil in Marion's mind, and thus transferring its own qualities to her.[32]

Indeed, this is a good example of Chion's notion of synchresis, where there is a spontaneous weld of sound and image irrespective of qualities of fitting together. As Cook notes, the correspondence of sound and image is tenuous at best. Perhaps the relationship between sound and image in this sequence ought to be approached as asynchronous, where each track has a strong sense of its own direction and part of the depth of effect comes from the music's repetitive and rhythmic purposefulness in the face of the image track's uncertainty. The less direct the connection between music and image, in terms of diegetic production, rhythmic concurrence, or emotional register, the more the music might appear to be anempathetic music—not emotionally engaged with the emotional character of events on-screen. In the American Film Institute's documentary film *Bernard Herrmann: Music from the Movies* (1992), film editor Paul Hirsch discusses this sequence and emphasizes the way that the audience's anxiety during the sequence does not stem from the image track, which merely has an alternation of a frontal medium shot of Marion driving and the reverse of car headlights hurtling toward her. Instead, Hirsch maintains it is solely Herrmann's music that provides the sense of apprehension. The music has a regular rhythmic and bar structure (a pulsing 2/4 with well-demarcated sections in alternation), so despite unconventional sound and harmony, in terms of temporal structure, it is very comprehensible, perhaps even facile. The two structures, the regular musical form and the regular alternation of two shots do not correspond and thus have no strong synch points. In other words, there is no palpable synchrony between sound and image in this sequence. I would contend that this attribute is a critical contributor to the anxious mood in this celebrated passage of Hitchcock's film.

Of course, these examples clearly are not incommensurate asynchrony or in any sense do they amount to any sort of contradiction between sound and image tracks.[33] They are, however, instances of a form of cinema beyond the dominant regime of synchronized dialogue sequences. Caryl Flinn rightly points out that the feting of asynchrony and positing of music as a 'disruptive' element have been overstated at times,[34] to some degree, perhaps under the inspiration of Eisenstein, but more following the line of amplifying (or perhaps even imagining) the subversive in culture.[35] On rare occasions, though, music unmistakably opens the possibility of dislocation with the image track. This may not necessarily be disruptive but often can take on a disturbing disposition. A notable example is *Silent Hill* (2006), where the videogame was transposed directly into film, and the sound rebuilt around the existing music for the game. This music embodies an essence of the *Silent Hill* character,[36] exemplifying the highly singular series of games produced by the Japanese company Konami. On the face of it, the games concern a third-person character's navigation through the misty ghost town of Silent Hill, under threat from various unsavory creatures while attempting to solve a compulsive mystery. It is a 'third-person survival horror game' in which the player explores a three-dimensional navigable environment, solves puzzles, collects items, stays alive, and endeavors to solve a central mystery. It contains a strong subtext of psychological disturbance, suggesting that it may all be a fantasy of the protagonist, along with a persistent suspicion that all is never quite what it seems.[37] The music *and* the entire sound design for each of the games was written and produced by Akira Yamaoka,[38] a specialist in videogame music.[39] As they say in the games industry, *Silent Hill* was 'ported' from one format to another, aiming at as little adaptation as possible.

The film imports its musical aesthetics directly from the videogame, and this has a significant impact on its character. Although much music in the game is interactive in that the player triggers music by certain acts or by entering certain locations, the music for *Silent Hill* is dominated by sustained music for 'cut scenes' (which are like film scenes depicting events) and repetitive pieces that, even if they are not looped, have a continuous character. There is no direct action matching by the music during gameplay, so the music appears as fairly distinct pieces with their own integrity. Thus the music makes the film a fragmentary experience—it contains little repetition and not much sense of a sonic continuity (i.e., no repeated themes, no orchestral, no songs, and no particular musical genre). However, for someone who has played these games and interiorized the game music, the experience is a constant evocation of memories of the game and feelings associated with it.[40] The music becomes like a long finger probing the memory and gaining direct access to feelings stemming from the game experience. The dominance of musical asynchrony enhances and develops a feeling of unease, disconnection, and uncertainty. The lack of repeated themes of a traditional film score makes for a feeling of schizophrenia (each second of the film is made anew) rather than intermittent return and the repose offered by the use of repeated themes or related musical material.[41] As an assemblage, the music might be divided between the dominant pieces with their own integrity, which are often ambiences (by Yamaoka, derived from the game) and momentary dramatics, notably isolated stingers and flourishes (Jeff Danna's few and newly added minimal, momentary action cues). The nature of the videogame music, as atmospheric musical loops often devoid of dynamics means that synchronization with images is precluded as an option. Furthermore, the sounds of ambience include drones, rumbles, distant clunked metal, bowed metal/microphone feedback, and echo and reverb, making for an effect far removed from traditional emotional film scoring. As this description suggests, there is also a strong tendency (imported directly from the games) to mix score and sound effects into a single unified sonic field.[42]

Songs can mismatch or dominate due to their solid form and regulated beat. We might imagine that conventional musical structures are just that—having come into being due merely to cultural traditions and the establishment of easy-to-follow rules. Yet Leonard Meyer notes that the commonplace use of four- to eight-bar structures is not merely a convention, but rather derived from what can be stored in short-term memory.[43] So, many have asserted that the conventional structure of popular music in essence may be much derived from human physical capabilities and requirements. Much accessible music uses four- and eight-bar structures, and so-called song form articulates these blocks in repetitive structures of alternation and variation (for instance, AABA, ABAB, ABACAB, etc.). These structures present a small amount of musical material in a highly comprehensive format. Though the understanding of these structures is largely unconscious, the familiarity of changes at certain points, the returns of choruses and verses, or the move to a 'middle eight' section for an instrumental solo, are all highly predictable to anyone who has listened to much popular music. This is massively important for the audience's anticipation of dramatic changes in the music and is regularly exploited by films.

Musical structures offer a preexisting frame into which musical content can be placed and developed. Alternation is a central strategy, as is the readability of certain important milestones throughout the piece that usually augur a different vector or tactic (the move to a sing-along chorus, the divisions between movements of symphonies, the triumphant return of the main musical material, for example). The sort of alternating structures evident in popular song (as well as in some classical forms) bears remarkable similarity to the bare bones structure of space in some films. Perhaps the best example is from television, when the soap opera *Dynasty* (1981–91) famously used a pared-down structure of establishing shot and then alternating shot-reverse shots, as nearly every scene was a dialogue-led, set-bound sequence. Of course, this repeated structure is evident in many mainstream films, but usually those that really deserve the title of talkie or those that are made with heavily restricted resources. Narrative and dialogue-based film language is a clear preexisting structure that showcases certain developments and leads to certain expectations, precisely in the manner of popular song form.[44]

The temporal aspect of a song can provide a film sequence with its central organizational spine. Musical time can replace film time. Yet musical time is profoundly different from the time schemes of cinema. It is continuous rather than flexible and gapped like time in films; time in pop music is, for the song's duration, a regime of the beat's rigorous reiteration. The continuity of the beat is the marker of time, held within song form's harnessing of the block repetitions of musical material that govern popular music. The most prevalent structure of repetition and variation is the sequence of AABA, with B as a variation and the A afterward as a return to what has already been established. This dynamic is clear in popular song where the chorus functions as a form of 'home'—the return to what we know and desire to hear. This is clearly essential in the psychological dynamics of the structure. Indeed, the structure might be seen at heart as a psychological structure, rather than merely a strategy from the point of view of production.

Films that use preexisting songs often evince a musical structure that marks the dramatic structure. This might be less on a large scale, but more in terms of image editing and visual movement. In the 1980s, some films had seemingly coherent musical scores built from a succession of pop songs. An example of this is *Manhunter* (1986) (figures 5.1–5.3), which foregrounds songs during certain key moments in the film, such as the Shriekback song that dramatically accompanies the sequence of serial killer Dollarhyde's intimacy with his blind colleague Reba. Although the film nominally has an underscore by Michel Rubini and the Reds (writing and recording separately), in effect it works as a number of pieces, most of them songs, that appear as blocks of music, unlike traditional scores written to fit action. Unlike most horror films, *Manhunter* by and large has less than scary music, although it has a fine example of anempathetic music, when the Iron Butterfly song "In-a-Gadda-Da-Vida" (figure 5.4) accompanies

Figures 5.1–5.3: *Manhunter* (1986).

the climactic sequence of investigator Will Graham's defeat of Dollarhyde. During emotionally heightened moments when Reba is on the verge of being killed and the police are converging on the house, the song's two-bar riff continues relentlessly, interrupted only by the song's chorus. As it appears diegetically, it is absent during the shots of the police but quickly

Figure 5.4: Iron Butterfly's "In-A-Gadda-Da-Vida," Main Riff.

takes on the high sound quality of non-diegetic music and articulates the action. At the point when Graham jumps through a plate-glass window, the images follow the music's dynamic. As he runs up in slow motion, "In-a-Gadda-Da-Vida" has a quiet dropout, but the organ builds in intensity as there is a showy slow-motion shot of Graham approaching the window (toward the camera). At the precise moment when he smashes through the window, the music explodes back into the main riff with all instruments, and the image track reverts to normal speed for the confrontation between investigator and serial killer. Despite the song being edited at times, it is not cut in this sequence, and the music's dynamic trajectory becomes that of the drama.

So-called song form is premised upon clear patterns of repetition and alternation, leading to an expectation of repeated musical material that provides pleasure when it reappears from a formal and temporal point of view. As Adorno has noted in his appraisal of popular music,

> The whole structure of popular music is standardized.... The whole is pregiven and preaccepted, even before the actual experience of the music starts.... The composition hears for the listener. This is how popular music divests the listener of spontaneity and promotes conditional reflexes.... The schematic build up dictates the way in which he [sic] must listen....[45]

Although Adorno is determinedly pejorative in his dealing with popular music, it is possible to glean some important points from his analysis. The comprehensive format of popular song form tends to dictate how various elements are understood, which means that much so-called popular music (and much other music as well) does not need to tax the listener's brain too much during consumption. Consequently, Adorno also—and characteristically—points toward the social implications of musical form. From the point of view of synchronization, clear musical structure often encompasses important moments that forge notable coupling points with impact in aesthetic or narrative terms.

AUDIOVISUAL CADENCES

Synch points are the name given in production to the points where sound is keyed precisely to image, to hold the two in place. These can fit lip movements on the one hand, or have the music hit a climax at the precise moment of a dramatic shot. They might be approached as the crucial pillars of structure in a film, the unapparent but architecturally and psychologically prime aspects that hold up a surface of content upon which we are directed to focus. In *Audio-Vision*, Michel Chion's compound of books edited and translated into one by Claudia Gorbman, he notes that synch points make "...a point where the effect of synchresis is particularly prominent, rather like an accented chord in music."[46] Synchronization thus has more to do with perceptual aspects than simply being a regular convention of the film editing process. There is no manual of staging and editing film for synchrony. Indeed, rather than being easily dismissed as merely a process followed by film technicians in post-production, synch points emerge from the essence of sound cinema: the confluence of sounds and images. Sounds will often seem to be keyed to images on-screen, and not necessarily as belonging to them. Non-diegetic music, emanating from a different (unrepresented) space from the world on-screen, still synchronizes and emphasizes significant moments. And as Chion suggests, significant words can cause a dramatic effect of synchronism with events on-screen, as indeed can the confluence of almost any visual and sonic activity. He goes on to state that while films contain an overwhelming number of synch points, only a few of these are of important structural significance:

> ...the primary synch points...are crucial for meaning and dynamics. In the case of synch dialogue, for example, you might find thousands of synch points, but only certain ones are important, the ones whose placement defines what we might call the *audiovisual phrasing* of the sequence.[47]

Certain synch points clearly function as sonic cadences, appearing at nodal points in the film, that call out for a musical hit or emphasis of some sort. These junctures are where the film changes gear or aims for some extra narrative redoubling or emotional impact. This process can be stylistic (in other words, material) or gestural, and regularly involves some combination of these elements. Often, the dynamics of a sequence are built up in visual terms through editing and interplay of space, such as shot contrast, although the dynamic line of a sequence can emanate primarily from the dialogue. Gestural aspects of the actors on-screen can also be imperative in the developmental progress of a sequence and dramatic movement by figures on-screen, as much as by camera or editing, which can provide a sense of plenitude or dramatic climax in a sequence no matter how short or small the dynamic change.

Synch points manifest something of an abstract line of dynamics and drama. This is often intimately related to narrative development but sometimes might purely have aesthetic determination (in the desire for momentary effect, for example). These points can be relatively regular. For example, in horror films such as *Halloween* (1978), there are regular build-ups in terms of tension that are capped by a moment of violence or an anticlimax, with the former usually accompanied by a loud musical stinger. Musical hits function in a similar manner to diegetic sound hits, with the diegetic sound of a knife stabbing into flesh being an equivalent of an accompanying stinger chord in the incidental music. Indeed, these are both synch points of the most precise order. If the visual impact of Michael Myers's blade on a victim was pre-empted slightly by a stinger (or missed momentarily), the effect would be highly bizarre. It would undermine the sense of aesthetic, as well as representational, unity at which such films wholeheartedly aim.

Cadences are points in the melodic and harmonic syntax where a conclusion is marked, however briefly. Often involving traditional chord changes (movements in harmony), cadences mark endings or pauses in a similar manner to commas, semi-colons, or periods. Indeed, temporal structures in music can often be subdivided into linguistic structures involving phrasing and cadence. The first sets up temporal units based on an interior logic in the music, while the latter marks changes and points to conclusions, be they temporary or final. Both film and music exhibit cadences. The most obvious one in traditional music involves a movement from the chord of the dominant to the tonic to mark a strong sense of ending, as illustrated in the common appearance of 'Amen' at the end of some Christian hymns (predominantly a plagal cadence [IV-I]). In film, the conclusion of a scene is sometimes underlined by fades (or cross-fades), which was a particularly common stylistic aspect of classical Hollywood filmmaking. Also, the end of a film might be signaled by a crane shot moving up and away from the event or place depicted. Audiences who have experienced even a few films will most likely understand this linguistic turn. Synch points are audiovisual cadences of a sort and, like musical cadences, might be conceived as more than simply punctuation. They might be conceived as the lynchpins holding the system firmly together. As Michel Chion points out, "Synch points...give audiovisual flow its phrasing, just as chords or cadences, which are also vertical meeting of elements, can give phrasing to a sequence of music."[48] Indeed, it seems fairly straightforward that films are structured through audiovisual cadences. In fact, cadence derives from the Latin *cadere*, meaning 'to fall,' and is most evident in spoken moments such as the end of sentences and emphasis through intonation. This structuration is evident in the accent in poetry but perhaps more clear in music, where a sense of finishing and starting sections is often extremely clear. When it comes to audiovisual cadences, significant elements appear to fall together, as evident in extremely dramatic synch points of sound and image, which yield a sense of great significance and intense aesthetic effect.

One paramount aspect of cadences is the sense of expectation. In *Emotion and Meaning in Music*, Leonard B. Meyer noted that music leads us to *expect* certain developments, most clearly through its use of melody, harmony, and tonal structure.[49] Of course, that expectation may not be fulfilled, but music will often lead in broadly predictable directions. Michel Chion noted that cadence in film is more than exclusively a musical advent:

> Musical form leads the listener to expect cadences; the listener's anticipation of the cadence comes to subtend his/her perception. Likewise, a camera movement, a sound rhythm, a change in an actor's behaviour can put the spectator in a state of anticipation. What follows either confirms or surprises the expectations established—and thus an audiovisual sequence functions according to this dynamic of anticipation and outcome.[50]

Sound and image often cohere cadentially to mark section boundaries, as well as to emphasize certain important moments in films. Indeed, films vary in how they use synchronized cadences. Some might use them as a succession or progression, while others may have more of a free flow of abstract dynamics. Indeed, a film's synch points might be thought of as an abstract line of dynamics and drama, much as pieces of music can often be mapped as a succession of cadential moments. Indeed, the audiovisual possibilities are, by and large, limited in mainstream films. As noted earlier, such nodal points, which ask for a musical or sonic hit or emphasis of some sort, might be where the film changes gear or aims for some narrative or emotional impact. This can be achieved through stylistic or gestural elements. The effect of such sequences is often not noted consciously by the audience, but in certain cases, they can be used as a self-conscious device. The British film *Bronson* for instance, discussed previously for its asynchrony, also employs an extreme form of precise and regimented synchronization. The film generally is very self-conscious about its music and the way it is used, exploiting a wide range of preexisting recordings, from Wagner's "Siegfried's Funeral March" from *Götterdämmerung* and Verdi's "Chorus of the Hebrew Slaves" from *Nabucco* to the Pet Shop Boys' song "It's a Sin." In fact, it is so self-conscious that its aesthetic strategies appear almost too unambiguously ironic. In the sequence where Bronson is released from prison, the action is edited and staged around the New Order song "Your Silent Face." The instrumental introduction to the song is protracted and has a regular structure that is used as the temporal foundation for the film's visual action. As the beat begins, a stylistic format takes shape where cuts or some notable visual movements on-screen take place at the important structural beats that begin each two- and four-bar strophic unit. Perhaps the most evident point is where the melodica enters as Bronson walks out into the sunlight of freedom. Thus the extremely clear structure of the song dictates the fall of the action, and the audience understands the temporal importance of these musical moments. This all seems too much, and such precise synchronization lays bare the effect and artifice of cinema.

Like songs, incidental music can take on a clear relationship of asynchrony with the image and other sound aspects of the film. Sometimes music in a film can persist following its own temporal logic that is not tied strongly, or indeed at all, to the events on-screen. For example, the highly dramatic conclusion of the cannibal western *Ravenous* (1999) involves a sustained and repetitive musical cue that relentlessly keeps its pulse going at a steady rate, while the dynamics, volume, and density of the music generally build throughout. This cue accompanies an extended duel between the film's two principal characters, the cannibal Colquhoun/Ives (Robert Carlyle) and Boyd (Guy Pearce). This sequence lasts over nine minutes, moving through a succession of violent acts perpetrated by the lead characters on each other, culminating in both of them being caught in a large bear trap that appears to spell their doom. During this long and varied sequence, which contains only a few lines of dialogue, there is loud and foregrounded music on the soundtrack that refuses to follow the ebb and flow of narrative activity but instead goes on its own course, based on its own musical logic. This is a repeated loop of eight bars in 3/4 time and runs for over nine minutes—covering the whole concluding action of the film, the confrontation between Boyd and the formidable cannibal Colquhoun/Ives. It concludes with them apparently both dying. The music is a waltz that with each repetition adds successive layers of electronic keyboard, electronic drum, synthesizer drones, and sustained deep bass notes. The commencement of the two characters' confrontation is startling in that the music repeats with absolutely no development for nearly two minutes. The sound of electronic keyboards with a distinctive wobbly pitch begins at 1.19:43 in the film's running time, during dialogue between Boyd and Colonel Hart (Jeffrey Jones). At the point when the latter asks the former, "Can you be trusted?" to which Boyd replies "Of course not," the regular pulse of three notes of the waltz's foundation commences but continues without development as Boyd cuts Hart's throat and proceeds to seek out Colquhoun/Ives.[51] It is almost two minutes before the first change to the musical ostinato when some echoed percussion and dulcimer enters. The piece follows an additive logic, with each new layer of music accumulating density. In succession, there is a deep synthesizer drone (on Eb) with a very modern-sounding filter sweep (sounding something like a wah wah pedal) that accompanies the swordfight between the two characters, along with a descending high synthesizer line,[52] dulcimer, and finally vocal chorus. Each development takes place within the repeated bar structure, often entering on the first beat. The point where the dulcimer enters matches the cut and dramatic appearance in close-up of Colquhoun/Ives with a sinister red cross in blood painted on his forehead (figure 5.5). The image track directly exploits the structure of the music. Indeed, this procedure has been evident throughout *Ravenous*, where dramatic events are underscored by the entry of a particular instrument in a repetitive (and usually additive) piece of music. The building of drama in the music is through an additive process that also exploits the cumulative effect of extreme repetition. The conclusion of the duel occurs at 1.28:56 when a large bear trap shuts loudly trapping both of the characters in a deadly embrace. The music that has been building interminably halts precisely at this moment, although a deep synthesizer drone remains and continues through the ensuing sequence, joined by a deep Native-American wail, as the film humorously concludes with the arriving general eating the stew containing human meat and presumably inadvertently allowing the cannibal weendigo spirit to enter him.

During this sequence, the music develops very slowly. Each successive addition is a musical loop that builds the density of the music. The image

Figure 5.5: *Ravenous* (1999).

track is full of variation, running from close-ups, to traveling camera shots and POV shots. However, as table 5.1 indicates, developments are keyed to progress in the additive piece of music. This table demonstrates how closely the structures of the action and the music are interlocked. The music has a highly logical and systematic structure, developing almost automatically with regular and mechanical additions of successive layers.[53] Narrative developments parallel musical developments. Changes in music match changes in activity; this is different from the usual arrangement in most mainstream films where points of impact and important words are underscored and emphasized musically. This sequence of confrontation has some moments of distinct inspiration from Sergio Leone's spaghetti westerns, with the dramatic facial close-ups and slow buildup to a duel being reminiscent of the denouements of *The Good, the Bad and the Ugly* (1967) and *Once Upon a Time in the West* (1968).

Table 5.1. TIME NARRATIVE: EVENTS AND MUSIC.

1.19:43	Dialogue between Boyd and Hart.	Three notes rising in pitch and in waltz time begin as Boyd says, "Of course not." The texture is sparing at this point. Dialogue continues.
1.21:40		Echoed percussion hits and dulcimer tremolos are added.
1.22:45	Boyd cuts Hart's throat and a swordfight ensues between Boyd and Colquhoun.	A deep droning synthesizer tone enters, and the continuous pitch is elaborated through filter sweeping that accompanies the swordfight.
1.23:34	Boyd goes out into the fort's yard looking for Colquhoun.	A sustained high note enters and then develops into a loop of high synthesizer notes sounding like a female voice playing a descending melody.
1.25:08	Cutting to a dramatic close-up shot of Colquhoun turning to reveal he has a cross daubed in blood on his forehead.	Loud dulcimer is added at the precise point of cutting.
1.25:39	The pair reengage.	The music becomes louder; rhythmic triplets in the voices are added.
1.27:45		Voices clearly enounce the words "Save Our Souls Lissa."
1.28:56	The bear trap shuts loudly, trapping the two fighting men.	The music stops at precisely the same moment, but the deep synthesizer drone remains.

There are broad dynamic changes in the music matched directly through film editing to events. The piece remains a repeated loop of eight bars in 3/4 time, its regularity expressing some of the inevitability of the negative outcome of the fight. The piece has a formal character, with something emotionally cold about the music's indifference to the events depicted. The additive structure of the music, where an extra layer is added every four bars, makes the music relentless and not geared toward visual events. Indeed, it seems to pull along those events through the synchronizations (cuts or action movements) at the onset of each four-bar section. The lack of emotion in the music is doubled by its mechanical progression that is matched in the imagery, which imparts a comic edge to a disturbingly violent scene while retaining a firm sense of the unresolved until the resolution through termination.

Films that are dominated by musical processes can be a source of anxiety for the audience, particularly when expectations might be confounded. For instance, Led Zeppelin's concert documentary *The Song Remains the Same* (1975) spices up the recording of a live performance at Madison Square Garden with fantasy sequences for each member of the group. The startling aspect of this is that, although the sound remains diegetic, the images become non-diegetic, inserted as a different diegesis from elsewhere. Making sense of these sections as traditional film is not a viable undertaking. For instance, guitarist Jimmy Page's visual sequence occurs during his extended guitar solo in "Dazed and Confused." It clearly was shot with little regard for accompanying the music but edited for some broad moments of synchronization, where dramatic turns in the music are matched to significant developments in the image track, including a shadowy figure's ascent of a hill with him swinging a multi-imaged and colored sword, and the return from this 'holiday' in the images to remarry with the continuous soundtrack. The latter marks the point when the extended guitar solo concludes and the rest of the band rejoins to continue with the song. The fantasy section accompanies an unconventional guitar solo, using violin bow and echo unit, with some wordless vocal accompaniment from singer Robert Plant. The moment of rejoining involves the guitar abandoning its extended techniques for a more straightforward exciting rock guitar solo with muscular rhythm from drums and bass guitar. This rejoinder is not just a coming home technically (away from avant garde noise and back to the traditional attractions of rock music); it is a dramatic coming home in the image track, and its synchronization with the sound track redoubles the effect.

This sequence manifests a certain anxiety on the levels of the music and the film's aesthetics. Attempts to find a pattern in the images and music as a unit fail, and instead there is merely disjunction. The point at which the corresponding images return feels almost like a relief, bringing the audience back to what it knows and indeed, what it probably wanted to see in the film: a direct packaging of the concert experience. The key is that this is not a mainstream film but more an autonomous soundtrack with image accompaniment. This tells us that it is less a part of film tradition and probably more a part of the music industry. This example—and indeed, most of the film—illustrates how far we assume that we are confronted with a unitary event when in fact we are not. The whole logic of the film is to present itself as a record of an event, and yet both soundtrack and image track are collages of different recordings of different events. The fantasy sequences thus become the most divergent, and in fact perhaps the least deceptive, of the film.[54] It is a mark of their lack of requirement for establishing veracity that these are almost wholly unsynchronized, in direct contrast with the precise synchronization achieved throughout the sequences of Led Zeppelin onstage. The fact that these sections of the film, and particularly the section just discussed, seem anomalous to mainstream film aesthetics illustrates the conventional manner in which most dramatic films attempt to regulate aesthetically induced anxiety. Mainstream film works hard to ameliorate uncertainty and manages anxiety through its careful and judicious use as an occasional device. Sustained asynchrony fosters diegetic uncertainty, leading to an unfulfilled expectation of the return of synchronization and the normality of dominant film style.

An exceptional illustration of heightened anxiety through sustained asynchrony is the version of Victor Sjöström's *The Phantom Carriage* (1921, *Körkarlen*) with a soundtrack by KTL made in the 2000s. The film is an anxious-enough encounter, with many tense and disturbing moments. But with an added soundtrack of droning music, it becomes an almost unbearably unnerving experience. The score is, loosely speaking, 'drone rock,' although it lacks drums and consists primarily of distorted electric guitar and programmed electronics. Broadly speaking, the music follows the dynamics of the action, but its movement is often almost negligible. It usually retains a sense of droning throughout most scenes and owes something to musical minimalism in its recourse to repetition as essence. The repetitive, continuous nature of the music means that it does not aim at precise synchronization, revealing sustained asynchrony as terror induced by the music's lack of connection. Significantly, the audience has trouble finding audiovisual patterns and for extended periods, the film seems to de-constitute into a representational image track and a disconnected and traumatized soundtrack. The KTL version of *The Phantom Carriage* embodies Robert Fink's description of cultural repetition as an embodiment of the

Figure 5.6: *Decasia* (2002).

Freudian death drive: a terror of stasis,[55] where there appears to be little or no prospect of progress or of return to the normality of synchronization (unless it is the surrender of image to sound and its redirection into mechanized stereotypical movement). A step or two away is Bill Morrison's film *Decasia* (2002) (figure 5.6) and its associated music by Michael Gordon. Although this is usually referred to as a film and sold on DVD, it was initially more of an art event, and perhaps this near misrecognition adds to the effect of expectation. Subtitled "The State of Decay" and compiled from old disintegrating nitrate silent film images from film archives, it appears to be on the verge of collapse itself. *Decasia* is the point at which *representation* disintegrates into *abstraction*. However, this sense is enhanced by Michael Gordon's repetitive phase and drone-based music, which at times gradually changes pitch but seems to have little direct relation to the images, and in fact none that might be described as synchronized. The lack of synchronization and the consequent relentless marching apart of sound and image tracks make for an incoherent single experience, despite the fact that both tracks might well make sense on their own.

CONCLUSION

One of the earliest theorizations of sound cinema, by Russian film director-theorist Sergei Eisenstein, appeared inspired predominantly by music, which he applied as a guiding principle and a metaphor that he sustained across his analyses. As discussed in chapter 3, this rightly stands as one of the foundational considerations of the essential relationship between sound and image, although Eisenstein's theories of montage have inspired more in the way of debate. He diagrammed the similarity between film and an orchestral score on music manuscript paper, with horizontal (in temporal succession) and vertical (simultaneous) relations apparent, what semiologists call the syntactic and paradigmatic dimensions that are evident in time-based cultural objects such as film or music.

An isomorphic relationship between film and music, where aesthetics are shared, assumes that on some level there is a common heart. A more abstract approach to film than is fashionable can yield insights. In recent years, notions like the 'music of the spheres' have returned to art and popular conceptions of aesthetics. Since the success of Dan Brown's *The Da Vinci Code* and its film adaptation (2006), the notion of the 'divine proportion' or 'golden section' has been more widely appreciated than ever. The ratio of 1 to 1.618 was used by classical Greek mathematicians Pythagoras and Euclid, as well as later artists like Leonardo Da Vinci. It is has even been discovered in art and culture that had little idea of consciously following any such 'magic' formula. Pre-existing abstract formulas abound though. Charles Barr discussed the mathematics of narration in Hitchcock's films and pointed to how the systematic use of numbers of frames was applied in editing, and that such abstract formalism was utilized covertly in mainstream cinema, rather than being solely the preserve of avant garde filmmakers such as Peter Kubelka.[56] It seems almost an accepted reality that music is essentially mathematical on a fundamental level. The Schillinger system of learning musical composition is based on mathematical structures and principles, and William Rosar notes what Fred Steiner called Bernard Herrmann's 'module technique' for film music composition, which used an arithmetical and symmetrical structure of bars: multiples of two bars within eight-bar structures. This is flexible and fits the momentary format of films with ease.[57] Hsu and Hsu note that music can be understood mathematically on a complex rather than simple level: "...the musical effects of a composition can be expressed as deviations from fractal geometry,"[58] proceeding from natural harmonies, and analysing a piece by Bach with reference to Benoit Mandelbrot's 'fractal' equations. Copernicus suggested that, given the stars move across space, they must make a sound. This celestial music may be inaudible, and some have suggested it is musical merely in its fundamental nature. It denotes an essential harmony of the universe and thus music in the extreme of its abstract sense, but also its most natural. This esoteric (although dominant until the Renaissance) philosophy about proportions and mathematical/geometrical relations was premised upon an idea of natural essences, with astral bodies, their relationships, and movements being as mathematically predictable and significant as the relationships of musical harmonics. These are all part of a universal sacred geometry. All of this adds up to a sense of underlying structure that is not merely functional but has the potential to be profound—irrespective of content or other significant aspects. Such a focus on abstract structure also points to a potential shared level for cultural products, a platform shared with nature and all objects of the universe, from the sacred to the profane.

While the book's discussion has focused on the implications of synchronization between sound and image, we would do well to remember that synchronization is also at the heart of music and thus central to film's sonic aspects. All musical ensembles have to be in time, and much studio recording is done to click tracks derived from those used in film music production from the 1930s onward. Though on occasion, music may segue poorly into a film or involve seemingly crude processes of sound and image editing, it is far from uncommon to have sequences structured around music, if not from the perspective of production, from the perspective of how a sequence is perceived. Sometimes music can be the structure around which film footage is edited—a situation far more common than many realize—or it can be the hook and beat that furnish cohesion to a sequence for its audience. Indeed, the whole soundtrack for a film perhaps ought to be conceived in musical terms. After all, centuries of development in musical theory provide one of the most highly developed means of analyzing sound and thinking in sonic terms. Furthermore, developments in electronic and avant garde music have absorbed sound effects and pursued inclusive theory and practice. So perhaps synch points are essentially sonic moments. After all, synch points are regularly geared around sound and sonic structure, and therefore constitute the key moments in sound film as a coherent unity.

CHAPTER 6
'Visual' Sound Design
The Sonic Continuum

Film sound has experienced some radical developments in both technological and aesthetic terms over the last 30 years or so. The traditional basic speaker system in cinemas in many cases has been replaced by a multi-speaker system that involves a significant spatialization of film sound allied to a remarkable improvement in sound definition. These changes augur an altered psychology at the heart of much new cinema, instilled by sound's increased importance for films:

> The sound of noises, for a long time relegated to the background like a troublesome relative in the attic, has therefore benefited from the recent improvements in definition brought by Dolby. Noises are reintroducing an acute feeling of the materiality of things and beings, and they herald a sensory cinema that rejoins a basic tendency of … the silent cinema. The paradox is only apparent. With the new place that noises occupy, speech is no longer central to films.[1]

Michel Chion points to technological developments in cinema that have had a notable impact on film aesthetics. Any movement from a speech-centered cinema to one that allows more prominence to 'noises' is potentially a shift from a cinema dominated by synchronized dialogue to one with significant amounts of asynchrony and sound as an effect in itself, whether through loud music or featured sounds. James Lastra comments on the emergence of sound design since the 1970s as a distinctive aspect of film: "Technological and economic factors surely exerted a determining pressure, and the stylistic norms that emerged surely derived from existing techniques in both the film and music recording worlds."[2] Indeed, in the increasing cohesion between sonic elements in film, it has rarely been recognized how far musical imperatives have determined the final product. While film scores and featured songs are an obvious result of the impact of music on contemporary film, a less obvious one is the degree to which sound effects and dialogue are marshaled in a quasi-musical manner. Perhaps the clearest indication of this is that sounds like music are increasingly classified as timbre (the particularities of individual solo sound) and structure (what fits where within the continuum).

UNIFIED SOUNDTRACKS

Cinema over the last few decades has evinced an unmistakeable fusing of the soundtrack elements.[3] Much as classical film musicals fused music with dialogue (or more accurately, we should use the term 'voices'), some recent films have fused music with sound effects, creating a sonic continuum. Music in film has a significant interaction with other elements of the soundtrack, as well as with the images, and one might even argue that its interaction with dialogue outweighs its interaction with images. In recent years, the development of converging digital sound technology has allowed sound designers to use musical software to enhance sound effects in films and allowed music composers to produce their own music incorporating elements of sound effects. Such developments, in line with technological convergence, aesthetic convergence, and harmonizing platforms and industries have meant that music is no longer simply an 'add-on' to films, but rather integrated almost genetically on a conceptual level: instigating film titles and narratives, and perhaps even having films as spin-offs from existing music, while continuing to inspire and articulate the most emotional and exciting moments of the overwhelming majority of films and other audiovisual media.

Technology has played a critical part in recent developments in film sound and music, and technological determinism is always an attractive, if too-easy, answer to questions of change. The availability of relatively cheap and easily programmed keyboard synthesizers at the turn of the 1980s led to an explosion of popular music and musicians exploiting the potential of these instruments. This had a notable impact on films. In the 1970s, John Carpenter's scores for his own films sounded unique in their use of simple textures with monophonic synthesizers, but by the next decade, they were sounding more like some of the contemporary pop music they had partly inspired. Greek keyboard player Vangelis came to some prominence for his scores for *Chariots of Fire* (1981) and *Blade Runner* (1982), and while rock keyboard players like Rick Wakeman and Keith Emerson had dipped their toes into film scoring, by the mid-1980s, pop groups using drum machines and synthesizers were producing scores, such as Wang Chung's for *To Live and Die in L.A.* (1985). The revolutionary development from analogue to digital sound has had a notable impact on many aspects of cinema[4] and on music and sound perhaps more than most other areas, allowing minute alteration and precise manipulation of all aural aspects. By the turn of the millennium, it was possible for musical scores to be constructed and fitted to a film on a computer screen at home, using AVID (or similar) and digital audio workstation (DAW) technology. Consequently, filmmakers like Robert Rodriguez are easily able to construct the scores for their films themselves, making film less of a collaborative medium, and making music less collaborative perhaps than ever. The elevation of the DAW has revolutionized music production, allowing easy construction of high-quality music on a home computer, although most of the top Hollywood film composers only use them for mock-ups until the final recording with an expensive orchestra (although one that is usually digitally beefed up). The development of sequencing software has had a direct influence on the styles of music being produced in the popular music arena. Examples of the dominant types of software sequencers include Steinberg Cubase, Sony Logic, Ableton Live, and Propellerheads Reason. One of the central tenets of such computer technology is that music can be reduced to recorded components that are then processed, through audio enhancement/distortion and looping, with a passage of music repeated verbatim. This latter aspect was responsible for the proliferation of dance music in the 1990s that was developed in home studios, with an emphasis on the manipulation of sound samples, pre-recorded passages of music that could be adapted, treated, and woven together into a new musical composition. Such music technology instils an awareness of sound and the ability to manipulate it electronically. This encourages a 'sound for sound's sake' approach focusing on the treatment of sound on a basic level (e.g., reverb, filters, positioning in the stereo mix, etc.) more than the traditional virtues of composition enshrined in so-called classical training (harmony, counterpoint, orchestration, etc.). This can lead to a confusion about what might constitute music and what might constitute non-musical sound, and at the very least has challenged the limited notions of music that were in wide circulation. Such technology is not only used by musical people but also by sound designers and editors, who use digital technology and techniques to manipulate sound effects the same way that composers use the same methods to compose music. While on the one hand, composers are more aware of sound as an absolute than perhaps ever before, film sound people are approaching soundtracks in a manner that might be deemed musical, or at the very least betrays a musical awareness of the interaction of elements and their particular individual sonic qualities.

Many contemporary films contain a unified and intricate field of music and sound effects. This inspires a certain sonic (and audiovisual) complexity, while the more self-contained nature of the soundtrack inspires less in the way of extended passages of synchronization. One context for this is the use of digital electronics for both music and sound effects, which means that music is increasingly conceptualized in sonic terms (or at least in electronic terms of basic sound manipulation, dealing with concepts such as envelope, filtering, etc.). On the other side of the coin, there is an increasingly musical conceptualization of sound design in such films, where sound elements are wielded in an artistic manner, manipulated for precise effect rather than merely aiming to duplicate and complement screen activity. Consequently, the distinct psychologies of music and sound effects mix. There is a notable collapse of the *space* between diegetic sound and non-diegetic music. This manifests a collapse of mental space, between the film's 'conscious' and its 'unconscious.' Rick Altman wrote about the differences between diegetic and non-diegetic music: "By convention, these two tracks have taken on a quite specific sense: the diegetic reflects reality (or at least supports cinema's referential nature), while the [non-diegetic] music track lifts the image into a romantic realm far above the world of flesh and blood."[5] In a similar manner, the unified field of sound merges these distinct channels, potentially mixing (by the film's terms) the objective and subjective, fantasy and reality, fixed perception and unstable reverie, conscious and unconscious, and not least, musical aesthetic and communicational aesthetic.

The convergence of music with ambient sound and sound effects contravenes the cinematic tradition of solid demarcation between such elements. As I have suggested, modern sound design in films might be understood as essentially musical in nature. After all, sound designers use musical software and digital products designed primarily for the production of music (such as the industry standard Pro Tools). This has led to a more *aesthetic* rather than *representational* conception of sound in the cinema. For a long time, cinema sound was thought of essentially in terms of clarity of dialogue and the uncluttered and functional composition of diegetic sound elements. A new impetus is particularly evident in films that have recourse to technical, as well as representational, extremity, most notably in the horror film.

Traditionally, film incidental music's effects include eliciting and affirming emotion, clarification or provision of information (such as mood and setting), furnishing a sound bath that immerses the audience in the film world, as well as the more traditional functional aspects that include attempting to provide continuity across edits and joins between shots and time-spaces. As such, the score can also furnish a sense of filmic movement while also functioning to clarify and articulate a formal structure for the film (through punctuation, cadence, and closure). Related structural functions might also include anticipating subsequent action in the film and commenting on screen activities or providing a further symbolic dimension not evident in other aspects of the film. In separate writings, Noel Carroll, Jeff Smith, and Roy Prendergast all quote a newspaper article from the 1940s wherein the respected composer Aaron Copland posited five categories of film incidental music function[6]: "...creating atmosphere; highlighting the psychological states of characters; providing neutral background filler; building a sense of continuity; sustaining tension and then rounding it off with a sense of closure."[7] Music has many material functions. It regularly has an enormous influence on the pacing of events and 'emphasizing the dramatic line.'[8] David Raksin notes that it was common to enter before the required emphasis with what was called 'neutral' music in the trade,[9] before being more emphatic with the music or making a specific musical effect. Such neutral music has given rise to pejorative descriptions of film music as 'wallpaper' or 'window dressing,' which, perhaps in some cases, is justified. Music regularly performs an instructive role, creating meaning by representing ideas, objects, and emotions. Indeed, it performs a primary role in eliciting emotional responses in the audience and in providing consent and encouragement for the audience's emotional responses.

Without assuming an unassailable cinematic ideal of sound and image in harmony, it should be admitted that in mainstream films, sound is overwhelmingly functional. It works to elide itself as contract more perhaps than any other element of film. Some theorize that we perceive the diegetic world on-screen as an unproblematic reality (on some level),[10] and sound is one of the principal elements that convinces us that the space on-screen is real. After all, one might argue that most sounds in films exist essentially to bolster or 'make real' the images we see on-screen and the surrounding world we imagine. Consequently, when we see faces on-screen talking, we expect to hear what they are saying; when a car drives past, we expect to hear those corresponding sounds. The fact that we hear a representation of those sounds, a convention that allows crisply heard voices and unobtrusive car engine sounds rising and then falling in pitch and volume, but not intruding on the important conversation, underlines just how conventional film sound is. Certainly, this is apparent if it is compared to the sounds recorded from an integrated microphone mounted on a home video camera.

However, having stated this, film sound still retains a principal function: to guarantee the illusionistic world on-screen. Random sound effects used in avant garde films might serve as an obtrusive reminder of the fabricated nature of film sound (and indeed synchronized cinema more generally) and point to our expectation of film sound to be merely a vehicle for the illusions on-screen. Now this is a very different traditional function from that of music in films. Perhaps such a unity of sound effects and music might be approached as moments of aesthetic effect, whereby sound effects are precisely sonic effects, such as the disconcerting noise coming from the attic early in *The Exorcist* (1973). This instance is not simply a sound; it is an emotional effect, more like an emanation from the id, a manifestation of primary psychology. Such opportunities are opened up by the recession of sound's representational function, which frees it to fulfil more in the way of direct emotional and aesthetic roles, in short, making film sound more like, or perhaps even a part of, the musical dimension of films. Consequently, great care can be taken with qualitative aspects of certain sounds—as the sounds have value in themselves rather than merely being conventionally representative of sounds from a small, stereotypical repertoire (a tradition that remains the case in much television production).

Michel Chion describes the new sonic space offered by directional multi-speaker surround sound as a 'superfield' that changes the perception of space and thereby amends the rules for constructing audiovisual scenes.[11] Although it retains much of traditional monaural film, he insists that it is an extension of off-screen space and qualitatively different from previous sonic space. Along similar lines, Philip Brophy uses the term 'acousmonium' to articulate the new tactile and multidirectional space.[12] Chion continues with his description:

> I call superfield the space created, in multitrack films, by ambient natural sounds, city noises, music, and all sorts of rustlings that surround the visual space and can issue from loudspeakers outside the physical boundaries of the screen. By virtue of its acoustical precision and relative stability this ensemble of sounds has taken on a kind of quasi-autonomous existence with relation to the visual field, in that it does not depend moment by moment on what we see onscreen.[13]

This new expanded field is beyond the simple space of dialogue and sound effects, but it is one where their interaction with music might prove to be the key to its organization. This development has inspired new aesthetics. According to Chion, Dolby multitrack favors passive off-screen sound, which works to establish a general space and permits more free movement for shots (more of which are close-ups) within that space, without any spatial disorientation of the viewer-auditor,[14] although there is a corresponding tendency to keep speaking characters on-screen as spatial anchors.

A further part of this process, evident in some films, is the convergence of music and sound effects, with a concomitant collapse of the strict demarcation between the two that reigned earlier. Of course, to a degree, it has always been impossible to fully and clinically separate the musical score from sound effects. Musical scores regularly have mimicked, emphasized, or suggested certain sound effects in the diegesis. Similarly, sound effects in films are regularly more than simply an emanation from the illusory diegetic world constructed by the film. They often have symbolic or emotional valences that outweigh their representational status. Indeed, it might be argued that much music in general has spent a lot of time and energy in attempting to approximate, or at least take inspiration from, the natural world and human ambiences, from birdsong to the rhythmic sounds of machinery. So talking in terms of a solid distinction between the diegetic sound effect and musical accompaniment becomes difficult upon closer scrutiny and deeper thought. However, in terms of film production, there has been a relatively solid divide: Musicians and composers produce music for film, and Foley artists and sound editors are responsible for constructing a conventional series of sound effects to accompany on-screen action. The advent of digital sound technology and the relative accessibility of complex sound-treating equipment had a notable impact on the production process. An early example of this was the development of special sound for *Evil Dead 2* (1987), where the sound of a creaking rocking chair was merged with sound recordings of a scream, using digital synthesizers to fuse the sounds on a genetic level. A more recent example of the process is *Resident Evil* (2002). The film begins with a voiceover narration accompanied by metallic and booming non-musical sounds, leading into a loop of one of the electronic themes Marilyn Manson wrote for the film as the action follows the events of a laboratory accident. Shortly afterward, when protagonist Alice studies what appears to be her wedding photograph, we hear music that sounds like it was composed from various non-musical sound samples, in other words, reorganized and repeated shards of sound effects. Her contemplation is halted abruptly by a nearby door opening. Sonically, this involves a very loud and percussive sound matched to the image of an automatic door. Yet the consistency of the sound is certainly not at odds with the preceding music, firmly supplying the impression of a continuum of organized sound that is able to be more rhythmic and more melodic while retaining a foot in diegetic sound effects and ambiences.

Such a unified field of music and sound effects is evident in a good number of recent films, although this once-marginal tradition might profitably be traced back to an origin in silent cinema, where the live music performed to accompany the film in many cases did the sound effects. This is probably more evident in the film scoring tradition where music will mimic or suggest certain diegetic sound effects, even though they may well be present on the soundtrack anyway. There was a minor tradition of certain sound films having a clear sonic continuum that fully merged music and sound effects. Probably the best example is *Forbidden Planet* (1956), which had a soundtrack of 'electronic tonalities' by Louis and Bebe Barron. For the purposes of film production, this could not be credited as music, and indeed, its origins in recordings of 'cybernetic sound organisms' that were then collaged to fit the film evinces a process far removed from the dominant traditions of Hollywood film scoring. There is a direct confusion over the sources of sounds. Some of the electronic sounds appear to be functioning like incidental music, and some are clearly synchronized with images on-screen (such as the monster, for example). Others appear to be environmental, marking the ambience of the unfamiliar alien planet and adding to the sense of the exotic and uncharted that the film represents. In his study of the sound and music for *Forbidden Planet*, James Wierzbicki notes that this was not an isolated case, and by traversing the membrane of conventional sound functions pointed to a new psychology:

> In contrast [with traditional orchestral scores of the time], electronic sounds in scores for many 1950s science-fiction films were strikingly non-traditional, and thus they tended to blur the long-standing boundary between non-diegetic underscore and diegetic sound effect. Electronic sounds did not simply accompany 'foreign' narrative objectives; in many cases, they seemed to emanate directly *from* them.[15]

Similarly, Alfred Hitchcock's *The Birds* (1963) has a soundtrack that mixes sound effects and music. It contained no underscore in the traditional sense. Instead it used electronic sound design (apparently Herrmann's idea), which was recorded in Munich with experimentalists Remi Gassmann and Oskar Sala. Herrmann, Hitchcock's regular composer at the time, was the advisor, and the final product, while using synthetic bird noises, remains related to the *musique concrète* produced by experimenters like Pierre Schaeffer and Pierre Henry in the 1940s and '50s. *The Birds*' sound design approached music as merely another element of the soundtrack and replaced a musical underscore with sound effects that nevertheless are fairly musical in their inspiration. Although the soundtrack appears to represent bird sounds that match the action on-screen, they were in fact produced electronically and only vaguely synchronized with the birds on-screen. It might be more apt to characterize the soundtrack to *The Birds* as a continuum of ambient bird sounds that are most clearly emphasized in the sequences of bird attacks.

Another film that has a soundtrack that goes beyond simple sound effects and music is David Lynch's *Eraserhead* (1977), which makes particularly harrowing use of ambient sound in the background throughout the film. Alan Splet's sound design collaged industrial sounds, metallic noises, rumbles, and wind into a disturbing and continuous sonic backdrop for the film's action.[16] It is not unchanging and moves to the foreground at times. Arguably, it takes something from the general function of film scores, which provide a sonic backdrop and a vague mood for the action. The fact that these sounds were not easily classified as non-diegetic music meant that they were more satisfactorily accounted for as acousmatic sound effects: the sounds seemingly emanating from some dreadful but indistinct industrial machines somewhere in the distance. Indeed, Alan Splet's sound work was far more than merely recording and compiling sounds for use in films. An available three-disc set, *Sounds from a Different Realm*, showcases Splet's work along with his collaborator Ann Kroeber. Some of the pieces are called "Unusual Presences" and illustrate the construction of nearly autonomous sound environments, some of which were used in David Lynch's films. Despite the collection nominally being a set of sound effects, it manifests more of a sustained, canned atmosphere, rather than being simply recorded sound effects ready for general use.

FILM SOUND AS MUSIC (AND MUSIC AS FILM SOUND)

The effect of a unified field of sound and music is the destruction of conventional use of sound in films, with a concomitant questioning of the relationship of sound to image. Certain contemporary films evince a unified sound design that conceives of the film's sound in holistic terms rather than as the traditionally separate music, dialogue, and sound effects. Miguel Mera and David Burnand note:

> Modernism is inherent in the technologically enabled means of audio production in filmmaking that encourages the alliance of music and sound

design as a recorded and edited form, and thus is at odds with the rehashed nineteenth-century orchestral scores typical of classic cinema, flown into the virtual orchestra pit of the movie theatre.[17]

Such films with a unified sound field deal with it in highly sophisticated terms. Sound effects are not simply about matching what the screen requires to verify its activities. Instead, sound effects can take on more of the functions traditionally associated with music: emotional ambiences, provision of tone to a sequence, or suggestions of vague connections. In short, film sound as a unified field has taken a high degree of its logic from music, and more specifically from music in films in the form of non-diegetic or incidental music. Films such as *7even* (1997) or *Ju-On: The Grudge* (2002) contain notable sequences in which sound could be construed as music or as sound effects. In both cases, the ambiguity is doubtless part of the general effect of the film. In *Donnie Darko* (2001), a voice (belonging to 'Frank') appears in the night, telling Donnie to wake up. This is accompanied by deep ambiguous rumbles and what might be construed as supernatural sounds. It is certainly not easily recognizable as a film score, but it equally fails to identify itself as sound effects for anything in the diegetic world. There is a seemingly organic mixture of diegetic sound and music evident in the London underground-set *Creep* (2004). At the start of the film, one of a pair of sewer workers disappears down a tunnel and as the other searches for him, the soundtrack embraces deep sub-bass rumbles that are ambiguous as to whether they are diegetic or not.[18] As his desperation grows, the music grows in volume, featuring metallic sounds and developing from the deep rumbles into a more clearly organized pattern, and thus more clearly becomes music.[19] Like much of the film, this sequence exploits the dramatic and psychological possibilities of an extended range of bass tones available in 5.1 Dolby sound.

Indeed, since the advent of multi-track recording technologies in the 1960s, Dolby stereo and surround sound in the 1970s, and digital sound technology in the 1980s, soundtracks have become increasingly complex and sophisticated. Elisabeth Weis points to the exponential expansion of sound resources indicated by the number of sound technicians working on recent films in comparison with the number on a film during the heyday of the Hollywood studio system.[20] The division of labor is often quite precise, although the supervising sound editor or sound designer will tend to have dominion over all sonic resources. Many directors have a significant input to the final sonic character of their films, while ones like David Lynch also design the sound for their films. Film soundtracks are constructed with great care and creativity. Any attempt to approach the unified soundtrack as simply sound effects is doomed—to banal results. The only viable approach is from a musical point of view. After all, music has been the science of sound for a very long time, and it is clear that aesthetic impulses are highly significant in determining film soundtracks, rather than merely representational concerns (making sounds match screen actions).

Sometimes it seems easy to forget that for centuries we have had a theory of organized sound relevant to the cinema: music. Music is at heart about organizing sound events in time, and some of its dominant concepts are highly evident in sonic organization in films. For example, the general ambience assigned to a space is conceived as 'backing' to the 'aria' or singing voice of dialogue. A more recent tradition has been concerned with making sound recordings into music: *musique concrète*, which developed in France after the Second World War and was based on the manipulation and distortion of sound recordings on magnetic tape. Although it would be a massive reduction to suggest that it is similar to film sound, there nevertheless are shared points of interest and assumptions. It is hardly fortuitous that the primary theorization of film sound comes from an individual with a background in electroacoustic music and training in *musique concrète*. Michel Chion has introduced a large number of terms and theories from this body of thought and praxis into the study of film. As one of the few areas to deal with sound, often in musical terms, *musique concrète* should be a stopping-off point (however brief) for any analysis of film soundtracks.

SAW'S MUSICAL SOUNDS

The horror film *Saw* (2004) has a highly distinctive soundscape. There is often little solid demarcation between incidental music and sound design; consequently, sound effects can sound synthetic and music can sound like sound effects. The film's sonic elements have a very intimate relationship that marks the film as unconventional, although since the turn of the millennium, it has become more common for films to eschew the dominant convention of music/sound effects/dialogue atomization. *Saw*'s music was written and performed by first-time film music composer Charlie Clouser. Up to this point, he was known for his remixes of existing songs, adapting and rebuilding sonic material rather than creating as such. Hence, it might be possible to approach Clouser's work in the *Saw* films as an adaptation, a partial remix, of the sound world as a whole, rather than merely the music alone. His music in the films is often unmelodic and not immediately memorable or obviously empathetic; it focuses instead on texture and timbre and plays upon confusion between what might traditionally be termed film music and sound effects. The films often wield sound either explosively or in a disconcerting and semi-dislocated manner. Furthermore, *Saw* illustrates the assimilation of new technologies and techniques and the concomitantly different assumptions about cinema's diegetic world and the place of sound in it.

The *Saw* films center on the activities of the Jigsaw Killer, a serial killer who is at pains to threaten or kill people in creative and imaginative ways that are specific to each individual. This involves a high level of invention, as well as meticulous planning leading to a tortuous route of potential escape for the protagonists. The first film starts with two men waking in the basement of a deserted building, both handcuffed securely but with clues about possible escape (and, most significantly, redemption for their sins). *Saw* adopts a striking aesthetic of matching a sumptuous soundscape to what are often overwhelmingly static visuals. Apart from a welter of flashback sequences, the whole film takes place in this one basement room. The soundtrack thus serves to provide variation for the audience and remove the potential for boredom. Although the narrative is gripping, the visuals are often quite pedestrian and the soundtrack's use of unusual timbres and unfamiliar activities compensates for this to a degree. Thus the limited diegetic space inspires a sonic drama, where the aural elements encourage a feeling of space that is denied by the film's visual construction. The claustrophobia of the film is highly effective, but it is enhanced or thrown into relief by a feeling of expanded space in the soundtrack. There is copious use of reverb and echo, which make the film feel like it is taking place in a large arena of emptiness rather than an over-lit basement room. This provides a striking mismatch of claustrophobic visual space with expansive and echo-laden sonic space that is dramatic in itself. Furthermore, it makes for a psychological mismatch between the image track and the soundtrack that is further enhanced by the uncertain status of much of the sound (diegetic sound effect but also non-diegetic music). The limited diegetic space forces the sonic space's elevation in importance to the point where the film's sonic space manifests an expansion of experience and simultaneously a fragmentation of the vaguely coherent subject position of the spectator (as theorized long ago and far away). In *Saw*, the Jigsaw Killer hears (rather than sees) the proceedings throughout, unperceived by the two protagonists. Indeed, the film could be characterized as a 'point of audition sound' acousmonium for him, offering a sonic experience close to ours as the audience. (Could this be seen as an aural development of Hitchcock's *Rear Window* [1954]?) Thus the spectator-auditor position in the film might be construed in this way to furnish the auditory equivalent of the person sitting in the film theatre [21]

The film's music composer Charlie Clouser started off as an electronic music programmer involved in television incidental music before becoming known as a member of the industrial rock group Nine Inch Nails and subsequently as a remixer for many rock groups, producing new versions of recordings with a highly individual stamp on them.[22] Clouser joined the *Saw* project after director James Wan had used a number of Nine Inch Nails pieces in the films' temp tracks.[23] Clouser had been a member of that group in the mid to late 1990s. A background in electronic sound manipulation is advantageous for a film that requires something radically different from a conventional orchestral film score and, indeed, Clouser approached the score in a far from traditional manner. He was interested in using non-musical sounds, such as metallic clashing and banging, "[s]ounds that might have originated in the sound effects. Subconsciously, I think almost sound as though these might be unseen characters to attack, on the other side of the wall.... [There was also a concern with b]lurring the line, and having industrial sounds that spring from the background of the movie [which] might make the viewer less aware of the music as music and that more aware of the general sense of tension and anxiety we were trying to create."[24] Director James Wan wanted to use the score precisely as an effect, for psychological impact rather than merely for emotional impact. Clouser noted: "Usually, I don't try to use sounds that will clash against the sound design—doors slamming, gunshots, things like that. But because of the character of the music that James [Wan] wanted it would involve a lot of metal screeching and banging types of sounds, which were going to get in the way of the sound effects, so it was the skillful mix that kept everything together."[25] While the final mix may accommodate Clouser's sounds, as well as sound effects, it works with similar sonic material in what appears to be a unified field of sound and music. It is little surprise that when asked to list influences on his work, Clouser mentioned Louis and Bebe Barron's electronic sounds/music for *Forbidden Planet*.[26]

The likely main source of *Saw*'s temp track was Nine Inch Nails' 1999 double album *The Fragile*, which included slow atmospheric music, as well as more up-tempo and noisy songs. While Trent Reznor was (and remains) the principal player in the group, Clouser was a mainstay at this point. An indication of Clouser's importance for the textural and ethereal tracks is his credit on the track "The Great Below" for 'atmospheres.' The *Saw* scores are premised upon music as provision of atmosphere, although they might be characterized as a distinct alternation of non-musical sounds and spare synthesizer tones with kinetic mechanical drum patterns characteristic of certain industrial rock groups, particularly Nine Inch Nails. Clouser noted that he used the sections with energetic percussion patterns "...to build adrenaline."[27] These sections include the speeded-up images of a man caught in razor wire and some of the 'reverse bear trap' sequence, in which a character has to beat a time limit to remove a piece of potentially fatal headwear.

While the drum-based passages provide energy, much of the rest of the music is sparsely textured. The type of music Clouser concentrated on focuses on the vertical aspect:

> [Tracks]...usually have a level of density, which is greater than most scoring cues, in terms of the number of things happening and how much attention you have to pay to them to decode it all. That kind of works against a lot of people coming from a record background when they're scoring because they wind up making it sound like a record and it might be too busy or too dense to serve as 'background.'[28]

While many forms of music that work outside the cinema can be reined into films effectively, Clouser points to a concern with momentary texture and the vertical aspects rather than the melodic or developmental. In fact, *Saw* tends to use emotionally cold sound/music throughout, lacking all emotional warmth and expressing partial disconnection. This lack of empathy can be related to Michel Chion's notion of anempathetic music, where mechanical music or music that follows its own logic continues over emotional action without matching the mood of the images.[29] In *Saw*, the connection of sound to images can be vague, and the music provides atmosphere and energy that match screen mood and action, but it refuses to provide anything that connects with the characters on an emotional level, never taking advantage of one of the principal functions of film music, which is to allow the audience to empathize with the characters on-screen.

One aspect of Clouser's score that is instantly striking is the sheer variation of sounds. It utilizes a wealth of electronic tones, as well as sounds derived from samples. However, it is nevertheless scored, in certain ways, in the traditional sense. For example, it uses the deep drones that are conventional to horror films and dramatizes and punctuates the voice of the Jigsaw Killer as it heard on a tape. That Clouser conceived his music in terms of sound elements that would form a sonic foundation for each scene[30] denotes a process closer to soundscape creation than to traditional film scoring. A sound art infusion is further evident in *Saw* in Clouser's copious use of sounds originating from Chas Smith's metal sculptures that were designed to be bowed and scraped to create sounds.[31] Clouser used recordings of these as raw material, manipulated in digital samplers but often retaining their original metallic sonic character.

When the two protagonists notice a dead body lying on the floor between them, there is a revolving shot and close-ups of the body's bloodied head and the gun clasped in its hand. Each shot d is accompanied by a sonic hit, creating a regular rhythmic pulse of sound and image. Matching the dramatic and unusual visual, the sound also acts unconventionally, including some reversed sounds and music alternating between the front two speakers, a rarity in films and a highly obtrusive sonic activity.

When Adam tries to get the tape player from the dead body's hand, there is an echoed drum hit marking and synchronizing the action. In the wake of this, as Adam uses his shirt and a rag to get the tape player, the music moves through a number of fairly distinct sonic passages: a high, falling ethereal monody interrupted by a sound reminiscent of a distant train passing, a short, high-pitched squeaky sound, a deep drone (that sounds like an electronically treated male voice choir), and a brief burst of repeated guitar feedback. Then there is a synchronized metal sound, similar to that of a bowed cymbal, followed by deep echoed sounds (like a large water tank being hit). Sonically, this sequence seems very much a succession that emanates from the ease with which contemporary digital technology encourages the use of sonic loops (particularly from DAWs and their ease of manipulating samples and musical blocks). This is further underlined at the moment when Adam finds a saw in a bag in the toilet cistern, which is accompanied by what sounds like heavily echoed guitar feedback looped and repeated into a single musical figure.

As befits a film with narrative twists and turns and an aura of uncertainty, there are notable sections that lack synchronization between sound and image. Beginning at 38:26, there is a sustained sequence of asynchrony lasting nearly three minutes with only occasional synch points, starting where there is a non-diegetic sound hit to indicate that time has passed from the previous shot of Dr. Lawrence Gordon's daughter being menaced, first by seeing an eye in her open closet door while a voice says, "Goodnight, little girl" (figure 6.1). Next, Mrs. Gordon and her child appear tied up, and there are a few synched footsteps (of Zepp, whose face is not yet visible), while the little girl cries. Then there is a shot of the mother and child with synchronized crying and moaning sounds. Mrs. Gordon says, "Get away from her!" However, the overwhelming majority of this extended sequence is not synchronized. The sustained shots of the tied-up couple from behind, showing Zepp threatening the backs of their heads, has a continuity of crying sounds but fails to continue showing their origin. At 39:58, there is another non-diegetic sound hit signalling a cut to an outside shot (on closed-circuit television) of Zepp looking out the window, which moves

Figure 6.1: *Saw*: "Goodnight, little girl."

Figure 6.2: *Saw*: "Who are you, little man?"

from being on camera to being on a television set with an awkward reframing cut. This is accompanied by a voiceover of uncertain origin: "Who are you, little man? I see you..." (figure 6.2). As the camera pans right from the television set, it alights on a former policeman who investigated the Jigsaw Killer, as he stares out the window of a nearby building. Although we are unable to see that he is the origin of the voice (and the voice's close sound and profound bass tones sound similar to those of the Jigsaw Killer that we have heard on cassette recordings already). At 40:22, the ex-policeman is on-screen and rapidly it becomes apparent that he is the owner of the voice (despite the complete lack of shots that synchronize this voice with his moving lips). At 40:44, a shot of the back of his head exposes a wall covered with newspaper clippings about killings, beginning a substantial montage sequence with the words "I should never have let you go" (figure 6.3). As

[138] *Occult Aesthetics: Synchronization in Sound Film*

Figure 6.3: *Saw*: "I should never have let you go."

the montage sequence takes off, music based on the film's main theme with an insistent beat based on regular eighth notes begins to drive it along, although always ceding prominence to the voiceover and sound effects. This montage includes images of various aspects of the Jigsaw Killer case and Dr. Gordon (many of which we have already seen), including voices both synchronized and unsynchronized, close-ups of newspaper headlines synchronized precisely with the sound of a camera clicking or by an anvil hit, and some vague synchronization of sound and image in the shots repeated from Amanda's tribulation (with the reverse bear trap on her head) from earlier in the film. The montage sequence finishes at 41:22 with a shot of the policeman (before his discharge) and Dr. Gordon in a car, returning the film to a regime of regular synchronized dialogue and standard sound-image relations.

Saw contains sections with only sparse dialogue, which therefore lack the most regular and clear lynchpin of synchronized sound and image. Furthermore, the fact that *Saw* is based on two characters (Lawrence and Adam) chained up in one room allows for dialogue without showing the speaking characters. The audience is aware of the spatial setup and so the camera has more freedom of movement. Chion notes that the development of the sonic superfield has erased the tradition of spatial scene construction in films by losing the requirement for establishing (and re-establishing) long shots, "...because in a more concrete and tangible manner than in traditional monoaural films the superfield provides a continuous and constant consciousness of all the space surrounding the dramatic action... such that the image now plays a sort of solo part, seemingly in dialog with the sonic orchestra in the audiovisual concerto."[32] The sonic aspect of *Saw* certainly evinces much variation, but it also consistently uses sounds of obscure origin, such as drones, scrapes, and loud bumps, all of which could be construed as diegetic sounds but more likely are non-diegetic, lacking any origin in the film world on-screen. The concomitant lack of synchronization in this equation adds up to a degree of mental uncertainty, emphasized by the film for the purposes of horror. At times, *Saw* gives the impression of having a soundtrack with a dislocated nature, at least partially uncoupled from the image track of the film.

PSYCHOLOGICAL SOUND SPACE

Acousmatic sound is essentially ambiguous in that we are not sure of its precise origins.[33] While their origins may become apparent later, in psychological terms, such sounds can mark a distinct uncertainty and a potential threat. In *Saw*, we hear much in the way of metallic sounds that could well have diegetic origins. They certainly don't sound like a traditional film score. But then there is no indication of any diegetic origin for these sounds. They question the status of the diegesis and, significantly, add to a sense of ambiguity of environment by confusion of sound and image. Similarly, there are regular bass rumbles (almost sub-bass rumbles) on the film's soundtrack. Are these diegetic? That information is never furnished by the film. The potentially disturbing effect of such ambiguous sound is discussed by Chion, who points to the essential ambiguity of such sounds. Their origins are immediately obscure, although their source might be understood later. In psychological terms, such sounds are perceived as a potential threat in that they remain uncertain for the listener.

As an aural counterpart to the rare non-diegetic insert,[34] we might wonder if recent cinema is wielding the non-diegetic sound effect, which likely has the same ambiguity as acousmatic sound, although it sounds like it could emanate from the world on-screen, yet it *cannot* be retrospectively understood and placed in the surrounding (diegetic) world.[35] It indeed has lost its synchronization absolutely, in that there is no possibility of its matching the screen world, and thus it manifests an extreme of mental confusion and potential threat. The horror genre has often been premised upon the drama of off-screen space concealing the unknown, such as in films like Hitchcock's *Psycho* (1960). However, in *Saw*, these sounds are not only off-screen, they are 'off world.' They are sounds from nowhere, occupying the same space as the film's non-diegetic music, which also emanates from an obscure space somewhere that is not existentially connected to the world represented on-screen. Now, non-diegetic music is purely conventional and as such does not invite direct questions about its origins. However, sound effects are anchored to screen representations. They provide the spatial and confirming aspects of activities on-screen or nearby still in the diegetic world. From time to time, however, sound effects appear to come from outside the diegetic world, most notably in surreal or horror films. For example, in the remake of *The Fog* (2005), as DJ Stevie Wayne (played by Selma Blair) sits in her car, there are deep, threatening sounds. Their status is ambiguous. They might be part of Graeme Revell's non-diegetic music, or they could be diegetic sounds of the mysterious fog itself. However, in all likelihood, they are non-diegetic sound effects.[36] This appears literally to be an occult aesthetic, yet such general ambiences function emotionally and work to immerse the audience in the film more effectively in sonic terms than might be possible as a visual effect. There are highly effective low-volume continuums, such as Freddy Kruger's basement in the *Nightmare on Elm Street* films, or in spaceships like the Starship Enterprise in the *Star Trek* films and television series. Rick Altman, McGraw Jones, and Sonia Tatroe note that some Hollywood films in the 1930s had continuous low-volume atmosphere sound, which had the function of enveloping the audience in a film's sonic space.[37] Such enveloping is an effect of the extension of sonic space, which is a characteristic of surround sound but also an effect of the degree of reverberation (or reverb) evident on any recorded sound.[38] In audio terms, reverb expresses space as the equivalent of showing it visually. Furthermore, the use of electronic reverb, adding a sense of space around a recorded sound, might be seen as a prime signifier of sound as aesthetic in films rather than following any vague attempt to reflect the space represented visually on-screen. Philip Brophy notes that, "[p]sychoacoustically, reverb grants us an out-of-body experience: we can aurally separate what we hear from the space in which it occurs."[39] This inconsistency of sound space represented on the soundtrack and the expected sound ambience that would have emanated from the space represented on-screen is not only evident in *Forbidden Planet* but also in films like *Saw*. It illustrates a degree of mental separation emanating from the evident mismatch in *Saw* of expansive, reverb-drenched music and sounds with an enclosed and circumscribed visual space. We might go further and approach electronic reverb and echo as a manifestation of a state of mind more than it is a representation of anything. After all, it does not signify diegetic space but something beyond, an emotional and unconscious enveloping of sound. In his discussion of *Forbidden Planet*, Philip Brophy continues:

> Reverb is heavily applied to *Forbidden Planet*'s synthetic sound effects firstly to invoke the expansive opening of interplanetary frontiers, and secondly to invoke an imposing sense of size and space. At least fifteen centuries of European church architecture used reverb to conjure up thundering scale and omnipotent power; sci-fi movies followed suit with their own brand of technological mysticism and God-fearing morality.[40]

So it has nothing to do with representing the world on-screen and more to do with providing an effect and an emotional tone. Annabel Cohen notes that

> The affective quality [of music] is consistent [with the diegesis]; the acoustical aspects of the music are not. Although the affective associations produced by the music seem to belong to the corresponding images, the sounds that produced those associations do not. Somehow, the brain attends to this affective meaning, while ignoring or attenuating its acoustical source.[41]

As noted earlier, the unification of sound effects and music conjoins the distinct psychologies of music and sound effects. The use of electronic echo and reverb marks a *musical* appropriation of sound space, unifying diegetic and non-diegetic sound as a psychological effect more than as a representational counterpart of the images on-screen (and diegesis of recorded voices). Sound theorist David Toop points to the "...attraction to the synthetic mimicry of resonance, the structural potential of delays and the physicality of sound waves in enclosed space has evolved into a wider exploration of time, space and sound...."[42] This quotation may have been aimed at a certain tendency in music, but it is equally applicable to the use of sound in some films, films that are interested, in one way or another, in exploring mental and psychological space. In other words, these films are *about* mental space, enabled by the sonic dimension of the film that is beyond representational functions.

SONIC SYMPHONIES

The close relationship between music and sound effects is highly evident in mainstream films made after the second millennium. DJs and electronic musicians Mike Truman and Chris Healings worked with film composer

Harry Gregson-Williams on *The Chronicles of Narnia: The Lion, the Witch and the Wardrobe* (2005) and *The Chronicles of Narnia: Prince Caspian* (2008). As well as having programming duties and helping Gregson-Williams with digital sounds, they also provided sonic backdrops to his music that were less traditionally musical than related to film sound effects. Healings explains:

> For the first *Narnia*, he wanted all these effects where the girl first walks into the forest, so we used trees creaking, boats creaking, forest noises, cracking ice, wind and so on. We used lots from the Sony Pro Series Sound libraries of sound effects, taking them and running them through Reaktor [software], and mixing them with non-digital sounding pads to create these 'frozen' effects for Harry to lay his orchestra on top of.[43]

Increasing numbers of digital musicians are working in film. An early example of a musician who worked with sound as a raw resource and found his way to the cinema was Brian Williams (usually known artistically as Lustmord). Starting in left-field rock music, some of his early recordings were of specific spaces (such as the Dunster Abattoir in Bangor, Wales, and Chartres Cathedral in France on *Paradise Disowned* [1984]). He worked with the experimental rock group SPK when they were using 'found' metal percussion, and he went on to produce regular recordings that sounded like they were inspired by horror film soundtracks. His 1990 album *Heresy* is seen as inaugurating the 'dark ambient' subgenre, while albums such as *The Monstrous Soul* (1992) make copious use of horror film samples in their nightmarish soundscapes. Over the past decade or so, Williams has worked in Hollywood as a musical sound designer, usually in collaboration with composer Graeme Revell (with whom he collaborated in SPK in the 1980s). Williams's role in films like *The Crow* (1994) was to provide certain sounds and ambiences that can be used in the film or in Revell's score. This suggests a unified sound design that is musical in its origin, as testified to precisely by Williams's screen credit.

A musical approach is meticulous with orchestration of sounds matched by a fundamental concern with sound qualities. Jay Beck notes that "*The Exorcist* [1973] is unique in the evolution of film sound for how it blurred the boundaries between sound effects and music. [Certain distinctive sound effects]...took on the musical function of leitmotifs throughout the film, and their repetition carried an emotional connection to a prior scene."[44] Director William Friedkin had declared a desire not to use conventional musical scoring methods, and some of that function was adopted by sound effects. Beck points convincingly to the overriding interest in timbre that led to highly characteristic and singular sounds in such films. In *The*

Exorcist, for example, the attic sound whose origin we never see was made by mixing sounds of guinea pigs running on a sandpaper-covered board, fingernails scratching, and a bandsaw flying through the air.[45] Although Beck is right to declare *The Exorcist* a unique case, the blurring of the division between music and film sound is far from a new phenomenon. Edmund Meisel, who wrote the prominent score for Eisenstein's *Battleship Potemkin* (1925), was mixing music and 'noises' in the 1920s and '30s. In 1941, Marian Winter noted that

> In his use of percussion instruments Meisel anticipated many effects of sound film; the use of noise—*Geräuschmusik*—was his special interest, and after sound film was an actuality he made a series of six records for Polydor which incorporated various noises into 'effect music'—*Street Noises, The Start and Arrival of a Train, A Train Running till the Emergency Brake is Pulled, Noises of a Railway Station, Machine Noises, A Bombardment* and *Music of the Heavenly Hosts*.[46]

Such atmosphere was rarely pure music in the concert hall sense. Similarly, the sense of integrated sound design is not necessarily simply a development from digital technology and practices. Indeed, there is evidence of this aesthetic approach going back to the earliest years of synchronized sound cinema.

If we remember the basic sound capabilities available in 1931 when Josef von Sternberg's *Shanghai Express* (figures 6.4–6.16) was made, the aesthetic character of the film's soundtrack emerges as all the more remarkable. At this point, films were struggling with recording basic dialogue, and interest in sound beyond this was a rarity. *Shanghai Express* (like a number of von Sternberg's films) evinces an intermittent and powerful sense of dislocation between image and soundtracks. The film contains almost no music, as it was produced at a time when incidental music had yet not established itself as a mainstay of Hollywood sound cinema.[47] A startling sequence takes place near the film's beginning, when the train pulls out of Peking (Beijing) heading for Shanghai. The train is stopped by a crowd of people and animals as it traverses a heavily populated area. This sequence is extremely arresting in visual terms. A mass of lateral movement in the foreground of the frame, consisting of people moving in different directions, is gradually parted by the appearance of the train in the distance of the center of the frame and moving toward the camera. Slowly but surely, the mass of people disperses to reveal the train coming directly toward the camera but subsequently being halted by a cow standing on the tracks. This triggers the interpolation of shots of an old man speaking to the cow, encouraging it to move from the tracks, and the driver of the train regularly

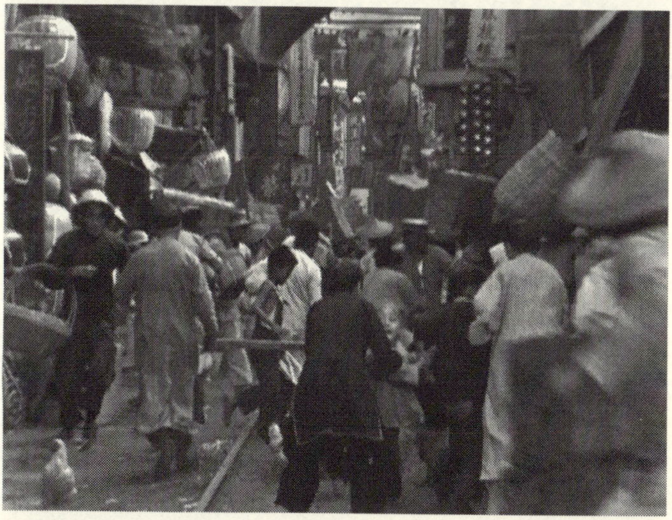

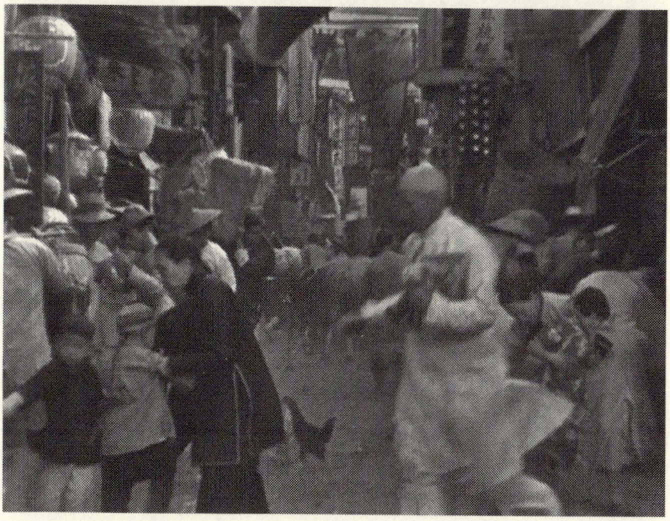

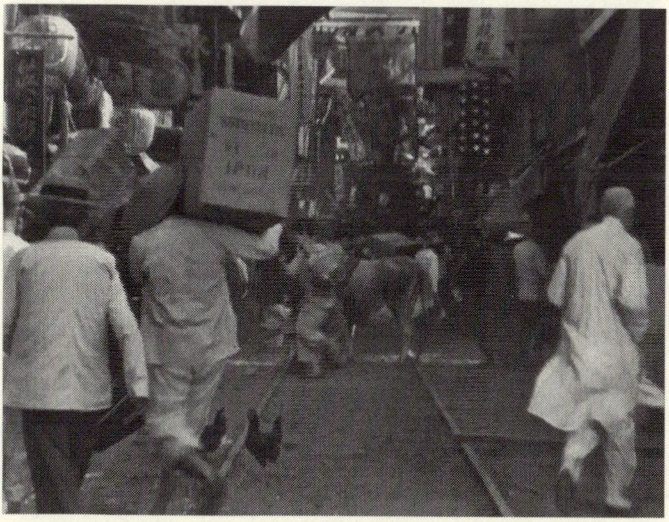

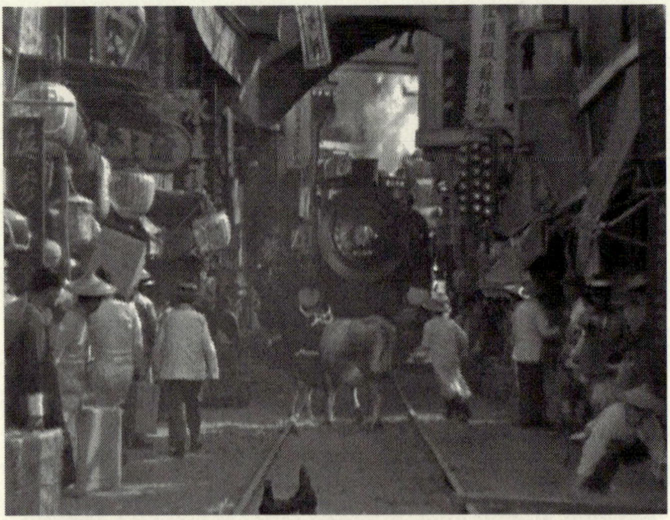

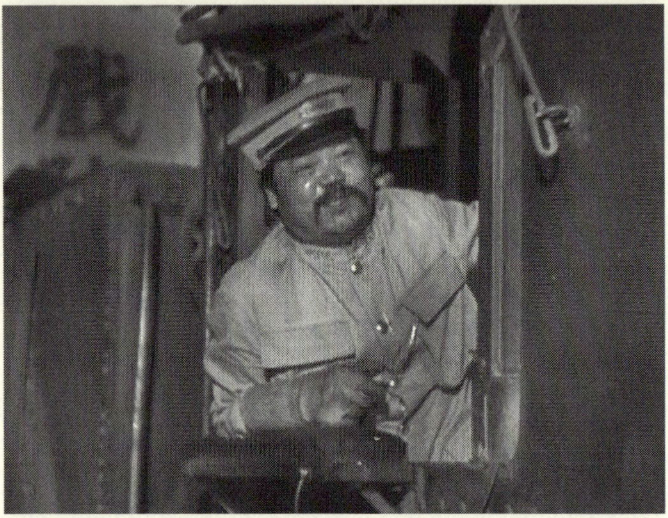

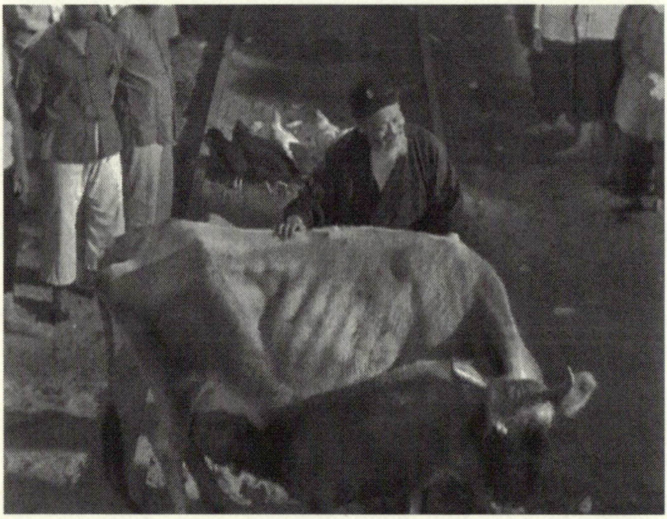

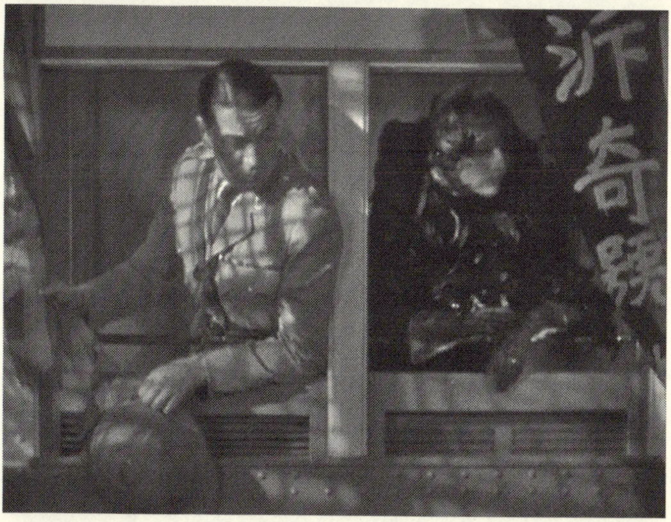

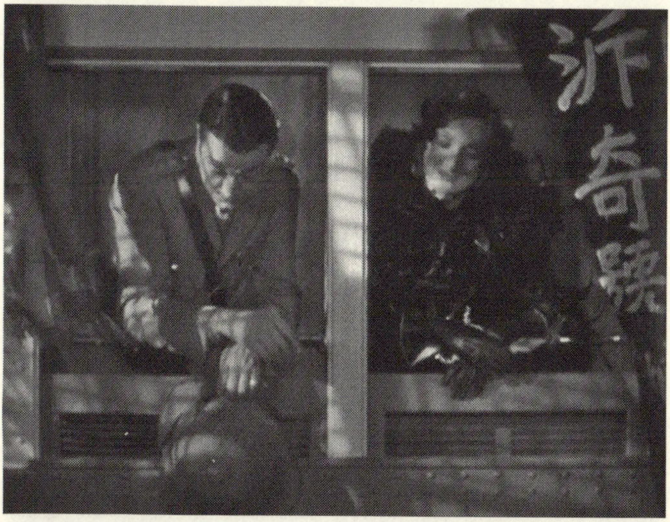

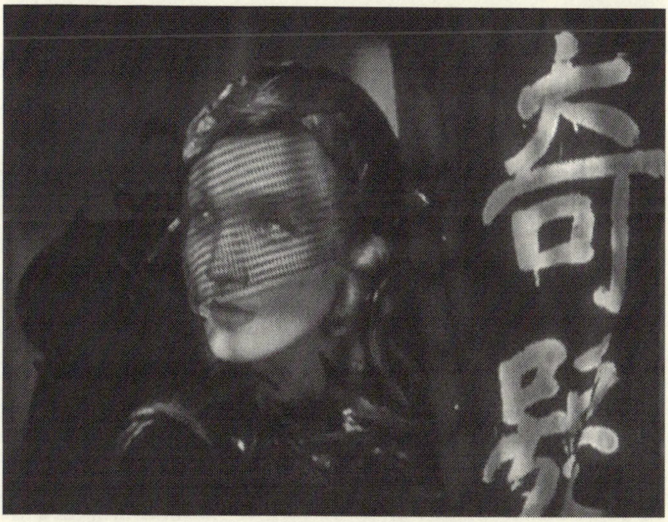

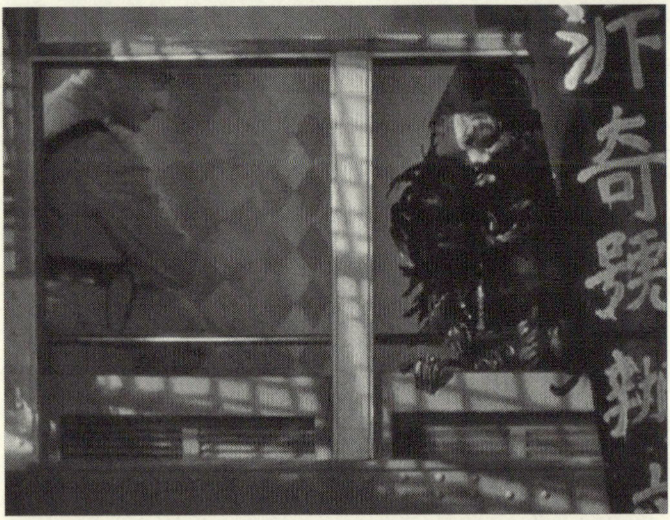

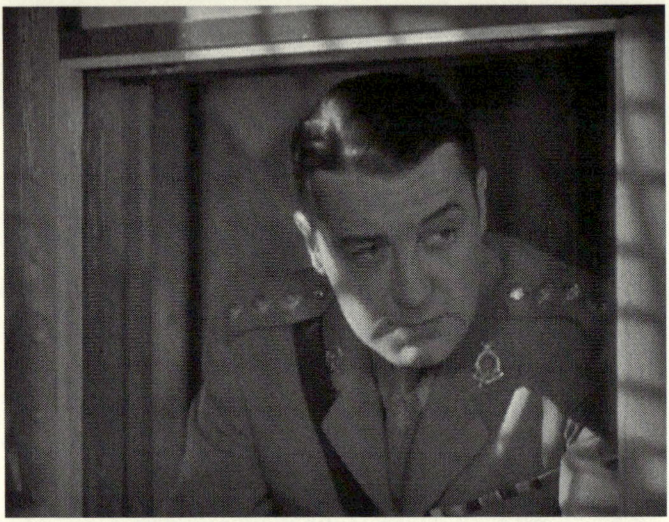

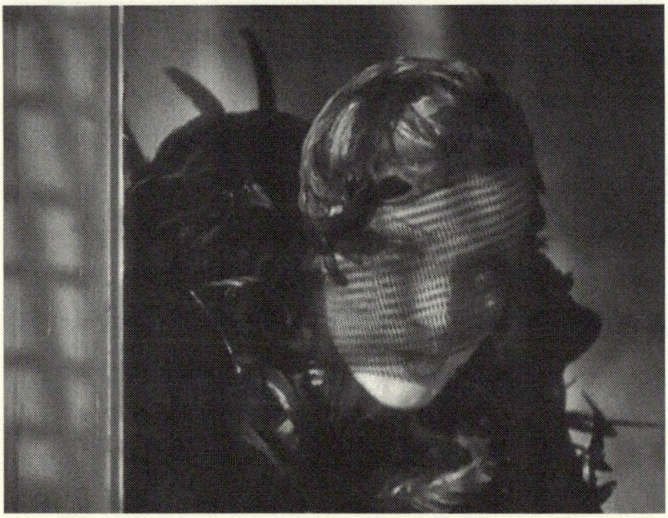

Figures 6.4–6.16: *Shanghai Express* (1931).

blasting the horn. The driver does this impassively without obvious annoyance, and the old man's words to the cow remain untranslated, as words in Chinese (although for the purposes of authenticity, it should be Mandarin, it is actually Cantonese) that for the overwhelming majority of the assumed audience would merely have been textural in effect, and a sign of exotic authenticity. This whole sequence is accompanied by the relentless, slow tolling of the bell on the train. Once the train halts, there is the sound of the steam engine. Whie a traditional analysis of the sequence might look for narrative cues and a sense of development along these lines, this would not account for the sequences in any satisfactory manner. The whole sequence is dreamlike and appears to contain little in the way of narrative information but much in the way of texture and abstraction. Indeed, extended sections of the film seem less interested in meaning in the semantic sense than they are in the play of aesthetics as a path toward internal mental states, or perhaps dream states. One remarkable aspect of the soundscape in this sequence is the repeated sound of the bell. This marks something of a slow rhythmic backdrop, dividing and structuring the sequence temporally. The bell appears as a referent sound, around which all else in the soundfield is keyed. There is a notably slow-paced dialogue scene between Magdalen (Marlene Dietrich) and Captain 'Doc' Harvey (Clive Brook) in a strange succession of frontal two-shots (containing both characters) and shot reverse shots, rather than conventionally intercutting a series of angled shot reverse shots. Some of the shots become closer but many are considerably obscured by pennant flags blowing in between the camera and the two actors. Director von Sternberg was celebrated for his baroque stagings and fetishized framings of Dietrich. He is also renowned for having a propensity for notably slow pacing matched by a sparse soundtrack. This is not to suggest that the film is silent, merely that sounds are often isolated or spaced apart by a lack of other sounds and continued ambient tone. Thus the soundtrack to *Shanghai Express* establishes a sense of quietude, something of the silence evident in dreams perhaps. Von Sternberg's films with Dietrich are all notably dreamlike, and the soundtrack often functions as one of the major contributors to this effect.

The pivotal and defining soundmark of the tolling bell (providing a regular key rhythm, with its iconic inevitability of persistence) in the first sequence and the ensuing literal polyphony of voices make for a rich soundtrack that does not miss the emotional dimension provided by incidental music that would have been the norm later in the decade. To a high degree, I would suggest, this soundtrack is organized in musical terms. While its dynamics remain largely on one level of volume and intensity, it structures a play of contrasts in organization of timbre. There is a distinct character to the timbres of different voices: the slow and deliberate English-accented diction of Clive Brook as Doc, the smoky thick-accented Dietrich as Shanghai Lily (who is also known as Magdalen), pert Anna Mae Wong as Hui Fei, languid and airily pitched Walter Oland as Henry Chang, and the rough and guttural barks of Eugene Pallet as Sam Salt. The contrast is most notable between the languid (Dietrich, Doc, Chang) delivery and the sharper (the more anxious Salt). Indeed, the qualities of Dietrich's voice are an attraction in themselves. The words she enunciates are sometimes hard to make out, yet that matters little as her voice is a sumptuous sonic texture, a timbre as distinctive as Miles Davis's horn or Jimi Hendrix's guitar. Dialogue sequences, rather than being perfunctory, at times clearly play around with sonic alternations and patterns: Dietrich's (and Wong's) non-Anglo-American (for the purposes of the film) diction and articulation, Oland's spurious Chinese accent, and Pallet's brash American Salt as the sonic foothold for the assumed American audience.[48] Clear contrasts exist between languid vocal delivery (Dietrich, Brook, and Oland) delivery and more urgent and angular (Pallet and the French soldier Lenard) delivery.

Apart from dialogue, there is little that is clearly synched to its origin: the horn blasts and the man's words to the cow stand out. Before this, there is a general noise from the crowd and the distant tolling of the train's bell, and then the indistinct rhythm from the static train's steam engine. This all builds a sense of disconnection between sound and image. We are presented with little that is directly synchronized until the dialogue sequence between Shanghai Lily and Captain Harvey, whom she calls 'Doc' in a wooden and unnatural, almost alienated manner. Apart from the ambiguity of multiple names and identities, the dialogue is stilted, befitting the bizarre history the two have as lovers, but more than this, there is a concentrated play upon the timbre of Dietrich's voice and her exotic accent. The film's visual fetishism is matched and sometimes eclipsed by its aural fetishism.[49] As was the case in other significant films of the time, such as *Frankenstein* (1931) and *Dracula* (1931), there are critical passages of silence. Indeed, the advent of synchronized recorded sound cinema allowed the appearance of silence as a structured aspect of films. This embodies an evident psychology of its own, encouraging the audience to be quiet and engage more deeply with the film.[50]

At times, the collusion of sounds mark almost a symphony, a sounding together of disparate elements corralled into a coherent whole. When there is a proliferation of sounds, it is tempting to discuss them as being orchestrated and indeed, they appear to be set out at least partly for their sonic qualities rather than any narrative necessity. Furthermore, such musical strategies as polyphony (the use of many distinct voices, often concurrently) and *klangfarbenmelodie* (the construction of a continuous melodic line through a diverse array of sounds) appear evident. That *Shanghai Express* achieved this with limited sound and synchronization technology, and at a time when basic sound and image relations dominated Hollywood, is astounding. Aesthetic possibilities divert the film, making the its visual structure fluid, in that it is not dependent on narrative and dialogue as agents of progression. *Shanghai Express* clearly illustrates an appreciation of sound beyond its immediate semantic content, most clearly when Chinese is spoken and not translated. This puts the sounds on the side of music (as part of the emotional) rather than as a functional agent of narrative development, and it is one of the reasons why the film has such a unique, dreamlike atmosphere.

CONCLUSION

Of course, music and sound effects have always been mixed despite efforts to keep them separate. Film scores have regularly imitated diegetic sounds (as indeed has music habitually imitated the sounds of nature). However, in recent years, there has been more radical confusion of score and sound effects. These two aspects of film sound, distinct since the coming of synchronized sound cinema, have converged and crossed what once was a fairly impermeable membrane between them. The personnel involved in their production often remain as distinct as in the heyday of the Hollywood studio system, but techniques and hardware have encouraged a convergence. Developments such as this need acknowledgment from those studying film. The increased depth of aestheticization evident in many recent film soundtracks renders many analyses that ignore their nuances little more than naïve descriptions of 'what happens' in those films. Narratological concerns should allow for the fact that sound-dominated films are essentially sensual experiences.

Now, on one level, some of this discussion might seem naïve. Austere music might well sound like sound effects to the uninitiated. I am aware of this—but there is a tradition of sound effects in film (and also in some television, and more prominently in videogames), and these recent scores/soundtracks engage those traditions more than they come from outside (from art music, for example). However, a number of recent films offer very rich sonic landscapes that work on their own independently of their films. This could be traced to the tradition of programmatic music, illustrating vistas and places through sound, a tradition reinvigorated by certain ambient and new-age music. There might also be an influence from sound art, which has been a burgeoning area of the art world over the past couple of decades. It is incontrovertible that the category of music has expanded to include many other sounds: for instance, CDs of natural sounds, not just of singing whales, but recordings of natural landscapes, such as the Global Journey CD *Nature Recordings: Thunderstorm*,[51] not to mention the recorded soundscapes of sonic artists like Hildegard Westerkamp. Such soundscaping has perhaps less to do with any attempt to objectively record a sound environment than it has to do with configuring sound psychogeographically as personal and emotional landscapes. To a degree, this process might also be identified in some films that aim to produce a mental and psychological aural landscape, as is the case in *Saw*, but this was also evident at the birth of sound cinema in a maverick film like *Shanghai Express*.

Freed from a functional role and the diegesis, and freely mixing diegetic sound with music, film sound is able to manifest direct emotion and a primary psychology. The tradition of sound mixing and construction developed by classical Hollywood and influential the world over was premised upon a solid demarcation of sound effects, dialogue, and music, and with a concomitant clarity of purpose for each stratum and the system as a whole. This appears to reflect a sense of clarity of purpose and solid understanding of the relationships between things in the world that marked protean American cinema of the time. By the same token, the collapse of consensus about sonic clarity might reflect social and political developments—perhaps the cultural confusion is a reflection of, or simply emanates from, a social and political confusion. We can speculate about such a reflection, but what is beyond doubt is that there is a remarkable collapse of the *space* between diegetic sound and non-diegetic music. This manifests a collapse of mental space between film's conscious and its unconscious, and perhaps not only between rational and irrational elements in horror films but also in cinema beyond.

Sounds are of interest in themselves and their individual qualities rather than simply affording general semantic value. Pierre Schaeffer's concept of 'reduced listening' encourages a focus on the sound itself instead of cause and meaning (sound as itself rather than as a vehicle for something else).[52] Although film sound offers much in the way of potential sensuality, there is nevertheless a mental search for origins and explanations, inculcated by the very audiovisual nature of film. Some acousmatic sounds pose questions, and on occasion, sounds can detract from diegetic effect and narrative development. In the early 1930s, British documentary filmmaker Basil Wright pointed out that, "Once orchestrated, [any sound] will become as abstract as music. Orchestrated abstract sound is the true complement to film.... It can intensify the value of, say, an aeroplane in flight in a way which natural aeroplane sound could not achieve."[53] His sense was that sound in the cinema was *not* the same as sound outside. We realize this: Sounds of punches and rain, among other things, have to be exaggerated in films, and we should never forget that many sounds are less a direct representation than an aesthetic construction.

Film scores traditionally have mimicked and bolstered sound effects, but increasingly, sound effects have become film music. Music in films has an intimately close relationship with the film's overall sound design: when there is a convergence of sound effects, ambient sound, and music. On the one hand, this might be attributed to the development of digital surround film sound and the corresponding importance of sound design in mainstream films. On the other, though, it might be accounted for by social and cultural aspects outside cinema: There has been a gradual but exponential increase in the degree of ambient sound and music over the past two decades.[54] Increasingly, film sound effects are often used less to bolster a sense of verisimilitude than they are to create an aesthetic effect as, for all intents and purposes, music. Sound design in these films might be understood as essentially musical in nature, following a musical logic rather than any other.

CHAPTER 7

'Pre' and 'Post' Sound

The cliché of the pianist playing a tune while delivering dialogue was a characteristic film phenomenon in the 1940s. *Casablanca* (1942) and *To Have and Have Not* (1944) had convincing pianists. Films such as *Dangerous Moonlight* (1941, U.S. title: *Suicide Squadron*) were less credible, with Anton Wallbrook's concert pianist-fighter pilot perched at the keyboard often facing the camera in order to avoid a close-up of inappropriate hand movements as he declaimed. Unconvincing pianists on-screen can undermine the illusion of a film's unity of sound and image. The problem was, of course, that filmmaking conceived of such piano playing as merely an incidental part of the action, of little importance. However, such details can be among the most important determinants in furnishing a sense of unity and illusion. Anticipation can look fake, as can exaggerated and out-of-time movement. More convincing performances (such as in Sam Peckinpah's *Bring Me the Head of Alfredo Garcia* [1974]) live less long in the memory than the less convincing (British film *Love Story* [1944]).[1] Considering these sequences discloses not just the illusionism central to cinema but the logic of connecting sound and associated image as an assumed source, as an organic cause-and-effect unity, one that was filmed and recorded as a single pro-filmic event.

Most sound in films is post-synchronized one way or another. Almost all music in films is added in post-production, most commonly a musical score. Since the earliest days of synchronized sound films, there has also been a process called 'tracking,' whereby library music (also known as stock music) or other existing music can simply be added to film footage in post-production, on occasion with little care for the precision of image and sound coherence exhibited by films that have music written to fit their precise dynamics. Sometimes films can shoot to music that defines the staging and decoupage of a sequence, as in film musicals, and sometimes film can be cut to music added in post-production. Although much music and sound appear to be synchronized to moving images on film, with the corresponding assumption that image and sound were created at the same time (or that music was created as a secondary supplement to the prime images), the reality of film production is often far from this. Animated films, for example, tend to record the soundtrack first so that it may be used as a guide for the actual animation. Achieving things the other way around is much more problematic, although far from impossible. Sound and music might predate a film and provide a blueprint for its staging, shooting, and editing or, as in most cases with sound and incidental music, they can be added onto a film that is, conceptually at least, not too far from being a finished product.

This chapter considers pre- and post-production sound, addressing the various conventional forms and degrees of synchronization in circulation. The opening section of this chapter looks into lip-synching, where screen actions are matched to preexisting sound and music. In these cases, the correspondence of image and sound is at the behest of the primary element: sound. Subsequently, this chapter considers the reverse of the lip-synching: dubbed dialogue, which replaces an original voice with another and emphasizes the artificiality of the audiovisual lock of sound cinema. Generally, this chapter addresses some of the practices that work against a notion of sound 'belonging' with its corresponding image and maintaining an organic relationship. Although we tend to perceive sound and image as a seamless unity, both pre- and post-synch sound are not fused organically with the image. Instead, the unity is formed in the moment of confluence and illustrates not only Michel Chion's notion of synchresis but also how far audiences are willing to accept sounds and images that do not belong to each other as unproblematic composites.

Synchronizing images to preexisting music involves the cutting of images to sounds or staging events in front of the camera to existing sound recordings (and in many cases both). On the other hand, post-synching of sound to images involves dubbing of voices and adding music later (as is the tradition in mainstream film scoring). While preexisting sound matched by images tends to be highly integrated, as sound dominates and image movements are motivated by sonic activity, it contains a grain of the uncanny. The regular lack of corresponding sound space between sound and image is highly conventionalized, but it can be disturbing if used in a manner that normally might require a realistic (a different convention) relationship of image and its attendant sounds. Similarly, there is also the slight potential for anticipation of the sounds by the images, where the staging of movements to fit the sounds might overeagerly preempt the sounds by a fraction of a second.

Post-synchronized sound might initially seem to be far less integrated than the norm: Voice dubbing often involves a lesser or greater degree of mismatch. Sometimes this involves anticipation but more often comprises lateness and failure to matching with any precision. Similarly, film scores can be loose in their relationship to actions on-screen, although there is a tradition of being perhaps too precise, embodied by Mickey Mousing, whereby actions are mimicked crassly with precise synchronization by the music. The use of preexisting music as a score can often go unnoticed. However, in certain cases (such as when pop songs are used as a non-diegetic score), the organization of the images bears closer relationship to the structure and texture of the music than to any notion of the film as an object with its own logic beyond music.

In these regimes of synchronization, the *gap* between seeing and hearing can be the defining aspect. The width of the gap is crucial, as is how far it can give without losing a sense of synchronization. In some cases, the loose bond can stretch impressively and the degree of give contained in the seeming unity of sound and image is proven to be highly robust and of momentous tensile strength. Michel Chion notes the difference in speed of cognition between the faster sound and the slower image.[2] The key to each approach is convention, permitting a wide variety of relationships to remain acceptable. Mainstream films by and large aim for a kind of sonic naturalism (as discussed in previous chapters) that arguably has come to fulfill Eisenstein's fears about the potential for sound in films to be reduced to the production of what is, in effect, filmed stage plays.[3] Rick Altman characterized the talkie as ventriloquism, with sound and image merely reproducing dialogue and prescribing standard visual style.[4] For many films, this remains the norm. This 'zero degree' style of sound cinema (the dominant, unremarkable conventions of sonic naturalism) is the format that goes unnoticed as seemingly natural in its overwhelming prevalence and simplicity. Proceeding from this zero degree style of sound cinema, this and the following chapter look at points of divergence from this norm.

Up to this point, the book has dealt with the process of movement between synchronized sound and images and asynchrony as a general process. This chapter encounters a number of strategies that, while not abrogating the dynamic, maintain distinct agendas of their own. The articulation of sound and image around synch points can lead to different economies of synchronization, whereby particular approaches yield idiosyncratic schemes of audiovisual unity and disunity. Rather than simply oscillating between simple synchronization and asynchrony, as described and investigated previously, some of the formats under discussion in this chapter are defined absolutely by their approach. For instance, the use of playback or so-called lip-synching in film musicals retains a constant synchronization (and for dance it is only slightly less). This chapter illustrates the strategies that often (although not in all cases) become *sustained* regimes of synchronization, and in the process mark a break from the convention of movement between synchronization and asynchrony. Indeed, each method of matching audio and visual detailed here is an exception one way or another (determined by genre, aesthetic approach, director's individual method, or cultural transformation) to the dominant modes of mainstream dramatic cinema.

LIP-SYNCH PLAYBACK

The influx of synchronized recorded sound to films in the wake of *The Jazz Singer* (1927) amazed audiences and enthralled them with the illusory synchronization of the images and voices of actors. It was hardly surprising that musicals should be one of the first film genres to boom in the earliest years of sound cinema. They were relatively easy to make and quite quickly had the option of a musical recording being played back for the actors to mime rather than relying on the vicissitudes of awkward dialogue recording on the set. In *Singin' in the Rain* (1952), much jollity is made of the turmoil caused in Hollywood by the arrival of the talkies 25 years before the film's release. Indeed, the film is illustrative of the absurdity of the illusion that lies at the heart of sound cinema. Successful silent actor Don Lockwood (Gene Kelly) attempts to rework his currently scheduled silent film as a synchronized sound film. When the finished product is screened, it has a comic effect on the audience members, who are driven into paroxysms of laughter by the use of melodramatic silent acting allied to repetitious and inane dialogue by the sound film format. The utter humiliation of Don and his attempt to cross over to sound films arise when the film falls out of synch and the audience is confronted with visual events made ridiculous by inappropriate dialogue and sounds. The film appears less interested in the disjunction of voice and image than in the comic effects of the inappropriateness of matched word and action. Of course, *Singin' in the Rain* bases this sequence on an apparently common occurrence in the early years of sound cinema that was particularly regular before the ousting of Vitaphone's sound-on-disc by the sound-on-film process: that of losing sound and image synchronization.

Figure 7.1: *Singin' in the Rain* (1952).

While interested in the disruption of synchronized sound and the process of early sound films, *Singin' in the Rain* is also concerned with voice and image synchronization in the form of the convention of lip-synching or playback. This is dramatized when Lina Lamonte's (Jean Hagen) inelegant voice is dubbed by Cathy Selden (Debbie Reynolds) (figure 7.1). However, the voice that we hear is not Debbie Reynolds's but rather Jean Hagen's. The film's final song, a version of the film's title song, appears to be sung on stage by Lina while it is lip-synched live by Cathy who is singing from behind a curtain as the former mimes.[5] However, in reality it is again not Reynolds's voice, as all her songs in the film were actually sung by Betty Noyes, who never appears on-screen.[6] So, not only does the film lie to us, it also tricks us with double-bluffs. With perception, Carol Clover notes that

> So wide is the gap between what *Singin' in the Rain* says and what it does that one is tempted to see a relation between the two—to see the moralizing surface of *Singin' in the Rain* as a guilty disavowal of the practice that went into its own making.[7]

The film's dramatization of its own deception illustrates a live process that can be similar to its screen counterpart. Some musical performers have had recourse to using live vocal doubles, although in more cases, they utilize playback recordings to which they can mime. Perhaps the most celebrated case is that of Whitney Houston at the opening ceremony for the 1991 Superbowl, as elucidated by Steve Wurtzler in his article named after the official explanation ("She Sang Live but the Microphone was Turned Off").[8] The concluding song of *Singin' in the Rain* very self-consciously indicates that the audience should be aware of artifice, and that popular culture objects like the film they are watching not only employ such modes of deception, but also playfully inform their audience of the fact that traditional musical films are made by filming actors miming to a playback of a sound recording.

Although *Singin' in the Rain* might be approached as an exception to the mainstream classical musical in some ways, it also exhibits more traditional procedures of song synchronization. Songs such as the iconic sequence of Don singing the title song as he dances in the rain entail him bursting into song accompanied by an invisible orchestra, while the concluding version of the same song mimed to by Lina appears as if it is a real recording of a song being performed live. In previous writing, I suggested two terms to differentiate between means of visual accompaniment to a song or dance sequence in musicals.[9] I used the term 'performance mode' to designate an attempt to express an ineluctable connection between images seen and sounds heard, indicating where images appear to confirm the *production* of simultaneous sounds. Moving away from this, sometimes images show only some of the music's production. The clearest example of this would be the bursting into song of the integrated film musical, for which I used the term 'lip synch mode,' deriving from the industrial process of matching the lips to a preexisting musical playback. Both the performance mode and the lip synch mode offer a greater or lesser degree of the experience of the performers of the song or dance for the implied audience. The performance mode references a documenting of 'the real,'[10] while the lip-synch mode tends to signify a hyperbolic move to 'fantasy,' the former being associated particularly with backstage musicals and the latter with integrated musicals such as *Seven Brides for Seven Brothers* (1954) or *South Pacific* (1958). Like many musicals, the film of Andrew Lloyd Webber's *Phantom of the Opera* (2005) mixes the two, with operatic arias sung in public at the opera house using the performance mode and songs sung intimately between characters using the lip-synch mode. As this description suggests, the two modes often work in different manners, with the former more amenable to use in mainstream dramatic films and the latter indicating a traditional integrated film musical. Indeed, the performance mode is a valid description of the filming of live performances in music documentary films like *The Last Waltz* (1978) with The Band or *Some Kind of Monster* (2004) with Metallica, or isolated musical performances in dramas, such as Lauren

Bacall singing *Sob Sister* while leaning on a piano at a party in *The Big Sleep* (1945). Perhaps a more recent instance of this would be Bill Murray singing karaoke at an apartment in Tokyo in *Lost in Translation* (2003). While the lip-synch mode has traditionally signified the genre of the film musical, there have still been isolated cases where its non-realistic aspects have graced films that follow less fantastic traditions than the musical. In most cases, however, it aspires to fantastical effect to a lesser or greater degree. In Bollywood and other popular Hindi films, there is a strong tradition of including fantastic songs using the lip-synch mode, which does not mean that these films should be approached using the body of thought accrued around the classical musical, although the similarities should not be disregarded. Bollywood film production focuses notably upon the song playback, using famous (indeed, very identifiable) singers whose sounds are then lip-synched by a different person on the screen. Such a situation is perhaps a rarity in mainstream Hollywood films, unless, of course, the film happens to be a biographical film or biopic about a famous singer, like *What's Love Got to Do With It* (1993), which starred Angela Bassett as singer Tina Turner. The songs Bassett appeared to sing were re-recordings completed for the film by Turner herself. The situation blurs slightly when it comes to some other musician biopics. Val Kilmer not only made a highly effective Jim Morrison, but he also did some of his own singing for Oliver Stone's *The Doors* (1991). Indeed, it is challenging to tell which of the singing is Kilmer's and which is Morrison's. The same goes for Andy Serkis as singer Ian Dury in *Sex & Drugs & Rock & Roll* (2009), where he sang Dury's songs throughout the film. A similar process also took place with *Control* (2007), the British biopic of the short and tragic career of Ian Curtis, the singer for Joy Division. Actor Sam Riley sang some of Curtis's lines in certain songs performed in the film while the group playing musical backing at times was clearly not Joy Division. There is some veracity in this artifice, though. Joy Division's studio sound was highly singular, whereas they sounded more generic when live, and it is in the film's live performances that the reality of Joy Division's sound is replaced by the reality of the actor's performance.[11]

In David Lynch's *Wild at Heart* (1990), Nicholas Cage (as Sailor) was originally going to mime to Elvis Presley songs but ended up actually using his own voice as it fitted the songs well enough. *Wild at Heart* broke one of the cardinal rules of serious mainstream cinema in that it borrowed directly from such a stylized and unrealistic form as the film musical. On a couple of occasions, the film indulges the audience with almost comic song moments (within the context of a film that at times has a tone of extreme gravity) that owe much to film musicals. Indeed, the film's opening appeared to be a denial of audience expectations. David Lynch had just come to some popular prominence due to the success of his television serial *Twin Peaks* (1990–91). Almost as if he wanted to deny the quirky and good-natured aspects of that program, the film opens with one of the most violent sequences imaginable, when lead character Sailor smashes another character's head repeatedly on a marble stairway. This violent action is synchronized to fast, rhythmic, thrash metal riffs. Such a heavily punctuated guitar-based rhythm is highly effective in an action sequence because it is particularly well-defined structurally, making for emphatic beats as quarter notes with regular 16th notes muted in between. At the time of *Wild at Heart*'s production, such music was almost never used as an accompaniment to action, but there has been a growing number of instances of its use in films, such as in the attempted rape scene in *Alien3* (1992).[12]

There are notable moments when *Wild at Heart* adopts the disposition of a film musical, although these are isolated occurrences. In the first musical sequence of the film, Sailor and girlfriend Lula (Laura Dern) are at a dancehall where the group Powermad is playing. Their fast, kinetic thrash punk inspires Sailor to do some energetic and gymnastic dancing. He then has a confrontation with another man and a potential altercation ends up being only narrowly avoided. The band has stopped playing and the focus is firmly on the confrontation between the two characters. Immediately after this, Sailor climbs up onto the stage with Powermad. They commence playing the Elvis Presley song "Love Me" and he provides the lead vocals for the song, singing directly to Lula who is standing in front of the stage. Little attempt is made to hide that this is a playback recording, even though it uses the performance mode and could be presented as if it is a real event. Although the sequence is not comic, it has an unmistakable sense of the ironic through its recourse to a technique distinctive of the more fantastic musical format. In terms of musical strategy, *Wild at Heart* goes further. At the conclusion of the film, after Sailor has walked away from Lula and his young son, he is beaten up by a gang of youths, and a fairy then appears to him, floating in the sky. Although the film has included some strange moments, this is unprecedented. The fairy tells him to return to his family, and Sailor runs through the street and catches up with them, whereupon he climbs onto the roof of a car and sings "Love Me Tender," another song associated with Elvis Presley. This song sequence follows the strategies of the traditional integrated musical form, where a character bursts into song with no musicians present (what I have termed the lip-synch mode). The musical backing is thus non-diegetic, like a musical score, while the singing is diegetic, like dialogue. There is a shift of audiovisual regime, via an audio dissolve,[13] where the dominant strategies of narrative cinema recede to be replaced by the modes of the film musical.

This sequence seems contradictory, as the rest of the film does not involve techniques that are associated so directly with the fantastical and stylized film musical. Indeed, some sections of the film appear to aim for quite hard-hitting impressions of the real rather than the stylized, particularly in terms of the aforementioned sequence of violence at the film's opening. However, in some ways, the "Love Me Tender" sequence fits the continued and exaggerated representation of emotional extremes that is a feature of *Wild at Heart*, and of course, music is a primary signifier and means of expressing extreme emotion in the cinema. These sections of the film come across as clear fantasy more than other sections, and they aim to engage with the golden age of Hollywood, both in terms of the referencing the film musical's aesthetic format and in terms of its dream factory optimism, a rarity in post-classical Hollywood films.

The "Love Me Tender" sequence at *Wild at Heart*'s conclusion embodies a not-uncommon trend in films that has become more prevalent in recent years, that of 'pre-fitting' a film, whereby existing recordings are integrated and visual sequences are filmed to fit them while they are being played back. Such playback sequences bear a notable resemblance to music videos and arguably mark one of the most obvious points of cross-fertilization between films and music videos. Such musical sequences can often take the form of a set piece and retain a notable demarcation from the rest of the film, like traditional film musical song sequences. An early example along such lines would be Charlie Chaplin's song and dance sequence near the end of *Modern Times* (1936), where he broke the film's defiant strategy of sonic limitation to incidental music and some featured sound effects, allowing the audience to hear his singing voice. A more recent example would be the dance competition sequence at Jackrabbit Slim's in *Pulp Fiction* (1994), where Vincent (John Travolta) and Mia (Uma Thurman) dance to Chuck Berry's "You Never Can Tell." Both sequences involve only diegetic sounds but remain distinct set pieces that are a reminder of the nomadic modes of the film musical, as well as making for integral sections that can easily be excised for publicity purposes.

The key ingredient of this process arguably takes place in the shooting of the sequence, where synchronization is aimed at by the actors. Music, however, is the primary object, seeing as it already exists and thus compels the film's visual aspects to cohere around its material aspects rather than vice versa. In discussing Fred Astaire's singing and dancing, Alan Williams notes: "The phenomenological effect is that the visuals become in some way an extension of the song. Astaire's body is not given as the point of origin of the music, but rather as the *sign* of the origin of the music, which thereby seems to emanate from the whole image."[14] Indeed, the process of pre-fitting casts the images as subordinate to the song or piece of music, which, to a lesser or greater extent, is interpreted by the staging and cutting of the images. The simple process of synching image and sound appears to signify or give an impression of 'the real' in films, yet the use of conventions connected to film fantasy in more dramatic contexts can prove to be innovative but also disruptive.

Overall, pre-fitting films by starting from the music can permit music to dominate, as in the case of film musicals, where the visuals are staged to fit preexisting sounds, namely the song recordings. The fact that music dominates the production in such sequences proves that this is in fact the *most* integrated that sound and image can be: retaining a regular sense of synchronism.[15] However, there is nonetheless the persistent potential for a mismatch of precise synchronization of sounds to their seeming origins on-screen. This can become an uncanny effect of nearly preempting sounds with corresponding movements. Miming actors might anticipate the sounds or music, a situation that readily can be identified in cheaply produced playback sequences. One of the clearest examples of this on British television was the BBC's *Top of the Pops* (1963–2006), a parade of best-selling records where singers and musicians with a few notable exceptions mimed to their records. In similar modestly budgeted films, such as the music revue *Gonks Go Beat* (1965), musicians' actions are not well matched to the recordings they attempt to visually accompany.

A fundamental issue in relation to the use of playback is how far the sequence aims to reproduce a performance that appears to be real (performance mode) or one that expresses fantasy (lip-synch mode). The former strives to convey the reality of the performance, particularly in the face of widespread and understood falsification of live performance.[16] The visual elements, most notably the style of camerawork and editing, function as guarantors of the reality of the event more than the sound. For instance, while accompanied by non-diegetic music, Fred Astaire's dances invariably entail little cutting and the consistent use of a full-stage 'tableau' long shot, in order to establish the space within which the reality of performance can take place.[17] Although it might be a moot point as to how much and what level of reality is present in such sequences, there is nevertheless an appeal to the camera and microphone as devices that capture an event. As an aesthetic of recording action, the use of long takes with synchronized sound guarantees the veracity of the event as transmitted. The key with playback sequences is the *staging* of visuals to complement an existing musical recording, expanding the notion of choreography beyond planned movement to embrace facial and bodily expression, as well as camera movement.[18] Central to such pre-fitting of film with music is that filmmakers (directors, music editors, sound designers, etc.) often maintain a strong concept of what is required from their knowledge about the music that will be used to animate the sequence.

MATCHING EXISTING MUSIC

The use of preexisting music in a film is known in the industry as 'tracking' and can take place with library music, written especially for use in films for general moods, or recordings of music that were not intended for use in film.[19] The preponderance of recordings used in mainstream films are instrumental classical music or jazz, or pop songs; in many cases, they are used as non-diegetic music, as a replacement for a specially written score to fit the film's requirements. In some cases, the film fits the music's requirements and there is a persistent feeling that these might less be films with musical accompaniment than they are music accompanied by images that to some degree might be seen as emanating from the sonic original. While pop songs are common in mainstream films, on occasion, classical music has been used as non-diegetic music, and the images can become choreographed to the rhythmic and dynamic patterns of the piece used.[20] A fine example is the renowned use of the Strauss waltz *The Beautiful Blue Danube* accompanied by the slow, graceful images of spaceships gliding in slow motion in Stanley Kubrick's *2001: A Space Odyssey* (1968). Initially, this might seem highly incongruous but in filmic terms, the images lack a sense of much movement and this is provided by the music.[21] The regime is not fully synchronized and lacks regular synch points, although the decoupage and staging are clearly dictated by the requirements of music more than anything else. In discussing *2001: A Space Odyssey*, Claudia Gorbman notes the sense of dislocation between music and images in Kubrick's "audio-visual choreography" of this sequence, commenting that both Michel Chion (music is "outside") and Royal S. Brown (a "parallel emotional/aesthetic universe") also indicate a lack of integration in the highly successful sequence.[22]

Kubrick's *The Shining* (1980), like his earlier *2001: A Space Odyssey* and *Barry Lyndon* (1975), predominantly used a soundtrack of preexisting pieces of music.[23] While it appears that these pieces were not played on set,[24] their place in the final product is prominent to the point of dominance. Kubrick had commissioned Wendy Carlos to provide a score for the film but then rejected almost all of it in favor of his selection of art music pieces, only some of which were used as the temp track for the rough cut of the film.[25] These pieces of music excerpted from larger pieces are dominated by dissonant and austere sounds, ranging from Béla Bartok's "Music for Strings, Percussion and Celesta" to Krzysztof Pendrecki's "Dream of Jacob." Although some of the pieces were adapted, cut, remixed, and combined for the film's requirements, they nevertheless have a significant impact on the sense of structure and articulation of elements in the image track, and perhaps to a lesser degree on the other elements of the soundtrack. It is difficult for a film to accommodate such pieces without adaptation.[26] The tendency is for such music to inspire the film's editing to cohere around the rhythms of the music, or for the action to be matched in a manner that makes it appear as if it had been staged and choreographed to the music. A good illustration of this in *The Shining* is the sequence where Jack Torrance (Jack Nicholson) is enraged after his wife accuses him of hurting their son. He walks toward the back-pedaling steadicam camera operator in one of the shorter corridors of the hotel (figure 7.2) and makes vigorous and violent arm movements, which ape but do not temporally match the stabs in the music. One violent movement is accompanied by a musical *sforzando* that appears like a classic horror film stinger chord. Other arm movements, however, are not matched by musical stabs. Yet more *sforzandi* appear in the music, disconnected from the action and seemingly out of synch, at least potentially. This is a bizarre and singular effect. It is like Mickeymousing knocked out of whack. This partial recognition of a well-worn and clichéd technique proves erroneous. Techniques here serve to disorientate the audience, partially through film syntactic disjunction but also through ambiguities about synchronization.

Figure 7.2: *The Shining* (1980).

This sequence inculcates the impression of the world out of synch. Indeed, Kubrick subtly follows such strategies of audience disconcertion throughout the film. One notable moment along these lines is the dialogue scene between Jack and Grady in the toilet, when the 180 degree line is traversed by the camera in the midst of a conventional shot reverse shot sequence. This breaks one of the cardinal rules of spatial continuity in cinema and has the effect of 'misusing' the audience's understanding of spatial conventions. Jack appears (following the expectations set up by continuity) to move positions from left to right. Of course, this is a significant moment in the narrative's progression, and such supernatural/psychological ruses are central moves in the film's development.

One memorable sequence involves Jack going to room 237, and the ensuing sequence is almost devoid of diegetic sound, instead containing loud music.[27] At times, the dislocation of the sound and image tracks works as a psychological effect. The sequence just described is highly unnerving, with events unfolding in a slow and almost dreamlike manner, while the music involves regular bursts of sound building to a slow pulse that is not synched with anything apparent on-screen. Perhaps one reason for the effectiveness of the music in this sequence specifically and in the film more generally is its relationship to primary physical aspects, notably the body's sound functions. The human heartbeat is homologized by regular intermittent blasts of musical and diegetic sound, including Danny's pedal car's alternation between the sounds of the floor and the carpet as he pedals down the endless corridors of the Overlook Hotel, and Jack rhythmically bouncing a ball against the wall. The heartbeat as part of the film's non-diegetic sound is most prominent when Jack meets the woman in room 237.[28] While this appears to unfold in slow motion, the soundtrack contains no corresponding diegetic sound and instead has a musical heartbeat that implicates a nervous audience in the body of the film (this appears to be a hangover from Wendy Carlos's almost totally rejected score). As a complement to the film's doubling of our own deep body sounds, we also hear a high-pitched whine not dissimilar to the sounds produced by our nervous systems. This is evident in the Ligeti and Penderecki pieces, although they have been sonically enhanced for the film. Such physical aspects are not necessarily rarities in music, which is often more organic (or at least more organically inspired) than many often realize. Here, the sound and music manifest in metaphorical form the beating heart and subjectivity of the film, as well as its nervous audience, suggesting an external force to the images (the evil in the hotel?).[29] The reuse of existing music usually does not allow for exceptionally precise synchronization. The sense of coalescence has to come from the overall tone of the action, music, and editing process.

The Shining's use of existing music derives from the filmmaking tradition of applying preexisting recordings of music as library or stock music, when off-the-shelf musical cue recordings are simply edited into film rather than having a composer manufacture a specially written score. It was not uncommon for Hollywood studios to cut up music from a film to facilitate the reuse of it in other (often lower prestige) productions. Perhaps the best example would be the use of edited sections from Franz Waxman's music for *The Bride of Frankenstein* (1935) in the adventure serials *Flash Gordon* (1936), *Flash Gordon's Trip to Mars* (1938), and *Flash Gordon Conquers the Universe* (1940), as well as in other films of the time. Originally, this cheaper form of film music construction was the domain of low-rent film productions, but in recent years, its status appears to have changed. Robynn Stilwell and Philip Powrie's edited book *Changing Tunes: the Use of Pre-Existing Music in Film* is dedicated to the prevalent use of existing recordings of music in films, as either non-diegetic or diegetic music.[30] It demonstrates that, although far from new, the process of using preexisting music in films has become a cultural norm and prevailing practice in recent years, with both pop songs and art music. Although some might be concerned with the potential jeopardy to the cultural status of some pieces of art music, there is not much concern with how existing music and new images are synchronized. Yet it is not respected concert hall music that dominates this process but commercial pop song recordings. Indeed, some films are assembled around a succession of pop songs that seem to manifest in some cases a more coherent unity (as a soundtrack compilation album) than the accompanying film does. Nonetheless, a series of songs can be used to sophisticated effect in films,[31] with directors like Quentin Tarantino wielding pop songs as centrally important elements in his films.[32]

The both celebrated and disparaged sequence in Tarantino's *Reservoir Dogs* (1992), when Mr. Blonde (Michael Madsen) cuts off the ear of a tied-up policeman, is soundtracked memorably with the 1970s pop song "Stuck in the Middle with You" by Stealer's Wheel. The song could easily have been presented as non-diegetic music, but instead appears diegetically played on a radio. Broadly, it serves the same function, but it crucially articulates diegetic, as well as narrative, action as the torturer dances to its inanely bopping rhythm. The song also adds a further sense of the grotesque to the horrific scene and embodies Michel Chion's notion of anempathetic music that remains indifferent and refuses to concur with the emotional disposition of events unfolding on-screen.[33] The actual moment of the captive policeman's ear being severed is particularly horrifying, even though there are no explicit shots of the act and indeed the camera turns coyly away into the corner to avoid capturing the event.[34] The fact that we get sound *without* images makes it all the more horrific.[35]

The point when Mr. Blonde steps outside of the claustrophobic torture room into the daylight provides momentary (and welcome) respite from the ongoing torture, but it also provides relief from the song playing on the radio. The music's decline in volume moves the audience away from horrific activity (as the camera follows the torturer), but soon Mr. Blonde returns, and the rise in the volume of the music signals to the audience that it should prepare for further beastliness. The music functions as the agent of torture in this sequence and forces other elements to synchronize with it, namely the movement of actors on-screen and points of narrative development. The continuity of sound is the skeletal backbone of the sequence rather than any narrative of torture; indeed, it closely resembles traditional song and/or dance sequences in film musicals in that the image almost becomes an accompaniment to the song. This is an intermittent strategy throughout *Reservoir Dogs*, where the fictional radio station 'K-Billy Super Sounds of the Seventies' with its deadpan-voiced DJ (comedian Steven Wright) imparts a sonic continuity across the film and affords the opportunity for audio dissolves into sequences with foregrounded music and marginal diegetic sound.

While the use of pop songs in films has been a customary practice since the 1980s,[36] there are few films that resort to such emphasis on the songs or foregrounding of the music more than *Reservoir Dogs*.[37] Much popular music can appear equally in the background in films. Indeed, for some years, there has been an area of music production that has had its eye on the possibility of being used as instrumental music in film or television.[38] D. J. Shadow's 1997 album *Endtroducing...* has supplied a few pieces that should be familiar from their constant use for atmospheric moments on television programs and in films. One of the pieces, *Stem/Long Stem*, was originally supposed to have singing on it, but instead, as D. J. Shadow himself observed:

> ...[I] opted for the instrumental version. It was probably a good thing, because the track is the one that somebody in Hollywood is always wanting to use for some scary movie. [laughs] Not that that's all that matters, but *Stem* was particularly important to articulate a cinematic feeling.[39]

The success of this piece among others demonstrates conclusively that incidental music need not precisely match and support the dynamics of a scene. Instead, the footage it accompanies might be cut to fit its temporal and dynamic impetus, or the matching of sound and images can assume a looser character.

In recent years, the process of fitting, staging, and cutting film to a piece of preexisting music has become common and more carefully crafted than in previous years. The rhythmic impetus of the music and its structure in most cases cannot be significantly altered, with the consequence that the images and the editing have to accommodate the temporal dynamics of the music. By and large, broad, sustained musical patterns accompany slow visual movements and occasional cuts, whereas active, busy music with strong rhythmic impetus usually accompanies sequences of rapid action with fast cutting.

Such use of existing music is a tradition with a long past. During the silent period, there were music libraries or compendiums of already existing sheet music that would then be woven together by a film theatre's musical director. These included Giuseppe Becce and Hans Erdmann's *Kinothek* (1919), Edith Lang and George West's *Musical Accompaniment of Moving Pictures* (1920), and Ernö Rapée's *Compendium* (1924, 1925). With the advent of recorded music for film, library music ceased to be written music on paper and became recordings to furnish general moods and provide aural wallpaper for low-budget film productions. Nonetheless, there is a legacy from these music libraries, not least in the manner that films can be 'fitted up' with music derived from an unrelated source. A sense of aesthetics, dynamics, and care in sequencing of music and image is essential to effective post-synchronization of sound with images. The process discussed above bears an unmistakable similarity to the routine of 'fitting up' or 'synchronization' as it was often known, when silent films were furnished with a fabric of existing pieces of music. This was a customary technique from the second decade of the 20th century until the displacement of silent cinema with live music by films with synchronized recorded soundtracks some two decades later.[40] Indeed, ambition led to some exceptionally artful musical scores built from compilations of musical material, such as Joseph Carl Breil's for D. W. Griffith's *Birth of a Nation* (1915), and William Axt and David Mendoza's for King Vidor's *The Big Parade* (1925), among many other films.

THE PERSISTENCE OF SILENT SOUND

One might argue that post-synching the images with sounds is a natural state of affairs in film, as this was the norm until the advent of sound cinema, and where sounds and music would be added live as the film was being projected. Silent cinema had a certain amount of autonomy for images and music respectively, which was conventionalized by the recorded soundtrack's domination by matching dialogue. However, as I noted in earlier chapters, there is certainly a strong case for the survival of the aesthetics of silent cinema in the margins of mainstream cinema, such as in montage sequences, where music can often take the foreground and diegetic sound often recedes to nothing. Generally speaking, foregrounded music tends to appear in sequences when dialogue has receded, or when there is a visual spectacle that requires something of an aural equivalent in terms of impressiveness.

In recent years, it has become possible and even quite popular again to experience silent films with live music. Rather than simply being superseded by the cinema of synchronized sound, perhaps silent cinema remained alive and well around the edges of dominant cinema.[41] Indeed, many avant garde films were distributed without soundtracks and were shown silently, and some came with only vague directions about how they should be accompanied.[42] Yet we might find something similar to silent films close at hand. During action sequences, mainstream films almost never record location sound, and in situations where filming is not completed easily, there is often no attempt to have a sound team there to record sound. Indeed, it remains the case that the heart of contemporary mainstream cinema is dialogue and the talking head shot (and variations), often held within a temporal structure of the shot reverse shot conversation. Mainstream cinema remains a talkie in the precise sense of the antiquated term. Outside of these interior shots where dialogic interaction between actors takes place, there is almost another form of cinema: one where the camera moves quickly and freely, where shots are less easily described than the standard terminology based on relation to human characters (long shot, medium shot, close-up), and where a divergence of sound and image tracks to a greater or lesser extent is allowed. This might be approached as a persistence of silent film aesthetics. Famously, Alfred Hitchcock's work is often charged with retaining something from his youth in silent films as evidence of visual storytelling.[43] This can be verified by looking for sequences without dialogue in his films that were clearly not shot with location sound and often rely heavily on music. Prime examples of this are the sequence of Marion driving in the rain in *Psycho* (1960), Melanie waiting outside the schoolroom as crows alight on the jungle gym behind her in *The Birds* (1963), and the fight on top of Mount Rushmore in *North by Northwest* (1959). Dialogue often can cease to be the motor of narrative development in favor of action, especially in the last few decades when genres such as horror films, war films, and action films have more generally prospered. In such films, when there are dedicated sequences of action, sound functions to convince the audience of special effects, and provide impact (loud sounds) and emotion (music), but there is not a regular reliance upon precise synchronization, apart from isolated moments. The soundtrack can become semi-independent and not dependent on synchronization with the image to the degree of the prevalent cinema fashion for sequences based on dialogue. Roger Manvell and John Huntley suggest that Kubrick's *2001: A Space Odyssey* returned to the modes of silent film through music and image independence and the marginalization of dialogue in the film.[44]

The persistence of silent film aesthetics might be identified elsewhere, in music videos and in the way that silent films from the past have been reformed for current consumption.[45] It may seem an incongruent aspect of this book to look at silent films when ostensibly dealing with synchronized sound cinema. However, we should bear in mind that we experience most silent films these days as DVDs or videos with locked, synchronized soundtracks. In some cases, these might be historically accurate in terms of what audiences at the time would have experienced, while in others, not.[46] F. W. Murnau's *Nosferatu: Eine Symphonie des Grauens* (1922) has proved to be something of a perennial silent horror film favorite and is available with a number of different assigned soundtracks. There is Gillian S. Anderson's meticulously researched and constructed historical score, and there is James Bernard's score, which uses a more recent musical argot: the one that was distinct to Bernard in his characteristic scores for many Hammer horror films from the 1950s to the 1970s. Yet another available version matches *Nosferatu* with music by the rock group Type O Negative.[47] This DVD amounts to an amateur tracking of the film, where the music is not made to fit at all, yet the overall outcome is generally one of interest and effectiveness. This is an independent production in a convincing sense of the term. The group's involvement was clearly small, perhaps even nonexistent. The DVD was put together by people who thought there was an essential compatibility between Type O Negative's music and the film. The group's music is gothic heavy rock, with deep declaiming vocals and distorted, overdriven electric guitar. The subject matter of the group's songs is what might be called dark, being concerned with vampirism (album *Bloody Kisses*) and werewolves ("Wolf Moon") along with constant themes of sex ("My Best Friend's Girlfriend") and death ("Red Water"). Some of these issues are certainly evident in *Nosferatu*, so perhaps there is a deep level where the music and images of the silent film cohere. However, the film is not cut in any way to fit the songs, and the songs are not noticeably adapted to fit the dynamics and temporal requirements of the film. Consequently, the degree of synchronization is not high, and the sound and image in many ways appear to plow separate furrows. There are moments of significant dynamic impact in the images that are not marked notably by the soundtrack. Also vice versa: When the soundtrack reaches a crescendo or highly dramatic moment, it is not reflected in the images. The majority of the music used in the film derives from Type O Negative's album *October Rust*, probably their most successful album, released in 1997, and this DVD release almost seems to function as a surrogate for a DVD release by the group tied to their album.

The modern manifestations of silent films can tell us a fair amount about synchronized sound cinema in that films can stand having large sections where there is little clear synchronization if the screen is not consistently peopled by human faces with moving lips. Gesticulating figures are not a problem, and outdoor vistas or street chases really require little in the way of precise synchronization of sound and image. However, in many cases when silent films are accompanied by music that is not written or adapted precisely to match action, there is a strong tendency to drift between points of synchronization and asynchrony. These points can often be where the music stops, starts, or noticeably changes character. Alternatively, this might be fortuitous. In an essay about soundtracking silent films with modern electronic music, Blair Davis quotes the response of one of his students who pointed to the tangible delight at the screenings when there appeared to be a serendipitous point of synchronization when a significant on-screen event was matched by one in the accompanying music.[48]

This did not prove to be the case with Giorgio Moroder's much discussed and often decried version of Fritz Lang's *Metropolis* (released in 1984),[49] which used some specially written synthesizer passages of incidental music between a succession of contemporary pop songs performed by different artists.[50] The songs follow their own musical structures and only rarely match the moments of emphasis in *Metropolis*, and indeed have an air of indifference to the film caused predominantly by a lack of regular and logical points of synchronization. The Pet Shop Boys' musical accompaniment for Eisenstein's *Battleship Potemkin*, which was first performed at a free concert and screening in Trafalgar Square in London in September of 2004, was, perhaps unexpectedly, an attempt to produce orchestral music of a character more consonant with the traditions of silent film accompaniment (at least with their manifestation at British establishments such as that arranged by the Institute of Contemporary Arts in 2004 and the Barbican in 2008). Its orchestral nature and precise scoring meant that it was more art than pop and followed fairly directly in the tradition of film-music live performances and DVD releases like Michael Nyman's score for Dziga Vertov's *Man With a Movie Camera* (1929) (released on DVD in

2002). Indeed, this angular, modernist film has proven to be highly popular with re-scorers, with DVDs available with a number of musical soundtracks, including those by the pop musicians Cinematic Orchestra and the silent film specialists Alloy Orchestra. While these last examples endeavor to synchronize musical events and dynamics with those of the screen, a number have followed the route described with respect to *Nosferatu*. In the late 1960s, there was a recording of *Häxan* (1922) with a jazz score and novelist William S. Burroughs's narration entitled *Witchcraft Through the Ages*. In 2004, there was a staging in New York for Black History Month of Oscar Micheaux's *Within Our Gates* (1920) with a new musical score by Fe Nunn, allied to simultaneous poetry reading and a jazz band playing, making a multi-media extravaganza out of the film rather than retaining any sense of its originally intended mode of screening. A year later, DJ Spooky presented his *Rebirth of a Nation* at the Lincoln Centre for the Performing Arts in New York, adding a soundtrack that at times did more to question than aid D. W. Griffith's *Birth of a Nation* (1915) and featuring critical commentary and on-screen graphics .

Clearly, such unsynchronized music works as a film accompaniment,[51] although arguably in a fundamentally different way from a dedicated score that aims at a solid melding of the character and effects of the film images and sound. In situations where there is less synchrony, actual moments of synchrony become all the more noticeable and powerful. There is an inevitability of moments when any images will match any random soundtrack that has been added. As I mentioned in the introduction, it is now well known that the Pink Floyd album *Dark Side of the Moon* (1973) appears to fit the images of *The Wizard of Oz* (1939) remarkably well if the two are synched up from the start (the composite often referred to as *The Dark Side of Oz*). However, there are few really notable synch points, although there appears to be synchrony where significant events and changes in image and soundtrack occur simultaneously. The lack of regular synch points allows for those seeming moments of synchronization to achieve a powerful impact. Furthermore, the complexity of the music in its own right can mean that more potential points of contact exist than in music that avoids sudden or dramatic changes, which often can prove to be easily synchronized with images in television reportage or documentaries. There is a further question of 'what fits what' in terms of character in film and music. Such broad matching of character is at the heart of the assumption that Type O Negative's brooding music fits the gothic atmosphere of *Nosferatu* as much as a bright, childlike jingle might fit an advertisement for a breakfast cereal. It might be argued that this match is at the heart of mainstream cinema's dominant use of orchestral film scores, where the patina of high art remains enough to impart a sense of artistry to the film product.[52] Equally, such specialist genre films as science fiction have a tradition of using unfamiliar and often electronic tones as an aural counterpart to the distinctive character of their imagery and themes.[53]

VOCAL DUBBING

Examining voice dubbing can provide much information about film sound processes and is of both metaphorical and descriptive value. In the early 1930s, film producers tried to work with MLV (multi-language versions) format, whereby films would be made in more than one language. Probably the most famous of these is Universal's *Dracula* (1931), which was shot back-to-back on set in English (with Bela Lugosi in the lead) and in Spanish (directed by George Melford with Carlos Villar in the lead). In Europe, there was an extensive program of production with films such as the German film *FP1 Antwortet Nicht* (1932) also being made back-to-back in English (released in 1933) and French. The expense of this mode of production led to its demise[54] and its replacement by the cheaper process of replacing the spoken part of the soundtrack, or dubbing as it is commonly known.

Sadly, scholars have neglected to attend to voice dubbing in much detail. Since the advent of synchronized sound cinema, there has of necessity been a conventional process to allow for dubbing into different languages. Certain countries (such as Greece, Sweden, and Holland) favor the use of subtitles and the retention of the original soundtrack for a film. Others, such as France, Italy, and Germany, have a fully developed industry to allow for the dubbing of foreign-language films into their native tongues. Indeed, we should remember that the tradition in the Italian film industry is that films are shot without location or studio sound, all of which is dubbed during post-production. Also, since the advent of ADR (automatic dialogue replacement) technology, mainstream films everywhere recreate the majority of their final dialogue during post-production.

In the earliest years of the talkies, voices were not unproblematic. Richard Maltby and Ruth Vasey describe negativity in Europe toward early American sound films in English. The front page of *The New York Times* on May 11, 1930, had an article about boycotts of American sound films that were being shown in countries including Hungary.[55] They also point to British criticisms of films with English spoken with an American accent. Indeed, the poster for Alfred Hitchcock's *Blackmail* (1929) not only boldly stated, "The first full-length all talkie film made in Great Britain," but also boasted, "See and hear it. Our mother tongue as it should be—spoken!" The emphasis was not only on hearing spoken words but also on which version of the English language was used. Ironically, the lead in Hitchcock's film was played by a Czech-born actress with a very strong middle-European accent when speaking English. Hitchcock decided that Annie Ondra's voice was not usable though her image was. So, while she acted her scenes, actress Joan Barry spoke her lines from off-camera, creating a remarkable composite person, and one hardly as English as critics of American films might have desired.

The dubbing of foreign-language films into other languages is not as uniform as it might appear to English-language audiences. For example, there are significant differences between the French and Italian modes of dubbing. The French tend to try and match as tightly as possible to the lip movements on-screen, while the Italians favor a more loose approach that will not sacrifice quality of vocal delivery to synchronization.[56] (This, of course, might be taken as proof that some countries are accustomed to less synchronization in sound and image to begin with.) Some techniques for aiding the dubbing process include removing frames from the film to allow the dubbed sounds to fit the lip movements better. Film purists blanch at the prospect, but popular audiences do not know or indeed care too much.

In the 1980s, Dario Argento's *Profondo Rosso* (aka *Deep Red*, 1975), now regarded as a horror film classic and in some quarters feted as an art film, was already on video release in Britain in an English-language version. In 1993, the film was re-released by Redemption Video in a version that repackaged the film and was seemingly aimed at an art-house audience. The film's English star David Hemmings was dubbed into Italian in this version, despite the fact that he is speaking English as can be verified from comparing the English language dub with his lip movements. Habitually, Italian films were shot without location sound, with the whole of the soundtrack being added in post-production. This not only made good use of Cinecitta's excellent sound facilities but also allowed for films to be shot using actors who could not speak Italian and the production of master dubs in post-production to facilitate easy export of the films. As with many other Italian horror films of the 1970s, the version of *Profondo Rosso* that had been in release in Britain and North America had contained a soundtrack in English, but this U.K. video release was aimed for an art-house audience, as evidenced by the fact that such cinemas in Britain always show films in an original-language version with subtitles and almost never knowingly show anything in a dubbed version, which is considered a rather philistine approach to cinema. The keys to this process for this film then were the retention of an 'original' Italian soundtrack to the film and the superimposition of subtitles in English. This not only denied the origins of the film in a world of post-synched soundtracks, but also led to the farcical spectacle of David Hemmings's voice being overdubbed by an Italian voice artist and then subtitled in English.

There is a notable difference between U.S. cinema and television, which prefer non-English-language films to be dubbed into English, and U.K. cinema and television, which almost uniformly prefer subtitled versions. Before the advent of the DVD and its multiple soundtrack capabilities, British cities often had cheap video shops that sold dubbed versions of foreign- language films derived from the U.S. market releases. Having already experienced the films in their native tongues, films such as *The Return of Martin Guerre* (1982), which had been known by its French title in the U.K., and Lasse Hallström's *My Life as a Dog* (1985) in their dubbed versions seemed slightly incongruous. The comic potential for dubbing is high, of course. The Japanese television shows *The Water Margin* (1973) and *Monkey* (1979–80) were broadcast in Britain with a soundtrack of ludicrous faux-Asian accents, while pornography's cheap and hurried dubbing has remained a perennial joke. *The Jesus of Montreal* (1989) has a comic scene of characters dubbing a porn movie, and in Britain there is a television show called *Badly Dubbed Porn* (2007–), which fashions comic narratives by adding a new soundtrack to non-explicit sequences from old pornographic films.

Similar humor derived from the soundtrack ridiculing the image track took place much earlier, in Woody Allen's *What's Up, Tiger Lily* (1966). He took a Japanese spy thriller and rebuilt the film as a comedy. This involved the shooting of some extra scenes that were inserted in the film but, perhaps most significantly, it involved the total re-recording of the soundtrack. The mix of sound effects and music was retained from the original, sold as part of the film for foreign dubs. The dialogue track was rewritten and performed by American actors to rescript the events depicted in the film as a series of gags. Some of the dubbed voices are as convincing in their synchronization with vocal movements as any dubbing.[57] There is also a significant extra musical input, from The Lovin' Spoonful, who provide songs, as well as appearing on-screen in an inserted scene. The group's music appears in no way alien to the film, though much of the dialogue does, and indeed, this is where a significant amount of the comedy lies. Allen saw the possibility for comic potential existing in the gap between visuals and soundtrack, and most precisely between comic dialogue and apparent seriousness in the image track.[58]

Post-synch sound is dominant in the international film industry. Some filmmakers create the soundtrack wholly in post-production, while some art film directors have retained the French tradition of 'son direct,' the real recording of sound that happens at the pro-filmic event when the camera is recording. Voice dubbing (usually from one language to another) can prove to be one of the most important ways to reorient a piece of film and surrounding ideas. As a child visiting Germany, I was taken to see a film starring some "famous American actors" called Terence Hill and Bud Spencer. I had never heard of them and only years later discovered that they were Italian and the films were not in the least American despite being westerns. Some 80 percent of foreign-language films in Germany are dubbed, with an aim to match lip movement as much as possible, including picking a translation that fits mouths better than the exact translation would. Daniel Meyer-Dinkgräfe notes how the dubbing of the television show *Magnum P.I.* (1980–88) involves an actor with a deeper voice (Norbert Langer) that fits Tom Selleck's image perhaps better than his actual voice, while Arne Eisholtz dubs the voices of Tom Hanks, Kevin Kline, and Bill Murray and makes them sound largely the same.[59] Dubbing can also allow for censorship (indeed, this is one reason for some countries insisting on subtitling). In Alfred Hitchcock's *Notorious* (1946), for example, the German dubbing changed the Nazi scientist into a Slavic drug dealer.

The U.K. film *Performance* (1970) has a different soundtrack in the U.S. than its British release, as the producers were worried that the Cockney accent of crime boss Harry Flowers would not be understood by American audiences. The U.K. release has actor Johnny Shannon's characteristic voice, but the U.S. soundtrack used an obscure English actor's voice, whose tones are clearer but highly disconcerting for a British audience familiar with the character actor on-screen. Oddly, a video release of the film in Britain in the mid-1990s was of the American version. This emphasized a side effect of the vocal replacement: that of seemingly suggesting that the gang boss is from a middle-class rather than a working-class background. This is not an insignificant development, enabled by recourse to the so-called RP (received pronunciation) tones spoken by the middle- and upper-class English.[60]

We need more suspension of disbelief than usual when it comes to clear voice dubbing in cinema. Indeed, if one is not used to dealing with films that have been dubbed, they can be an unnerving experience. (Of course, conversely, if you are used to them, they are nothing remarkable.) As John Belton noted: "The rather obvious intervention of technology involved with [foreign language] dubbing severely circumscribes our faith in both sound and image, provoking a crisis in their credibility."[61] Non-original dubbed sound poses a distinct question. On rare occasions, television news might broadcast footage in another language without the option of removing the soundtrack, and we can discern talking in another language at a lower volume than our channel's commentary. This not only emphasizes the lack of connection between the footage and the added voiceover but also gives the impression that our television station is merely using second-hand news footage, which is why footage aimed at being sold overseas often lacks an added commentary.[62] While it is likely that people in countries that habitually dub films might be more open to lack of synchronism than those in countries that subtitle films, such lack of synchrony merely illustrates how far films can vary as objects and how different audiences can be in approach and expectation. The overall effect of vocal dubbing is not one of Brechtian alienation that distances audiences from films and it also may well not be fully real, but it is *conventional* and thus naturalistic in its own way.

CONCLUSION

To summarize, pre-fitting films by beginning with music can permit music to dominate. Approaches include cutting images to fit the sounds (as in *The Shining*) and/or staging to sounds (as in *Singin' in the Rain*). Fitting up sound in post-production, be it post-synching dialogue, dubbing into another language, or adding music to a finished film, all open up questions of the specific production context and agency involved in the process of synchronizing sound and image. All the processes addressed in this chapter follow conventions, although they may vary in their manifestation of broad principles. Variations in acceptability of loose synchronization and what constitutes being 'in time' are most evident in instances of foreign-language dubbing but also apparent in other areas of film.

In the mid-2000s, editor Robert Ryang won a competition by recutting Stanley Kubrick's *The Shining* to make it appear to be a romantic comedy. The apocryphal film's title was changed to simply *Shining*, and the impression was given that it was a Nora Ephron film or similar heart-warming story of the positive developments in a family relationship. The raw material, images, and sounds from *The Shining* are reformulated into what convincingly appears to be a romantic comedy where Jack has a romance with Wendy and befriends her son Danny. While Ryang was highly selective about which shots to use, the key to reorientation was more through the soundtrack than the editing of the visuals. Indeed, the only additions are on the soundtrack. The first is the stereotypical Hollywood trailer extra-diegetic voiceover, which provides defining guidance for the new story and tone of the film. A crucial addition to the diegesis is an alien line of dialogue ("I'm your new father" allegedly said by Jack to Danny), which imparts a momentous and alternative narrative vector. Apart from the voice, music has a significant role to play, particularly in emotional terms. The trailer first tracks some unsynched comedy music and then (triumphantly) Peter Gabriel's "Solsbury Hill" to brighten the images. The music provides a distinct dynamic to the piece, with the first half being quirky and staccato like the music and the second being more sustained. Indeed, the second part begins with the film's opening, prolonged helicopter shots of the Torrance's car dwarfed by the spectacular Colorado scenery. Gabriel's song delivers a strong sense of emotional engagement with a smattering of obscure but meaningful lyrics sung with feeling, and the line 'I'm going to take you home' repeated as the song's conclusion. This vectorizes the recut footage from *The Shining* in a divergent direction, but the voiceover is crucial for anchoring its new meanings. Indeed, the trend for mock trailers uploaded on the Internet after significant recutting arguably relies essentially on sonic alterations that provide a wholly different idea of the film.

One of the clearest indications of the impact of CGI (computer generated imagery) is in the 'talking animal' film, which also illustrates the desire for precise synchronization of voice and lips. For instance, the films *The Cat from Outer Space* (1978) and *Look Who's Talking* (1989) included a cat and babies, respectively, whose voices could be heard but were not matched with their lip movements. Since CGI's widespread adoption, this minor film genre (if it even can be called that) has seen the precise matching of lips and sounds, as was the case in *Babe* (1995) and *Underdog* (2007). The movement is often effective but slightly uncanny, not quite convincingly real (to my eyes and ears, at least). Part of this may be due to the ultra-precise synchronization of voice and lip movements—it looks too precisely matched—as well as the difficulty of surmounting the widespread assumption of the impossibility of animal speech. Perhaps a rougher synchronization could be effective, like a foreign-language dub that aims at the overall spirit of the film rather than the technical meticulousness of an arid process. Indeed, there was an almost convincing television comedy starring a 'talking' horse, *Mister Ed* (1961), which (without CGI of course) was able to apply a process remarkably similar to foreign-language dubbing by attempting to match the horse's almost random lip movements with spoken dialogue.

The dubbing of voices to images bears a distinct resemblance to ventriloquism. During the 1980s and early '90s, the Northern Irish Republican Party Sinn Féin suffered British government censorship on television programs that showed their images speaking with their voices ludicrously replaced by actors.[63] Such a gap between sound and image is an everyday occurrence in countries that dub foreign films rather than subtitle them, but it is also an occasionally showcased aspect of horror films when scary voices are required. For example, in *The Exorcist* (1973), character actress Mercedes McCambridge provided the demonic voice for the possessed girl Regan (played by Linda Blair in most shots). Indeed, in some horror films, demonic possession often adds up to little more than replacement of a person's voice. Ventriloquism as a metaphor for sound cinema (as Rick Altman noted) reveals sound's capacity to animate the inanimate and make the inert visual. Animated films instantly confirm this peculiar and distinctive effect. Ventriloquism's vocal replacement can have a distinctly uncanny or unnerving effect. A horror film about ventriloquism, *Dead Silence* (2007), illustrates the unreliability of an assumption of direct causal connection between sound and image. Probably the most famous film that touches on ventriloquism is another horror film, *Dead of Night* (1945), where the synchronized sound is a better indicator of life and consciousness than the image. Since the advent of technology like ADR, an inorganic relationship of sound and tied image has been at the heart of almost all mainstream film production, in a form that retains—indeed *strengthens*—the illusory character of the synchronized film. Filmmaking dominated by pre- and post-production can question the illusion of sound cinema. The audiovisual contract can, however indirectly, be jeopardized by the material heterogeneity of sound and image. *Singin' in the Rain* may be partly about a lie, but it is itself precisely a lie of this order.

CHAPTER 8
Wild Track Asynchrony

It is possible to remove the soundtrack of a film and add one of your own choice, whether using an editing suite or roughly synchronizing sound and image hardware at home. Attempting this at random can have fascinating consequences. Adding live radio asserts the separation of sound and image, but recourse to a music disc can often have unanticipated consonances between sound and image. These may be moments of synchrony that seem to fit or a general sense of matching mood or tone, but on occasion, it is the very independence and lack of cohesion between sound and image that can be most effective.

Forms of disconnected sound include 'wild' disconnected sound, extra-diegetic (as in conventional non-diegetic film scores), off-screen sounds including acousmatic sound, and more subtle uses such as a general ambient sound. Some off-screen sound has no connection with screen activity, while other sounds may have an ambiguous connection. Acousmatic sound lacks an immediately traceable source. It emanates from an off-screen source that remains a mystery. The original term was used by Schaeffer and later electroacoustic musicians to describe sound that had lost its identifiable origin and thus might become a sound in itself—one not implying a specific source—or might remain mysterious and make the listener speculate as to its original origin. However, in film, the term is applicable to sounds that can remain an off-screen mystery for a period or have an off-screen origin that is never concretized.

PLESIOCHRONY

There are many situations when sound and image are not precisely matched at all and may only seem to be in general accordance. The term used to describe something comparable in scientific and engineering terms is 'plesiochrony.' For film, this might designate a rough, general synchronization that is not a proper matching of unified in-synch sound and image but fits a general soundtrack to particular images. Rick Altman briefly touches on the notion as 'semi-synch' in the concluding chapter of *Sound Theory, Sound Practice* as

> A characteristic of sound that is apparently synchronized with onscreen actions of secondary importance. This technique is often used for the linking of stock sound footage to mobs, parades, battles and other large-scale scenes where the viewer cannot possibly check whether each sound is actually synchronized to an onscreen image. Already employed in the early *Fox Movietone News*, this technique facilitates the use of generic sound and sound loops. It is heavily used by television news to accompany background action in still photographs.[1]

Altman's noting of the process as highly evident in *Fox Movietone News* dates it to the earliest days of sound cinema, when such newsreels were in a pioneering position, using the Movietone sound-on-film system before the industry's more general conversion. Documentary films, a close relative of newsreels, have dealt in plesiochronous relationships between sound and image by nature of their production background as much as their repertoire of accepted aesthetic strategies. Some television historical documentaries consist solely of silent film footage, such as *The Third Reich in Colour* (2001). This included footage of the Normandy landings that had been taken by either war correspondents or cine-film enthusiasts in the military, and had of course been shot without any corresponding sound. The footage was shown with sound accompaniments of gunfire, explosions, and general machine noise, assembling a general parallel to the images. The assumption was that audiences were unused to (and by implication, unhappy with) images that lacked a corresponding and appropriate sound. This artificial ambient sound has become a mainstay of television, and indeed has long been present in film, although often in a more sophisticated form.

Indeed, plesiochronous sound appears regularly in crowd scenes and in the background in city street scenes; in fact, it appears in all places where a general noise is required that is vaguely consonant with expectations of what should emanate from the visuals. In contemporary Hollywood films, it is the ambience of urban or rural settings, while in much historical television, it has a more basic psychological function: that of removing the silence of soundless footage and thus rendering it more 'normal.' This is remarkably similar to some early sound films. In Hitchcock's *Blackmail* (1929), this is most evident in the sequence in Alice's bedroom. Her mother enters and wakes her while removing the cover from her canary's cage. The soundtrack suddenly bursts into life with birdsong, although the sound does not appear precisely synchronized, and the sound quality and volume do not match the room space on-screen. It later finishes abruptly. More recent examples of such general sound include the horror comedy film *Severance* (2006), where, in its concluding scenes with a woman being attacked by an assailant and man being attacked by another, the soundtrack consists merely of a fairly undifferentiated fabric of seemingly diegetic grunts and hitting impact sounds. These form their own continuum and do not match image events precisely, much like the sounds of shouting and cracking impacts in screen fights.[2] Such sound is not uncommon. Indeed, it might also be easily argued that much incidental music in films has a plesiochronous character. This is because incidental music can be only approximately synchronized to action.

The term 'plesiochrony' might be applied to different situations in sound films. First, the term might be used for poor synchronization, when the intention of precise synchronization is clear but not achieved. This was endemic at the birth of sound cinema and remained a difficulty until the sound-on-film systems assured a good level of precision. However, this problem of delivery has never been fully vanquished, and such poor matching of sound and image is evident in many Internet-delivered audiovisual objects. What Altman is referring to might be approached as an ambient strategy, whereby images without distinct or synchronized sounds are accompanied by sound of a general but appropriate character. This aesthetic might be traced to part-sound films made during the years of transition between silent and sound cinema. In many cases, silent films were 'fitted up' with added sounds and had a handful of sequences reshot as dialogue scenes, producing a 'new' talkie film.

TRACKS DRIFTING APART

In some films, music and/or sound can drift apart from the image track. In this case, it becomes the soundtrack as a coherent and nearly independent entity. This is far more often the case with non-diegetic music, which already has a certain distance from the diegesis and on-screen activities. A striking aspect evident in many of French director Jean Rollin's films is that large sections not only appear to have been shot without synchronized sound recorded during shooting, but that the final product also retains a lack of synchronization between soundtrack and image track. At times, there is a remarkably high degree of separation, indeed autonomy, between the action on-screen and the loud and continuous music track. The music remains accompaniment, but it is part of an audiovisual regime that concentrates less on dialogue sequences than is the case with the overwhelming majority of mainstream dramatic films. A dreamlike and poetic slow tempo to action and cutting along with minimal and sometimes no dialogue characterize Rollin's films. His Lèvres de sang (Lips of Blood, 1975) starts with almost six minutes until there is any dialogue, the title card appearing in an unhurried manner across visual action and non-diegetic music. The film has protracted sequences of protagonist Frederic wandering around an almost silent town at night, and later, scantily clad female vampires move aimlessly around a deserted castle ruin. These sequences tend to contain little in the way of diegetic sound and often have non-diegetic music that does not match the dynamics of on-screen movement. There are few, if any, clear synch points, meaning that there is a strong degree of autonomy between music and image tracks and a sense of dislocation, reminiscent of watching a silent film with unrelated music played on a CD player. Indeed, these sequences are not far from Blair Davis's experiments mentioned in the previous chapter about students' reactions to screenings of silent films shown with unrelated modern music.[3]

This separation is often a symptom in low-budget filmmaking of the exigencies of shooting without a sound crew and the luxury of location sound. It is also testament to the ease with which post-production sound can be utilized in an effective manner. Sharing production techniques with many low-budget films, Herk Harvey's Carnival of Souls (1962) incorporated substantial sections that were shot without location sound. Consequently, the final film includes some sequences where dialogue and sound effects were post-synched and some substantial sections where there is no diegetic sound and loud non-diegetic music instead. These sequences, by and large, are the eerie, atmospheric ones, such as those of the old building accompanied by the sound of an organist (Gene Moore) playing a large theatre organ like a Wurlitzer.[4] Perhaps the most memorable non-synched sequences in Carnival of Souls are those near the conclusion when a group of people (or should that be souls?) chase the organist Mary and dance in the deserted carnival and bathhouse building, with a total lack of diegetic sound and accompaniment from the organ that has haunted the film's soundtrack. Such dissonant, atonal music is considered negatively. When Mary's church organ playing transmogrifies into discordant and eerie playing, the pastor declares, "Profane, sacrilege" and fires her. The film has a certain narrative ambiguity (are these simply ghosts or a temporal confusion of past and present?), which is doubled by the film style and the ambiguous relationship of images and sounds during the long periods lacking distinct points of synchronization. The effect of this is to provide significant cognitive and emotional dislocation, aiding the films in their dreamlike atmospheres. Perhaps these are indeed suitable representations or expressions of disembodied souls in both films, where sounds are literally disembodied while images are similarly disconnected, with the latter as spectral images outside the sense of space established by sound.

In Alain Resnais's *L'aneé dernière à Marienbad* (1961), there is a different form of divergence between image and soundtrack. As a film that consistently manipulates audience expectations and defies narrative and aesthetic conventions, it works to set up a gap between what is shown on-screen and what is heard on the soundtrack. This seems to be a distinct example of the sort of counterpoint that Eisenstein, Pudovkin, and Alexandrov called for in their "Statement on the Sound Film" (discussed previously). Here, they warned of the aesthetically—and by implication, socially—regressive potential of certain strategies in matching sound and image. For them, counterpoint was one of the progressive options that opened up possibilities for the development of cinema as art and communication. It is notable that *L'aneé dernière à Marienbad* is such an isolated example among feature films, and it might easily be argued that the dominant naturalism in narrative feature films manifests precisely the filmed stage plays against which Eisenstein, Pudovkin, and Alexandrov warned.

The key is the space between image track and soundtrack. This is where the real meaning is produced, where the real potential resides. *L'aneé dernière à Marienbad* is a film founded upon ambiguity in terms of narrative and depiction, and it contains extended passages of asynchrony along with sequences of conventionally synchronized sound and image. It is a startling and singular film, and it begins with a statement of intent in terms of sound and image relations. A voiceover starts while the film's titles are still being shown, and it continues for eight-and-a-half minutes, intermittently fading in and out. The audience is never told the source of the voice. Once the titles finish, we are given a succession of slow traveling shots, mostly of the elaborate ceilings of the palatial house that joins the voiceover and the organ music that began with the film's titles (Figure 8.1, 8.2 and 8.3).

The whole of the opening appears to move the audience toward an unfolding event: the performance of a play called *Rosmer*. The first synchronization of sound and image takes place nearly six-and-a-half minutes after the first shot of the house. Over a minute before this point, the image track has reached the space in which the play is being performed, but it has refused shots of events on the stage in favor of

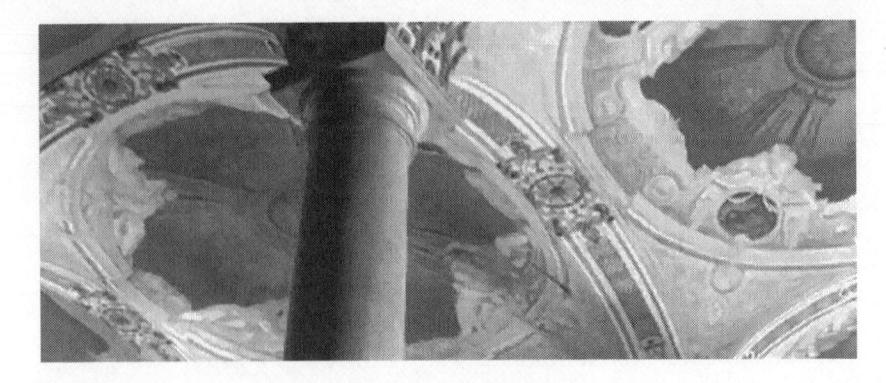

Figure 8.1

Figure 8.2

Figure 8.3

traveling shots of the static audience watching the play, accompanied by voices that have an ambient echo that differentiates them from the opening voiceover and sets them within the space on-screen despite their precise sources remaining absent. The first point of synchronization is when we see the lips of one of the actors match the words we hear, just before the play finishes. We have been shown these characters before, but with their mouths closed as words were heard. This establishes the film's dreamlike and dislocated atmosphere, with a sense of purposeful movement and structure largely denied. While the traveling shots appear to take us into the heart of the building and the play, there is a desire to hold off direct engagement. The sequence has been accompanied by organ music by Francis Seyrig, the brother of the film's star Delphine Seyrig. His music has a distinct and continuous slow pulse that matches the traveling shots in terms of character and provides a sense of continuous movement for the audience's guidance through sound and image.[5] The music lacks a clear sense of structural development, which is not to say that it is a repetitive continuum, but that its dissonant, but almost conventional, style provides a sense of emotional non-involvement with screen activities compounded by its rhythmic impetus as the driving force of the sequence, giving a sense of a slow walk toward a target. The use of extended passages of asynchrony as a policy wreathes *L'aneé dernière à Marienbad* in an emotional and cognitive dislocation, emanating from its lack of specific time and space. In a film such as this, counterpoints pile up, not just between sound and image tracks, but between dynamics, perception, and the film's conceptual terrain.

In these cases, there is a tendency for music to appear to be lacking in structure (or in some other cases, for it to seem nothing but structure) when disconnected from image, and to give the impression of continuity due to the repetitive, continuous nature of sound and image relations as much as any intrinsic character of the music or on-screen developments. Robert Fink notes that film incidental music regularly follows a clear pattern of tension and release that is less straightforward in minimalist art music, which appears closer to stasis. He relates this to Freud's notion of the death instinct, a reaction to the compulsion to repeat.[6] More clearly structured music (with well-defined repetition and variations) can furnish a stronger sense of holding the whole together. Yet in all cases like this, there is arguably something of a return to the modes of silent cinema. The independence of image and soundtracks, rather than forging a cohesive unity, adds up to more when put together than alone and creates distinctive effects through its lack of unanimity.

ASYNCHRONY

I was disappointed when I first found out the truth about natural history documentaries. Like most people, I imagine, I thought that I was experiencing a sound and image reality. Instead, of course, we are, in the overwhelming majority of cases, experiencing images and sounds that were not recorded at the same time and place. Indeed, it seems that the distance between the filming and sound recordings might not only be continental but can vary within each track and, for example, images of successive pandas might in fact be different ones that we assume are the same individual. Soundtracks can, if anything, be more of a composite, and indeed, since the advent of digital sound, might exhibit all manner of enhancements. The natural history film and television industries (and their relation to the natural history sound-recording industry) have specialist technicians for different jobs, and sound recording is highly specialized and cannot be completed in many cases with only a film camera crew in the vicinity. Indeed, it has often been something of a tradition in the field of documentary filmmaking that film images can be shot without any location sound, which can be 'faked' later in the studio or, on the other hand, the imagery might be accompanied by a different sound. There is an assumption here that the latter emboldens the narration of films, with a strong voiceover and some general ambient sound in the background, or even the use of recordings from different places in comparison with the images on-screen.

Wild track sound, as it is known in the film and television industries,[7] involves the accompaniment of the image track with unsynchronized sound derived from elsewhere. While in aesthetic terms, cohesion of some sort may be constructed between image and sound, there is no necessity for its existence. Sometimes wild track sound can have no connection at all with the image track, unifying highly diverse times and spaces. The use of wild track sound became fairly prominent in television documentaries in the 1970s. It allowed for images to be accompanied by voiceover narration, or in certain cases, by edited-together 'vox pops' (recordings of members of the public replying to questions). This latter strategy allowed both sound and image to appear to be mere recordings of reality with less of an apparent interfering hand from the filmmakers. It also opened a space between what was seen and heard by the audience. Doubtless a connection existed between what was said on the soundtrack and what was shown in the image track, although sometimes this might be less than apparent and allow for something along the lines of the 'intellectual montage' proposed by Eisenstein. Thus the soundtrack in a documentary is able to manifest a level of independent commentary to the image track, whether its relationship to the image is simple or oblique. Perhaps it is able to function as a further level of truth for the documentary discourse.

Andrew Kötting's faux-documentary road movie *Gallivant* (1996) uses the soundtrack to furnish something of an aural memory for the film. The film appears to be a documentary of a road trip around Britain that the director takes with his daughter and mother. The film intermittently utilizes wild track sound, with voices and other recordings cut in seemingly at random and not obviously or clearly connected to the activities on the image track. These destroy the illusion of sound and image naturalism. They appear unconnected but we, the audience, attempt to make mental connections between the sounds and images. Situations like this demonstrate an extreme of asynchrony, where the two tracks have become uncoupled and continue along their own paths independently. Sound perspective is aberrant. We are faced with two distinct spaces: that of the image and that within which the sound was (in most cases obviously) recorded. This leads to a propensity for fairly close-miked 'vox pop' anonymous comments that seem to defy the sense of space established on-screen.

In *Gallivant*, sound at times appears to directly represent memory. This appears less derived from an analogue to the abilities and processes of human memory than more derived from film language, where the extra-diegetic 'sound cut-in' (particularly with a line of dialogue) was developed in classical cinema to denote an aural memory. In *Gallivant*, these become sound flashes, literally sound bites where short phrases and short monologues interject into the film, seemingly from nowhere.

There is, of course, a well-established convention in mainstream film language that a snatch of extra-diegetic voice with a slightly echoed or reverberating quality signifies a memory for the character on-screen. However, Kötting appears to use such sonic memories as a counterpoint to visual memory. This makes for a film fabric that not only has regular discontinuity of sound and image but where each has the ability to question more than reinforce the other. In some cases, the performers are long dead, and even the limitations and distinctive sound characteristics of the recording medium come to manifest an important faculty of the music's status as a memory.[8] The encoding of memory experiences into songs that people associate with certain moments of private life in public can lead to Pavlovian emotional reactions at the unannounced appearance of certain pieces of music. Popular songs as manifestations of public memory are highly effective, and many embody consensus thumbnail memories of certain periods that can function for us even though we may lack or have radically different experiences of the era personally. Indeed, unsynchronized sound can often function as a manifestation of memory for a character in a film. These might be sonic flashbacks, aural counterparts to the more familiar flashbacks (either as memories for a diegetic character or as a means of indicating something to the audience), that often but not always include synchronized sound, although sound is often a principal means by which the audience is made aware that the diegesis has changed register.

An example of a film that on one level appears to be inspired by nightmares is David Lynch's debut feature film *Eraserhead* (1977). Yet on another level, the film might be interested in the disturbing processes of memory. Events seem to transpire without forewarning, and protagonist Henry does not appear to remember certain events taking place. His emotional disconnection from the film's bizarre parade of events is doubled by *Eraserhead*'s constant use of disconnected ambient sound. Indeed, one of the most alarming aspects of the film is the soundtrack. The images, activities, and representations are disturbing enough, but Alan Splet's sound design creates an ambient continuum of unease. Behind the foreground of isolated and awkward dialogue, there is almost continuous background noise. This is acousmatic in that we are uncertain of the ultimate source of the sounds, although some of them sound like they might emanate from heavy machinery of some sort.

Gestalt theory emphasizes the importance of the perceptual phenomenon of the figure and ground, the object we focus on in the foreground and its modest backdrop. We might focus on the figure, thinking that it is the important thing, but it *needs* the ground for its own definition. This should be kept in mind in relation to background ambiences in films. R. Murray Schafer discusses the idea of what he calls 'keynote sounds' in the sonic environment. Everything else in the soundscape takes on special meaning in relation to these, and they can often constitute a background that may remain unnoticed.[9] Such sounds form a ground for the figures of what he calls 'signals,' the more consciously noticed sounds that appear to be in the foreground. In *Eraserhead*, we constantly experience a ghostly background noise of industry. Schafer also refers to the 'flat line' in sound, which is sound on a fairly continuous, undynamic level of volume and intensity. He notes that this was introduced into daily life by the industrial revolution and its expansion.[10] The background ambience in *Eraserhead* marks a sonic continuity, yet there is little visual sign of the industrial activity that might constitute an origin for these sounds. It is almost as if they are a ghostly memory, an uncomfortable reminder of a collapsed industrial heritage. Splet's sounds constitute an unhealthy background of sound following Schafer's analysis, an amplification of the sort of soundscape that many people in cities experience as a matter of course.

It might also be easily argued that we are far more used to acousmatic sound and dislocated sounds and images than ever before. We are certainly used to passing moments of distinct asynchrony in certain types of television programs, although there has also been a tradition of its use in film documentaries since the coming of recorded sound. Julien Temple's two films about the Sex Pistols and punk rock, *The Great Rock'n'Roll Swindle* (1980) and *The Filth and the Fury* (2000), might be approached as two halves of a whole, or as a statement and its contradiction. The latter is a straightforward documentary while the former mixes documentary techniques with many others, including parodic drama, animation, and event reconstruction. There is a significant amount of shared footage between the two films. One perennial problem for rock documentary filmmakers is how to accompany song recordings. If there is no corresponding music video and the filmmakers want images of the group to accompany the song, they have to demonstrate some ingenuity. Matching live footage of a group performing with the sounds of songs recorded in studios can often prove less problematic than one might imagine. Audiences often fail to notice the plesiochrony of such a marriage, particularly if there is a dearth of footage that marks moments of synchronization, such as singing or distinct notes being played on instruments. Sometimes, the live footage appears seamlessly fitted to a song that is not being performed. In *The Great Rock'n'Roll Swindle*, there are some very poor-quality black-and-white images that accompany the group's version of Chuck Berry's "Johnny B. Goode." These images almost certainly were not recorded at the same time as the sound and are highly unlikely to even depict the Sex Pistols performing the same song. However, the images and sound are fairly well synchronized, to the point where we might easily miss the subtle aspects of sound and image that betray a lack of precise synchronization, and indeed, even the lack of possibility of it being a unified synchronization of image and sound. In this sequence, the images are rocked back and forth and almost manifest an animation of still images. A lack of usable images leads at times to such creative attempts to accompany the songs with an almost total lack of synchronization. This song was a dire, impromptu performance, a studio outtake that appears on the film's soundtrack album and clearly had been dug out of the dustbin for extra material to release after the group's demise. Similarly, another studio outtake that appears on the same album is used for a prominent and sustained sequence in *The Filth and the Fury*. A cover of Jonathan Richman and the Modern Lovers's song "Road Runner" plays for almost its full length, accompanied by disparate images of the group performing live. At times, the matching of the song to the images is fairly precise and gives the initial impression of being an authentic recording of a live performance by the Sex Pistols.[11] However, at other times, the synchronization is by necessity unconvincing, although other elements, including a voiceover commentary, obscure any sense of the film being a guaranteed recording of a live show.[12] The continuity of music means that we are willing to solely accept such general synchronization only in a handful of situations. These are in passing and thus not to be concentrated on. Otherwise we might well feel cheated as we realized that the unification of sound and image is not beyond the most cursory level. These moments follow to some degree the tradition of documentaries of wild track, which comes from the common procedure of recording sound and filming images separately, a common way of proceeding with some documentary films.

PULLING APART

Sometimes sound and image tracks pull apart to remain coupled only at isolated moments. Disparate synchronization transpires when the speed of image becomes slow motion yet the speed of the sound remains normal. This is a well-established convention. The use of slowed-time sound is rare to the point that audiences readily accept an extremity of difference between sound and image speeds in the representation of a single event. When a sequence goes into slow motion, it is almost never accompanied by diegetic sounds that match the speed of the action. Thus it moves into asynchrony. Its usual accompaniment is loud non-diegetic music that obliterates diegetic sound or diegetic sound at the normal speed, which creates something of a cognitive anomaly for the audience. While these two strategies allow for aesthetic synchronization and coherence between sound and image, the essential illusionistic synchronization of time and space represented on-screen and the time and space represented on the soundtrack are riven apart.

A good example of this occurs in the western *Breakheart Pass* (1976) when the train on which all the action has occurred is uncoupled and cars full of soldiers roll backward off the tracks and over a precipice to their demise. At this point, the images go into slow motion in order to show and emphasize to the audience the utter destruction of the cars and their contents. However, in contradistinction, the sound remains at the standard speed, most notably the shouts of the unseen soldiers as the first impacts take place. The divergence of image and soundtrack has nothing to do with space and everything to do with time. Yet this separation of the image and sound remains in the same space, depicting the same event, and it sets up a philosophical contradiction: Where is the reality of this event? Is it in the sound more than the images? It would seem so, but the widespread acceptance of slow motion means that we tend not to notice how far the image is aestheticized and moved into abstraction. The Maysles brothers and Charlotte Zwerin's *Gimme Shelter* (1970) includes a sequence in slow motion of the Rolling Stones seemingly performing Robert Johnson's "Love in Vain," although the song retains the normal tempo of the studio recording. In effect, there is no synchronization at all here, producing a sense of dislocation that is evident not only in the film's depictions but in its film style. Earlier sound films were more aware of stepping back from the image for contemplation and exploited it, but without the later convention of sound at normal speed. For example, Jean Vigo's *Zero de conduite* (1933) has a highly dramatic slow-motion dormitory battle in a school. This is accompanied by Maurice Jaubert's music, which was recorded and then played backward, thus without any direct synchronization with the images. This not only redoubled the bizarre effect of backward music and slow-motion imagery but also compounded the whole with a lack of synchronization.

Such disparate synchronization of sound and image speeds has become increasingly evident in the faddish use of so-called avid zooms and speed ramping, involving the sudden digital speeding up and slowing down of the image. Although not the first film to use it, *The Matrix* (1999) was noted for its use, while Darren Aronofsky's *Requiem for a Dream* (2000) was also a consistent showcase for the technique.[13] Many of the sequences that follow this strategy use prominent music as a sonic mask but also employ sound mixes both slowed and at normal speed. In the visually striking, classically set *300* (2007), there is a fine illustration of digital speed changing when the messenger of Persian King Xerxes is kicked into a pit by Spartan leader Leonidas. This is still synched to precise points—most obviously the impact of the kick; sounds fail to slow down and speed up but retain temporal continuity. Such different speeds of sound and image became a characteristic of the television show *The Dukes of Hazzard* (1977–85), when car chases and crashes took place. Of course, this process also became something of a signature for Sam Peckinpah's films, with sequences of extreme violence being time-stretched to allow for the exquisite detail of the choreography of violence.[14] A similar situation of detached sound and image track is the climactic shootout in John Woo's *Face/Off* (1997). A child listens to "Somewhere over the Rainbow" on a personal stereo, which occupies most of the film soundtrack and contrasts sharply with the slow-motion violent action.

A singular but related example of this process of detachment is the conclusion of *Butch Cassidy and the Sundance Kid* (1969) when, as the two outlaws run out of a house to their deaths, the image freezes, preventing (perhaps sparing) the audience from seeing the demise of the film's protagonists. However, the soundtrack continues, allowing the audience to hear that they have been killed by a massive volley of gunfire. This is a psychologically complex moment, with the soundtrack telling the audience that they are dead but the image retaining a view of them alive. Crucially, it is the soundtrack that carries the burden of representation, and the audience is forced into using its visual imagination to understand what is happening. Characterized by occasional but crucial synch points between sound and image, almost all of a disparate synchronized sequence is clearly not synchronized, yet an audience is unlikely to register that it is asynchrony. Other forms of spectacle-based sequence do similar things. Indeed, sequences that remove most diegetic sound often allow a strong interaction between a loud piece of non-diegetic music and a succession of images, returning momentarily to the aesthetics of silent cinema.

Hearing without seeing is more prominent in the cinema than seeing without hearing. While this strategy has been used to express the world as perceived by a deaf character, it can also be used as a disquieting strategy in thrillers or horror films. Of course, infants are able to hear before they can see, and the removal of this primary stimulus can have a substantial effect. Anthony Storr notes in *Music and the Mind*:

> A dark world is frightening. Nightmares and infantile fears coalesce with rational anxieties when we come home at night through unlit streets. But a silent world is even more terrifying. Is no one there, nothing going on at all? We seldom experience total silence, except in artificial conditions... we are dependent on background sound of which we are hardly conscious for our sense of life continuing. A silent world is a dead world. If 'earliest' and 'deepest' are in fact related, as psychoanalysts have tended to assume, the priority of hearing in the emotional hierarchy is not entirely surprising; but I think it unlikely this is the whole explanation.[15]

The withholding of sound is certainly able to have a horrifying effect. In the horror film *Dead Silence* (2007), protagonist Jamie drives in a car with the ventriloquist's dummy Billy sitting in the backseat. Suddenly, the car and all other diegetic sounds disappear leaving total silence. In the midst of the eerie lack of sound, an acousmatic—unsynched and offscreen, possibly even non-diegetic—metallic scraping sound occurs, and the dummy Billy subsequently turns his head to look at Jamie. Later, Jamie digs up Billy's grave. Again and equally suddenly, diegetic sound and non-diegetic music halt abruptly; Jamie then looks around concerned, after which we hear a gradual and quiet return of diegetic sound. Exactly the same thing happens in the ghost story *The Innocents* (1961) when the possible appearance to the governess of a ghostly figure on top of the building leads to a withdrawal of diegetic sound and a later appearance of uncanny electronic sounds, both emphasizing the disconcerting effect of the apparition. These examples manifest a dead soundtrack, which emphasizes the filmic event through the removal of the contractual convention for sound and image relations. Such blind spots are on some level an audio equivalent to the dead image track evident when Quentin Tarantino turned his camera to the wall and the audience heard the sounds of Marvin the policeman having his ear cut off by Mr. Blonde in *Reservoir Dogs* (1992), as discussed in the previous chapter. Other examples of moments when the sound track 'dies' occur in *Saving Private Ryan* (1998), where an explosion makes the audience deaf along with the protagonist, and in Woody Allen's *Manhattan* (1979), where in an isolated sequence of memory or fantasy, a boy in a cape flies off upward in a seeming moment of magical realism.

The real silence of a dead soundtrack is not the same as a perceived silence, where room tone (a certain amount of quiet ambient diegetic sound) is added to give the impression that events on-screen are in virtual silence. Of course, non-diegetic music also has to recede for these moments to be effective. David Sonnenschein notes that in moments when we expect music but merely receive diegetic sound, a similar process is in operation: "...the spectators...are drawn into examining the image more carefully and actively, seeking to explain the strangeness of the silence."[16] In the context of films that habitually contain a lot of sound, its absence certainly can seem strange, if not at times a disconcerting reminder of the unstable union of sound and image. Furthermore, these moments exploit the social feelings of unease generated by awkward silences, engendering a desire for the normality of a soundscape not bereft of sounds.

OFF-SCREEN SOUND

By definition, off-screen sound is not synchronized with on-screen sources, yet it often is synchronized with on-screen events. It emphasizes a world beyond the film frame, which also might undermine film's restriction to that narrow space for much of its duration. The most common form of off-screen sound is unproblematic and includes immediate sounds or sounds emanating from objects momentarily off-screen. This involves retrospective motivation where we discover the origin of the sound, or situations where sound is unremarkable ambient sound that does not call itself into question as an ambiguity. Other forms of off-screen sound are more ambiguous. The use of non-diegetic or extra-diegetic sound is conventional, most apparent in the habitual use of non-diegetic incidental music and less so in voiceover narration. The origins of these are well off-screen, as the space of its sound is fundamentally different from that represented on-screen. Further conventional use of off-screen sound includes subjective internal sounds, where we might hear the voice of a letter being read silently or a character's thoughts (which can be more ambiguous), although, of course, much film sound (and images) might indeed be construed as subjective. Such off-screen sound also has particular cinematic functions concerning time (when the memory sound of a voice or place is depicted). Objective off-screen sound regularly has a function relating to space, extending on-screen space (we always hear more than we see) and providing a wider ambience. This embraces the general sounds of spaces immediately beyond sight and those farther afield, with the qualities of recorded sound providing important depth cues for the audience. Beyond these, off-screen sound has distinct dramatic functions tied to acousmatic status in that sounds can be ambiguous or puzzling and then subsequently receive retrospective motivation once we are allowed to see the origin of the sound—which can be important for the audience or for diegetic characters alone. This is most common in detective and mystery narratives, while in the horror genre, ghostly sounds can remain unaccounted for, although they most often constitute a symptom of a potential future threat.

Celebrated films premised upon narratives concerning recorded sound, such as Francis Ford Coppola's *The Conversation* (1974) and Brian DePalma's *Blow Out* (1981), use retrospective motivation to allow the protagonist and the audience to understand ambiguous sound recordings that lack images. Indeed, both films mark a virtual treatise on the possibilities and the limitations of conventional film sound. In *The Conversation*, detective Harry Caul (Gene Hackman) bugs a couple and gradually pieces together their conversation and its implications, while in *Blow Out*, film sound effects recorder Jack Terry (John Travolta) accidentally records the sounds of what might be an assassination. In a sense, these films do not require much analysis as they provide their own within the films themselves. They are both premised upon the ambiguities posed by sound recordings, and the understanding of such situations more generally, and of course the dramatic withholding of information that is gradually revealed. In each case, retrospective motivation is crucial.

Michel Chion's (after Pierre Schaeffer) development of the notion of the acousmatic, where a sound's nature and origin may not be apparent, points to a fundamental ambiguity created by sound cinema. The acousmatic certainly has a source off-screen, but more significantly, it has an unapparent source. It emanates from an uncertain origin, furnishing it with an insistent ambiguity. A crucial further characteristic of acousmatic sound is that, by necessity, it lacks any distinct synchronization with on-screen elements. This is not to say that it appears as an unsynched element as it may well synchronize with off-screen activity, or in addition may synch with non-diegetic elements such as music or voiceover. However, the most common manifestation of the acousmatic, certainly the form discussed by Chion, involves sound that lacks notable synchronization with other elements. Consequently, we should approach the acousmatic as commonly a form of asynchronous sound that is not part of the dominant illusionistic regime in synchronized sound cinema.

Acousmatic sound triggers the imagination. Doherty and Berry noted that Acousmatic art is the art of mental representations triggered by sound,[17] while Robert Normandeau referred to acousmatic sound as "cinema for the ears."[18] Off-screen sounds can certainly make us imagine spaces and objects, but in many films they are used in a manner that does not call attention to themselves, merely constituting a backdrop of ambience. Acousmatic film sound, on the other hand, wishes to be noticed, even if the origins of the sound seem fairly straightforward. For instance, off-screen enemies and threats are common in horror films. They also supply a psychological backdrop to films set in war trenches, as signs of the enduring off-screen threat of the enemy, who are otherwise only evident through their artillery shelling or the occasional appearance of their infantry. Sounds are often a more tangible sign; artillery, gunfire, and shouts across the trenches provide anticipation for the run 'over the top' and eventual contact with the invisible enemy. Indeed, the trench-set horror film *Deathwatch* (2002) played upon this invisible threat, with a British unit facing a malevolent enemy that they only later realize is not the German army but rather a supernatural force. That the loose relationship between sound and source is not only a narrative device but a psychological disturbance is emphasized by Peter Hutchings:

> Even when sounds are connected to their sources within horror films, there is still sometimes a sense that sound and image are operating in relation to different registers. The frequent mismatching of sound to image in horror clearly offers the film-makers opportunities not only to denote the beyondness or otherness of its monsters but also to dramatise extreme emotional

states—especially that of terror —in ways not bounded by the limitations of any particular performance.[19]

Acousmatic sound is a staple horror device as a threatening or anxiety-producing off-screen effect. Indeed, a good example is the sound from the attic early in *The Exorcist* (1973), which does not suggest an identifiable source and is thus even more disturbing and affecting. In the Australian horror film *The Long Weekend* (1978), a couple with marriage problems has gone to spend a weekend camping near the shore in the outback. Everything about the natural environment appears as a potential threat to them, and they are plagued by harrowing wails at night that they eventually decide have been coming from a dugong. Even this retrospective motivation is not fully without reservation, yet there are cases where origins of sounds remain completely unexplained. In *Alien* (1979), there is a synchronized off-screen sound of maximum equivocality. During the landing shuttle's descent to the planet to investigate the distress beacon, there is an ambiguous sound of unclear origin. This sound appears to be unsynchronized with anything on-screen or in the diegetic world. It clearly takes place in the on-screen diegetic, however, as one of the crew (Yaphet Kotto as Parker) declares, "What the hell was that?" The speaker and the audience receive no answer. There is startling ambiguity about the origin of this sound. While at least one of the shuttle's crew seems to hear it, the others are not noticeably concerned. Is this a sound from the landing ship, a form of stress creaking? Or is it non-diegetic in origin,[20] a stray piece of the musical score that has wandered into earshot of one of the crew? As such, it might well be a sonic flash-forward to the alien, a premonition sound. This example appears to be an absolute definition of the acousmatic in its original sense. "What the hell was that?" might refer to its timbre as much as its origin. It is in fact a Tibetan thighbone trumpet sound, and the audience will soon hear it more as a thematic accompaniment to the alien in Jerry Goldsmith's film score. This moment marks a rarity in mainstream narrative cinema, with sound effects colonized directly by music, proving the musical aspects of other areas of film sound. The audience does not focus on this instance with apprehension, as conventionally, such acousmatic sound will be retrospectively motivated. But, of course, on some occasions, it is not explained later, and these are the moments when the acousmatic manifests a most radical form of film asynchrony.

CONCLUSION

Perhaps it is more natural for sound and image tracks to de-constitute into their separate channels than it is for them to form a cohesive unity and illusion. In discussing Luis Buñuel's *Les Hurdes* (*Land without Bread*, 1933), which was shot without synch sound due to lack of finance, Barry Mauer notes that "Each 'track' of Buñuel's film—the visuals, the music, the narration, and the text—does more than merely avoid synchresis; each represents a different register of discourse."[21] When sound and image tracks drift apart into states of some independence, they may well become more like cohesive objects with their own integrity, as can be the case with footage from a real event, for example, or a highly prominent piece of music. They also, however, illustrate how far the principles of the McGurk effect apply: Different impulses in sound and image add up to a third term, where a new effect is produced that is more than the sum of the two parts. Mediocre songs can appear far more pleasing in a film, and there is an assumption in the film industry that good music can save a poor film. There is always some sort of effect—as attested to by random soundtracking of films with CDs—precisely the sort of research I recommend for idle moments (what Michel Chion calls 'forced marriage'[22]). This works particularly well with silent films because it illustrates the persistence of a silent film aesthetic, which remains strong if unacknowledged in contemporary cinema and other audiovisual culture.

One effect of the increasing integration of film soundtracks is that they may gain a degree of independence in themselves and endanger the unity of the film as a coherent object. This can certainly be the case with highly featured music, which can render the rest of the film as little more than visual accompaniment. In some art films, there has been a move toward disjunction as a matter of aesthetic choice. Annette Davison points to Derek Jarman's *The Garden* (1990) as a film that uncouples the "...unity of the sound and image track."[23] Jarman often made films on 8mm with no synchronized soundtrack and sometimes publicly showed them silently. This is not to suggest that Jarman had no interest in soundtracks. His final film, completed as he was going blind, was *Blue* (1993), which had an image track consisting of a blue screen throughout while accompanied by an expansive and varied soundtrack. Much earlier, Walter Ruttmann's early sound film *Week-End* (1930) had also consisted solely of soundtrack with a blank screen. While it might be argued that Ruttmann's and Jarman's films were more like radio plays than films, and that this is no longer audiovisual culture, they seem to suggest that just as it is possible for silent film to be meaningful without sonic accompaniment, film can lose the image and survive as an object.[24]

CHAPTER 9

Conclusion

Final Speculations

There are two ways to look at the world: imagining that everything is apparent, real, and on the surface, or imagining that everything is hidden, unapparent, and conspiratorial. If I had to choose between these two poles, I would certainly take the second. Of course, we can never negate either position, but the more sophisticated view of the world is that processes and mechanisms are not immediately apparent and unproblematically existing in consciousness. Film's processes are far from straightforward, even if its final product can appear to be so. The occult of cinema garners a massive psychological effect from the chemical amalgamation of two elements causing a new and vital outcome.

During the final stages of writing this book, I was plagued with illness that caused temporary but profound deafness. The irony was not lost on me. Watching television, I was happy to find that some channels have subtitles for the hard of hearing. However, I quickly realized that news and current affairs programs had subtitles that were well in temporal arrears to what was being discussed. This led to a strong and confusing disjunction, where images and people were coupled with the wrong thing. However, quite quickly, I adjusted. It seems that human perception is able to compensate—after all, we already mix in our heads as impulses from sound reach the brain before impulses from vision. Making a whole does not necessarily require synchronized input. After all, watching films with subtitles makes for a processing experience far different from films otherwise. Furthermore, one of the dominant instruments of contemporary audiovisual culture, the website YouTube, which hosts a cornucopia of easily accessible video imagery and sound, is inclined to have noticeably poor synchronization between sound and image. This suggests that people are increasingly able to accept slight lags between corresponding sound and images. Yet this also might imply that people concentrate on the images less and value their unity less than in the cinema. Indeed, we should remember that small screens such as television are rarely attended to with the same psychological intensity as in film theatres, where sound and image can be an enveloping and total experience.

Recent advances in digital technology have made the manipulation of sound in the cinema much easier and hastened certain aesthetic developments in relation to sound and image. While these have enabled an unprecedented degree of control for filmmakers, they have inaugurated a progressively complex aesthetic experience for cinema audiences, with increased use of asynchrony but a retention of the paramount keystones of so-called synch points, creating a pulsating heart of cinema. Synchronization is not just a mechanical process of projection and editing conventions. It is a way of thinking and a psychological state of mind. Taking inspiration from phenomena of human perception, most obviously the McGurk effect, we should understand film's combination of sound/music and image as a synergy of human senses that exploits not only the specifics of perception but also cross-references in various locations of the brain. Neuroaesthetics suggests that culture emanates from and engages with perceptual, cognitive, and neurological patterns of the human brain, which suggests a fruitful potential for analysis less in the cultural and ideological sphere than in the physiological and perceptual sphere.[1]

The increasing use of asynchronous relations between sound and image has seemingly served to corral soundtrack elements together. Or, on the other hand, perhaps the increasing convergence of sonic elements has hastened the use of asynchrony more in audiovisual culture. The amalgamation of incidental music and sound effects in film has become more insistent in recent years, although it was always a tradition in certain more challenging films. This unifies the different impulses and motivations of the two sonic discourses. This collapse of the *space* between diegetic sound and non-diegetic music instigates a collapse of mental space between the film's conscious and its unconscious, if you like, by bringing together the different traditional characters of sound effects (often banal and everyday, in the real world) and music (soaring, emotional, and fantastical). This removes a solid division between such aspects as not only fantasy and reality, but also the objective and the subjective, fixed perception and unstable reverie, and the aesthetic and the communicational.

This book is premised upon the notion that film is precisely audiovisual and that the aesthetics of sound are at the heart of the medium. This provides a starting point for all its analysis and theorization. Such a perspective allows for a rethinking of film, precisely as an aesthetic medium rather than one where analysis can simply describe 'people' and 'what happens' as if the critic or analyst were confronted with real events unfolding in front of them. This is the most undemanding approach to an illusion. Theory and criticism, one might argue, have focused on the wrong thing, assuming that the heart of cinema is the illusion of continuity rather than the lock of image and sound. This is why there are so many books on film that merely focus on the narrative—following André Bazin's influential notion of film's essence being that it on some level shows reality (an illusion of the real world, at least[2])—to the detriment of the many other aspects of film. Indeed, film soundtracks are a powerful element of film, one that is still underestimated in accounts of cinema, despite the prodigious amount of money spent on film scores at the intersection of the film and music industries (two of the biggest cultural industries). The psychological importance of film sound is borne out by experiments such as Repp and Penel's, where test subjects tapped their fingers in time with seemingly unified sound and image events. The conclusion drawn was that the subjects relied more on sound for the task than vision.[3] Indeed, film audiences are more reliant on sound than people might think; the majority of films may be based on hearing spoken dialogue, but contemporary film can often house sumptuous soundscapes.[4] Lipscomb and Kendall concluded from an experiment looking into musical accompaniment that there was "...evidence of the powerful effect a musical soundtrack has on the motion picture experience."[5] Also, the perception of the same sequence changed when different musical accompaniment was used, while Bullerjahn and Güldenring found "...that each musical soundtrack creates its own particular type of film and plot...[and that] film music polarizes the emotional atmosphere and influences the understanding of the plot."[6] Precise points of synchronization between sound and image are the lynchpins of film, television, and audiovisual culture more generally. It is almost inconceivable to have visuals accompanied by sounds that are not intended in any way to match, and in the vast majority of cases, a great deal of time and mental energy are expended in working out how sounds will match images. This notion is far older than the development of recorded and synchronized sound in the late 1920s. And now, with the proliferation of audiovisual culture through the Internet and portable devices, synchronization remains a crucial issue. At a time when the aesthetics of cinema have been extruded to television, videogames, and Web 3.0 (and beyond), it is a significant juncture to address the fundamental psychology of audiovisual culture. Rather than simply following the dominant psychological frameworks in film studies (cognitive psychology or psychoanalysis), discussions of the psychology of sound film here have followed the inspiration of phenomenology in a broad sense, seeing the essence of cinema as an act of perception induced by an intimate relationship between a film and a committed viewer-auditor. Generally speaking, my approach followed such lines, although my concerns embarked from the scientific and the physical, more interested in the body and unapparent effects in sound and image than in more traditional models of the cognitive spectator/auditor or studies of any empirical audience.

Progressively, since the introduction of synchronized recorded sound, technological developments have allowed for more precise editing and synchronizing of sound and image. Developments in digital technology over the last decade or so have enabled a previously unimagined degree of control for filmmakers and an increasingly complex aesthetic experience for cinema audiences. Part of this has included direct exploitation of non-synchronized sound. Concurrently, in the world outside the cinema, we are in increasingly more situations where sound does not immediately match our visual perception. One effect of being in a world where there is increasingly less synch, where things seem more out of synch, is increased mental disturbance, cognitive dissonance, and stress.

AESTHETIC SOCIAL PSYCHOLOGY

Adorno notes that we should not see culture as merely a symptom of society but as concentrated social substance,[7] and indeed, we might find processes in film and music that can tell us much about the social aspects of which they are a part. Film in essence is a psychological process whereby we are transported to different worlds and provided with some degree (a lot or a little) of emotional involvement in what is represented on-screen. Consequently, any investigation of the complexities of film as a process has to have psychological inspiration, if not an explicit theory of psychology. And, of course, any psychology of culture, or indeed, any consideration of culture more generally, is at heart social. Eisler and Adorno see a central connection between film music aesthetics and the social, where

> ...the alienation of the media from each other [film from its music] reflects a society alienated from itself, men [sic] whose functions are severed from each other even within each individual, therefore, the aesthetic divergence of the

media is a potentially legitimate means of expression, not merely a regrettable deficiency that has to be concealed as well as possible.[8]

Although it seems like an unfounded statement, it is merely a minor step to encounter broader human processes evident in aesthetic procedures. Significantly, they point to the central position of synchronization between sound and image as the heart of a social unity, if perhaps only in poetic form. In some broad manner, this might also partially account for the independence of image and soundtracks evident in some films. Chion backs this up:

> Basically, the question of the unity of sound and image would have no importance if it didn't turn out, through numerous films and numerous theories, to be the very signifier of the question of human unity, cinematic unity, unity itself.... It is not I but the cinema that, via films like *Psycho* and *India Song*, tells us the impossible and desired meeting of sound and image can be an important thing.[9]

So, whether this has viability on a social level or not, film sets out its importance as a *social* feature on the stage of films themselves. The primary but difficult relationship between scientific and physical facts about sound and theoretical speculation into the imaginary zone of film furnishes a tension, a dialectic, rather than a fully formed theory that requires proving at some later date. These are speculations that likely will never be proven to the satisfaction of scientists or staunch social science positivists. One of the key points to retain here is that there is a clear relationship between film's occult processes and the world outside of the screen and speakers.

The adding together of the two tracks forms a new unity that is more powerful than each on its own. Eisenstein quoted Kurt Koffka: "It has been said: The Whole is more than the sum of its parts. It is more correct to say that the whole is something else than the sum of its parts, because summing is a meaningless procedure, whereas the whole-part relationship is meaningful."[10] This sets up an early connection with Gestalt psychology, although Eisenstein's ideas are premised upon behaviorist principles. Indeed, though, Pavlovian principles of conditioned stimuli eliciting conditioned responses are clearly relevant for discussions about film and sound synchronization. The central concern with simultaneity of sound and vision stimuli was evident in Pavlov's work, where conditioned responses were elicited by the association of buzzers with the appearance of dogs' meals. This synchronization of sound and vision stimuli to create strong conditioned association is evident in American psychologist John B. Watson's famous behaviorist experiment with a little boy and a rat. A little boy named Albert was given a tame white rat to play with. He liked the rat, but Watson then made a disturbing noise by hitting a metal bar with a hammer each time Albert touched the rat. The boy was soon associating the rat with startling and scary blasts of sound, and he became afraid of the rat. As Watson had predicted, generalization then took place, where Albert became afraid of similar white furry things, including Santa Claus's beard.[11] The point of synchronizing sound and vision at a single point was clearly crucial to the whole endeavor.

So these moments of coalescence are crucial, in psychological and by implication social terms. Chion coined the term 'synchresis' to describe the phenomenon of spontaneous magnetic clamping together of sound and image into a seemingly single event. There is an associated form of psychology attached to the synchronization of sound and image, wherein the illusion of unity is enough to engender a sense of reality on some level. This cultural configuration according to Wolfgang Köhler is underlined by "…the fact that sensory fields have in a way their own social psychology."[12] Aesthetics have solid psychological implications, and social integration/inclusion is implied through aesthetic integration (as Eisler and Adorno noted). Large-scale consumerism, of course, has a vested interest in integrated social inclusivity, and the mainstream film products of Hollywood and other popular cinemas reflect this. Audiovisual techniques, and audiovisual culture more generally, work for social inclusion as consumerist inclusion, yet the threat of exclusion hangs in the air (embodied by avant garde film's alienation effects). It is not simply consumer culture that desires an integrated, non-alienated audience; for the state of social order and stability, good consumers and happy citizens are vital. Film, like some other areas of audiovisual culture, harbors potential worry in the possibility for the collapse of aesthetics into constituent elements, the failure of illusion, and the alienation of the audience. Yet such aesthetics are exciting, at least partly because of their ambiguity and threat of collapse, and asynchrony is a fundamental element of film, with inevitable occasional appearances and more sustained use as a device of anxiety. Its overuse can be shocking and even fatiguing. In music, if there is too much concentration in high-frequency ranges, the effect is tiring for the listener. Equally, the use of sustained asynchrony might prove tiring for audiences not versed in its extended use.

Characterizing film as a combination of intellectual image corralled with emotional music and sound, Mary Ann Doane contends that film sound

...risks a potential ideological crisis. The risk lies in the exposure of the contradiction implicit in the ideological polarisation of knowledge. Because sound and image are used as guarantors of two radically different modes of knowing (emotion and intellection), their combination entails the possibility of exposing an ideological fissure—a fissure which points to the irreconcilability of two truths of bourgeois ideology. Practices of sound editing and mixing are designed to mask this contradiction through the specification of allowable relationships between sound and image.[13]

Mainstream narrative films strive to remove uncertainty (unless it drives the film forward) and attempt to contain anxiety through its rare and careful use as a device. The appearance of sustained asynchrony cultivates uncertainty about the illusory diegetic world on-screen, fostering an unfulfilled expectation of the return to the normality of synchronization and dominant invisible film style. This dynamic of alternation follows a generally logical relationship, one of antecedent-consequent, and the essential cause-and-effect logic of cinema.

An ecological approach to film soundtracks looks not only to an integrity and autonomy of elements in themselves, but also sees/hears their interrelation as primary. In film, there are a number of different acoustic spaces, often superimposed and simulated. For example, the space of recorded dialogue, the space of replaced (post-production) dialogue, the space of recorded music, and the space of prerecorded sound effects. Most of these will not impose themselves in any immediately noticeable way on the unfolding of a film diegesis in time. Yet they are nevertheless present and might be perceived by the persistent and meticulous listener as a potential destruction of the illusory composite of sound and image.

Of course, music is the terrain where all sound might be unified. The music industry has had a big impact on neighboring industries, and music as an aesthetic has had a significant impact on the audiovisual arts. This has been recognized far less than it might have been. In films, music has had an increasing but unacknowledged influence in recent years, due not only to music's ubiquity but also to the dominance of musical (in the extended sense) ways of thinking about sound more generally.

For years, the sonic dimensions of society have been ignored as an aspect of relevance to social analysis. All aesthetics have social implications; they are never neutral. In a rush to find personal psychology behind cinema, theorists have neglected social function or mass psychology in recent years, which means that we fail to see cinema as a palliative, something to make us feel better and confirm our worldviews. Approaching synch points as a form of harmony, on one level at least, involves seeing them as an underlying philosophy of aesthetics, thus potentially a philosophy of life itself. This might be termed a Pythagorean approach, in that it sees a human or natural essence in the complexities and logics of mathematics, or in this case, in aesthetic conventions. After all, much in the way of writing and spoken words has been expended upon the essential connections between mathematics and music, and we might conclude that both are expressive of an underlying level of human existence and experience. Edward R. Lippman notes that,

> ...in a type of Pythagoreanism, [composer Jean-Philippe] Rameau eventually finds that music gives the law to every manifestation of human thought and creativity. And...the structure of the music is indissolubly connected with its expressiveness: its technical theory, that is, with its aesthetics, but also with its metaphysical foundation.[14]

Lippman also notes that an understanding of the underlying principles of arts such as music opens us to the realization that there are implications beyond simply a practice: "A vibrating string is an audible unity of number and length, of arithmetic and geometry, while the moral and emotional influence of music suggests that its corresponding mathematical study may possess ethical powers of its own."[15] This consideration of ancient Greek musical theory highlights how theorists were unwilling to see culture shut off from its wider implications. More recently, there has been a tendency to ignore harmony (on whatever level) or the related senses of aesthetic normality as psychological states that mainstream culture promotes.

Synchronization is a philosophy of society, embodying its veneer of social harmony but also its requirement of some social discord. What is the effect of being in a world where there is increasingly less synch? Quite likely, as I noted earlier, it is mental disturbance and stress. Others might wish to take this further. Cinema's alternation of synchronization and seemingly sourceless sound is a conventional dynamic that is a central characteristic of sound cinema, but an existence without matching sound and vision risks tipping into Schafer's schizophonia as less a slightly anxious condition and more a pathological state.

FINAL WORDS

This book has been concerned with synchronization and the associated psychology suggested or constituted. It aimed to reassess film from the point of view of it being less about representation and more about the *combination* of sound and image. To a degree, this has had the effect of moving analysis into a more abstract constituency. Arguably, the first book on film theory, Hugo Münsterberg's *The Photoplay* (published in 1916), theorized that film manifested an analogue of the workings of the human mind.[16] The synchronization of hearing and vision mark a fundamental mechanism of perception, which therefore constitutes its own psychological mechanism. It is upon this foundation that the magic contrivance at the heart of cinema and other audiovisual culture is instigated. Mary Ann Doane theorized that 'invisible' synchronization hides film's 'material heterogeneity,' unifying mechanical elements into a breathing, believable illusion. Keyed around synch points, this holds a stable position for the audience, warding off the trauma of realizing the truth behind cinema.[17] The potential catastrophic collapse of audiovisual unity into technological components that lose the ability to hide their technological basis and unemotional character is suggestive of a form of the Freudian death drive (Thanatos), a tendency toward an inorganic and inert state. Against this, synchronization of sound and image aims to retain an ordered, sensible, and comforting experience from irrational chaos and the psychological terror of meaninglessness and futility.

It seems to me that a contemporary form of alchemy is the mixture of scientific ideas, physics, and physical facts with more aesthetic arguments that are founded upon different principles, ontologies, and epistemologies. Rather than necessarily using one to justify the other, this book has aimed to pull together theoretical speculation about a highly ephemeral object through the means of accepted fact and contemplative conjecture. Broadly blending scientific and critical theory components generates a tension, a dialectic, rather than a theory that requires proving at some later date. And these are speculations that will likely never be proven to the satisfaction of died-in-the-wool scientists, social science positivists, or methodological conservatives.

After all, methodological marriage (forced, shotgun, or otherwise) matches this book's interest in the marriage of sound and image tracks. Indeed, the pulling together of these two separate technologies, impulses, and sense stimuli marks the union of two separate ideas and the production of something different. The concept of 'synch' involves the conjoining of two ideas. In the process, something is gained in meaning, but something is lost as well. These two things are not necessarily unified, for example, the sounds of punches in films, dubbed dialogue, or birds in natural history programs. So synch is not about the natural but about *belief* (not nature/realism but culture). Synchronization requires *faith*. We must provide our own belief for the system of suturing sound and vision to work.

We fit the words we hear to the lips that move—as in the perennial favorite TV outtake in which a horse's lips move and match the words of a talking man standing next to it. The joke betrays something of the truth: that it is we who connect the horse's movements with the sounds, rather than there being any immutable bond between the two. Montage is the basic principle. Eisenstein noted:

> The basic fact was true, and remains true to this day, that the juxtaposition of two separate shots by splicing them together resembles not so much a sum of one shot plus another shot—as it does a *creation*. It resembles a creation—rather than a sum of its parts—from the circumstance that in every such juxtaposition *the result is qualitatively* distinguishable from each component element viewed separately.[18]

Like the horizontal (across time) Kuleshov effect, which alternated the same image of actor Ivan Mosjoukhine with images of different objects to yield a sense of emotional and logical connection between the two, McGurkian synchronization works vertically (of the moment) to conjoin separate ideas into a whole, not unlike a so-called Hegelian synthesis, with two terms combining to produce a third term. The outcome in film can be far less predictable and often more abstract and elusive. The effect of this third term can be enough to blind us, but it is undoubtedly a piece of mechanical natural magic built around moments of sometimes unlikely unity.

NOTES

PREFACE
1. Gershom Sholem, *Walter Benjamin: the Story of a Friendship* (London: Faber and Faber, 1982), 59.
2. Michel Chion, *Audio-Vision: Sound on Screen*, edited and translated by Claudia Gorbman (New York: Columbia University Press, 1994), 63, 64.
3. Maurice Merleau-Ponty, *The Phenomenology of Perception* (London: Routledge, 1962), 232.

CHAPTER 1
1. T. W. Adorno, *Minima Moralia: Reflections from a Damaged Life* (London: Verso, 1978), 222.
2. Although this screen activity may not actually be against the beat (but rather slow and not synchronized), it demonstrates how it can be difficult for film to be 'out of time' to music.
3. A number of theorists have been interested in this phenomenon, including Gilles Deleuze in *Cinema 1 : The Movement Image* (London: Athlone, 1986) and *Cinema 2: The Time Image* (New York: Continuum, 2005), although his interest remains visual.
4. Sergei M. Eisenstein, *The Film Sense*, edited and translated by Jay Leyda (London: Faber and Faber, 1943); Hanns Eisler and Theodor Adorno, *Composing for the Films* (London: Athlone, 1994).
5. It should be noted that this book is discussing cinema as distinctly perceptual. Films shown on television lack the strength of the immersive effect of big screen, big sound, and directed concentration. Consequently, effects are likely to be much reduced.
6. Rick Altman, "Introduction" in *Yale French Studies*, no. 60, 1980, 6.
7. Of course, even this can vary. For example, the French tend to be more tightly synched to mouth movements than the more free Italians.
8. Michel Chion, *Audio-Vision: Sound on Screen*, translated and edited by Claudia Gorbman (New York: Columbia University Press, 1994), 223.
9. Ibid., 59.
10. Mary Ann Doane, "Ideology and the Practice of Sound Editing and Mixing" in Teresa de Lauretis and Steve Neale, eds., *The Cinematic Apparatus* (London: Macmillan, 1980), 47–48.

11. Semir Zeki investigated the notion of a biological foundation to aesthetics, seeing art as exploiting modular aspects of the brain and the structure of nerve cells. *Inner Vision: An Exploration of Art and the Brain* (Oxford, UK: Oxford University Press, 1999).
12. Leonard B. Meyer, *Emotion and Meaning in Music* (Chicago: University of Chicago Press, 1961), 207.
13. Philip Ball, *The Music Instinct: How Music Works and Why We Can't Do Without It* (London: Vintage, 2011).
14. See further discussion in Michael Shermer, *The Believing Brain: From Ghosts and Gods to Politics and Conspiracies* (London: Robinson, 2012).
15. Albert S. Bregman, *Auditory Scene Analysis: the Perceptual Organization of Sound* (Cambridge, MA: MIT Press, 1990), 459–460.
16. Chion, op. cit., 63, 224.
17. Ibid., 63–64.
18. Lipscomb and Kendall point to essential perceptual marking by points of synchronization between sound and image. Scott D. Lipscomb and Roger A. Kendall, "Sources of Accent in Musical Sound and Visual Motion" in *Proceedings of the 4th ICMPC* (Liege, BE: 1994), 451–452.
19. Harry McGurk and John W. MacDonald, "Hearing Lips and Seeing Voices" in *Nature*, no. 264, 1976, 746–748.
20. I first became aware of this phenomenon in the mid-1990s, when word-of-mouth became translated to Websites. Since then, many have looked for synchronies between various films and records. Pink Floyd's music appears amenable: Their song "Echoes" (from *Meddle*, 1971) appears to fit the final section of *2001: A Space Odyssey* (1968), which almost wholly lacks dialogue. This has been bolstered by the persistent rumor that Kubrick originally asked Pink Floyd to score the film. Recounted in Nicholas Schaffner, *Saucerful of Secrets: The Pink Floyd Odyssey* (London: Harmony, 1991), 127.
21. This is when two events seem related but are not related according to regular principles of causality, but rather by an acausal connection. Carl Gustav Jung, *Synchronicity—An Acausal Connecting Principle* (Princeton, NJ.: Princeton University Press, 2010).
22. There are small companies, such as the DeVille Workshop (syncmovies.com), that sell DVDs that add albums to the visuals of films, also including among others *The Black Matrix*, soundtracking *The Matrix* with Metallica's *Black Album*; *The Ozzorcist* (*The Exorcist* and Black Sabbath's eponymous debut album); and *Planes, Trains and Candy-O* (*Planes, Trains and Automobiles*, and The Cars' *Candy-O*).
23. John Belton notes that in *The Wizard of Oz*, the wizard's unmasking occurs at the precise moment when synchronization is established, completing a hermeneutic chain in the film. "The Technology of Film Sound" in Elisabeth Weis and John Belton, eds., *Film Sound: Theory and Practice* (New York: Columbia University Press, 1985), 65.
24. Sergei M. Eisenstein and Sergei Yutkevich, "The Eighth Art: On Expressionism, America, and of course, Chaplin" in Richard Taylor, ed. and trans., *Sergei M. Eisenstein, Selected Works, Volume 1, Writings 1922–1934* (London: BFI, 1988), 30.
25. Maurice Merleau-Ponty, *The Phenomenology of Perception* (London: Routledge, 1962), xiii, xiv.
26. Mary Ann Doane, "The Voice in Cinema: the Articulation of Body and Space" in *Yale French Studies*, no. 60, 1980, 45.

27. Sergei M. Eisenstein, Vsevolod Pudovkin, and Grigori Alexandrov, "Statement on Sound" in Richard Taylor, ed. and trans., *Sergei M. Eisenstein: Selected Works, Volume 1, Writings 1922–1934* (London: BFI, 1988), 113.
28. Silent cinema had a certain amount of autonomy for images and music respectively, which was conventionalized by recorded soundtracks' domination by matching dialogue. However, there is certainly a case for the survival of the aesthetics of silent cinema in the margins of mainstream cinema, such as in montage sequences, where music can often take the foreground, and diegetic sound often recedes to nothing. Generally speaking, foregrounded music tends to appear in sequences where dialogue has receded, or where there is a visual spectacle that requires something of an aural equivalent in terms of impressiveness. The advent of music video allowed more scope for a sustained sense of counterpoint among communication, character, or aesthetics of sound and image.
29. Foley is the name given to effects produced by a person with a range of sound-producing devices, such as coconut shells and a cat litter tray.
30. John Belton, "Technology and Aesthetics of Film Sound" in Elisabeth Weis and John Belton, eds., *Film Sound: Theory and Practice* (New York: Columbia University Press, 1985), 66.
31. Noel Burch, *Theory of Film Practice* (Princeton, NJ: Princeton University Press, 1981), 90.
32. Although modern medicine can use the term to describe a conflict-free state, Freud originally discussed it in terms of the death drive. Sigmund Freud, *The Interpretation of Dreams* (New York: Empire, 2011), chapter 7; Fatima Caropreso and Richard Theisen Simanke, "Life and Death in Freudian Metapsychology: A Reappraisal of the Second Instinctual Dualism" in Salman Akhtar and Mary Kay O'Neil, eds., *On Freud's 'Beyond the Pleasure Principle'* (London: Karnac, 2011), 100–101.
33. Despite their vocal silence, they have their own associated music.
34. Ernest Walter (from *The Technique of the Film Cutting Room*), quoted in Doane, op. cit., 49.

CHAPTER 2

1. "The pronounced misgivings in the period of transition to sound can be traced to the rising awareness that films with sound live up to the spirit of the medium only if the visuals take the lead in them. Film is a visual medium." Siegfried Kracauer, *Theory of Film: The Redemption of Physical Reality* (Oxford, UK: Oxford University Press, 1960), 103.
2. Indeed, some of the most prominent film scholars have helped to perpetuate this problem. For instance, Bordwell, Staiger, and Thompson's *The Classical Hollywood Cinema* devotes only a small handful of its epic wordage to sound and music, an unforgivable exclusion in an otherwise excellent volume. The same goes for Bordwell's outstanding book *Narration in the Fiction Film*, which wholly ignores narration in film musicals, despite his having addressed film music in other writing. David Bordwell, Janet Staiger, and Kristin Thompson, *The Classical Hollywood Cinema: Film Style and Mode of Production to 1960* (London: Routledge, 1988); David Bordwell, *Narration in the Fiction Film* (London: Routledge, 1987).
3. W. K. L. Dickson, "A Brief History of the Kinetograph, the Kinetoscope and the Kineto-Phonograph" in *Journal of the SMPTE*, vol. 21, December 1933, reprinted in Raymond Fielding, ed., *A Technological History of Motion Pictures and Television* (Berkeley, CA: University of California Press, 1967), 12.

4. Martin Koerber, "Oskar Messter, Film Pioneer: early Cinema between Science, Spectacle and Commerce" in Thomas Elsaesser and Michael Wedel, eds., *A Second Life: German Cinema's First Decades* (Amsterdam: Amsterdam University Press, 1996), 56.
5. Leo Enticknap, *Moving Image Technology: From Zoetrope to Digital* (London: Wallflower, 2005), 110.
6. Rick Altman, "Sound History" in Rick Altman, ed., *Sound Theory Sound Practice* (London: Routledge, 1992), 121.
7. Michel Chion, *Audio-Vision: Sound on Screen*, Claudia Gorbman, ed. and trans. (New York: Columbia University Press, 1994), 5.
8. Ibid., 63, 64.
9. Chion's synchresis matches the ideas of Lipscomb and Kendall, both of which note perceptual 'marking' by synch points. S. D. Lipscomb and R. A. Kendall, "Sources of Accent in Musical Sound and Visual Motion" in the *Proceedings of the 4th ICMPC* (Liege, BE: 1994), 451–452.
10. Roy Armes, "Entendre, C'est Comprendre: in Defence of Sound Reproduction" in *Screen*, vol. 29, no. 2, Spring 1988, 11.
11. Such neuroimaging tomography (looking inside something) is often fMRI, functional magnetic resonance imaging, which uses radio frequency waves to find activity in the brain, but it could also be PET, positron emission tomography, or SPECT, which uses gamma rays.
12. Mariano Sigman and Stanlislas Dehaene, "Brain Mechanisms of Serial and Parallel Processing during Dual-Task Performance" in *Journal of Neuroscience*, vol. 28, no. 30, July 2008, 7585.
13. 'Perceptual expectancy' or a 'perceptual set' is a preexisting blueprint that allows the rapid perception of similar things and situations.
14. Joseph Ledoux, *The Emotional Brain: The Mysterious Underpinnings of Emotional Life* (New York: Simon and Schuster, 1996), 265.
15. Ibid., 69.
16. Only a handful of books have attempted to pull emotions into a cognitive frame, with various degrees of success. One of the first and most interesting was Carl Plantinga and Greg M. Smith, eds., *Passionate Views: Film, Cognition, and Emotion* (London: Johns Hopkins University Press, 1999), which included a chapter about film music written by Jeff Smith.
17. An example of this is James J. Gibson's 'ecological model,' which assumes that the mapping of stimulus to cognition is absolutely one to one. Gibson, *The Ecological Approach to Visual Perception* (Boston: Houghton Mifflin, 1979).
18. Evolutionary psychology (EP) suggests that the brain uses a significant proportion of the body's energy input (about 25 percent) and so must be its most significant part for survival. J. C. Steven and Donald McBurney, *Evolutionary Psychology* (London: Prentice Hall, 2003), chapter 4.
19. In recent years, there has been an amending of earlier cognitive psychology approaches to emphasize the physiological level and even consciousness through the notion of 'embodiment.' Francisco J. Varela, Evan Thompson, and Eleanor Rosch, *The Embodied Mind* (Cambridge, MA: MIT Press, 1991).
20. However, more recently, the notion of 'embodiment' increasingly has been taken seriously to address lived experience for cognitive approaches, suggesting that the human mind and experience have a crucial physical character rather than being 'Descartian' mental abstraction. Cf. Francisco J. Varela, Evan Thompson, and Eleanor Rosch, *The Embodied Mind* (Cambridge, MA: MIT Press, 1991).

21. Gestalt psychology contradicted the dominant form of psychology of the time, 'structuralism' (not to be confused with the approach in critical theory), which saw the mind as comprised of separate modular functional constituents.
22. Gestalt psychologist Max Wertheimer discussed in detail the phi phenomenon at the heart of the illusion of film. Accounting for the apparent movement of a succession of still images in film projection, phi phenomenon has now replaced the notion of the persistence of vision as an explanation. Its focus is on the process of perception rather than the other's premise that images are retained on the retina for only a short period, blurring them together. "Experimentelle Studien über das Sehen von Bewegung" in *Zeitschrift für Psychologie*, no. 61, 1912, 161–265.
23. Rudolf Arnheim, "The Gestalt Theory of Expression" in Mary Henle, ed., *Documents of Gestalt Psychology* (Los Angeles: University of California Press, 1961), 308.
24. Meraj Dhir, "A Gestalt Approach to Film Analysis" in Scott Higgins, ed., *Arnheim for Film and Media Students* (Abingdon, UK: Routledge, 2011), 89–90.
25. This is called 'Prägnanz,' which is often translated as 'pithiness,' whereby we alight on the simplest and most balanced pattern to register.
26. Claude Alain, Karen Reinke, Yu He, Chenghua Wang, and Nancy Lobaugh, "Hearing Two Things at Once: Neuropsychological Indices of Speech Segregation and Identification" in *Journal of Cognitive Neuroscience*, vol. 17, no. 5, 2005, 811.
27. C. Redies, J. Crook, and O. Creutzfeld, "Neuronal Response to Borders with and without Luminance Gradients in Cat Visual Cortex and Lateral Geniculate Nucleus" in *Experimental Brain Research*, no. 61, 1986, 469–481; Lothar Spillmann and Walter H. Ehrenstein, "Gestalt Factors in the Visual Neurosciences" in L. Chalupa and J. S. Werner, eds., *The Visual Neurosciences* (Cambridge, MA: MIT Press, 2003); L. Spillmann and J. S. Werner, eds., *Visual Perception: the Neuropsychological Foundations* (San Diego, CA: Academic Press, 1990).
28. Kurt Koffka, "On the Structure of the Unconscious" in *The Unconscious: A Symposium* (New York: Alfred A. Knopf, 1928), 60.
29. John G. Benjafield, *A History of Psychology* (Needham Heights, MA: Simon and Schuster, 1996), 173.
30. Kurt Goldstein, *The Organism. A Holistic Approach to Biology Derived from Pathological Data in Man* (New York: Zone, 1995), 292.
31. Chion states that synch points generally "... obey the laws of gestalt psychology." Chion, op. cit., 59.
32. Sandra K. Marshall and Annabel J. Cohen, "Effects of Musical Soundtracks on Attitudes Toward Animated Geometric Figures" in *Music Perception*, vol. 6, no. 1, 1988, 95–112.
33. Scott D. Lipscomb and Roger A. Kendall, "Perceptual Judgments of the Relationship Between Musical and Visual Components in Film" in *Psychomusicology*, no. 13, 1994, 60–98.
34. Harry McGurk and John W. MacDonald, "Hearing Lips and Seeing Voices" in *Nature*, no. 264, 1976, 746–748.
35. D. Alais and D. Burr, "The Ventriloquist Effect Results from Near-Optimal Bimodal Integration" in *Current Biology*, vol. 14, no. 3, 2004, 257–262.
36. V. J. Bolivar, A. J. Cohen, and J. C. Fentress, "Semantic and Formal Congruency in Music and Motion Pictures: Effects on the Interpretation of Visual Action" in *Psychomusicology*, no. 2, 1994, 38–43.
37. R. Sekuler, A. B. Sekuler, and A. B. Lau, "Sound Alters Visual Motion Perception" in *Nature*, no. 385, 1997, 308; J. Vroomen and B. de Gelder, "Sound Enhances Visual Perception: Cross-Modal Effects of Auditory Organization on Vision" in

Journal of Experimental Psychology: Human Perception and Performance, vol. 26, no. 5, 2000, 1583–1590.

38. A. O'Leary and G. Rhodes, "Cross-Modal Effect on Visual and Auditory Object Perception" in *Perception and Psychophysics*, no. 35, 1984, 565–569.
39. L. Shams, Y. Kamitani, and S. Shimojo, "Visual Illusion Induced by Sound" in *Cognitive Brain Research*, 14, 2002, 147–152.
40. This was exploited by the TV comedy *Mister Ed* (1961–66), which had a horse's random lip movements vaguely matched to a human voice.
41. *The Incredible Journey* (1963) and its remake *Homeward Bound: The Incredible Journey* (1993) were both made by Disney; they were both about a long and perilous journey made by two dogs and a cat. The later version has the animals' lips moving. This is effortless because of current computer software that uses the existing soundtrack to 'match' newly generated mouth movements.
42. John Belton, "Technology and Aesthetics of Film Sound" in Elisabeth Weis and John Belton, eds., *Film Sound: Theory and Practice* (New York: Columbia University Press, 1985), 70.
43. Charles O'Brien, *Cinema's Conversion to Sound: Technology and Film Style in France and the U.S.* (Bloomington, IN: Indiana University Press, 2005), 2.
44. Ibid., 1.
45. Rick Altman, "Sound Space" in Rick Altman, ed., *Sound Theory, Sound Practice* (London: Routledge, 1992), 58–59.
46. A good example is the sound of a werewolf howl off-screen as we follow a potential victim on-screen.
47. Siegfried Kracauer, *Theory of Film: The Redemption of Physical Reality* (Oxford, UK: Oxford University Press, 1960), 111–112.
48. Ibid.
49. Sergei Eisenstein, *The Film Sense*, Jay Leyda, ed. and trans. (London: Faber and Faber, 1943), 67–68.
50. Ibid., 68.
51. Ibid.
52. Ibid., 69.
53. Ibid.
54. Robert Spadoni, *Uncanny Bodies: the Coming of Sound Film and the Origins of the Horror Genre* (Berkeley, CA: University of California Press, 2007), 14.
55. Sergei M. Eisenstein, Vsevolod Pudovkin. and Grigori Alexandrov, "Statement on Sound" in Richard Taylor and Ian Christie, eds,. *The Film Factory: Russian and Soviet Cinema in Documents 1896-1939* (Cambridge, MA: Harvard University Press, 1988), 234–5.
56. D. M. Neale, *How to Do Sound Films*, revised by R. A. Hole (London: Focal Press, 1969), 25.
57. Barry Salt, "Film Style and Technology in the Thirties: Sound" in Elisabeth Weis and John Belton, eds., *Film Sound: Theory and Practice* (New York: Columbia University Press, 1985), 39.
58. Roy M. Prendergast, *Film Music: A Neglected Art* (New York: Norton, 1992), 263.
59. Punching film gives clicks and scratching a frame diagonally, making so-called streamers, allowing for more free timings as they appear and fade and give a sense of where musical events should be happening. Flashes conventionally aligned with circles above staff in the conductor's score indicate the precise moments required. Often, complex calculations were involved using a reference book often known as 'The Knudson book' (written by Caroll Knudson in 1965).

60. T. G. Blackham, "Film Sound Technique" in *Studio Sound*, vol. 13, no. 4, April 1971, 188.
61. The development and availability of the Nagra and Uher portable recorders allowed for far easier location sound recording. Enticknap, op. cit., 127.
62. Blackham, op. cit., 188.
63. "If... the projector speeds up or slows down, the switches become out of phase, the relationship is altered, and depending on the direction they are out of phase, the value of the motor control resistance is altered and the projector is speeded up or slowed down." Neale, op. cit., 90.
64. Belton, op. cit., 68.
65. Some widescreen films retained the 'sound on film' system, which was far easier for distribution and exhibition.
66. Ashley Shepherd, *Pro Tools for Video, Film and Multimedia* (Boston: Muska and Lipman, 2003), 53.
67. Originally this was 25 per second in Europe (the 'EBU Timecode') and 30 per second in North America, although revisions were made in 2008. Such timecodes are not only for audiovisual products; they are also endemic in the production of music. So the SMPTE's is not the only timecode.
68. Slight variations can have impact. One apparent problem is that the speed of light is faster than the speed of sound, meaning that with synchronized filming, a distant sound source will appear to be slightly behind its corresponding image.
69. During the first decade of the second millennium, AVID's Media Composer became the dominant sound editing program, while Apple's Final Cut Pro also gained in popularity.
70. Pro-MPEG is a body that has aimed to standardize industrial approaches to audiovisual compressed digital media. It was founded just after the millennium and replaced the earlier MPEG (Moving Picture Experts Group), which gave the name to the digital audiovisual format.
71. A limitation is that with cheap capture cards in computers, frames can be 'dropped' from the digital copy that is worked on by the composer, and this will mean that music can become out of synch with the film.
72. Shepherd, op. cit., 196.
73. See, for instance, Gianluca Sergi, *The Dolby Era: Film Sound in Contemporary Hollywood* (Manchester, UK: Manchester University Press, 2004); Mark Kerins, *Beyond Dolby (Stereo): Cinema in the Digital Sound Age* (Bloomington, IN: Indiana University Press, 2011).
74. Indeed, it is most common for film music composers to use software that has an essentially musical function for creation and is also suited to the image and the mixing stage. According to a number of composers I spoke with, dominant software at the time of the book's writing include industry standard Pro Tools, Apple FinalCut Pro, and Digital Performer (although often importing basic material from Logic or Cubase).
75. "Significant audio changes are automatically detected; similarly the source video is automatically segmented and analyzed for suitability based on camera motion and exposure.... High quality video clips are then automatically selected and aligned in time with significant audio changes." Jonathan Foote, Matthew Cooper, and Andreas Girgensohn, "Creating Music Videos Using Media Analysis" in *Multimedia '02 Conference Proceedings*, December 1–6 (Juan-les-Pins, FR), 553.

76. One also might argue similarly for music video, which often consists of separate sound and image channels, meaning that it is unremarkable sometimes to remain unsynched for sustained periods.
77. Armin G. Kohlrausch, Steven L. D. J. E. van de Par, Rob L. J. Eijk, and James F. Juola, "Human Performance in Detecting Audio-Visual Asynchrony" in *Journal of Acoustical Society of America*, vol. 120, no. 5, 2006, 3048–3085; C. N. J. Stoelinga, D. J. Hermes, and A. G. Kohlrausch, "On the Influence of Interaural Differences on Temporal Perception of Masked Noise Bursts" in *Journal of the Acoustical Society of America*, vol. 120, no. 5, 2006, 2818–2829.
78. Although individual responses vary, auditory information is processed faster (the brain activates 30–50 msecs earlier for sound than for image). Rob L. J. van Eijk, Armin Kohlrausch, James F. Juola, and Steven van de Par, "Audiovisual Synchrony and Temporal Order Judgments: Effects of Experimental Method and Stimulus Type" in *Perception and Psychophysics*, vol. 70, no. 6, 2008, 966, 955.
79. This exhibits smaller thresholds than in many previous experiments using impact stimulus for results. Steven van der Par, Armin Kohlrausch, and James F. Juola, "Some Methodological Aspects for Measuring Asynchrony Detection in Audio-Visual Stimulus" in A. Calvo-Manzano, A. Perez-Lopez, and J. S. Santiago, eds., *Proceedings of the Forum Acousticum 2002*, CD-ROM (Porto, PT: Universidade de Porto, Faculdade de Engenharia, 2002), 4, 2.
80. Neale, op. cit., 80.

CHAPTER 3

1. Lev Manovich, *The Language of New Media* (Cambridge, MA: MIT Press, 2001).
2. Dominated by what is now commonly known as Soviet montage cinema of the 1920s and '30s.
3. Siegfried Kracauer, *Theory of Film: the Redemption of Physical Reality* (Oxford, UK: Oxford University Press, 1960), 115.
4. Although the coming of sound to cinema has been well documented in U.S. cinema, it has received rather less of a focus in cinema elsewhere. To some degree, it might be argued that this makes sense because all other countries the world over had to follow the patterns established in the U.S. However, there were significant local variations in activity, as testified to by Michael Allen's discussion about multiple turntable disc players in British cinema before the widespread adoption of U.S. synchronized sound technology in film. Allen, "In the Mix: How Electrical Reproducers Facilitated the Transition to Sound in British Cinema" in K. J. Donnelly, ed., *Film Music: Critical Approaches* (Edinburgh, UK: Edinburgh University Press, 2001).
5. In the second and third decades of the 20th century, George Beynon wrote a manual for cinema accompanists that aimed to make standardized and precise synchronizations of live music with silent films. Beynon, "From Musical Presentation of Motion Pictures" [1921], reprinted in Julie Hubbert, ed., *Celluloid Symphonies: Texts and Contexts in Film Music History* (Berkeley, CA: University of California Press, 2011), 61.
6. Rick Altman, "Introduction: Four and a Half Film Fallacies" in Rick Altman, ed., *Sound Theory, Sound Practice* (London: Routledge, 1992), 36.
7. Altman, "Sound Space" in Rick Altman, ed., *Sound Theory, Sound Practice* (London: Routledge, 1992), 46–58.
8. Wesley C. Miller, "Basis of Motion Picture Sound" in *Motion Picture Sound Engineering* (London: Chapman and Hall, 1938), 7.

9. Altman, op. cit., 46–47.
10. Kenneth F. Morgan, "Dubbing" in Lester Cowan, ed., *Recording Sound for Motion Pictures* (New York: McGraw Hill, 1931), 145.
11. Ibid., 147–148.
12. Ibid., 148.
13. Anon., "The Debut of the Talkies: What Happened at 'The Jazz Singer'" in *Melody Maker*, November 1928, 1277.
14. Ibid., 1278.
15. Anon., "Sound Film Activity" in *Melody Maker*, October 1928, 1150.
16. Sergei M. Eisenstein, *The Film Sense*, Jay Leyda, ed. and trans. (London: Faber and Faber, 1943), 18.
17. Kristin Thompson pointed out that there were in fact few Soviet 'counterpoint' films made during the era of Soviet montage cinema in the 1920s and '30s. Thompson, "Early Sound Counterpoint" in *Yale French Studies*, no. 60, 116.
18. Vsevolod Pudovkin's writings were published as *Film Technique and Film Acting* (London: Grove Press, 1958).
19. Eisenstein, *Film Form: Essays in Film Theory*, Jay Leyda, trans. (New York: Harcourt Brace, 1949).
20. Ibid., 72–79.
21. There is a celebrated homage in Francis Ford Coppola's *Apocalypse Now* (1979), where a ritual killing of a cow is crosscut with Kurtz's assassination.
22. The montage of attractions was later recast by Eisenstein as a more general dialectical montage. He saw cinema as a crucial synthesis of the human endeavors of art and science, whereas Pudovkin believed that film was more natural, with editing and visual techniques being derived from aspects of human perception.
23. Eisenstein's article on vertical montage, written in 1940, appeared in *Selected Writings, Volume II*, Michael Glenny and Richard Taylor, eds. and trans. (London: BFI, 1991).
24. Eisenstein, "A Course in Treatment" (1932) in *Film Form: Essays in Film Theory*, Jay Leyda, trans. (New York: Harcourt Brace, 1949), 64–65.
25. Eisenstein, "The Filmic Fourth Dimension" (1929) in *Film Form: Essays in Film Theory*, Jay Leyda, trans. (New York: Harcourt Brace, 1949), 71.
26. Eisenstein, Vsevolod Pudovkin, and Grigori Alexandrov, "Statement on Sound" in Richard Taylor, ed. and trans., *S. M. Eisenstein: Selected Works, Volume 1, Writings 1922–1934* (London: BFI, 1988), 113.
27. Ibid.
28. Ibid.
29. Ibid.
30. Ibid.
31. Eisenstein, 1943, op. cit., 67.
32. Ibid., 62. Aimée Mollaghan notes the diagram's similarity to the screen format of elements in current digital editing software (such as Final Cut Pro or Avid). *The Musicality of the Visual Film* (Ph.D. diss., University of Glasgow, 2011), 40.
33. Robert Robertson, *Eisenstein on the Audiovisual: The Montage of Music, Image and Sound in the Cinema* (London: I. B. Tauris, 2009), 175.
34. David Bordwell, Janet Staiger, and Kristin Thompson, *The Classical Hollywood Cinema: Film Style and Mode of Production to 1960* (London: Routledge, 1988), 303.
35. Royal S. Brown, *Overtones and Undertones: Reading Film Music* (Los Angeles: University of California Press, 1994), 10.

36. George Burt, *The Art of Film Music* (Boston: Northeastern University Press, 1994), 81.
37. Music in British films over the years has often seemed far less precisely synchronized than music in Hollywood films. I have discussed this to some degree elsewhere. One of a handful of reasons for this looser synchronization of music to image was that respected art music composers often refused to write to precise timings. They clearly did not think they should be subordinating their compositional talents to the requirements of film, although they often were more than happy at the degree of remuneration they received.
38. Michel Chion, *Audio-Vision: Sound on Screen* (New York: Columbia University Press, 1994), 38.
39. For discussions of anempathetic music, see Claudia Gorbman, "Anempathy: Hangover Square" in *Unheard Melodies: Narrative Film Music* (London: BFI, 1987); and Chion, op. cit., 123.
40. Caryl Flinn, quoted in James Buhler and David Neumeyer, "Film Music/Film Studies" in *Journal of the American Musicological Society*, vol. 47, no. 2, 1994, 44; cf. Annette Davison, *Hollywood Theory, Non-Hollywood Practice: Cinema Soundtracks in the 1980s and 1990s* (Aldershot, UK: Ashgate, 2004), 34.
41. Burt, op. cit., 6.
42. Richard Maltby, *Hollywood Cinema* (Oxford, UK: Wiley-Blackwell, 2003), 239.
43. Tim Anderson, "Reforming Jackass Music: the Problematic Aesthetics of Early American Film Music Accompaniment" in *Cinema Journal*, vol. 37, no. 1, Fall 1997, 12–14; James Wierzbicki, *Film Music: A History* (Oxford, UK: Oxford University Press, 2009), 34.
44. This is the sonic equivalent of the anachronistic piece of mise-en-scène in historical films, such as the typewriter and more in Derek Jarman's *Caravaggio* (1986) and a large number of objects in Alex Cox's *Walker* (1987).
45. Basil Wright and Vivian Braun, "Manifesto: Dialogue on Sound" in Elisabeth Weis and John Belton, eds., *Film Sound: Theory and Practice* (New York: Columbia University Press, 1985), 96.
46. Ibid., 97.
47. Rene Clair, "The Art of Sound" [1929] in Elisabeth Weis and John Belton, eds., *Film Sound: Theory and Practice* (New York: Columbia University Press, 1985), 92.
48. Ibid., 94.
49. David Bordwell, *On the History of Film Style* (Cambridge, MA: Harvard University Press, 1998), 36.
50. Kracauer, op. cit., 116.
51. Ibid., 106.
52. This is reminiscent of the overlapping lines of dialogue evident in some of Robert Altman's films.
53. With, for example, Ives's *Fourth Symphony* requiring two conductors, and the second movement quoting at least six tunes from elsewhere.
54. Dimitri Shostakovich, *The Missing Symphony* (V/Vm/ Test Records, VVMTCD10, no year of release stipulated, but somewhere in the early to mid-2000s).
55. Albert S. Bregman, *Auditory Scene Analysis* (Cambridge, MA: MIT Press, 1990), 459.
56. The "Restored Collector's Edition" from Image Entertainment, DVD in 2005 and Blu Ray in 2008.

57. Criticized heavily by many, including Nicholas Cook, who suggests replacing this notion with three terms: "conformance, complementation, and contest." *Analysing Musical Multimedia* (Oxford, UK: Oxford University Press, 2000), 65, 103–104.
58. Eisenstein, Pudovkin, and Alexandrov, op. cit., 113.
59. Alexander Graf, *The Cinema of Wim Wenders: The Celluloid Highway* (London: Wallflower, 2002), 140.
60. Béla Balázs, *Theory of the Film: Character and Growth of a New Art* (New York: Dover, 1970), 218–219.

CHAPTER 4

1. See, for example, Tom Ruffles, *Ghost Images: Cinema of the Afterlife* (Jefferson, NC: McFarland, 2004).
2. Stephen Bottomore, "The Panicking Audience?: Early Cinema and the 'Train Effect'" in *Historical Journal of Film, Radio and Television*, vol. 19, no. 2, 1999, 177.
3. André Gaudreault, "Theatricality, Narrativity and 'Trickality': Re-Evaluating the Cinema of Georges Méliès" in *Journal of Popular Film and Television*, vol. 15, no. 3, 1987, 110–119.
4. Peter Brooks, *The Melodramatic Imagination: Balzac, Henry James, Melodrama, and the Mode of Excess* (New Haven, CT: Yale University Press, 1995), 5.
5. Tom Gunning, "Doing for the Eye What the Phonograph Does for the Ear" in Richard Abel and Rick Altman, eds., *The Sounds of Early Cinema* (Bloomington, IN: Indiana University Press, 2001), 16.
6. Robert Spadoni, *Uncanny Bodies: The Coming of Sound Film and the Origins of the Horror Genre* (Berkeley, CA: University of California Press, 2007), 17.
7. Ibid., 30.
8. David Toop, *Sinister Resonance: the Mediumship of the Listener* (London: Continuum, 2010), 126–127.
9. Harry McGurk and John W. MacDonald, "Hearing Lips and Seeing Voices" in *Nature*, no. 264, 1976, 746.
10. Andy Hamilton, "Adorno" in Theodore Gracyk and Andrew Kania, eds., *The Routledge Companion to Philosophy and Music* (New York: Routledge, 2011), 393.
11. Rudolf Arnheim, *Visual Thinking* (Berkeley: University of California Press, 2004), 139.
12. Leonard B. Meyer, *Emotion and Meaning in Music* (Chicago: University of Chicago Press, 1961), 261, 268.
13. John Belton, "Technology and Aesthetics of Film Sound" in Elisabeth Weis and John Belton, eds., *Film Sound: Theory and Practice* (New York: Columbia University Press, 1985), 65.
14. The human ear consists of three chambers. Sound enters from the ear flap (the pinna or auricle), follows into the outer ear, a cavity that leads to the tympanic membrane or eardrum, which vibrates as the sound wave hits it. Beyond the ear drum, the middle ear contains air (and thus becomes pressurized during flight). This contains three bones: the stapes (stirrup), the incus (anvil), and the malleus (hammer). The vibrating eardrum causes movement in the malleus, which in turn moves the other two bones, with the stapes pushing the oval window, which causes movement of the liquid in the inner ear. The liquid-filled cochlea is the central organ of hearing in the inner ear and is sensitive to the effects of motion and gravity, affecting the sense of balance. Here, movements in the liquid are converted by sensitive hairs on the surface into an electrical impulse, which is then fed into the neurological system.

15. Mariano Sigman and Stanlislas Dehaene, "Brain Mechanisms of Serial and Parallel Processing during Dual-Task Performance" in *Journal of Neuroscience*, vol. 28, no. 30, July 2008, 7585.
16. The primary sensory areas of the brain include areas of the upper brain, primarily the auditory section of the temporal lobe and insular cortex, the somatosensory section of the parietal lobe, and the visual section of the occipital lobe. The association areas of the cortex are involved in primary perception and also more complex thought.
17. Indeed, activities in the parietal lobe are often associated with meditative states. Cinema arguably might take on some of the characteristics of meditation and offers something perhaps related to an out of body experience.
18. Vernon B. Mountcastle, *Medical Physiology* (St. Louis, MO: C. V. Mosby, 1974), 579.
19. Anthony Storr, *Music and the Mind* (London: Harper Collins, 1997), 35.
20. Jennifer A. McMahon, "Perceptual Constraints and Perceptual Schemata: the Possibility of Perceptual Style" in *Journal of Aesthetics and Art Criticism*, vol. 61, no. 3, Summer 2003.
21. Michael Shermer, *The Believing Brain: From Ghosts and Gods to Politics and Conspiracies—How We Construct Beliefs and Reinforce Them as Truths* (London: Times Books, 2011). Also see Daniel Dennett, *Consciousness Explained* (Boston: Back Bay Books, 1992).
22. Graham Reed, *The Psychology of Anomalous Experience: A Cognitive Approach* (Buffalo, NY: Prometheus, 1988).
23. This human tendency toward 'patternicity' is discussed in detail by Shermer, op. cit.
24. The shapes are without structure, which is provided by the patient's mind, illustrating unconscious concerns. The test's scientific status is not agreed upon.
25. This phenomenon can be taken advantage of by audio equipment that wishes to provide lower notes than the system appears capable of delivering.
26. Particularly so, given that auditorium sound is not necessarily even originating from the same direction in which the audience is facing.
27. The notion of synchresis is an attempt to make a theoretical replacement for the illusory sense of 'reality' found in cinema.
28. Wolfgang Köhler, *Gestalt Psychology. An Introduction to New Concepts in Modern Psychology* (New York: Liveright, 1947), 20.
29. R. Murray Schafer, *Our Sonic Environment and the Soundscape: The Tuning of the World* (Rochester, NY: Destiny, 1994), 91.
30. The Institute of Sound and Vibration Research at the University of Southampton has a particularly impressive 'live' echo chamber, where even short spoken sentences are unintelligible through sound reflection.
31. There is a constant danger of re-experience through a trigger. After a while, emotional exhaustion might take over. This can lead to a state of complete lack of emotions, communicational distance, and even problems with memory.
32. Freud's work centred on psychological trauma. This is not the same as Jacques Lacan's work, which is more concerned with understanding through language. For instance, Lacan's "the Real" has a traumatic capability outside symbolization, where categories fail. It is thus an object of anxiety par excellence. Jacques Lacan and Wladimir Lanoff, "Fetishism: The Symbolic, the Imaginary and the Real" in *Journal for Lacanian Studies*, vol. 1, no. 2, 2003, 299–308.
33. Lionel Festinger, *A Theory of Cognitive Dissonance* (Stanford, CA: Stanford University Press, 1957).

34. Some have suggested that Festinger's original formulation needs rethinking. For example, Elliot Aronson, "The Theory of Cognitive Dissonance: A Current Perspective" in Leonard Berkowitz, ed., *Advances in Experimental Social Psychology*, vol. 4 (New York: Academic Press, 1969), 1–34; Joel M.Cooper, *Cognitive Dissonance: 50 Years of a Classic Theory* (London: Sage, 2007).
35. In the television series *Space 1999* (1975) "End of Eternity" episode, alien Balor fights the inhabitants of Moonbase Alpha to a fully silent soundtrack. Later, when lead characters Konig, Bergman, and Helena wonder about the art in Balor's asteroid prison, we are shown shots of paintings of chaos with tortured and aggressive faces, accompanied by extra-diegetic sounds of screaming and terror.
36. These pieces also appear in Van Sant's following film *Last Days* (2005), which is based on the days leading up to the suicide of a rock star clearly based on Nirvana's Kurt Cobain.
37. According to Randolph Jordan's extensive analysis, Westerkamp's pieces, rather than simply expressing alienation, connect interior subjectivity in the film to a plane outside the diegesis, indeed outside the film. "The Schizophonic Imagination: Audiovisual Ecology in the Cinema" (Ph.D. diss., Montreal: Concordia University, 2010), 263. See further discussion in Danijela Kulezic-Wilson, "Sound Design is the New Score" in *Music, Sound and the Moving Image*, vol. 2, no. 2, Autumn 2008, 129.
38. Edward Tatnall Canby, "Sound Minus Synch: Part Two" in *Studio Sound*, vol. 13, no. 8, August 1971, 403.
39. Alan Williams, "The Musical Film and Recorded Popular Music" in Rick Altman, ed., *Genre: The Musical* (London: Routledge and Kegan Paul, 1981), 149.
40. John Cotner, "Careful with that Axe, Eugene" in Kevin Holm-Hudson, ed., *Progressive Rock Revisited* (London: Routledge, 2001), 84.
41. While it may not necessarily be 'filmic,' it certainly has a representational dimension. The screams suggest that the care urged in the title was not taken, while the live version of the song on *Ummagumma* has the snare drum produce a 'chopping axe' rim-shot sound. Programmatic music, which had extra-musical inspiration, perhaps entered popular music from art music, yet one could also argue that the 'program,' the music's representational aspects, could have been inspired at least as much if not more by film.
42. Indeed, in 2009, a direct attempt to copy the visuals of this sequence was used in a British television advertisement for home insurance.
43. Barry Salt calls it the "…first shock cut in cinema…." *Film Style and Technology: History and Analysis* (London: Starword, 1983), 284.
44. Hanns Eisler and Theodor Adorno, *Composing for the Films* (London: Athlone, 1994 [1947]), 73–74.
45. Charles Barr, "A Conundrum for England" in *Monthly Film Bulletin*, vol. 51, no. 607, August 1984, 234–235.
46. McGurk and Macdonald, op. cit., 746.

CHAPTER 5

1. Don Warburton, "Cinema for the Floating Ear" [interview with Michel Chion] in *The Wire*, no. 294, August 2008, 26.
2. For instance, Danijela Kulezic-Wilson's work, including "The Musicality of Film Rhythm" in John Hill and Kevin Rockett, eds., *National Cinema and Beyond* (Dublin, UK: Four Courts Press, 2004) and "A Musical Approach to Filmmaking: Hip

Hop and Techno Composing Techniques and Models of Structuring in Darren Aronofsky's *Pi*" in *Music and the Moving Image*, vol. 1, no. 1, 2008.
3. Royal S. Brown, *Overtones and Undertones: Reading Film Music* (Los Angeles: University of California Press, 1994), 18.
4. Sergei M. Eisenstein, *The Film Sense*, Jay Leyda, ed. and trans. (London: Faber and Faber, 1963), 67.
5. Evident in his discussions of "nonindifferent nature," the "musicality of landscape," and the "musicality of color and tone." Sergei M. Eisenstein, *Nonindifferent Nature: Film and the Structure of Things*, Herbert Marshall, trans. (Cambridge, UK: Cambridge University Press, 1987), 389.
6. However, Stan Link suggests that to understand the complex interactions of sound and moving image, theorists might not need the concept of synaesthesia. "Nor the Eye Filled with Seeing: the Sound of Vision in Film" in *American Music*, Spring 2004, 90.
7. Peter Kivy, *Sound and Semblance: Reflections on Musical Representation* (Princeton, NJ: Princeton University Press, 1984), 33.
8. Immanuel Kant, *Critique of Judgment* (Indianapolis, IN: Hackett, 1987), 82.
9. Rudolf Arnheim, "The Gestalt Theory of Expression" in Mary Henle, ed., *Documents of Gestalt Psychology* (Los Angeles: University of California Press, 1961), 308.
10. Andre Habib and Frederick Peltier, "An Interview with Peter Kubelka" in *Off Screen*, vol. 9, issue 11, November 2005 [www.offscreen.com/index.php/phile/interview_kubelka/], accessed September 17, 2010.
11. Jon Dale, review of Guy Sherwin, "Optical Sound Films 1971–2007" DVD in *The Wire*, no. 294, August 2008, 72.
12. This is similar to interactive iPhone applications for generative music, such as Brian Eno and Peter Chilvers's *Bloom*.
13. The loose movement of cultural primitivism at this same time suggested that human processes were being bypassed by conventional, undynamic, and banal developments, often assigned to the standardization of mass culture.
14. Suzanne K. Langer, *Philosophy in a New Key: A Study in the Symbolism of Reason, Rite and Art* (Cambridge, MA: Harvard University Press, 1957), 228.
15. Kivy, op. cit., 143.
16. Francois Truffaut, *Hitchcock* (London: Secker and Warburg, 1968), 335.
17. Alfred Hitchcock, "On Style" in Sidney Gottlieb, ed., *Hitchcock on Hitchcock: Selected Writings and Interviews* [original interview published in *Cinema*, 1963] (London: Faber and Faber, 1997), 298.
18. Is this staking a claim on the most significant contribution to his films that was beyond his control? Ironically, Bernard Herrmann, Hitchcock's most famous musical collaborator, was conductor of the CBS Symphony Orchestra for 15 years and saw himself more as a conductor than composer.
19. Robynn J. Stilwell, "'Bad Wolf': Leitmotif in *Doctor Who*" in James Deaville, ed., *Music in Television: Channels of Listening* (London: Routledge, 2011), 137.
20. D. M. Neale, *How to Do Sound Films*, revised by R. A. Hole (London: Focal Press, 1969), 109–110.
21. Noel Burch, *Theory of Film Practice* (Princeton, NJ: Princeton University Press, 1981), 95.
22. David Bordwell, "The Musical Analogy" in *Yale French Studies*, no. 60, 1980, 141–156.
23. Eisenstein, op. cit., 1985, 216.
24. Eisenstein, op. cit., 1943, 62.

25. Sergei Eisenstein, "From Lectures on Music and Colour in Ivan the Terrible" in *Selected Writings, Volume III* [1946–7], Richard Taylor, ed. and trans. (London: BFI, 1996), 319, 321.
26. "Playing the Green Cathedral: the Music of Geoffrey Burgon," DVD extra on *Doctor Who: the Seeds of Doom*, BBCDVD3044, 2010.
27. Eisenstein, op. cit., 1943, 69.
28. R. Murray Schafer, *The Soundscape: Our Sonic Environment and the Tuning of the World* (Rochester, NY: Destiny, 1994), 5.
29. John Cage, *Silence: Lectures and Writings* (London: Marion Boyars, 1980), 3. On p. 83, Cage notes that Edgard Varèse had used the term 'organized sound' to describe music before him.
30. George Burt, *The Art of Film Music* (Boston: Northeastern University Press, 1994), 88–89.
31. Ibid., 100.
32. Nicholas Cook, *Analysing Musical Multimedia* (Oxford, UK: Oxford University Press, 2000), 66.
33. The degree of difficulty of contradiction is well illustrated by a sketch in the second series of the British comedy show *Big Train* (1998), where a film editor has accompanied a director's sad funeral scene with Status Quo's "Rocking All Over the World."
34. Caryl Flinn, *Strains of Utopia: Gender, Nostalgia and Hollywood Film Music* (Princeton, NJ: Princeton University Press, 1992), 139.
35. A central strategy particularly for Gramscian Marxist-inspired cultural studies approaches.
36. Indeed, director Christophe Gans initiated the film project by creating a demo that he sent to Konami. This was cut to the game's music, so the music was the absolute foundation of the film.
37. The game series includes *Silent Hill* (1999, Playstation, later versions ported for PC); *Silent Hill 2* (2001, PS2, PC, Xbox); *Silent Hill 3* (2003, PS2, PC); *Silent Hill 4: The Room* (2004, PS2, PC, Xbox), *Silent Hill Origins* (PSP); *Silent Hill: Homecoming* (2008, PS3, Xbox, PC); *Silent Hill: Shattered Memories* (2009, Wii, PS2, PSP); *Silent Hill: Downpour* (2010, PS3, Xbox); and *Silent Hill: Book of Memories* (2012, PS Vita). A sequel to the film was released after a long wait: *Silent Hill: Revelation 3D* (2012).
38. He was trained at an art school rather than a music school (so he was not classically trained). He joined Konami as a roster composer and musician at the age of 25 in 1993 (working on *Castlevania: Symphony of the Night* [1997]). By the time of *Silent Hill 3*, Yamaoka had become the game producer for the PC version of the whole thing. Composers such as Yamaoka and Nobuo Uematsu (*Final Fantasy*) are cult celebrities among dedicated videogame players.
39. "Every sound and every line of sound that is in the game is done by me. And, I make all my own sound effects...," "GDC [Game Developers Conference] 2005: Akira Yamaoka Interview" in *Game Informer* magazine [www.gameinformer.com/News/Story/200503/N05.0310.1619.39457.htm], accessed March 7, 2007.
40. Strangely, the music was credited solely to Jeff Danna, and Akira Yamaoka, the composer of almost all the incidental music that appeared in the film, was instead credited as executive producer of the film itself. Perhaps this suggests that the music's role in the transition from small to large screen was more important than its merely incidental status. On first analysis, the music appears simply to 'port'

Yamaoka's game music into the film—as a temp track like Kubrick's *2001: A Space Odyssey* (1968). However, upon closer inspection, some of the music has been remixed and some re-recorded, although Kevin Banks's credit as music editor suggests that there was a need to cut pieces together.

41. The track "Promise: Reprise" is repeated, but the musical strategy is about presentation rather than structural cohesion.
42. *Silent Hill*'s world appears to emanate from the neurotic mind of the game's central character. Indeed, the constant dislocation of sound and image establishes the sense of aberrant psychology at the heart of the game. This might account for the game and the film's mismatch of expansive reverb-drenched music and sounds, with misty visuals in the deserted town of Silent Hill, where we would expect sound to be muffled and close-sounding.
43. Leonard B. Meyer, *Emotion and Meaning in Music* (Chicago: University of Chicago Press, 1961), 207.
44. However, it should be noted that films based on the transmission of a pro-filmic event, such as rock documentaries, are defined perhaps to a lesser degree by, or certainly in different ways from, narrative film form. These might be construed as visual emanations from music, something like song sequences in film musicals.
45. Theodor Adorno, "On Popular Music" in Andrew Goodwin and Simon Frith, eds., *On Record: Rock, Pop and the Written Word* (London: Routledge, 1990), 306.
46. Michel Chion, *Audio-Vision: Sound on Screen*, Claudia Gorbman, ed. and trans. (New York: Columbia University Press, 1994), 59.
47. Ibid., 190.
48. Ibid., 59.
49. Meyer, op. cit., 138; see also David Huron, *Sweet Anticipation: Music and the Psychology of Expectation* (Cambridge, MA: MIT Press, 2007).
50. Chion, op.cit., 55.
51. E♭ followed by B♭ a fifth higher, and then E♭ a fourth higher than that, with each on the downbeat of the looped bar of 3/4.
52. It sounds a little like a female voice and runs down a minor scale, including a chromatic sixth, from E♭ to B♭ (E♭ D♭ C C♭ B♭). This melodic motif (in different rhythmic formation) appeared earlier in the film at the first appearance of Colquhoun, who puts his face to the window.
53. Musical pieces throughout the film tend to be structured in this way. Although pop music and Nyman's particular form of orchestral music often have structures like this, electronic 'soft studios' also encourage the construction of music in this way, as proven by much electronic dance music.
54. An extraordinarily detailed analysis of album and film is provided by Eddie Edwards. This illustrates how the soundtrack was a combination of edited parts of different musical performances, while the image track is also a combination of different performances, part of which was restaged at Shepperton Studios in London. "The Garden Tapes" [www.thegardentapes.co.uk/], accessed May 8, 2011.
55. Robert Fink, *Repeating Ourselves: American Minimal Music as Cultural Practice* (Berkeley, CA: University of California Press, 2005), 5.
56. Charles Barr, "Hitchcock, Music and the Mathematics of Editing," unpublished paper from Hitchcock and Herrmann, Partners in Suspense conference, York, UK, June 2011.
57. William H. Rosar, "Bernard Herrmann: The Beethoven of Film Music?" in *Journal of Film Music*, vol. 1, nos. 2–3, Fall–Winter 2003, 136–137.

58. Kenneth J. Hsu and Andreas J. Hsu, "Fractal Geometry of Music: From Birds to Bach" in *Proceedings of the National Academy of Sciences of the United States*, vol. 87, no. 3, February 1990, 938.

CHAPTER 6
1. Michel Chion, *Audio-Vision: Sound on Screen*, Claudia Gorbman, ed. and trans. (New York: Columbia University Press, 1994), 155.
2. James Lastra, "Film and the Wagnerian Aspiration: Thoughts on Sound Design and History of the Senses" in Jay Beck and Tony Grajeda, eds., *Lowering the Boom: Critical Studies in Film Sound* (Chicago: University of Illinois Press, 2008), 125.
3. Michel Chion notes that there was a desire for the full unification of film's sound elements from the early years of sound film, embodied by directors like Jean Epstein, and then later among theorists of the 1970s, such as Jacques Aumont. He comments that "...the dream, statistically speaking, has proven a total failure." *Film, A Sound Art*, Claudia Gorbman, trans. (New York: Columbia University Press, 2009), 204.
4. Gianluca Sergi, *The Dolby Era: Film Sound in Contemporary Hollywood*. (Manchester, UK: Manchester University Press, 2004), 30.
5. Rick Altman, *The American Film Musical* (London: BFI, 1987), 11.
6. Noel Carroll, *Theorising the Moving Image* (Cambridge, UK: Cambridge University Press, 1996), 139; Jeff Smith, *The Sounds of Commerce: Marketing Popular Film Music* (New York: Columbia University Press, 1998), 6; and Roy M. Prendergast, *Film Music: A Neglected Art* (New York: Norton, 1992), 213–222.
7. Aaron Copland, "Tip to the Moviegoers: Take Off Those Ear-Muffs" in *The New York Times*, November 6, 1949, section six, 28.
8. George Burt, *The Art of Film Music* (Boston: Northeastern University Press, 1994), 79.
9. Ibid., 80.
10. Siegfried Kracauer, *Theory of Film: The Redemption of Physical Reality* (Oxford, UK: Oxford University Press, 1960), 33–34.
11. Chion, op. cit., 149–150.
12. Philip Brophy, *100 Modern Soundtracks* (London: BFI, 2004), 38.
13. Chion, op. cit., 150.
14. Ibid., 85.
15. James Wierzbicki, *Louis and Bebe Barron's* Forbidden Planet: *A Score Guide* (London: Scarecrow, 2005), 26–27.
16. Cf. Liz Greene, "The Unbearable Lightness of Being: Alan Splet and Dual Role of Editing Sound and Music" in *Music and the Moving Image*, vol. 4, no. 3, Fall 2011, 1–13.
17. Miguel Mera and David Burnand, "Introduction" in Miguel Mera and David Burnand, eds., *European Film Music* (London: Ashgate, 2006), 5.
18. The burst of internationally successful Japanese horror films at the turn of the millennium, such as *The Ring* (*Ringu*, 1998), *Dark Water* (2002), and *Ju-On: The Grudge* (2002), all used low-frequency sound as an important part of their arsenal of disturbing effects.
19. When protagonist Kate runs along the deserted underground train, the music consists of a rhythmic loop of treated metallic sounds that are more sound effects than musical in origin. This piece has notable similarities with some of Charlie Clouser's kinetic music in the *Saw* films.

20. Elisabeth Weis, "Sync Tanks: The Art and Technique of Postproduction Sound" in *Cineaste*, vol. 21, nos. 1–2, 1995, 42–48.
21. Such as in other celebrated sonically based films like Coppola's *The Conversation* (1974) or DePalma's *Blow Out* (1981).
22. Clouser composed and produced television music with Australian composer Cameron Allen in the late 1980s before working with Nine Inch Nails and remixing other musical artists. He worked on television shows, including *Las Vegas* (2005) and *American Horror Story* (2011), and he also scored films, including *Death Sentence* (2007), *Resident Evil: Extinction* (2007), and *Dead Silence* (2007).
23. Rob Sacks, "Charlie Clouser's Scary Soundtrack for *Saw*" (interview with Charlie Clouser) in *NPR*'s "Day to Day," October 9, 2004 [http://www.nrp.org/templates/story/story.php?storyId=4132853], accessed November 15, 2006.
24. Ibid.
25. Charlie Clouser, "Interview" at *ign.com* [http://music.ign.com/articles/562/562509p1.html], accessed December 3, 2004.
26. Ibid.
27. Sacks, op. cit.
28. Clouser, op. cit.
29. Chion, op. cit., 8.
30. Sacks, op. cit.
31. Ibid.
32. Chion, op. cit., 150–151.
33. Ibid., 71.
34. These are the proverbial shots of trains going into tunnels that allegedly implied sex in silent films. They are likely apocryphal stories and the fodder of comedy. Probably the most famous non-diegetic insert is during the violent riot that concludes Eisenstein's *Strike* (1925), where a shot from elsewhere of a bull being slaughtered is inserted in the middle of the action..
35. See further discussion in K.J. Donnelly, "*Saw* Heard: Musical Sound Design in Contemporary Cinema" in Warren Buckland, ed., *Contemporary Film Theory* (London: Routledge, 2009), 103–123; and Klas Dykhoff, "Non-Diegetic Sound Effects" in *The New Soundtrack*, vol.2, 2012, 169–179.
36. A philosophical problem is posed by the notion of the non-diegetic sound effect. The concept of diegesis is itself highly questionable, being dependent on an assumption made by an idealized audience member about the illusory world on-screen.
37. Rick Altman, McGraw Jones, and Sonia Tatroe, "Inventing the Cinema Soundtrack: Hollywood's Multiplane Sound System" in James Buhler, Caryl Flinn, and David Neumeyer, eds., *Music and Cinema* (Middletown, CT: Wesleyan University Press, 2000), 352.
38. See further discussion of endemic use in recorded music in Peter Doyle, *Echo and Reverb: Fabricating Space in Popular Music Recording, 1900–1960* (Middletown, CT: Wesleyan University Press, 2005).
39. Brophy, op. cit., 108.
40. Ibid., 108.
41. Annabel J. Cohen, "Film Music: Perspectives from Cognitive Psychology" in James Buhler, Caryl Flinn, and David Neumeyer, eds., *Music and Cinema* (Middletown, CT: Wesleyan University Press, 2000), 373–374.
42. David Toop, *Haunted Weather: Music, Silence and Memory* (London: Serpent's Tail, 2004), 64.

43. Anon., "CM Producer Masterclass: Hybrid" in *Computer Music*, no. 129, Summer 2008, 48.
44. Jay Beck, "William Friedkin's *The Exorcist* and the Proprietary Nature of Sound" in *Cinephile*, vol. 6, no. 1, Spring 2010, 6.
45. Ibid., 7.
46. Marian Hannah Winter, "The Function of Music in Sound Film" in *The Musical Quarterly*, vol. 27, no. 2, April 1941, 151.
47. Although, in Sweden, incidental music was established immediately with recorded sound, foreshadowing the fashion in Hollywood. Christopher Natzén, "The Coming of Sound Film in Sweden 1928–1932, New and Old Technologies" (Ph.D. thesis, Stockholm University) in *Stockholm Cinema Studies*, no. 10, 2010.
48. While Hollywood films always sold internationally, their primary target audience was the U.S. market. It is difficult to imagine that a Chinese audience was ever even considered for the film.
49. Josef von Sternberg's films inspired some significant theory, discussed by Laura Mulvey in her landmark article "Visual Pleasure and Narrative Cinema" in *Screen*, vol. 16, no. 3, Autumn 1975, 6–18.
50. The sudden use of silence makes the audience more interested in what is being depicted. David Sonnenschein, *Sound Design—The Expressive Power of Music, Voice, Sound* (Studio City, CA: Michael Wiese Productions, 2001), 127.
51. Global Journey record GJ3638, 2001.
52. Chion, op. cit., 29.
53. Basil Wright and Vivian Braun, "Manifesto: Dialogue on Sound" in Elisabeth Weis and John Belton, eds., *Film Sound: Theory and Practice* (New York: Columbia University Press, 1985), 97.
54. Film has increasingly influenced television aesthetics and set up a gold standard for audiovisual quality. On the other hand, it might also be argued that aesthetics more at home in television—asynchrony included—are increasingly evident in film.

CHAPTER 7

1. In *The Mission* (1986), when Father Gabriel (played by Jeremy Irons) plays the oboe, his movements and fingering are convincing, but not for the music that is heard on the soundtrack. Irons clearly mimed to a different piece of music during the shooting of the film.
2. Michel Chion, *Audio-Vision: Sound on Screen* (New York: Columbia University Press, 1994), 11.
3. Sergei M. Eisenstein, Vsevolod Pudovkin, and Grigori Alexandrov, "Statement on Sound" in Richard Taylor, ed. and trans., *S. M. Eisenstein: Selected Works, Volume 1, Writings 1922–1934* (London: BFI, 1988), 114.
4. Rick Altman, "Moving Lips: Cinema as Ventriloquism" in *Yale French Studies*, no. 60, 1980, 67–79.
5. Jeff Smith relates the extraordinary dubbing of the singing voices of Harry Belafonte, Dorothy Dandridge, and Joe Adams by (often) white opera singers who try to "blacken their voices." "Black Faces, White Voices: The Politics of Dubbing in Carmen Jones" in *The Velvet Light Trap*, no. 51, Spring 2003, 28.
6. Laura Wagner, "'I Dub Thee': A Guide to the Great Voice Doubles" in *Classic Images*, November 1998 [www.classicimages.com/past-issues/view/?x=/1998/November98/idibthee.html], accessed February 2, 2009.

7. Carol Clover, "Dancin' in the Rain" in *Critical Enquiry*, vol. 21, no. 4, Summer 1995, 725.
8. Steve Wurtzler, "She Sang Live but the Microphone was Turned Off" in Rick Altman, ed., *Sound Theory, Sound Practice* (London: Routledge, 1992).
9. K. J. Donnelly, *Pop Music in British Cinema: A Chronicle* (London: BFI, 2001), viii; see also K. J. Donnelly, *British Film Music and Film Musicals* (Basingstoke, UK: Palgrave, 2007), 10–11.
10. A sense of the reality of performance can also be achieved through imperfection. Jeff Smith notes that off-key singing in *Popeye* (1980) and *Everyone Says I Love You* (1996) provided 'amateurish charm' and broke conventions of the Hollywood musical. Op. cit., 29.
11. The live performances are clearly based on those recorded in the live film/video *Here Are the Young Men* (Factory Video, FACT 37, 1982).
12. While there are isolated cases of thrash metal being used as incidental music in films (such as John Carpenter's *Ghosts of Mars* [2001]), it appears more readily in television programs, particularly those that require the expression of energy, such as the criminal entrapment documentary TV series *Bait Car* (2008).
13. Heather Laing points to the "simultaneous dual existence" of such songs as semi-diegetic. "Emotional By Numbers: Music, Song and the Musical" in Bill Marshall and Robynn Stilwell, eds., *Musicals: Hollywood and Beyond* (Exeter, UK: Intellect, 2000), 8.
14. Alan Williams, "The Musical Film and Recorded Popular Music" in Rick Altman, ed., *Genre: The Musical* (London: Routledge and Kegan Paul, 1981), 152.
15. A highly singular example of sound's primacy is Chris Morris's television program *Jaam* (2000), which retrofitted images to an original radio show soundtrack.
16. The boom in live rock albums in the 1970s was accompanied by persistent (and seemingly well-founded) rumors of live recordings at best being 'sweetened' by studio remixing and at worst being extensively re-performed in the studio.
17. It is a bit more problematic when it comes to guaranteeing that singing is a real event. There has been a trend for 'warts and all' singing, which announces its ontological status as sub-professional, in contrast with the perfection of playback singers in Hindi cinema. This method is embodied by Lee Marvin's rough baritone version of "I was Born under a Wondering Star" in *Paint Your Wagon* (1969) or Michael Caine's distraught singing of "It's Over" at the conclusion of *Little Voice* (1998).
18. The notion of pre-soundtracks (not to be confused with temp tracks) is discussed further in K. J. Donnelly, *The Spectre of Sound: Music in Film and Television* (London: BFI, 2005), 39–40.
19. Siegfried Kracauer notes that scoring a film with known music can have a negative effect, what he calls a 'blinding effect.' *Theory of Film: the Redemption of Physical Reality* (Oxford, UK: Oxford University Press, 1960, 141.
20. Kristi A. Brown points to Grieg's "In the Hall of the Mountain King" being reused in Joseph Carl Breil's score for *Birth of A Nation* (1915), as a whistled tune in Fritz Lang's *M* (1931), in the horror film *Demons* (1986), in the TV miniseries *Stephen King's Needful Things* (1993), and in the comedy *Rat Race* (2001). "The Troll Among Us" in Phil Powrie and Robynn J. Stilwell, eds., *Changing Tunes: The Use of Pre-Existing Music in Film* (Aldershot, UK: Ashgate, 2006), 74–75. I would add the Norwegian film *Trollhunter* (2010).
21. Chion notes that "sound endows the shot with temporal linearization... [and] vectorizes or dramatizes shots," orienting them toward a future or goal. Op. cit., 13.

22. Claudia Gorbman, "Ears Wide Open: Kubrick's Music" in Phil Powrie and Robynn J. Stilwell, eds., *Changing Tunes: The Use of Pre-Existing Music in Film* (Aldershot, UK: Ashgate, 2006), 4–5; Royal S. Brown, *Overtones and Undertones: Reading Film Music* (Los Angeles: University of California Press, 1994), 10.
23. In his films, there is only a loose connection between the existing pieces of music and the images, with each retaining some autonomy. This is profoundly different from Disney's *Fantasia* (1940), where images were composed precisely as an accompaniment to the musical pieces. For further discussion, see Kate McQuiston, "An Effort to Decide: More Research into Kubrick's Music Choices for *2001: A Space Odyssey*" in *Journal of Film Music*, vol. 3, no. 2, 2010, 145–154; Irena Paulus, "Stanley Kubrick's Revolution in the Usage of Film Music: *2001: A Space Odyssey* (1968)" in *International Review of the Aesthetics and Sociology of Music*, vol. 40, no. 1, June 2009, 99–127.
24. Vivian Kubrick's short documentary about the making of the film shows some of Stravinsky's *The Rite of Spring* being played as they shoot the chase in the maze.
25. Carlos's score included Sibelius's *Valse Triste*, which was not used in the final film. For more insight into the use of temp tracks, cf. Ron Sadoff, "The Role of the Music Editor and the 'Temp Track' as Blueprint for Score, Source Music, and Source Music of Films" in *Popular Music*, vol. 25, no. 2, 2006, 165–183.
26. Musical pieces are not only used in fragmentary fashion but altered, for instance, at times through superimposition of an electronic heartbeat that was in Carlos's original music.
27. Most obviously here, but arguably the rest of the film can also be interpreted as Danny's fantasy.
28. For further discussion of the heartbeat added to the music, see K. J. Donnelly, *The Spectre of Sound: Film and Television Music* (London: BFI, 2005), 35; and Ben Winters, "Corporeality, Musical Heartbeats, and Cinematic Emotion" in *Music, Sound and the Moving Image*, vol. 2, no. 1, Spring 2008, 14–21.
29. In the conclusion of the film, when Danny is chased in the maze by his father, Jack's voice has changed, transformed as a principal signifier of his change as a person.
30. Phil Powrie and Robynn J. Stilwell, eds., *Changing Tunes: The Use of Pre-Existing Music in Film* (Aldershot, UK: Ashgate, 2006).
31. Ian Garwood, "Must You Remember This?: Orchestrating the 'Standard' Pop Song in *Sleepless in Seattle*" in *Screen*, vol. 41, no. 3, 2000.
32. Ken Garner, "'Would You Like to Hear Some Music?': Music in-and-out of Control in the Films of Quentin Tarantino" in K. J. Donnelly, ed., *Film Music: Critical Approaches* (Edinburgh, UK: Edinburgh University Press, 2001).
33. Chion, op. cit., 8.
34. A similar sequence takes place in *Oldboy* (2003), where Oh Dae-Su cuts his tongue off but the camera does not show the act.
35. Indeed, the effect is akin to Pavlovian classical conditioning, welding the association of the song with extreme violence. The song's re-release as a single and appearance on television ads served only to remind listeners of *Reservoir Dogs*. Or was the assumption that most people seeing the ads had not seen the film?
36. The process of pre-fitting such music nevertheless relies on post-production, where high sound quality music is dubbed onto the guide track to which actors have been synchronizing their actions.
37. Tarantino's building of scenes around songs is discussed in Garner, op. cit., 188–205; and Ronald Rodman, "The Popular Song as Leitmotif in 1990s Film" in Phil

Powrie and Robynn J. Stilwell, eds., *Changing Tunes: The Use of Pre-Existing Music in Film* (Aldershot, UK: Ashgate, 2006), 126.

38. See further discussion in K. J. Donnelly, *The Spectre of Sound: Music in Film and Television* (London: BFI, 2005), 150–171.
39. Eliot Wilder, *Endtroducing...* (London: Continuum, 2006), 76–77.
40. As Martin Miller Marks notes, before 1910, accounts of cinema are only rarely specific about the music used as accompaniment. *Music and the Silent Film: Contexts and Case Studies, 1895–1924* (Oxford, UK: Oxford University Press, 1997), 31.
41. There are eccentric exceptions, such as the Canadian director Guy Maddin, who has made extensive (and signature) use of antiquated silent film style and early sound film style in his films.
42. Indeed, those with 8mm home movie equipment up until the 1960s would have shown the film silently or with their own improvised soundtrack. The format that became known as Regular 8 lacked a soundtrack on the film itself, unlike its later development, the so-called Super 8.
43. Donald Spoto, *The Art of Alfred Hitchcock: Fifty Years of his Motion Pictures* (London: Doubleday, 1992), 130.
44. Roger Manvell and John Huntley, *The Technique of Film Music* (London: Focal Press, 1975), 253.
45. Indeed, there has been an occasional but persistent stylistic legacy of silent films, for instance the direct influence of German Expressionist silent films on the music video for The Kaiser Chiefs' *I Predict a Riot*, Rob Zombie's *Living Dead Girl*, and in the Metz Schnapps 'Judder Man' advertisement of the early 2000s.
46. For instance, Gillian S. Anderson's work includes reconstructing and conducting a large number of silent era scores including De Mille's *Carmen* (1915), Pabst's *Pandora's Box* (1925), and Griffith's *Way Down East* (1920). In the U.K., Ed Hughes has composed new orchestral music for silent films, even replacing Edmund Meisel's famous and celebrated score for Eisenstein's *Battleship Potemkin* (*Bronenosets Potemkin*, 1925).
47. *Nosferatu: The First Vampire* (Arrow Home Entertainment, ARRO219DVD, 2000).
48. Blair Davis, "Old Films, New Sounds: Screening Silent Cinema With Electronic Music" in *Canadian Journal of Film Studies*, vol. 17, no. 2, Autumn 2008, 88.
49. *Metropolis* (1928, Fritz Lang), new edition overseen by Giorgio Moroder and released in 1984. One of the only scholars to come out in favor of the film is Thomas Elsaesser, who applauds Moroder's attempt to refresh the film rather than leave it as a museum piece. *Metropolis* (London: BFI, 2000), 59.
50. It should be noted that Moroder's seeming lack of credentials for this project, as a successful disco record producer (most prominently for Donna Summer), damned him in the eyes and ears of many.
51. Claudia Gorbman notes that any music added to any image will work to a lesser or greater degree and have some sort of effect. *Unheard Melodies: Narrative Film Music* (London: BFI, 1987), 15.
52. It might also be convincingly argued that the orchestra provides a wide range of tone color and dynamics, as well as an emotional tone that is often lacking in other musical formats.
53. For further discussion on the matter, see K. J. Donnelly, "Constructing the Future through Music of the Past: the Software in *Hardware*" in Ian Inglis, ed., *Popular Music and Film* (London: Wallflower, 2003), 131–147.

54. Cf. Joseph Garncarz, "Versions" in Andrew Higson and Richard Maltby, eds., *'Film Europe' and 'Film America': Cinema, Commerce and Cultural Exchange 1920–1939* (Exeter, UK: Exeter University Press, 1999).
55. Richard Maltby and Ruth Vasey, "The International Language Problem: European Reactions to Hollywood's Conversion to Sound" in David W. Ellwood and R. Kroes, eds., *Hollywood in Europe: Experiences of a Cultural Hegemony* (Amsterdam: University of Amsterdam Press, 1994), 68–93.
56. Charles O'Brien notes that both American and French films are tightly synchronized. *Cinema's Conversion to Sound: Technology and Film Style in France and the U.S.* (Bloomington, IN: Indiana University Press, 2005), 1; while Michel Chion notes this and contrasts it with Italian dubbing. Op. cit., 64–65.
57. In the late 1960s, it clearly was difficult to see holding a foreign cultural product up to ridicule in this manner as being in poor taste.
58. This is not to suggest that there is no comedy in the image track. The film opens with a female dancer in a club taking off her clothes. Her naked body is obscured by superimposed print denoting that this is available only in the 'foreign version' of the film.
59. Daniel Meyer-Dinkgräfe, "Thoughts on Dubbing Practice in Germany: Procedures, Aesthetic Implications and Ways Forward" in *Scope*, issue 5, June 2006 [www.scope.nottingham.ac.uk/article.php?id=131&issue=5], accessed March 27, 2009.
60. As Colin MacCabe notes in his study. The consequence is most likely lost on North American audiences. *Performance* (London: BFI, 1998), 42.
61. John Belton, "Technology and Aesthetics of Film Sound" in Elisabeth Weis and John Belton, eds., *Film Sound: Theory and Practice* (New York: Columbia University Press, 1985), 65.
62. Questions of direct connection between sound and image are less important in television than in film because of differences in the mediums and traditions of mode and place of consumption. Cf. Chion, op. cit., 37.
63. Cf. Liz Greene, "The Gentle Gunman: Stephen Rea—Voicing Republicanism" in the proceedings from Sounding Out 5 (Bournemouth University, UK, 2011).

CHAPTER 8

1. Rick Altman, "Baker's Dozen" in Rick Altman, ed., *Sound Theory, Sound Practice* (London: Routledge, 1992), 251.
2. Michel Chion, *Audio-Vision: Sound on Screen*, Claudia Gorbman, ed. and trans. (New York: Columbia University Press, 1994), 11.
3. Blair Davis, "Old Films, New Sounds: Screening Silent Cinema With Electronic Music" in *Canadian Journal of Film Studies*, vol. 17, no. 2, Autumn 2008, 88.
4. Julie Brown notes the organ's spectral presence throughout the film. "*Carnival of Souls* and the Organs of Horror" in Neil Lerner, ed., *Music in the Horror Film: Listening to Fear* (London: Routledge, 2010), 3.
5. Although perhaps not narrative guidance. As Michel Chion notes, the music has "...no discernible direction, it acts to create a feeling that those long tracking shots in the baroque palace aren't going in any particular direction either...." *Film, A Sound Art*, Claudia Gorbman, trans. (New York: Columbia University Press, 2009), 267.
6. Robert Fink, *Repeating Ourselves: American Minimal Music as Cultural Practice* (Berkeley, CA: University of California Press, 2005), 5.
7. I have always wondered if the term was derived from wildlife filmmaking, where habitually there is no location sound recorded to accompany the images, with

the completion of the footage with library or specially produced recordings during post-production. It seems more likely that it is sound untamed by the image, perhaps.
8. David Toop has written about soundtracks as a form of memory. *Haunted Weather: Music, Silence and Memory* (London: Serpent's Tail, 2004), 94–98.
9. R. Murray Schafer, *Our Sonic Environment and the Soundscape: The Tuning of the World* (Rochester, NY: Destiny, 1994), 9.
10. Ibid., 78.
11. David Laderman coined the term 'slip synch' to describe miming musicians failing to match the lip-synch on purpose to keep their credibility. "(S)lip-Sync: Punk Rock Narrative Film and Postmodern Musical Performance" in Jay Beck and Tony Grajeda, eds., *Lowering the Boom: Critical Studies in Film Sound* (Chicago: University of Illinois Press, 2008), 272. The biographical documentary about the Sex Pistols' bass guitarist, *Sid Vicious: the Final 24 Hours* (2006), clearly could not afford to use their music and had vague sound-alike punk rock in the background throughout.
12. Some of the songs in the film have extra sounds dubbed onto them. The persistent complaints by Johnny Rotten (John Lydon) ("Oh fuck it's awful I hate songs like that. The Pits. Stop it. It's fuckin' awful. Fuckin' ridicularse. Wish I had the words.") sound as if they have been taken from the previous outtake under discussion.
13. Cf. the discussion of the musicality of similar sound and image interaction in Aronofsky's previous film, in Danijela Kulezic-Wilson, "A Musical Approach to Filmmaking: Hip Hop and Techno Composing Techniques and Models of Structuring in Darren Aronofsky's *Pi*" in *Music and the Moving Image*, vol. 1, no. 1, 2008.
14. Cf. Jason Jacobs, "Gunfire" in Karl French, ed., *Screen Violence* (London: Bloomsbury, 1996), 171–178.
15. Anthony Storr, *Music and the Mind* (London: Harper Collins, 1997), 27.
16. David Sonnenschein, *Sound Design—The Expressive Power of Music, Voice, Sound* (Studio City, CA: Michael Wiese Productions, 2001), 127.
17. Douglas Doherty and Ron Berry, "Sound Diffusion of Stereo Music Over a Multi Loud-Speaker Sound System, From First Principles Onwards to a Successful Experiment" in *Journal of Electroacoustic Music*, vol. 11, Spring 1998, 9.
18. Robert Normandeau, "...Et vers un cinema pour l'oreille" in *Circuit, (Revue Nord-Américaine de Musique du XXe Siècle)*, vol. 4, nos. 1–2, 1993, 113.
19. Peter Hutchings, *Hammer and Beyond: the British Horror Film* (Manchester, UK: Manchester University Press, 1993), 134.
20. Thus jumping the divide between incidental music and diegetic sound effects—see some discussion of non-diegetic sound effects in chapter 6.
21. Barry Mauer, "Asynchronous Documentary: Buñuel's *Land Without Bread*" in Jay Beck and Tony Grajeda, eds., *Lowering the Boom: Critical Studies in Film Sound* (Chicago: University of Illinois Press, 2008), 143.
22. Chion, op. cit, 188.
23. Annette Davison, *Hollywood Theory, Non-Hollywood Practice* (Aldershot, UK: Ashgate, 2004), 71.
24. This is perhaps the inverse of the BBC's sound CD releases of the soundtracks without images from some of their lost *Doctor Who* serials from the 1960s. The BBC had destroyed their copies of the programs, but enthusiasts had used tape recorders to preserve the experience of the broadcast for themselves. The soundtracks tend to work remarkably well without the images, with only slight and intermittent interventions from a narrating voiceover. This is the point when

the soundtracks of audiovisual productions start to become radio plays, as testified to by the similarity of these CDs to *Doctor Who* "Audio Adventures" made by Big Finish Productions.

CHAPTER 9

1. Cf. Semir Zeki, *Inner Vision: An Exploration of Art and the Brain* (Oxford, UK: Oxford University Press, 1999); Dahlia Zeidel, *Neuropsychology of Art: Neurological, Cognitive and Evolutionary Perspectives* (London: Psychology Press, 2012).
2. There are influential writings about the realistic nature of film, such as those of André Bazin in *What is Cinema?: Volume 1* (Berkeley, CA: University of California Press, 2004).
3. B. H. Repp and A. Penel, "Auditory Dominance in Temporal Processing: New Evidence from Synchronization with Simultaneous Visual and Auditory Sequences" in *Journal of Experimental Psychology: Human Perception and Performance*, vol. 28, no. 5, 2002, 1085–1099.
4. Gianluca Sergi, "The Sonic Playground: Hollywood Cinema and its Listeners" at *Filmsound.org* [www.filmsound.org/articles/sergi/index.htm], accessed June 6, 2011; Barbara Flueckiger, "Sound Effects: Strategies for Sound Effects in Films" in Graeme Harper, Ruth Doughty, and Jochen Eisentraut, eds., *Sound and Music in Film and Visual Media* (New York: Continuum, 2009), 155.
5. Scott D. Lipscomb and Roger A. Kendall, "Perceptual Judgment of the Relationship between Musical and Visual Components in Film" in *Psychomusicology*, vol. 13, Spring/Fall 1994, 92.
6. Claudia Bullerjahn and Markus Güldenring, "An Empirical Investigation of Effects of Film Music Using Qualitative Content Analysis" in *Psychomusicology*, vol. 13, nos. 1–2, 1994, 110.
7. T. W. Adorno, *The Philosophy of Modern Music* (New York: Continuum, 2003), 130; Andy Hamilton, "Adorno" in Theodore Gracyk and Andrew Kania, eds., *The Routledge Companion to Philosophy and Music* (New York: Routledge, 2011), 393.
8. Hanns Eisler and Theodor Adorno, *Composing for the Films* (London: Athlone, 1994), 74.
9. Michel Chion, *Audio-Vision: Sound on Screen*, Claudia Gorbman, ed. and trans. (New York: Columbia University Press, 1994), 97.
10. Kurt Koffka, *Principles of Gestalt Psychology* (London: Kegan Paul, 1935), quoted in Sergei M. Eisenstein, *The Film Sense*, Jay Leda, ed. and trans. (London: Faber and Faber, 1943), 19.
11. Despite the ease with which Watson instilled this response, he was unable to remove it, and Albert remained frightened. Denise Winn, *The Manipulated Mind: Brainwashing, Conditioning and Indoctrination* (London: Octagon Press, 1983), 59.
12. Wolfgang Köhler, *Gestalt Psychology. An Introduction to New Concepts in Modern Psychology* (New York: Liveright, 1947), 20.
13. Mary Ann Doane, "Ideology and the Practice of Sound Editing and Mixing" in Teresa de Lauretis and Steve Neale, eds., *The Cinematic Apparatus* (London: Macmillan, 1980), 50.
14. Edward A. Lippman, *The Philosophy and Aesthetics of Music* (Lincoln, NE: University of Nebraska Press, 1999), 111.
15. Ibid., 85.

16. Hugo Münsterberg, *The Photoplay: A Psychological Study* (London: Appleton, 1916). Although in recent years, I have heard this idea inexplicably assigned to far more recent sources.
17. Mary Ann Doane, "The Voice in Cinema: The Articulation of Body and Space" in *Yale French Studies*, no. 60, 1980, 45.
18. Sergei M. Eisenstein, *The Film Sense*, Jay Leyda, ed. and trans. (London: Faber and Faber, 1943), 18.

BIBLIOGRAPHY

Adorno, Theodor W. *Minima Moralia: Reflections from a Damaged Life* (London: Verso, 1978).
Adorno, Theodor W. "On Popular Music" in Andrew Goodwin and Simon Frith, eds., *On Record: Rock, Pop and the Written Word* (London: Routledge, 1990), 301–314.
Adorno, Theodor W. *The Philosophy of Modern Music* (New York: Continuum, 2003).
Alain, Claude, Karen Reinke, Yu He, Chenghua Wang, and Nancy Lobaugh. "Hearing Two Things at Once: Neuropsychological Indices of Speech Segregation and Identification" in *Journal of Cognitive Neuroscience*, vol. 17, no. 5, 2005, 811–818.
Alais, David, and David Burr. "The Ventriloquist Effect Results from Near-Optimal Bimodal Integration" in *Current Biology*, vol. 14, no. 3, 2004, 257–262.
Allen, Michael. "In the Mix: How Electrical Reproducers Facilitated the Transition to Sound in British Cinema" in K. J. Donnelly, ed., *Film Music: Critical Approaches* (Edinburgh, UK: Edinburgh University Press, 2001), 62–87.
Altman, Rick. *The American Film Musical* (London: BFI, 1987).
Altman, Rick. "Baker's Dozen" in Rick Altman, ed., *Sound Theory, Sound Practice* (London: Routledge, 1992), 249–254.
Altman, Rick. "Introduction: Four and a Half Film Fallacies" in Rick Altman, ed., *Sound Theory, Sound Practice* (London: Routledge, 1992), 35–45.
Altman, Rick. "Introduction" in *Yale French Studies*, no. 60, 1980, 3–15.
Altman, Rick, McGraw Jones, and Sonia Tatroe. "Inventing the Cinema Soundtrack: Hollywood's Multiplane Sound System" in James Buhler, Caryl Flinn, and David Neumeyer, eds., *Music and Cinema* (Middletown, CT: Wesleyan University Press, 2000), 339–359.
Altman, Rick. "Moving Lips: Cinema as Ventriloquism" in *Yale French Studies*, no. 60, 1980, 67–79.
Altman, Rick. "Sound History" in Rick Altman, ed., *Sound Theory, Sound Practice* (London: Routledge, 1992), 113–125.
Altman, Rick. "Sound Space" in Rick Altman, ed., *Sound Theory, Sound Practice* (London: Routledge, 1992), 46–64.
Altman, Rick, ed. *Sound Theory, Sound Practice* (London: Routledge, 1992).
Anderson, Tim. "Reforming Jackass Music: the Problematic Aesthetics of Early American Film Music Accompaniment" in *Cinema Journal*, vol. 37, no. 1, Fall 1979, 3–22.
Anon. "CM Producer Masterclass: Hybrid" in *Computer Music*, no. 129, Summer 2008, 48.

Anon. "The Debut of the Talkies: What Happened at *The Jazz Singer*" in *Melody Maker*, November 1928, 1277.
Anon. "Sound Film Activity" in *Melody Maker*, October 1928, 1150.
Armes, Roy. "Entendre, C'est Comprendre: in Defence of Sound Reproduction" in *Screen*, vol. 29, no. 2, Spring 1988, 9–22.
Arnheim, Rudolf. *Film as Art* (Los Angeles: University of California Press, 1957).
Arnheim, Rudolf. *Film Essays and Criticism*, Brenda Bethiem, trans. (Madison, WI: University of Wisconsin Press, 1997).
Arnheim, Rudolf. "The Gestalt Theory of Expression" in Mary Henle, ed., *Documents of Gestalt Psychology* (Los Angeles: University of California Press, 1961), 301–323.
Arnheim, Rudolf. *Visual Thinking* (Berkeley, CA: University of California Press, 2004).
Aronson, Elliot. "The Theory of Cognitive Dissonance: A Current Perspective" in Leonard Berkowitz, ed., *Advances in Experimental Social Psychology*, vol. 4 (New York: Academic Press, 1969), 2–34.
Balázs, Béla. *Theory of the Film: Character and Growth of a New Art* (New York: Dover, 1970).
Ball, Philip. *The Music Instinct: How Music Works and Why We Can't Do Without It* (London: Vintage, 2011).
Barr, Charles. "A Conundrum for England" in *Monthly Film Bulletin*, vol. 51, no. 607, August 1984, 234–235.
Barr, Charles. "Hitchcock, Music and the Mathematics of Editing," unpublished paper from Hitchcock and Herrmann, Partners in Suspense conference, York, UK, June 2011.
Bazin, André. *What is Cinema?: Volume 1* (Berkeley, CA: University of California Press, 2004).
Beck, Jay. "William Friedkin's *The Exorcist* and the Proprietary Nature of Sound" in *Cinephile*, vol. 6, no. 1, Spring 2010, 4–10.
Beck, Jay, and Tony Grajeda, eds. *Lowering the Boom: Critical Studies in Film Sound* (Chicago: University of Illinois Press, 2008).
Belton, John. "Technology and Aesthetics of Film Sound" in Elisabeth Weis and John Belton, eds., *Film Sound: Theory and Practice* (New York: Columbia University Press, 1985), 63–72.
Benjafield, John G. *A History of Psychology* (Needham Heights, MA: Simon and Schuster, 1996).
Beynon, George. "From Musical Presentation of Motion Pictures" [1921], reprinted in Julie Hubbert, ed., *Celluloid Symphonies: Texts and Contexts in Film Music History* (Berkeley, CA: University of California Press, 2011), 74–83.
Blackham, T. G. "Film Sound Technique" in *Studio Sound*, vol. 13, no. 4, April 1971, 188.
Bolivar, Valerie J., Annabel J. Cohen, and John C. Fentress. "Semantic and Formal Congruency in Music and Motion Pictures: Effects the Interpretation of Visual Action" in *Psychomusicology*, no. 2, Spring/Fall 1994, 38–43.
Bordwell, David, Janet Staiger, and Kristin Thompson. *The Classical Hollywood Cinema: Film Style and Mode of Production to 1960* (London: Routledge, 1988).
Bordwell, David. "The Musical Analogy" in *Yale French Studies*, no. 60, 1980, 141–156.
Bordwell, David. *Narration in the Fiction Film* (London: Routledge, 1987).
Bordwell, David. *On the History of Film Style* (Cambridge, MA: Harvard University Press, 1998).
Bottomore, Stephen. "The Panicking Audience?: Early Cinema and the 'Train Effect'" in *Historical Journal of Film, Radio and Television*, vol. 19, no. 2, 1999, 177–216.
Bregman, Albert S. *Auditory Scene Analysis* (Cambridge, MA: MIT Press, 1990).

Brooks, Peter. *The Melodramatic Imagination: Balzac, Henry James, Melodrama, and the Mode of Excess* (New Haven, CT: Yale University Press, 1995).
Brophy, Philip. *100 Modern Soundtracks* (London: BFI, 2004).
Brown, Julie. "*Carnival of Souls* and the Organs of Horror" in Neil Lerner, ed., *Music in the Horror Film: Listening to Fear* (London: Routledge, 2010), 1–20.
Brown, Kristi A. "The Troll Among Us" in Phil Powrie and Robynn J. Stilwell, eds., *Changing Tunes: The Use of Pre-Existing Music in Film* (Aldershot, UK: Ashgate, 2006), 74–90.
Brown, Royal S. *Overtones and Undertones: Reading Film Music* (Los Angeles: University of California Press, 1994).
Buhler, James, and David Neumeyer. "Film Music/Film Studies" in *Journal of the American Musicological Society*, vol. 47, no. 2, 1994, 364–85.
Bullerjahn, Claudia, and Markus Güldenring. "An Empirical Investigation of Effects of Film Music Using Qualitative Content Analysis" in *Psychomusicology*, no. 13, 1994, 99–118.
Burch, Noel. *Theory of Film Practice* (Princeton, NJ: Princeton University Press, 1981).
Burt, George. *The Art of Film Music* (Boston: Northeastern University Press, 1994).
Cage, John. *Silence: Lectures and Writings* (London: Marion Boyars, 1980).
Canby, Edward Tatnall. "Sound Minus Synch: Part Two" in *Studio Sound*, vol. 13, no. 8, August 1971, 403.
Carlsson, Sven E. "Synchresis—Om syntesen mellan synkrona rorelser i bild och ljud" in *Filmhäftet*, no. 4, 1994,.reprinted online at[http://fototips.se/filmljud/synchres.htm] accessed April 3 2008.
Caropreso, Fatima, and Richard Theisen Simanke. "Life and Death in Freudian Metapsychology: A Reappraisal of the Second Instinctual Dualism" in Salman Akhtar and Mary Kay O'Neil, eds., *On Freud's 'Beyond the Pleasure Principle'* (London: Karnac, 2011), 86–107.
Carroll, Noel. *Theorising the Moving Image* (Cambridge, UK: Cambridge University Press, 1996).
Chion, Michel. *Audio-Vision: Sound on Screen*, Claudia Gorbman, ed. and trans. (New York: Columbia University Press, 1994).
Chion, Michel. *The Voice in Cinema* (New York: Columbia University Press, 1998).
Chion, Michel. *Film, A Sound Art*, Claudia Gorbman, trans. (New York: Columbia University Press, 2009).
Christie, Ian. "Asynchrony" in Larry Sider, Diane Freeman, and Jerry Sider, eds., *Soundscape: The School of Sound Lectures, 1998–2001* (London: Wallflower, 2003), 161–169.
Clair, Rene. "The Art of Sound" [1929] in Elisabeth Weis and John Belton, eds., *Film Sound: Theory and Practice* (New York: Columbia University Press, 1985), 92–95.
Clouser, Charlie. "Interview" at *ign.com* [http://music.ign.com/articles/562/562509p1.html], accessed December 3, 2004.
Clover, Carol. "Dancin' in the Rain" in *Critical Enquiry*, vol. 21, no. 4, Summer 1995, 360–376.
Cohen, Annabel J. "Film Music: Perspectives from Cognitive Psychology" in James Buhler, Caryl Flinn, and David Neumeyer, eds., *Music and Cinema* (Middletown, CT: Wesleyan University Press, 2000), 360–376.
Coleman, Mark. *Playback: From the Victriola to MP3, 100 Years of Music, Machines and Money* (Cambridge, MA: Da Capo Press, 2003).
Connor, Stephen. *Dumbstruck: A Cultural History of Ventriloquism* (Oxford, UK: Oxford University Press, 2000).

Cook, Nicholas. *Analysing Musical Multimedia* (Oxford, UK: Oxford University Press, 2000).
Cooper, Joel M. *Cognitive Dissonance: 50 Years of a Classic Theory* (London: Sage, 2007).
Copland, Aaron. "Tip to the Moviegoers: Take Off Those Ear-Muffs" in *The New York Times*, November 6, 1949, section six.
Cotner, John S. "Careful with that Axe, Eugene" in Kevin Holm-Hudson, ed., *Progressive Rock Revisited* (London: Routledge, 2001), 65–90.
Cowan, Lester, ed. *Recording Sound for Motion Pictures: AMPAS* (New York: McGraw-Hill, 1931).
Dale, Jon. Review of Guy Sherwin, "Optical Sound Films 1971–2007" DVD in *The Wire*, no. 294, August 2008, 72.
Davis, Blair. "Old Films, New Sounds: Screening Silent Cinema with Electronic Music" in *Canadian Journal of Film Studies*, vol. 17, no. 2, Autumn 2008, 77–98.
Davison, Annette. *Hollywood Theory, Non-Hollywood Practice: Cinema Soundtracks in the 1980s and 1990s* (Aldershot, UK: Ashgate, 2004).
Deleuze, Gilles. *Cinema 1: The Movement Image* (London: Athlone, 1986).
Deleuze, Gilles. *Cinema 2: The Time Image* (New York: Continuum, 2005).
Deleuze, Gilles, and Felix Guattari. *A Thousand Plateaus: Capitalism and Schizophrenia*, Brian Massumi, trans. (Minneapolis: University of Minnesota Press, 1987).
Dennett, Daniel. *Consciousness Explained* (Boston: Back Bay Books, 1992).
Dhir, Meraj. "A Gestalt Approach to Film Analysis" in Scott Higgins, ed., *Arnheim for Film and Media Students* (Abingdon, UK: Routledge, 2011), 89–106.
Dickinson, Kay. *Off Key: When Film and Music Won't Work Together* (New York: Oxford University Press, 2008).
Dickson, W. K. L. "A Brief History of the Kinetograph, the Kinetoscope and the Kineto-Phonograph" in *Journal of the SMPTE*, vol. 21, December 1933, reprinted in Raymond Fielding, ed., *A Technological History of Motion Pictures and Television* (Berkeley, CA: University of California Press, 1967), 9–16.
Doane, Mary Ann. "Ideology and the Practice of Sound Editing and Mixing" in Teresa de Lauretis and Steve Neale, eds., *The Cinematic Apparatus* (London: Macmillan, 1980), 47–56.
Doane, Mary Anne. "The Voice in Cinema: the Articulation of Body and Space" in *Yale French Studies*, no. 60, 1980, 33–50.
Doherty, Douglas, and Ron Berry, Dhomont, Francis. "Sound Diffusion of Stereo Music Over a Multi Loud-Speaker Sound System, From First Principles Onwards to a Successful Experiment" in *Journal of Electroacoustic Music*, vol. 11, Spring 1998, 9–11.
Donnelly, K. J. *British Film Music and Film Musicals* (Basingstoke, UK: Palgrave, 2007).
Donnelly, K. J. "Constructing the Future through Music of the Past: the Software in Hardware" in Ian Inglis, ed., *Popular Music and Film* (London: Wallflower, 2003), 131–147.
Donnelly, K. J. *Pop Music in British Cinema: A Chronicle* (London: BFI, 2001).
Donnelly, K. J. *The Spectre of Sound: Film and Television Music* (London: BFI, 2005).
Doyle, Peter. *Echo and Reverb: Fabricating Space in Popular Music Recording, 1900–1960* (Middletown, CT: Wesleyan University Press, 2005).
Dreher, Carl. "Recording, Re-recording and the Editing of Sound" in *Journal of the Society of Motion Picture Engineers*, vol. 16, no. 6, June 1931, 756–765.
Dykhoff, Klas, "Non-Diegetic Sound Effects" in *The New Soundtrack*, vol.2, 2012, 169–179.

Edwards, Eddie. "The Garden Tapes" [www.thegardentapes.co.uk/], accessed May 8, 2011.

Eisenstein, Sergei M. *Film Form: Essays in Film Theory*, Jay Leyda, trans. (New York: Harcourt Brace, 1949).

Eisenstein, Sergei M. *The Film Sense*, Jay Leyda, ed. and trans. (London: Faber and Faber, 1943).

Eisenstein, Sergei M. *Nonindifferent Nature: Film and the Structure of Things*, Herbert Marshall, trans. (Cambridge, UK: Cambridge University Press, 1987).

Eisenstein, Sergei M. *Sergei M. Eisenstein, Selected Works: Volume 1, Writings 1922–1934*, Richard Taylor, ed. and trans. (London: BFI, 1988).

Eisenstein, Sergei M. *Selected Writings, Volume II*, Michael Glenny and Richard Taylor, eds. and trans. (London: BFI, 1991).

Eisenstein, Sergei M. *Selected Writings, Volume III* [1946–7], Richard Taylor, ed. and trans. (London: BFI, 1996).

Eisenstein, Sergei M., Vsevolod Pudovkin, and Grigori Alexandrov. "Statement on Sound" in Richard Taylor, ed. and trans. *S.M.Eisenstein: Selected Works, volume 1, Writings 1922-1934* (London: BFI, 1988).

Eisler, Hanns, and Theodor Adorno. *Composing for the Films* (London: Athlone, 1994).

Elsaesser, Thomas. *Metropolis* (London: BFI, 2000).

Enticknap, Leo. *Moving Image Technology: From Zoetrope to Digital* (London: Wallflower, 2005).

Festinger, Lionel. *A Theory of Cognitive Dissonance* (Stanford, CA: Stanford University Press, 1957).

Fink, Robert. *Repeating Ourselves: American Minimal Music as Cultural Practice* (Berkeley, CA: University of California Press, 2005).

Flinn, Caryl. *Strains of Utopia: Gender, Nostalgia and Hollywood Film Music* (Princeton, NJ: Princeton University Press, 1992).

Flueckiger, Barbara. "Sound Effects: Strategies for Sound Effects in Films" in Graeme Harper, Ruth Doughty, and Jochen Eisentraut, eds., *Sound and Music in Film and Visual Media* (New York: Continuum, 2009), 151–179.

Foote, Jonathan, Matthew Cooper, and Andreas Girgensohn. "Creating Music Videos Using Media Analysis" in *Multimedia '02 Conference Proceedings*, CD-ROM (Juan-les-Pins, FR), npn.

Freud, Sigmund. *The Interpretation of Dreams* (New York: Empire, 2011).

Garncarz, Joseph. "Versions" in Andrew Higson and Richard Maltby, eds., *'Film Europe' and 'Film America': Cinema, Commerce and Cultural Exchange 1920–1939* (Exeter, UK: Exeter University Press, 1999), 57–80.

Garner, Ken. "'Would You Like to Hear Some Music?': Music in-and-out of Control in the Films of Quentin Tarantino" in K. J. Donnelly, ed., *Film Music: Critical Approaches* (Edinburgh, UK: Edinburgh University Press, 2001), 188–205.

Garwood, Ian. "Must You Remember This?: Orchestrating the 'Standard' Pop Song in Sleepless in Seattle" in *Screen*, vol. 41, no. 3, 2000, 282–298.

Gaulin, Steven J. C., and Donald H. McBurney. *Evolutionary Psychology* (London: Prentice Hall, 2003).

Gibbs, Tony. *The Fundamentals of Sonic Art and Sound Design* (Lausanne, CH: AVA, 2007).

Gibson, James J. *The Ecological Approach to Visual Perception* (Boston: Houghton Mifflin, 1979).

Goldsmith, L. T. "Re-recording Sound Motion Pictures" in *Journal of the Society of Motion Picture Engineers*, vol. 39, no. 11, November 1931, 277–283.

Goldstein, Kurt. *The Organism. A Holistic Approach to Biology Derived from Pathological Data in Man* (New York: Zone, 1995).

Gorbman, Claudia. "Ears Wide Open: Kubrick's Music" in Phil Powrie and Robynn J. Stilwell, eds., *Changing Tunes: The Use of Pre-Existing Music in Film* (Aldershot, UK: Ashgate, 2006), 3–18.

Gorbman, Claudia. *Unheard Melodies: Narrative Film Music* (London: BFI, 1987).

Graf, Alexander. *The Cinema of Wim Wenders: The Celluloid Highway* (London: Wallflower, 2002).

Greene, Liz. "The Gentle Gunman: Stephen Rea—Voicing Republicanism" in the proceedings from *Sounding Out 5*, USB stick (Bournemouth University, UK, 2011).

Greene, Liz. "The Unbearable Lightness of Being: Alan Splet and Dual Role of Editing Sound and Music" in *Music and the Moving Image*, vol. 4, no. 3, Fall 2011, 1–13.

Habib, Andre, and Frederick Peltier. "An Interview with Peter Kubelka" in *Off Screen*, vol. 9, issue 11, November 2005 [www.offscreen.com/index.php/phile/interview_kubelka/], accessed September 17, 2010.

Hamilton, Andy. "Adorno" in Theodore Gracyk and Andrew Kania, eds., *The Routledge Companion to Philosophy and Music* (New York: Routledge, 2011), 391–402.

Hayward, Philip, ed. *Terror Tracks: Music, Sound and Horror Cinema* (London: Equinox, 2009).

Hitchcock, Alfred. "On Style" in Sidney Gottlieb, ed., *Hitchcock on Hitchcock: Selected Writings and Interviews* [original interview published in *Cinema*, 1963] (London: Faber and Faber, 1997), 285–302.

Hsu, Kenneth J., and Andreas J. Hsu. "Fractal Geometry of Music: From Birdsong to Bach" in *Proceedings of the National Academy of Sciences of the United States*, vol. 87, no. 3, February 1990, 938–941.

Hubbert, Julie, ed. *Celluloid Symphonies: Texts and Contexts in Film Music History* (Berkeley, CA: University of California Press, 2011).

Huron, David. *Sweet Anticipation: Music and the Psychology of Expectation* (Cambridge, MA: MIT Press, 2007).

Hutchings, Peter. *Hammer and Beyond: the British Horror Film* (Manchester, UK: Manchester University Press, 1993).

Jacobs, Jason. "Gunfire" in Karl French, ed., *Screen Violence* (London: Bloomsbury, 1996), 171–178.

Jordan, Randolph. "The Schizophonic Imagination: Audiovisual Ecology in the Cinema" (Ph.D. diss., Concordia University, Montreal, 2010).

Jung, Carl Gustav. *Synchronicity—An Acausal Connecting Principle* (Princeton, NJ: Princeton University Press, 2010).

Kalinak, Kathryn. *Settling the Score: Narrative Film Music* (Madison, WI: University of Wisconsin Press, 1992).

Kant, Immanuel. *Critique of Judgment* (Indianapolis, IN: Hackett, 1987).

Kerins, Mark. *Beyond Dolby (Stereo): Cinema in the Digital Sound Age* (Bloomington, IN: Indiana University Press, 2011).

Kivy, Peter. *Sound and Semblance: Reflections on Musical Representation* (Princeton, NJ: Princeton University Press, 1984).

Koerber, Martin. "Oskar Messter, Film Pioneer: Early Cinema between Science, Spectacle and Commerce" in Thomas Elsaesser and Michael Wedel, eds., *A Second Life: German Cinema's First Decades* (Amsterdam: Amsterdam University Press, 1996), 51–61.

Koffka, Kurt. "On the Structure of the Unconscious" in *The Unconscious: A Symposium* (New York: Alfred A. Knopf, 1928), 43–68.

Koffka, Kurt. *Principles of Gestalt Psychology* (London: Kegan Paul, 1935).

Köhler, Wolfgang. *Gestalt Psychology. An Introduction to New Concepts in Modern Psychology* (New York: Liveright, 1947).

Kohlrausch, Armin G., Steven L. D. J. E. van de Par, Rob L. J. Eijk, and James F. Juola, "Human Performance in Detecting Audio-Visual Asynchrony" in *Journal of Acoustical Society of America*, vol. 120, no. 5, 2006, 3048–3085.

Kozloff, Sarah. *Overhearing Film Dialogue* (Berkeley, CA: University of California Press, 2000).

Kracauer, Siegfried. *Theory of Film: the Redemption of Physical Reality* (Oxford, UK: Oxford University Press, 1960).

Kulezic-Wilson, Danijela. "A Musical Approach to Filmmaking: Hip Hop and Techno Composing Techniques and Models of Structuring in Darren Aronofsky's *Pi*" in *Music and the Moving Image*, vol. 1, no. 1, 2008. [www.press.uillinois.edu/journals/mmi.html, accessed April 7, 2009.

Kulezic-Wilson, Danijela. "The Musicality of Film Rhythm" in John Hill and Kevin Rockett, eds., *National Cinema and Beyond* (Dublin, Ireland : Four Courts Press, 2004, 115–124).

Kulezic-Wilson, Danijela. "Sound Design is the New Score" in *Music, Sound and the Moving Image* 2, no. 2, Autumn 2008, 127–131.

Lacan, Jacques, and Wladimir Granoff. "Fetishism: The Symbolic, the Imaginary and the Real" in *Journal for Lacanian Studies*, vol. 1, no. 2, 2003, 299–308.

Laderman, David. "(S)lip-Sync: Punk Rock Narrative Film and Postmodern Musical Performance" in Jay Beck and Tony Grajeda, eds., *Lowering the Boom: Critical Studies in Film Sound* (Chicago: University of Illinois Press, 2008), 269–288.

Laing, Heather. "Emotional By Numbers: Music, Song and the Musical" in Bill Marshall and Robynn Stilwell, eds., *Musicals: Hollywood and Beyond* (Exeter, UK: Intellect, 2000), 5–14.

Langer, Suzanne K. *Philosophy in a New Key: A Study in the Symbolism of Reason, Rite and Art* (Cambridge, MA: Harvard University Press, 1957).

Lastra, James. "Film and the Wagnerian Aspiration: Thoughts on Sound Design and History of the Senses" in Jay Beck and Tony Grajeda, eds., *Lowering the Boom: Critical Studies in Film Sound* (Chicago: University of Illinois Press, 2008), 123–140.

Lastra, James. *Sound Technology and the American Cinema: Perception, Representation, Modernity* (New York: Columbia University Press, 2000).

Ledoux, Joseph. *The Emotional Brain: The Mysterious Underpinnings of Emotional Life* (New York: Simon and Schuster, 1996).

Lerner, Neil, ed. *Music in the Horror Film: Listening to Fear* (London: Routledge, 2010).

Link, Stan. "Nor the Eye Filled with Seeing: the Sound of Vision in Film" in *American Music*, Spring 2004, 76–90.

Lippman, Edward A. *The Philosophy and Aesthetics of Music* (Lincoln, NE: University of Nebraska Press, 1999).

Lipscomb, Scott D., and Roger A. Kendall. "Perceptual Judgments of the Relationship Between Musical and Visual Components in Film" in *Psychomusicology*, no. 13, 1994, 60–98.

Lipscomb, Scott D., and Roger A. Kendall. "Sources of Accent in Musical Sound and Visual Motion" in the *Proceedings of the 4th ICMPC* (Liege, BE, 1994), npn.

MacCabe, Colin. *Performance* (London: BFI, 1998).

Maltby, Richard. *Hollywood Cinema* (Oxford, UK: Wiley-Blackwell, 2003).

Maltby, Richard, and Ruth Vasey. "The International Language Problem: European Reactions to Hollywood's Conversion to Sound" in David W. Ellwood and

R. Kroes, eds., *Hollywood in Europe: Experiences of a Cultural Hegemony* (Amsterdam: University of Amsterdam Press, 1994), 68–79.

Manovich, Lev. *The Language of New Media* (Cambridge, MA: MIT Press, 2001).

Manvell, Roger, and John Huntley. *The Technique of Film Music* (London: Focal Press, 1975).

Marks, Martin Miller. *Music and the Silent Film: Contexts and Case Studies, 1895–1924* (Oxford, UK: Oxford University Press, 1997).

Marshall, Sandra K., and Annabel J.Cohen. "Effects of Musical Soundtracks on Attitudes Toward Animated Geometric Figures" in *Music Perception*, vol. 6, no. 1, 1988, 95–112.

Massaro, Dominic W., Michael M. Cohen, and Paula M. T. Smeele. "Perception of Asynchronous and Conflicting Visual and Auditory Speech" in *Journal of the Acoustical Society of America*, vol. 100, no. 3, September 1996, 1777–1786.

Mauer, Barry. "Asynchronous Documentary: Buñuel's *Land Without Bread*" in Jay Beck and Tony Grajeda, eds., *Lowering the Boom: Critical Studies in Film Sound* (Chicago: University of Illinois Press, 2008), 141–151.

McGurk, Harry, and John W. MacDonald. "Hearing Lips and Seeing Voices" in *Nature*, no. 264, 1976, 746–748.

McMahon, Jennifer A. "Perceptual Constraints and Perceptual Schemata: The Possibility of Perceptual Style" in *Journal of Aesthetics and Art Criticism*, vol. 61, no. 3, Summer 2003, 259–272.

McQuiston, Kate. "An Effort to Decide: More Research into Kubrick's Music Choices for *2001: A Space Odyssey*" in *Journal of Film Music*, vol. 3, no. 2, 2010, 145–154.

Mera, Miguel, and David Burnand. "Introduction" in Miguel Mera and David Burnand, eds., *European Film Music* (London: Ashgate, 2006), 1–12.

Merleau-Ponty, Maurice. *The Phenomenology of Perception* (London: Routledge, 1962).

Meyer, Leonard B. *Emotion and Meaning in Music* (Chicago: University of Chicago Press, 1961).

Meyer-Dinkgräfe, Daniel. "Thoughts on Dubbing Practice in Germany: Procedures, Aesthetic Implications and Ways Forward" in *Scope*, issue 5, June 2006. [www.scope.nottingham.ac.uk/article.php?id=131&issue=5], accessed March 27, 2009.

Miller, Wesley C. "Basis of Motion Picture Sound" in *Motion Picture Sound Engineering* (London: Chapman and Hall, 1938), 101–108.

Mollaghan, Aimée. "The Musicality of the Visual Film" (Ph.D. diss., University of Glasgow, UK, 2011).

Morgan, Kenneth F. "Dubbing" in Lester Cowan, ed., *Recording Sound for Motion Pictures* (New York: McGraw Hill, 1931), 145–148.

Mounce, E. B., C. Portman, and M. Rettinger. "The Vocal Room and Scoring Operations at RKO Radio Pictures" in *Journal of the Society of Motion Picture Engineers*, vol. 42, no. 1, June 1944, 375–378.

Mountcastle, Vernon B. *Medical Physiology* (St. Louis, MO: C. V. Mosby, 1974).

Mulvey, Laura. "Visual Pleasure and Narrative Cinema" in *Screen*, vol. 16, no. 3, Autumn 1975.

Mulvey, Laura. "Cinema, SyncSound and Europe 1929: Reflections on Coincidence" in Larry Sider, Diane Freeman, and Jerry Sider, eds., *Soundscape: The School of Sound Lectures, 1998–2001* (London: Wallflower, 2003), 15–27.

Münsterberg, Hugo. *The Photoplay: A Psychological Study* (London: Appleton, 1916).

Natzén, Christopher. *The Coming of Sound Film in Sweden 1928–1932, New and Old Technologies* (Stockholm, SE: Stockholm Cinema Studies, 2010).

Neale, D. M. *How to Do Sound Films*, revised by R. A. Hole (London: Focal Press, 1969).

Neale, Steve. *Cinema and Technology: Image, Sound, Colour* (London: BFI, 1985).

Normandeau, Robert. "...Et vers un cinema pour l'oreille" in *Circuit (Revue Nord-Américaine de Musique du XXe Siècle)*, vol. 4, nos.1–2, 1993, 113–127.

O'Brien, Charles. *Cinema's Conversion to Sound: Technology and Film Style in France and the U.S.* (Bloomington, IN: Indiana University Press, 2005).

O'Leary, A., and G. Rhodes. "Cross-Modal Effect on Visual and Auditory Object Perception" in *Perception and Psychophysics*, no. 35, 1984, 565–569.

Paulus, Irena. "Stanley Kubrick's Revolution in the Usage of Film Music: *2001: A Space Odyssey* (1968)" in *International Review of the Aesthetics and Sociology of Music*, vol. 40, no. 1, June 2009, 99–127.

Petric, Vlada. "Sight and Sound: Counterpoint or Entity?" in *Filmmakers Newsletter*, vol. 6, no. 7, May 1973, 27–31.

Plantinga, Carl, and Greg M. Smith, eds. *Passionate Views: Film, Cognition, and Emotion* (London: Johns Hopkins University Press, 1999).

Powrie, Phil, and Robynn J. Stilwell, eds. *Changing Tunes: The Use of Pre-Existing Music in Film* (Aldershot, UK: Ashgate, 2006).

Prendergast, Roy M. *Film Music: A Neglected Art* (New York: Norton, 1992).

Prince, David. "The Aesthetics and Practice of Sound" in *Wide Angle*, 1978, 68–72.

Pudovkin, Vsevolod. *Film Technique and Film Acting* (London: Grove Press, 1958).

Pudovkin, Vsevolod. "Asynchronism as a Principle of Sound Film" in Elisabeth Weis and John Belton, eds., *Film Sound: Theory and Practice* (New York: Columbia University Press, 1985), 86–91.

Redies, Christoph, Jeremy M. Crook, and Otto D. Creutzfeldt. "Neuronal Response to Borders with and without Luminance Gradients in Cat Visual Cortex and Lateral Geniculate Nucleus" in *Experimental Brain Research*, no. 61, 1986, 469–472.

Reed, Graham. *The Psychology of Anomalous Experience: A Cognitive Approach* (Buffalo, NY: Prometheus, 1988).

Repp, Bruno H., and Amandine Penel. "Auditory Dominance in Temporal Processing: New Evidence from Synchronization with Simultaneous Visual and Auditory Sequences" in *Journal of Experimental Psychology: Human Perception and Performance*, vol. 28, no. 5, 2002, 1085–1099.

Rettinger, M. "Reverberation Chambers for Re-recording" in *Journal of the Society of Motion Picture Engineers*, vol. 15, no. 5, November 1945, 375–378.

Robertson, Robert. *Eisenstein on the Audiovisual: The Montage of Music, Image and Sound in the Cinema* (London: I. B. Tauris, 2009).

Rodman, Ronald. "The Popular Song as Leitmotif in 1990s Film" in Phil Powrie and Robynn J. Stilwell, eds., *Changing Tunes: The Use of Pre-Existing Music in Film* (Aldershot, UK: Ashgate, 2006).

Rosar, William H. "Bernard Herrmann: The Beethoven of Film Music?" in *Journal of Film Music*, vol. 1, nos. 2–3, Fall/Winter 2003, 121–150.

Ruffles, Tom. *Ghost Images: Cinema of the Afterlife* (Jefferson, NC: McFarland, 2004).

Sacks, Rob. "Charlie Clouser's Scary Soundtrack for *Saw*" (interview with Charlie Clouser) in *NPR*'s "Day to Day," October 9, 2004 [http://www.nrp.org/templates/story/story.php?storyId=4132853], accessed November 15, 2006.

Sadoff, Ron. "The Role of the Music Editor and the 'Temp Track' as Blueprint for Score, Source Music, and Source Music of Films" in *Popular Music*, vol. 25, no. 2, 2006, 165–183.

Salt, Barry. *Film Style and Technology: History and Analysis* (London: Starword, 1983).

Salt, Barry. "Film Style and Technology in the Thirties: Sound" in Elisabeth Weis and John Belton, eds., *Film Sound: Theory and Practice* (New York: Columbia University Press, 1985), 37-43.

Schaeffer, Pierre. "Le Contrepoint, Le Son et Le Image" in *Cahiers du Cinema*, no. 108, 1960, 7-22.

Schafer, R. Murray. *Our Sonic Environment and the Soundscape: The Tuning of the World* (Rochester, NY: Destiny, 1994).

Schaffner, Nicholas. *Saucerful of Secrets: The Pink Floyd Odyssey* (London: Harmony, 1991).

Seifert, Marsha. "Image/Music/Voice: Song Dubbing in Hollywood Musicals" in *Journal of Communication*, vol. 45, issue 2, June 2005, 44-64.

Sekuler, R., A. B. Sekuler, and A. B. Lau. "Sound Alters Visual Motion Perception" in *Nature*, no. 385, 1997, 308.

Sergi, Gianluca. *The Dolby Era: Film Sound in Contemporary Hollywood* (Manchester, UK: Manchester University Press, 2004).

Sergi, Gianluca. "The Sonic Playground: Hollywood Cinema and its Listeners" at Filmsound.org [www.filmsound.org/articles/sergi/index.htm], accessed June 6, 2011.

Shams, L., Y. Kamitani, and S. Shimojo. "Visual Illusion Induced by Sound" in *Cognitive Brain Research*, 14, 2002, 147-152.

Shepherd, Ashley. *Pro Tools for Video, Film and Multimedia* (Boston: Muska and Lipman, 2003).

Shermer, Michael. *The Believing Brain: From Ghosts and Gods to Politics and Conspiracies* (London: Robinson, 2012).

Sholem, Gershom. *Walter Benjamin: the Story of a Friendship* (London: Faber and Faber, 1982).

Sigman, Mariano, and Stanlislas Dehaene. "Brain Mechanisms of Serial and Parallel Processing during Dual-Task Performance" in *Journal of Neuroscience*, vol. 28, no. 30, July 2008, 7585-7598.

Silverman, Kaja. *The Acoustic Mirror: The Female Voice in Psychoanalysis and Cinema* (Bloomington, IN: Indiana University Press, 1988).

Smith, Jeff. "Black Faces, White Voices: The Politics of Dubbing in Carmen Jones" in *The Velvet Light Trap*, no. 51, Spring 2003, 29-42.

Smith, Jeff. *The Sounds of Commerce: Marketing Popular Film Music* (New York: Columbia University Press, 1998).

Sonnenschein, David. *Sound Design—The Expressive Power of Music, Voice, Sound* (Studio City, CA: Michael Wiese Productions, 2001).

Spadoni, Robert. *Uncanny Bodies: The Coming of Sound Film and the Origins of the Horror Genre* (Berkeley, CA: University of California Press, 2007).

Spence, Charles, and Sarah Squire. "Multisensory Integration: Maintaining the Perception of Synchrony" in *Current Biology*, vol. 13, issue 13, 1 July 2003, R519–R521.

Spillmann, Lothar, and Walter H. Ehrenstein. "Gestalt Factors in the Visual Neurosciences" in L. Chalupa and J. S. Werner, eds., *The Visual Neurosciences* (Cambridge, MA: MIT Press, 2003), 1573–1589.

Spillmann, Lothar, and John S. Werner, eds. *Visual Perception: The Neuropsychological Foundations* (San Diego, CA: Academic Press, 1990).

Spoto, Donald. *The Art of Alfred Hitchcock: Fifty Years of his Motion Pictures* (London: Doubleday, 1992).

Sterne, Jonathan. *The Audible Past: Cultural Origins of Sound Reproduction* (Durham, NC: Duke University Press, 2003).

Steven, J. C., and Donald McBurney. *Evolutionary Psychology* (London: Prentice Hall, 2003).

Stilwell, Robynn J. "'Bad Wolf': Leitmotif in *Doctor Who*" in James Deaville, ed., *Music in Television: Channels of Listening* (London: Routledge, 2011), 119–142.

Stoelinga, C. N. J., D. J. Hermes, and A. G. Kohlrausch, "On the Influence of Interaural Differences on Temporal Perception of Masked Noise Bursts" in *Journal of the Acoustical Society of America*, vol. 120, no. 5, 2006, 2818–2829.

Storr, Anthony. *Music and the Mind* (London: Harper Collins, 1997).

Tasker, Homer G. "A Dubbing Rehearsal Channel" in *Journal of the Society of Motion Picture Engineers*, vol. 24, no. 1, January 1935, 286–289.

Thom, Randy. "Designing a Movie for Sound" in Larry Sider, Diane Freeman, and Jerry Sider, eds., *Soundscape: The School of Sound Lectures, 1998–2001* (London: Wallflower, 2003), 121–137.

Thompson, Kristin. "Early Sound Counterpoint" in *Yale French Studies*, no. 60, 1980, 115–140.

Toop, David. *Haunted Weather: Music, Silence and Memory* (London: Serpent's Tail, 2004).

Toop, David. *Sinister Resonance: The Mediumship of the Listener* (London: Continuum, 2010).

Truax, Barry. *Acoustic Communication* (Norwood, NJ: Ablex, 2000).

Truffaut, Francois. *Hitchcock* (London: Secker and Warburg, 1968).

Van der Par, Steven, Armin G. Kohlrausch, and James F. Juola. "Some Methodological Aspects for Measuring Asynchrony Detection in Audio-Visual Stimulus" in A. Calvo-Manzano, A. Perez-Lopez, and J. S. Santiago, eds., *Proceedings of the Forum Acousticum 2002* CD-ROM (Porto, PT: Universidade de Porto, Faculdade de Engenharia, 2002), npn.

Van Eijk, Rob L. J., Armin G. Kohlrausch, James F. Juola, and Steven van der Par. "Audiovisual Synchrony and Temporal Order Judgments: Effects of Experimental Method and Stimulus Type" in *Perception and Psychophysics*, vol. 70, no. 6, 2008, 955–968.

Van Leeuwen, Theo. *Speech, Music, Sound* (Basingstoke, UK: Macmillan, 1999).

Varela, Francisco J., Evan Thompson, and Eleanor Rosch. *The Embodied Mind* (Cambridge, MA: MIT Press, 1991).

Vroomen, J., and B. de Gelder. "Sound Enhances Visual Perception: Cross-Modal Effects of Auditory Organization on Vision" in *Journal of Experimental Psychology: Human Perception and Performance*, vol. 26, no. 5, 2000, 1583–1590.

Wagner, Laura. "'I Dub Thee': A Guide to the Great Voice Doubles" in *Classic Images*, November 1998 [www.classicimages.com/past-issues/view/?x=/1998/November98/idibthee.html], accessed February 2, 2009.

Warburton, Dan. "Cinema for the Floating Ear" (interview with Michel Chion) in *The Wire*, no. 294, August 2008.

Weis, Elisabeth, and John Belton, eds. *Film Sound: Theory and Practice* (New York: Columbia University Press, 1985).

Weis, Elisabeth. *The Silent Scream: Alfred Hitchcock's Soundtracks* (Rutherford, NJ: Fairleigh Dickinson University Press, 1982).

Weis, Elisabeth. "Sync Tanks: The Art and Technique of Postproduction Sound" in *Cineaste*, vol. 21, nos.1–2, 1995, 56–81.

Weis Elisabeth. "The Sound of One Wing Flapping" in *Film Comment*, vol. 14, no. 5, September–October 1978, 42–48.

Wertheimer, Max. "Experimentelle Studien über das Sehen von Bewegung" in *Zeitschrift für Psychologie*, no. 61, 1912, 161–265.

Wetzel, Edwin. "Assembling a Final Sound-Track" in *Journal of the Society of Motion Picture Engineers*, vol. 29, no. 4, October 1937, 374–375.

Whittington, William. *Sound Design and Science Fiction* (Austin, TX: University of Texas Press, 2007).

Wierzbicki, James. *Film Music: A History* (Oxford, UK: Oxford University Press, 2009).

Wierzbicki, James. *Louis and Bebe Barron's Forbidden Planet: A Score Guide* (London: Scarecrow, 2005).

Wilder, Eliot. *Endtroducing...* (London: Continuum, 2006).

Williams, Alan. "The Musical Film and Recorded Popular Music" in Rick Altman, ed., *Genre: The Musical* (London: Routledge and Kegan Paul, 1981), 147–150.

Winn, Denise. *The Manipulated Mind: Brainwashing, Conditioning and Indoctrination* (London: Octagon Press, 1983).

Winter, Marian Hannah. "The Function of Music in Sound Film" in *The Musical Quarterly*, vol. 27, no. 2, April 1941, 146–164.

Winters, Ben. "Corporeality, Musical Heartbeats, and Cinematic Emotion" in *Music, Sound and the Moving Image*, vol. 2, no. 1, Spring 2008, 14–21.

Wollen, Peter. "24 Mismatches of Sound and Image" in Larry Sider, Diane Freeman, and Jerry Sider, eds., *Soundscape: The School of Sound Lectures, 1998–2001* (London: Wallflower, 2003), 221–230.

Wright, Basil, and B.Vivian Braun. "Manifesto: Dialogue on Sound" in Elisabeth Weis and John Belton, eds., *Film Sound: Theory and Practice* (New York: Columbia University Press, 1985), 96–97.

Wurtzler, Steve. "She Sang Live but the Microphone was Turned Off" in Rick Altman, ed., *Sound Theory, Sound Practice* (London: Routledge, 1992), 87–103.

Zeidel, Dahlia. *Neuropsychology of Art: Neurological, Cognitive and Evolutionary Perspectives* (London: Psychology Press, 2012).

Zeki, Semir. *Inner Vision: An Exploration of Art and the Brain* (Oxford, UK: Oxford University Press, 1999).

Zettl, Herbert. *Sight, Sound, Motion: Applied Media Aesthetics* (Belmont, CA: Wadsworth, 1999).

INDEX

300 (2007), 193
2001: A Space Odyssey (1968), 58, 164, 171, 211n, 225n, 230n
7even (1997), 132

A nous la liberté (1932), 59
action films. *See* genre.
'active perception', 20
acousmatic, 131, 140, 153, 181, 190–1, 194, 196, 197–8
acousmonium, 128, 134
acoustics, 15, 80, 85, 104, 142
  psychoacoustic, 21, 78, 141
Adam and the Ants, 58
Adorno, Theodor W., xi, 1, 2, 14, 75, 91, 111, 203, 205
ADR (automatic dialogue replacement), 174, 180
The Adventures of Don Juan (1926), 16, 34, 45
akinesthesia (akinetopsia), 81
Alexander Nevsky (1938), 52, 104
Alien (1979), 198
Alien 3 (1992), 161
Allen, Woody, 176, 195
  Manhattan (1979), 195
  What's up, Tiger Lily? (1966), 176
Alloy Orchestra, 173
Alexandrov, Grigori, 9, 34, 50, 51, 52, 53, 68, 69, 185
  'Statement on Sound', 9, 50, 51, 52, 58, 68, 185
Altman, Rick, 3, 15, 16, 29, 46, 126, 141, 156, 180, 182, 183, 219n
amateur films. *See* genre.
anempathetic music, 34, 54–5, 57, 106, 109, 136, 167

antiphony, 55
American Beauty (1999), 55
An American in Paris (1951), 96
L' Aneé derniere a Marienbad (1961), 55, 185, 187
Anderson, Gillian S., 171, 231n
animated films. *See* genre.
Anger, Kenneth, 87, 100
  Kustom Kar Kommandos (1965), 100
  Scorpio Rising (1964), 87, 100
antiphony, 55
Antonioni, Michaelangelo, 1, 82, 87
  Blow Up (1966), 1
  The Passenger (Professione Reporter) (1975), 82–3
  Zabriskie Point (1970), 87–9
Aphex Twin, 58
apophenia, 6, 79
Apocalypse Now (1979), 40–1, 218n
Argento, Dario, 175
  Profondo Rosso (AKA *Deep Red*, 1975), 175–6
Armes, Roy, 17
Armstrong, Craig, 58
  Plunkett and Macleane (1999), 58
Aronofsky, Darren, 193, 233n
  Requiem for a Dream (2000), 193
Arnheim, Rudolf, 19–20, 98,
  Film as Art (1958), 19
  "The Gestalt Theory of Expression" (1949), 19–20, 98
art films. *See* genre.
L' arrive d'un train en gare de la Ciotat (1895), 70
Assault on Precinct 13 (1976), xi, 61, 65–7
Astaire, Fred, 162–3
asynchrony. *See* synchronization.

atonal, 184
Atonement (2007), 54
audiovisual, 2–4, 8–9, 12–13, 25, 33–34, 55, 68, 94, 101, 112–4, 119, 124, 126, 128, 139, 153, 155–156, 161, 180, 183, 184, 202, 205–6, 208, 216n, 228n, 234n
  audiovisual cadence, 114
  audiovisual culture, 2, 4, 8, 15, 23, 38, 41, 73, 93, 95, 199, 200–3, 205, 208
  audiovisual naturalism, 42, 81
  audiovisual phrasing, 112
  audiovisual score, 52
  audiovisual synchronization, 9
auditory capture, 26
avant garde. *See* genre.
AVI (Audio Video Interleave), 39
AVID Technology, Inc., 39, 125, 216n, 218n
  Avid zooms, 193
Axt, William, 169

Babe (1995), 179
Bach, Johann Sebastian, 100–1, 121
  Brandenburg Concerto No. 3, 100
  Goldberg Variations, 101
Badly Dubbed Porn (2007 - present), 176
Balázs, Béla, 69
Ball, Philip, 5
Barr, Charles, 91, 121
Barron, Louis and Bebe, 130, 135
  Forbidden Planet (1956), 130, 135, 141–2
Barry Lyndon (1975), 164
Bartok, Béla, 165
  Music for Strings, Percussion and Celesta, 165
Battleship Potemkin (1925), 144, 172, 231n
Bazin, André, 29, 55, 202
Bax, William, 96
  Tintagel, 96
Becce, Giuseppe, 169
  Kinothek (1919), 169
Beck, Jay, 133–4, 233n
Beethoven, Ludwig van, 86, 97
  6th Symphony, 97
  Moonlight Sonata, 86
Belton, John, 15, 29, 38, 76, 177, 211n

Benjafield, John, 22
Bernard Herrmann: Music from the Movies (1992), 106
Bernard, James, 171
Berry, Chuck, 162, 191
  "You Never Can Tell", 162
  "Johnny B. Goode", 191
The Big Parade (1925), 169
The Big Sleep (1945), 160
'Biophon', 15
The Birds (1963), 57, 130, 131, 170
Birth of a Nation (1915), 169, 173
Black Water (2008), 92
Blackham, T.G., 36
Blackmail (1929), 90, 174, 182
Blade Runner (1982), 125
Blow Out (1981), 196, 227n
Blow Up (1966), 1
Blue (1993), 199
body model, 18
Bolivar, Valerie, 26
Bollywood, 160
Boogie-Doodle (1948), 99
Bordwell, David, 53, 59, 103, 212n
bounce inducing effect, 25–6
Bow Wow Wow, 58
Bram Stoker's Dracula (1992), 67
Brakhage, Stan, 101
Breakheart Pass (1976), 192
Bregman, Albert, 6, 67
Breil, Joseph Carl, 169, 229n
The Bride of Frankenstein (1935), 167
Bring me the Head of Alfredo Garcia (1974), 154
Bronson (2009), 85, 114–5
Brooks, Peter, 71
Brophy, Philip, 128, 141–2
Brown, Royal S., xi, 15, 53, 95, 164
Browning, Tod, 72
  Freaks (1932), 72
Bullerjahn, Claudia, 201
Buñuel, Luis, 199
  Les Hurdes (*Land without Bread*, 1933), 199
Burch, Noel, 10, 103
Burgon, Geoffrey, 104
Burnand, David, 131
Burroughs, William S., 173
  Witchcraft Through the Ages (*Häxan* [1922]) 173

Burtt, Ben, 41
Burt, George, 56, 105
Butch Cassidy and the Sundance Kid (1969), 193

Cage, John, 105, 224n
Candyman (1992), 58
Canon (1964), 99
Carlos, Wendy, 164, 166
Carnival of Souls (1962), 184, 232n
Carpenter, John, xi, 61, 124, 229n
    Assault on Precinct 13 (1976), xi, 61, 65–7
Carroll, Noel, 127
Casablanca (1942), 154
The Cat From Outer Space (1978), 179
CGI (computer generated imagery), 179
Chariots of Fire (1981), 91, 125
Chion, Michel, vii, ix, xi, 4, 6, 12, 14–16, 55, 79, 94, 106, 112–14, 123, 128–9, 133, 136, 139–40, 155–6, 164, 167, 197, 199, 204–5, 213n, 214n, 226n, 229n, 232n
The Chronicles of Narnia: The Lion, the Witch and the Wardrobe (2005), 143
The Chronicles of Narnia: Prince Caspian (2008), 143
CinemaScope (1953), 38
Cinematic Orchestra, 173
Cinerama (1952), 38
Clair, René, 59
    Sous le toits de Paris (1930), 59
    Le Million (1931), 59
    A nous la liberté (1932), 59
classical films. *See* genre.
classical music (and scores), 5, 10, 54, 97–8, 164
click tracks, 36, 55, 122
A Clockwork Orange (1971), 57
Clouser, Charlie, 133, 135–6, 226n, 227n
    Saw (2004), 133–141, 152, 226n, 227n
Clover, Carol, 158
Cocktail party effect, 78
Coen Brothers, 57
    Miller's Crossing (1990), 57
cognitive dissonance, 81–2, 89, 203
cognitive psychology (or Cognitive Science). *See* psychology.
Cohen, Annabel, 24–6, 142

comedy films. *See* genre.
The Committee (1967), 88
congruence-associationist model, 24
contrary motion, 56
Control (2007), 160
The Conversation (1974), 196, 227n
Cook, Nicholas, 106, 220n
Copland, Aaron, 127
Coppola, Francis Ford, 196, 218n, 227n
    The Conversation (1974), 196, 227n
    Apocalypse Now (1979), 40–1, 218n
Coppola, Sofia, 58
    Marie Antoinette (2006), 58
Cotner, John S., 87, 222n
counterpoint, 1, 9, 31, 34, 42, 43, 45, 50, 52–61, 68–9, 83, 125, 185, 187, 212n
Creep (2004), 132
cross-modal effect, 24
Cubase, 40, 125, 216n
Curtis, Ian, 160
    Control (2007), 160

The Da Vinci Code (2006), 121
Da Vinci, Leonardo, 121
Dangerous Moonlight (1941) (*Suicide Squadron* [US title]), 154
Danna, Jeff, 108, 224n
Davis, Blair, 172, 184
Davis, Miles, 150
Davison, Annette, 199
DAW technology, 40, 125, 137
Dead of Night (1945), 28, 180
Dead Silence (2007), 180, 194, 227n
'Dead soundtrack', 34, 195
Deathwatch (2002), 197
Debussy, Claude, 97
    La Cathedrale engloutie, 97
Decasia (2002) 'The State of Decay', 120
DePalma, Brian, 196, 227n
Dern, Laura, 161
Dhir, Meraj, 20
dichotic listening (dual hearing), 22
Dickson, W.K.L., 15
Dietrich, Marlene, 149–51
Digital Audio Workstations, 40
direct coupling, 37
direct sound ("*son direct*"), 29, 176
disparate synchronisation. *See* synchronisation.

dissonance, 81–3, 89, 203
D.J. Shadow, 168
   Endtroducing, 168
D.J. Spooky, 173
   Rebirth of a Nation, 173
Doane, Mary Anne, 4, 8, 205, 208
Doctor Who (TV series), 102, 233n, 234n
documentaries. *See* genre.
Dolby sound, 40, 41, 123, 129, 132
Donnie Darko (2001), 132
The Doors (1991), 160
Dr Strangelove (1964), 57
Dracula (1931), 45, 59, 151, 174
The Draughtsman's Contract (1982), 58
Dreyer, Carl Theodor, 59
   Vampyr (1932), 59
dual listening, 67
dubbing, 3, 10, 41, 45–7, 60, 72, 155, 156, 158, 174–9, 208, 228n, 232n
The Dukes of Hazzard (1977–85), 193
Dynasty (1981–91) (TV series), 109

Ealing Studios, 28
   Dead of Night (1945), 28, 180
The Eye and the Ear (1945), 100
Edison, Thomas, 15
Egoyan, Atom, 90
   The Sweet Hereafter (1997), 90
Eisenstein, Sergei, vii, xi, 1, 7, 9, 14, 15, 31–4, 42, 43, 48, 49, 50–2, 55, 60, 61, 68, 69, 89, 93, 96, 103, 104, 107, 120, 121, 144, 156, 172, 185, 188, 204, 209, 218n, 223n, 227n, 231n
   Alexander Nevsky (1938), 52, 104
   Battleship Potemkin (1925), 144, 172, 231n
   "A Dialectic Approach to Film Form" (1929), 48
   The Film Sense, 31, 52
   'Montage Anglais', 91
   montage of attractions, 49, 218n
   "Methods of Montage" (1929), 49–50
   montage theory, 44, 48–9, 103–4
   The Old and the New (1929), 103–4
   rhythmic montage, 49
   sound montage, 48–52, 103–4
   Soviet film, 44, 48–9, 59, 69, 217n, 218n
   "Statement on Sound", 9, 50–2, 58, 68, 185
   Strike (1925), 49, 89, 227n

Eisler, Hanns, 2, 14, 59, 91, 203, 205
electroacoustic music, 133, 181
Elephant (2003), 85
Emerson, Keith, 125
Enthusiasm (1930), 59
Ephron, Nora, 178
Eraserhead (1977), 131, 190
Erdmann, Hans, 169
   Kinothek (1919), 169
Eustache, Jean, 29
Evil Dead 2 (1987), 129
The Exorcist (1973), 128, 143–4, 180, 198
experimental films. *See* genre.
experimental music, 104, 143

Face/Off (1997), 193
Fentress, John, 26
Festinger, Lionel, 81, 222n
Fiddle-Dee-Dee (1947), 99
film structure, 5, 7, 23, 49, 97–8, 101–3, 109, 122, 127, 151, 156, 165, 172, 187
Filter Beds (1998), 100
The Filth and the Fury (2000), 191
Fink, Robert, 119, 187
Fischinger, Oskar, 100
Flash Gordon (1936), 167
Flash Gordon Conquers the Universe (1940), 167
Flash Gordon's Trip to Mars (1938), 167
Fleischer, Richard, 105
Flinn, Caryl, 55–6, 107
The Fog (2005), 141
Foley, 10, 129, 212n
Forbidden Planet (1956), 130, 135, 141, 142
'forced marriage', 199
Fox/Western Electric, 34, 38, 182
   'Movietone', 34
   Fox Movietone News, 182
FP1 Antwortet Nicht (1932), 174
Frankenstein (1931), 59, 151
Freaks (1932), 72
Freud, Sigmund, viii, ix, 11, 120, 187, 208, 212n, 221n
   Nirvana Principle, 11
Friedhofer, Hugo, 105
   Fugue on *Dies Irae*, 105
Friedkin, William, 143

Gabriel, Peter, 179
Gallivant (1996), 189
Garcia-Abril, Anton, 60
The Garden (1990), 199
Gassmann, Remi, 130
genre (film):
   action films, ix, 170–1
   amateur films, 43, 171, 229n
   animated films, 12, 71, 99, 100–1, 155, 180, 191
   art films, 175–6
   avant garde, 11–3, 42–4, 81, 84, 87, 89, 92, 94, 99, 100, 104, 118, 121, 122, 128, 170, 205
   classical films, 19, 55, 68, 124, 159, 160, 189
   comedy films, 56, 90, 176, 178–9, 183, 215n, 224n, 227n, 232n
   documentaries, 12, 29, 58–9, 99, 106, 118, 153, 159, 173, 182, 188–9, 191–2, 225n, 229n, 230n, 233n
   experimental films, 12
   horror films, 11, 24, 32, 33, 60, 70, 72, 98, 109, 113, 126, 133, 136, 140, 141–3, 153, 165, 170–1, 175, 180, 183, 194, 196–8, 226n
   modernist films, 173
   musicals, 12–3, 28, 95, 97, 155, 157–63, 168, 212n, 225n, 229n
   music videos, 92, 95–7, 162, 171, 191, 212n, 217n, 231n
   silent films, 11, 16, 36, 45–6, 48, 50, 56, 58, 59–60, 69, 71, 103, 120, 123, 130, 157, 169–73, 182–4, 187, 194, 199, 212n, 217n, 222n, 227n, 231n
   video art, 42
   westerns (incl. Spaghetti), 115, 117, 177, 192
Geräuschmusik, 144
Gestalt psychology, 18–24, 26, 28, 75–6, 79, 98, 190, 204, 214n
Gimme Shelter (1970), 193
Glass, Philip, 58
The Go Between (1970), 91
Godard, Jean-Luc, 29, 84
Gold, Ernest, 54
The Golden Compass (2007), 71
Goldsmith, Jerry, 198
Goldstein, Kurt, 23

Gonks Go Beat (1965), 163
The Good, the Bad and the Ugly (1967), 117
'good Gestalt', 20, 23–4, 26
Gorbman, Claudia, xi, 14, 15, 55, 112, 164, 231n
Gordon, Michael, 120
   Decasia (2002) 'The State of Decay', 120
Graf, Alexander, 69
The Great Rock 'n' Roll Swindle (1980), 191
Gregson-Williams, Harry, 143
Griffith, D.W., 169, 173
   Birth of a Nation (1915), 169, 173
Gunning, Tom, 71

Halloween (1978), 32, 113
Hallström, Lasse, 176
   My Life as a Dog (1985), 176
Harry Potter (Films), 71
Harvey, Herk, 184
   Carnival of Souls (1962), 184, 232n
Healings, Chris, 142–3
Hendrix, Jimi, 150
Henry, Pierre, 130
Herrmann, Bernard, 106, 121, 130, 223n
Hirsch, Paul, 106
Hitchcock, Alfred, 57, 90, 102, 106, 121, 130, 134, 140, 170, 174–5, 177, 182, 223n
   The Birds (1963), 57, 130, 131, 170
   Blackmail (1929), 90, 174, 182
   North by Northwest (1959), 170
   Notorious (1946), 177
   "On Style" (1963), 102
   Psycho (1960), 22, 57, 76, 106, 140, 170, 204
   Rear Window (1954), 134
Holm-Hudson, Kevin, 88
   Progressive Rock Revisited, 88
Honegger, Arthur, 97
   Pacific 231, 97
horror films. *See* genre.
Houston, Whitney, 159
Huillet, Danièle, 29
human psychology. *See* psychology.
Huntley, John, 171
Les Hurdes (*Land without Bread*, 1933), 199
Hutchings, Peter, 197

India Song (1975), 204
The Innocents (1961), 195
iPod, 5
Iron Butterfly, 109, 111
   "In-a-Gadda-Da-Vida", 109, 111
The Iron Foundry (1928), 97
Ivens, Joris, 59
   Song of Heroes (1931), 59
Ives, Charles, 67, 219n

Jarman, Derek, 199, 219n
   The Garden (1990), 199
   Blue (1993), 199
Jaubert, Maurice, 193
The Jazz Singer (1926), 16, 34, 45, 47, 157
The Jesus of Montreal (1989), 176
Johnson, Robert, 193
   "Love in Vain", 193
Jones, McGraw, 141
Ju-On: The Grudge (2002), 132, 226n
Jung, Carl Gustav, 7, 211n

Kamitani, George, 27
Kant, Immanuel, 102
   Kantian idealism, 79, 98
Kelly, Gene, 157
Kendall, Roger, 25, 202, 211n, 213n
Kepler, Johannes, 95
   Harmonices Mundi (1619), 95
Kilar, Wojchiech, 67
   Bram Stoker's Dracula (1992), 67
Kivy, Peter, 97, 102
Klangfarbenmelodie, 151
Koffka, Kurt, 22, 204
Köhler, Wolfgang, 79, 205
Kötting, Andrew, 189
   Gallivant (1996), 189
Kracauer, Siegfried, 31, 45, 60–1, 212n, 229n
Kroeber, Ann, 131
KTL, 119
Kubelka, Peter, 99, 100, 121
   Mosaik im Vertrauen (1955), 99
   Unsere Afrikareise (1966), 99–100
Kubrick, Stanley, 57, 164, 166, 171, 178, 211n, 225n, 230n
   2001: A Space Odyssey (1968), 58, 164, 171, 211n, 225n
   Barry Lyndon (1975), 164
   A Clockwork Orange (1971), 57

Dr Strangelove (1964), 57
The Shining (1980), 164–7, 178–9
Kuleshov experiment/effect, 43, 209
Kustom Kar Kommandos (1965), 100

Lang, Edith, 169
Lang, Fritz, 27, 59, 172, 229n, 231n
   M (1928), 59, 229n
   Metropolis (1927, re-released 1983), 27, 172, 231n
Langer, Suzanne K., 101
The Last Waltz (1978), 159
Lastra, James, 123
Lauste, Eugene-Auguste, 15
'law of minimum principle', 22–3
Led Zeppelin, 118–9
   Jimmy Page, 118
   Robert Plant, 118
   The Song Remains the Same (1975), 118
Ledoux, Joseph, 18
Leone, Sergio, 117
   The Good, the Bad and the Ugly (1967), 117
   Once Upon a Time in the West (1968), 117
Lèvres de sang (*Lips of Blood*, 1975), 184
lip-synching. *See* synchronisation.
Lippman, Edward R., 207
Lipscomb, Scott, 25, 202, 211n, 213n
Liszt, Franz, 100
   Second Hungarian Rhapsody, 100
   Motion Painting No. 1 (1947), 100
live performance, 9, 29, 30, 38, 46, 56, 68, 100, 118, 130, 158–60, 163, 169–70, 172, 191–2, 217n, 222n, 229n
Lloyd Webber, Andrew, 159
   Phantom of the Opera (2005), 159
London, Kurt, 14
The Long Weekend (1978), 198
Look Who's Talking (1989), 179
The Lord of the Rings (Films), 71
Losey, Joseph, 91
   The Go Between (1970), 91
Lost Highway (1997), 80
Lost in Translation (2003), 160
Love Story (1944), 154
Lovin' Spoonful, The, 176
Lumière brothers, 70
   L' arrive d'un train en gare de la Ciotat (1895), 70

Lye, Len, 99, 101
Lynch, David, 80, 131, 132, 160, 190
  Lost Highway (1997), 80
  Eraserhead (1977), 131, 190
  Wild at Heart (1990), 160–2
  Twin Peaks (1990–91), 161

M (1928), 59, 229n
MacDonald, John W., 6, 25
magnetic tape, 36–8, 133
Magnum P.I. (1980–88), 177
Maltby, Richard, 56, 174
Man with a Movie Camera (1929), 172
Mandelbrot, Benoit, 121
Manhattan (1979), 195
Manhunter (1986), 109–11
Manovich, Lev, 44, 69
Manson, Marilyn, 129
Manvell, Roger, 171
Marianelli, Dario, 54
  Atonement (2007), 54
Marie Antoinette (2006), 58
  Adam and the Ants, 58
  Aphex Twin, 58
  Squarepusher, 58
  The Strokes, 58
Marshall, Sandra, 24–5
The Matrix (1999), 193
Mauer, Barry, 199
Maysles Brothers, 193
  Gimme Shelter (1970), 193
McCambridge, Mercedes, 180
McCormack, John, 91
McGurk, Harry, 6, 14, 24, 25, 27, 28, 43, 73, 79, 92, 199, 201, 209
'The McGurk effect' (or 'the McGurk-MacDonald Effect'), 24, 25, 27, 28, 43, 79, 92, 199, 201
McLaren, Norman, 99, 101
  Boogie-Doodle (1948), 99
  Canon (1964), 99
  Fiddle-Dee-Dee (1947), 99
  Synchromy (1972), 99
Meisel, Edmund, 144, 231n
Méliès, Georges, 71
Melody Maker, 47
Mendel, George, 15
Mendoza, David, 169
mental model, 18
Mera, Miguel, 131
Merleau-Ponty, Maurice, x, 8

Messter, Oskar, 15
Metallica, 159, 211n
Metropolis (1984), 27, 172, 231n
Meyer, Leonard B., 5, 75, 108, 114, 211n, 220n, 225n
Meyer-Dinkgräfe, Daniel, 177, 232n
Micheaux, Oscar, 173
'Mickeymousing', 5, 10, 32, 36, 53–4, 57, 98, 100, 156, 165
MIDI (Musical Instrument Digital Interface), 40
Miller's Crossing (1990), 57
Le Million (1931), 59
Mister Ed (1961), 179, 215n
MLV format (Multi-Language Versions), 174
Modern Times (1936), 162
modernism, 131
modernist films. *See* genre.
Monkey (1979–80), 176
'Montage Anglais', 91
montage, 9, 22, 32, 34, 43, 48, 50–1, 61–2, 68, 89, 91, 93, 103–4, 121, 138, 170, 188, 209, 212n, 217n, 218n
  metric montage, 49
  Montage Anglais, 91
  montage theory, 44
  rhythmic montage, 49
  sound montage, 49, 52, 59, 62
Moor, Gene, 184
Morgan, Kenneth F., 47, 218n
  Recording for Motion Pictures (1931), 47
Moroder, Giorgio, 28, 172, 231n
  Metropolis (1983), 27, 172, 231n
Morrison, Bill, 120
  Decasia: The State of Decay (2002), 120
Morrison, Jim, 160
Mosaik im Vertrauen (1955), 99
Mosjoukhine, Ivan, 209
Mossolov, Alexander, 97
motion bounce illusion, 26
MOV (digital video format), 39
Moviola, 35
MPEG (digital video format), 39, 216n
Multistability, 20
Münsterberg, Hugo, 208
  The Photoplay (1916), 208
Murnau, F. W., 171
  Nosferatu: Eine Symohonie des Grauens (1922), 171

musicals. *See* genre.
music software, 39–40, 124–5, 143, 215n, 216n, 218n
musicvideos. *See* genre.
musical structure, 5, 23, 31, 41, 49, 61, 67, 88, 98, 100–3, 105–6, 108–9, 111, 113–8, 121–2, 127, 150, 156, 172, 187, 207, 225n
musique concrete, 130, 133
My Life as a Dog (1985), 176

Nagra portable tape recorder, 37, 216n
Narnia (Films), 71, 143
  The Golden Compass (2007), 71
  The Chronicles of Narnia: The Lion, the Witch and the Wardrobe (2005), 143
  The Chronicles of Narnia: Prince Caspian (2008), 143
Neale, D.M., 43, 215n, 216n
Necker cube, 20–1
neurology (incl. neuropsychology and neurophysiology), ix, 22, 81, 201, 220n
  neuroaesthetics, 5, 201
  neuroscience, 17, 27, 42, 74, 77
  neuroimaging, 17, 213n
  human neurology, 17, 27, 74, 77, 81, 201, 213n, 220n
A Nightmare on Elm Street (1984), 141
Nine Inch Nails, 135, 227n
non-diegetic, 2, 4, 28, 32, 42, 51, 53–4, 57, 61–2, 66, 78, 85–9, 91–2, 111–12, 118, 126, 130–2, 134, 137, 140–2, 153, 156, 161, 163–4, 166–7, 181, 183–4, 192, 194–8, 201, 227n, 233n
non-functional harmony, 61
non-linear editing, 39
non-musical films. *See* genre.
Normandeau, Robert, 197
North by Northwest (1959), 177
Nosferatu: Eine Symphonie des Grauens (1922), 171, 173
Notorious (1946), 177
nouvelle vague, 84
Nunn, Fe, 173
Nyman, Michael, xi, 58, 172, 225n
  The Draughtsman's Contract (1982), 58
  Man with a Movie Camera (1929), 172

O'Brien, Charles, 29, 232n
occult, ix, 1–3, 70–2, 93, 141, 200, 204
off-screen sound, 2, 30–1, 33, 38, 76, 129, 140, 181, 195–8, 215n
The Old and the New (1929), 103–4
Once Upon a Time in the West (1968), 117

Pacific 231, 97
parallelism, 1, 9, 17, 20, 27, 31, 42, 52–6, 60, 68, 77, 87, 117, 164, 182
pareidolia, 6, 79
The Passenger (Professione Reporter) (1975), 82–3
pattern finding, 5–6, 21–4, 28, 78–9, 101, 118–9, 201, 214n
Pavlov, Ivan, 204
  Pavlovian theory, ix, x, 16, 24, 189, 204, 230n
Peckinpah, Sam, 154, 193
  Bring me the Head of Alfredo Garcia (1974), 154
Pendrecki, Krzysztof, 165
Performance (1970), 177
The Phantom Carriage (1921, *Körkarlen*), 119
Phantom fundamentals, 21, 79
Phantom of the Opera (2005), 159
'phi phenomenon', 19, 214n
Phonotone, 47
The Photoplay (1916), 208
Picnic at Hanging Rock (1975), 91
Pierrot le fou (1965), 84
Pink Floyd, 7, 87–8, 173, 211n
plagal (cadence), 113
plastic music, 103
plesiochrony, 31, 181–3, 191
Plunkett and Macleane (1999), 58
Point Blank (1967), 83–4, 90
polyphony, 62, 103, 150–1
pop music, 47, 57–8, 87, 108–9, 111, 124–5, 156, 163–4, 167–8, 172–3, 189, 222n, 225n
post-production, 10, 39, 74, 86, 112, 154, 155, 174–6, 178, 180, 184, 206, 230n, 233n
post-synch. *See* synchronization.
Powell, Michael, 91
  Wings of the Morning (1937), 91
Powermad, 161
Powrie, Philip, 167

Prägnanz, 23, 214n
Prendergast, Roy, 127
Presley, Elvis, 160–1
pre-recording, 30, 34, 99, 125, 206
Profondo Rosso (AKA *Deep Red*, 1975), 175–6
programme music, 97, 152, 222n
Propellerheads Reason, 125
ProTools, 39–40, 126, 216n
proximal stimulus, 17
Psycho (1960), 22, 57, 76, 106, 140, 170, 204
psychology: ix-x, 2, 5, 8–9, 11–12, 14–23, 28, 42–3, 54, 73, 75, 79, 81–2, 87, 90, 93, 107, 109, 112, 123, 126–8, 130, 132, 134–5, 140, 142, 151–2, 166, 182, 194, 197, 200–8, 213n, 214n, 221n, 225
   cognitive psychology (or Cognitive Science), 18–19, 23, 203, 213n
   Gestalt psychology, 18–20, 22–3, 75, 79, 98, 204, 214n
   human psychology, ix, 5–6, 18–21, 23, 28, 74–5, 78–9, 101, 166, 200–1, 204, 208, 213n, 223n
   psycho-acoustics, 21, 78
   psychoacoustic phantom effect, 78
   psychogeography/ emotional landscape, 103, 152
   psychophysical parallelism, 20
   schizophrenic listening, 67
   synaesthesia, 96, 223n
Pudovkin, Vsevolod, 9, 31, 34, 48–52, 59–60, 68–9, 185
   Technique of the Film, 48
   "Statement on Sound", 9, 50, 51, 52, 58, 68, 185
   Deserter (1933), 59
Pulp Fiction (1994), 162
Pythagoras, 121

Raksin, David, 127
Rameau, Jean-Philippe, 207
Rapée, Ernö, 169
   Compendium (1924, 1925), 169
Ravenous (1999), xi, 115–6
RCA (Radio Corporation of America), 16, 34
   RCA Photophone, 34
Reaktor (software), 143

Rear Window (1954), 134
Reed, Lou, 57
reference synch. *See* synchronization.
reification, 20
Reservoir Dogs (1992), 57, 167–8, 195, 230n
Resident Evil (2002), 129, 227n
Requiem for a Dream (2000), 193
Resnais, Alan, 185
   L'Aneé derniere a Marienbad (1961), 55, 185, 187
The Return of Martin Guerre (1982), 176
Revell, Graeme, 141, 143
reverb, 108, 125, 134, 141–2, 189, 225n
Reynolds, Debbie, 158
Reznor, Trent, 135
Rhodes, Gillian, 26
Rivette, Jacques, 29
rock music, 58, 88, 118, 119, 125, 135, 143, 160, 171, 191, 222n, 224n, 225n, 229n, 233n
Rodriguez, Robert, 125
Rollin, Jean, 183–4
   Lèvres de sang (*Lips of Blood*, 1975), 184
Rolling Stones, 193
Rorschach blot test, 79
Rosar, William, 121
Rossini, Gioachino, 57
   La Gazza Ladra, 57
Rothko, Mark, 101
RP tones (received pronunciation), 177
Rubin vase, 20–1
Ruttman, Walter, 101, 199
   Week-End (1930), 199
Ryang, Robert, 178

Sala, Oskar, 130
Salt, Barry, 35
Saving Private Ryan (1998), 195
Saw (2004), 133–41, 152, 226n
Scary Movie 3 (2003), 90
Schafer, R. Murray, 80, 104, 190, 207
   The New Soundscape, 80
   'Schizophonia', 80, 207, 222n
Schaeffer, Pierre, 130, 153, 181, 197
Schillinger system, 121
'schizophonia', 80
schizophrenic listening. *See* psychology.
Schlesinger, John, 83
   Point Blank (1967), 83–4, 90

Scorpio Rising (1964), 87, 100
Screen Test no. 1 (1965), 100
Screen Test no. 2 (1965), 100
Selsyn motors, 37
Seven Brides for Seven Brothers (1954), 159
Severance (2006), 183
Sex & Drugs & Rock & Roll (2009), 160
Sex Pistols, 191–2, 233n
The Filth and the Fury (2000), 191
Seyrig, Francis, 187
Shallow Grave (1994), 57
Shams, Ladan, 27
Shanghai Express (1931), 144, 149–52
Shepherd, Ashley, 38
Sherwin, Guy, 100
Shimojo, Shinsuke, 27
The Shining (1980), 164–7, 178–9
Shostakovich, Dmitri, 67
Shriekback, 109
silent films. See genre.
Silent Hill (2006), 107, 224n, 225n
Singin' in the Rain (1952), 158–9
Sinn Fein, 179
Simba (1928), 47
Sjöström, Victor, 119
    The Phantom Carriage (1921, Körkarlen), 119
Sleep (1963), 100–1
Smith, Chas, 136
Smith, Jeff, 127, 213n, 228n, 229n
Snow, Michael, 101
Society of Motion Picture and Television Engineers (SMPTE), 39
The Song Remains the Same (1975), 118
sonic cadences, 112
song form, 88, 108–9, 111
Sonnenschein, David, 195
Sony, 125, 143
Sony Logic, 125
    Sony Pro Series Sound libraries, 143
sound design, xi, 30, 41, 107, 123–7, 130–3, 135, 143–4, 153, 164
sound diffusion, 40
sound-effect, 3–4, 10, 12, 16, 30, 32, 36, 40, 43, 46–7, 53, 55, 61, 74, 86, 105, 108, 122, 124–6, 128–135, 151–3, 162, 176, 184, 196, 198, 201, 206, 224n, 226n, 227n, 233n
sound naturalism, 31, 42, 51, 59, 69, 80, 128–9, 152, 156, 185, 189
sound on sound
soundtrack, viii, 4, 9–10, 14, 28–30, 33–5, 39, 44, 46, 49, 56, 58, 60–1, 68–9, 74, 83, 85, 86–7, 91, 99–100, 104, 115, 118–19, 124, 126, 130–4, 140–1, 143–4, 150, 152, 155, 164–7, 169–78, 181–5, 187–95, 199, 201–2, 204, 206, 211n, 212n, 215n, 222n, 225n, 228n, 229n, 231n, 233n, 234n
Sous le toits de Paris (1930), 59
South Pacific (1958), 159
Spadoni, Robert, 33, 72–3
Spaghetti Western, 117
    The Good, the Bad and the Ugly (1967), 117
    Once Upon a Time in the West (1968), 117
speaker systems, 34, 123
speed ramping, 193
SPK, 143
Splet, Alan, 131, 190
    Sounds from a Different Realm, 131
spotting, 32, 40, 41, 47
Squarepusher, 58
Star Trek (films and TV series), 141
Star Wars (1977), 30, 41
Stealer's Wheel, 57, 167
Steinberg Cubase, 125
Steiner, Fred, 121
Steiner, Max, 36, 55
Stilwell, Robynn, 120, 167
Stone, Oliver, 160
    The Doors (1991), 160
Storr, Anthony, 194
Straub, Jean-Marie, 29
Strauss, Johan, 58, 62, 66, 164
Strike (1925), 44, 89, 227n
The Strokes, 58
Sunset Boulevard (1950), 55, 84
Superfield, 128, 139
surroundsound cinema, 38, 41, 74, 128, 132, 141
The Sweet Hereafter (1997), 90
synaesthesia. See psychology.
'synchresis'. See synchronization.
Synchromy (1972), 99

synchronization:
   asynchrony, 2, 9–11, 28, 31, 33, 38, 42, 44–5, 48, 50–1, 53, 59, 67, 69, 71, 73–5, 77–8, 81, 83–4, 86, 89, 92–3, 99–100, 106–8, 114, 119, 123, 137, 156–7, 172, 181, 187–9, 191–2, 197–8, 201, 205–6, 217n
   disparate synchronisation, 33, 192–4
   levels of synchronisation, 31–2
   lip-synching, 3, 27, 30–1, 43, 45, 72, 138, 155, 157–63, 175, 179, 209, 233n
   post-synch, 11, 30, 154–6, 169, 176–8, 184
   reference synch, 39–40
   'synchresis', x, 6, 16, 27–8, 79, 106, 112, 115, 205, 213n, 221n
   Trigger synch, 39
Szymanowski, Karol, 100

Tarantino, Quentin, 57, 167, 195, 230n
   Reservoir Dogs (1992), 57, 167–8, 195, 230n
   Pulp Fiction (1994), 162
Tatroe, Sonia, 141
Television (TV), viii, 3, 8, 16, 28–30, 32, 38–9, 42, 51, 76, 87, 95, 98, 102, 109, 128, 135, 137–8, 141, 152, 161, 163, 168, 173, 176–9, 182, 188, 193, 200–2, 209, 210n, 215n, 222n, 227n, 228n, 229n, 230n, 232n
Temple, Julien, 191
   The Great Rock 'n' Roll Swindle (1980), 191
   The Filth and the Fury (2000), 191
texture, 3, 117, 124, 133, 136, 149, 150, 156
Thanatos, 208
Themerson, Franziska, 100
   The Eye and the Ear (1945), 100
Themerson, Stefan, 100
   The Eye and the Ear (1945), 100
'Theory of Ocular Music', 104
The Third Reich in Colour (2001), 182
Thirty-Two short films About Glen Gould (1993), 100
timecode, 39–40, 216n
To Have and to Have Not (1944), 154

To Live and Die in L.A. (1985), 125
Todd-AO/70mm (1955), 38
The Tombs of the Blind Dead (1971), 11, 60
tonality, 10, 32, 49, 51, 101, 114
tracking, 154, 164, 171, 232n
Trainspotting (1995), 57
transduction, 17
trauma, 81, 90, 119, 208, 221n
trigger synch. *See* synchronization.
Truman, Mike, 142
Turner, Tina, 160
Twin Peaks (1990–91), 161
Tyler, Bonnie, 28
Type O Negative, 171–3

Uncle Josh at the Moving Picture Show (1902), 70
Under the Freeway (1995), 100
Underdog (2007), 179
Unsere Afrikareise (1966), 99–100

Vampyr (1932), 59
Van Sant, Gus, 85, 222n
Vangelis (Evangelos Papathanassiou), 125
   Blade Runner (1982), 125
   Chariots of Fire (1981), 91, 125
Varèse, Edgard, 105, 224n
Vasey, Ruth, 174
ventriolquism, 28, 80, 156, 179–80, 194
'ventriloquist effect', 25–6
Verdi, Giuseppe, 144
Verfremdungseffekt, 84
Vertov, Dziga, 44, 49, 59, 99, 100, 172
   Enthusiasm (1930), 59
   Man with a Movie Camera (1929), 172
   Soviet Film, 44, 49, 59
video art. *See* genre.
videogames, 16, 107–8, 152, 202, 224n
videotape, 38–40
Vidor, King, 169
   The Big Parade (1925), 169
Vigo, Jean, 193
   Zero de Conduite (1933), 193
viseme, 26, 79
visual music, 99
Vitaphone, 15–6, 34, 38, 157
Von Sternberg, Josef, 144, 150, 228n
V/Vm, 'The Missing Symphony' (Shostakovich adaptation), 67

Wagner, Richard, 47, 97, 114
   Tannhäuser, 47
   Siegfried's Funeral March
      (*Götterdämmerung*), 117
Wakeman, Rick, 125
Walter, Ernest, 12
Wan, James, 135
Wang Chung, 125
   To Live and Die in L.A. (1985), 125
Warhol, Andy, 100–1
   Sleep (1963), 100–1
   Screen Test no. 1 (1965), 100
   Screen Test no. 2 (1965), 100
The Water Margin (1973), 176
Watson, John B., 205, 234n
Wavelength (1967), 101
Waxman, Franz, 167
   The Bride of Frankenstein (1935), 167
   Flash Gordon (1936), 167
   Flash Gordon's Trip to Mars (1938), 167
   Flash Gordon Conquers the Universe
      (1940), 167
Week-End (1930), 199
Weis, Elisabeth, xi, 15, 132
Wenders, Wim, 69
Wertheimer, Max, 19, 214n
West, George, 169
Westerkamp, Hildegard, 85–6, 152, 222n
   "Türen der Wahrnehmung" ("Doors of
      Perception") (1989), 85
   "Beneath the Forest Floor" (1992), 85
westerns (incl. Spaghetti). *See* genre.
Western Electric, 15–6, 34

What's Love Got to Do With It (1993), 160
What's Up, Tiger Lily (1966), 176
White, Frances, 85
   "Walk Through Resonant Landscape
      no. 2" (1992), 85
Wierzbicki, James, 130
Wild at Heart (1990), 160–2
wildtrack sound, 181, 188–9, 192
Williams, Alan 87, 162
Williams, Andy, 57
Williams, Brian (AKA Lustmord), 143
   The Crow (1994), 143
Wings of the Morning (1937), 91
Winter, Marian, 144
Within Our Gates (1920), 173
The Wiz (1978), 7
The Wizard of Oz (1939), 7, 76,
   173, 211n
Woo, John, 193
   Face/Off (1997), 193
Wright, Basil, 58, 153
Wurlitzer, 184
Wurtzler, Steve, 159
   "She Sang Live but the Microphone
      was Turned Off", 159

Yamaoka, Akira, 107–8, 224n, 225n
Yutkevich, Sergei, 7

Zabriskie Point (1970), 87–9
Zero de Conduite (1933), 193
Zwerin, Charlotte, 193
   Gimme Shelter (1970), 193

Printed in Great Britain
by Amazon.co.uk, Ltd.,
Marston Gate.